Essential ZBrush®

Wayne Robson

Wordware Publishing, Inc.

Library of Congress Cataloging-in-Publication Data

Robson, Wayne
    Essential ZBrush / by Wayne Robson.
      p. cm.
    Includes index.
    ISBN-13: 978-1-59822-059-9
    ISBN-10: 1-59822-059-4 (pbk., companion cd)
    1. Computer graphics. 2. ZBrush. 3. Three-dimensional display systems.
    I. Title.
    T385.R5792 2008
    006.6'93--dc22   2008035078
                                         CIP

© 2008, Wordware Publishing, Inc.

All Rights Reserved

1100 Summit Avenue, Suite 102
Plano, Texas 75074

No part of this book may be reproduced in any form or by
any means without permission in writing from
Wordware Publishing, Inc.

Printed in the United States of America

ISBN-13: 978-1-59822-059-9
ISBN-10: 1-59822-059-4
10 9 8 7 6 5 4 3 2 1
0808

All inquiries for volume purchases of this book should be addressed to Wordware Publishing, Inc., at the above address. Telephone inquiries may be made by calling:

(972) 423-0090

Dedication

To those who helped fix what was once broken and repair the irreparable.

To my other half, Katrina, my son Kane, my brother Simon, and not forgetting my mam and dad.

An extra special dedication to my unborn child, who is currently lying safe and warm inside Katrina. I look forward to being your daddy and loving you as much as any human can.

Special Thanks to:

Pixologic, for creating the best tool any artist could wish for. In the words of Mr. Spock, "Live long and prosper."

Glen Southern, who I count as a good friend and who has been my inspiration since day one, a man truly without limitations.

Katrina, my other half, for being my inspiration and helping to find the soul I needed to be an artist. (Remember Dover.)

My son Kane, for bringing the light and shade into each day with his smile and wonder at all things I do.

My mother, without her I wouldn't be here and you'd have saved some money on this book. So any blame lies at her door, I'm afraid (lol). Seriously though, she taught me that with enough time and dedication anything is possible, something that I'll always treasure.

My father, for helping (along with my mother) to make me into a good person despite having to deal with a "teenaged Wayne" many years back (as a teenager I was a complete nightmare of epic proportions).

Simon, my brother, who is the yin to my yang and is also the logic to my artistic side at times.

Ryan Kingslien, a friend, advisor, and the hardest working man I know.

Neil Simpson, who as my best mate since school days has seen me through both good times and really amazingly bad ones, who kept me sane when life went "pear-shaped," and who I owe more than I can ever repay.

The members of ZBrushCentral, for putting up with the endless streams of bad models when I first started without ever saying "Give up, you damn loser."

Most importantly of all, Tim McEvoy and Wordware Publishing, without whom this book wouldn't exist. Thank you.

Finally, special thanks has to go out to the endless stream of "Wayne made" computers I've owned, made, modified, and then blew up in showers of sparks in the name of "art" over the years. I give them my thanks and hope they are enjoying silicon heaven.

Contents

Part III: Projects

Introduction

Well, here it is… much of my last few months sitting condensed into a book that you now hold in your hands. ZBrush has given me both something I love to do (digital sculpting) and an income. I've tried to fit within this book as many things as possible that users both new and old, those starting out and more experienced, would all find of interest. I hope its conversational style will help to make reading it enjoyable as well as instructional.

As digital artists we are living in interesting times, when sculpting has escaped the confines of a sculptor's workshop and entered homes and businesses around the world. Thanks to programs like ZBrush, people who would never have dreamed a few years back that they would be artists are now highly successful and respected digital sculptors.

The world of digital art is something that one can never know everything about, as it is forever changing and expanding. In ZBrush, Pixologic has produced the perfect sculpting tool. It's a joy to work with and has a depth that inspires as well as continued innovations and free plug-ins.

This book can be used either as a reference or read from cover to cover. For the projects in this book, I decided to take on the challenge of creating a number of models, both hard surface and organic, as well as environments and props that come together to form the scene that you see on the front cover. I hope that it gives those just starting out enough to really get their teeth into, but also contains helpful information for more experienced users.

Everything is explained in as much detail as possible to instill in new users confidence in their abilities. For more experienced users, a large project hopefully shows them new and different ways in which to work. In this book I use only default alphas so that everyone starts on an equal footing.

We cover rendering our displacement maps in both Maya and 3ds Max, as well as importing and using normal maps. We also cover a number of other areas, such as ZMapper, in great detail. In addition to a simple "help guide," I've tried to make this book something that you refer to time and time again to help you keep improving. So enjoy *Essential ZBrush*, and should you see me on a 3D forum online (as DarthWayne), be sure to say hi.

Note: The companion files for this book as well as full-color versions of all the images within this book are included on the DVD. There are also a few extras that may help to make your journey in ZBrush interesting, and tutorial videos that help show many of the processes.

1 About ZBrush

Who Should Use ZBrush?

This may seem to be a strange question, or indeed title for this section, but for those unfamiliar with ZBrush this section outlines some of the ways that ZBrush can be of use to you as an artist or in your company's pipeline.

FIGURE 1-1

ZBrush is capable of a great many things and is much more than just a digital sculpting tool. As the market leader in its area, it is a tool that everyone who wants to get into making next-generation computer games must learn. While the most obvious users of ZBrush are digital sculptors, game artists, and those who work in the film industry, its appeal is much broader than that.

More and more traditional sculptors and artists are making the transition from traditional materials to digital sculpting. Their reasons range from reducing the cost of materials such as clay to simply wanting to try something a little different or more advanced.

ZBrush is also starting to make an impact in the matte painting world as more and more artists in film pipelines use it for 2D matte painting. In fact, this pipeline was used to great effect in a number of recent movies.

To artists just starting out in digital sculpting from a traditional polygon modeling background, the program can seem rather alien at first. Instead of moving edges, polygons, or vertices around, ZBrush is more similar to traditional clay sculpting. Although the transition can be difficult at first, with a little perseverance (like anything in life) it does pay off in the end with much more complex and accurate models.

For those modelers working in the computer game industry, ZBrush offers a host of useful features. Apart from the obvious digital sculpting aspect, it also allows the creation of normal maps and the ability to paint textures. Artists can start with a simple base mesh and sculpt in the details they need. ZBrush also allows you to retopologize your model to ready it for output to riggers and animators.

So as you can see, while it is not quite a "one-stop shop" for next-generation game artists, it certainly isn't that far away. In fact, many of the models used in games today could not be produced without ZBrush.

ZBrush is one of the most amazing success stories in the whole of digital art. It has grown from a small hobbyist tool to a sophisticated production application that is used in just about every film and game production house in the world.

So is it just an organic sculpting program? Although certainly best known as a tool for organic digital sculpting, it is capable of much more. As more and more artists find they can use ZBrush for very high-end hard surface sculpting and detailing, you will see it used more and more on projects other than organic forms. It is already used in many pipelines and for detailing sets, props, buildings, and more.

As you can see, ZBrush has a very broad appeal to artists regardless of the type of sculpt or model that needs to be created. By reading this book and following along with the projects, I'm confident that you will soon feel at home with it and see many more possibilities.

Learning to Be a Digital Sculptor

When you first decide that digital sculpting and 3D are the things that you wish to learn, there are a number of decisions to make early on that can affect your long-term development as an artist. Choosing a way to learn to become a good digital sculptor is probably the most important decision you will face, as the way you choose to study will affect how fast you develop.

The choices you have are:

- Learn by yourself without any outside help
- Learn by yourself with the use of DVDs, online tutorials, and books
- Take a specialized course in 3D
- One-on-one tutoring
- Using a combination of the above

Which route is the best one depends on the artist, where he or she lives, how much they want to spend on learning, and a great many other things. So a route that is right for one person may be totally wrong for another. Whereas some people need the discipline that comes with a regular course with its timetables and routines, others may find that learning at a set speed along with other students actually hinders them.

It is important that you choose the way to learn that fits you as both a person and an artist. Go for a way that will best suit your needs, and not just the way that may be popular at the time. Let's take a look at the good and bad points of each way of learning so that those starting out can have a better idea of which way to go. Even though I do have a great deal of experience teaching 3D and digital sculpting to users of all skill levels, I do not know your personal situation so I can only give you some guidelines.

Self-based Learning

Nearly every user starts out learning alone. From the time you first open up ZBrush, every step you take is a journey into a land of self-based learning. How well you learn and take in the information you come across is up to you, and it requires a certain amount of dedication to advance beyond a certain level.

You may choose to learn by yourself because you live in a remote location or simply because you find that you learn much better that way. While it is certainly possible to learn to be a great digital sculptor in ZBrush without ever taking lessons, watching an instructional DVD, or reading books or articles, it will probably be a long and difficult process.

The positive aspect of learning by yourself without additional resources is that you have complete control of how, where, and when you learn. If you find you learn much better in the very early hours, you can set this time as your learning period each day. On the other hand, it requires more determination and dedication to learn by yourself without the input of others who have similar interests around you all the time. It can be very easy to get stuck in a rut if you aren't careful, or to simply spend time learning the wrong thing that in the long term can slow down your progress.

Self-based learning is also very good for those who may have to work during the day and are trying to change their current career. This means that you can still go out and earn a crust to survive while you spend your free time learning. When I started out there were no 3D courses in universities or colleges (in fact, in the part of England where I currently live they are still few and far between), so the only way left to learn was to learn by myself.

Learning by yourself without the benefit of DVDs, books, online tutorials, and the help of others can be a much richer and more rewarding learning experience though. And the many free tutorials on the Pixologic web site can give you a bit of a head start on things regardless of the direction you decide to take.

Course-based Learning

There are a number of things to bear in mind if you are considering taking the path of course-based learning. First of all, make sure that the course curriculum focuses not only on the skills that you require as an artist but also those that will enable you to get a job. Although the syllabus outlines the course of study, it is difficult for someone with little to no experience to decide if a particular class is the right one. I would disregard "brand-name" courses and judge based on a few simple criteria, such as the reputation of the instructors and the institution.

Is the course taught by an experienced teacher? This may seem odd, but being a good artist and being good at teaching art are totally different things that do not often come in the same package. So where a teacher has worked and what cool things he has worked on are of much less importance than excellent recommendations from previous students. The ability of a teacher can often be judged by how well he or she conveys complex ideas to the pupils. A good tutor will teach not just to your strengths, but also to your weaknesses. It is no good only improving what a person can already do well; a good tutor will seek to improve those problem areas a pupil may have.

Is the syllabus geared toward those with less than brilliant traditional art skills, or toward people who are already accomplished artists? You must be very honest with yourself and not overestimate your strengths if you want to get the very best out of any course.

Which area of the industry are you interested in? Unless you are planning on being an animator, taking a course on animation may not be a good idea unless you are sure that the skills you will learn are portable in some way. Certain skills in 3D and digital sculpting are crossover areas that can be covered in courses of different types. Don't let the fact that you really want to focus exclusively on one skill color your judgment about the rest of a course.

Does the school promise to find you a job on graduation? This is a common claim in many course publicity materials, and some get around this by mentioning that they have "contacts" in many top firms. The only time a course can guarantee you a job is if it is basically little more than a glorified recruitment service. These "schools" are probably less interested in upping your skill set than they are at having a fast turnover of pupils to keep the money rolling in. Your ability to find a job depends on your skills as well as intangibles such as how easy you are to get along with, if you fit into the mindset of the current group of employees, and where you reside. Of course knowing people in the right firms can often help, so don't discount that advantage.

Probably the biggest advantage of taking a course is in fact the contacts made while you are there. Inevitably, some former students will end up in positions of power and influence at firms you may want to work for.

A good course should give you a decent skill set in a certain amount of time. Combined with the expense of the tuition, you must include the cost of your time off work to attend, which can certainly add up.

What is the school's accreditation? Unlike many industries, the qualifications you receive may not stand for much outside the industry. For example, getting a diploma in "digital sculpting" may be worthless in another industry. Also, a course in one country may not prove that you are skilled in that area in a different country. So until some industry recognized qualifications are introduced (which hopefully will be soon), it is still a bit of a risk if you end up not being able to get a job.

Another drawback or at least something to watch out for is schools and courses that pressure pupils to brand themselves as graduates of college "X." While in some ways this may be a "stamp of quality" if the previous graduates were talented individuals that were taught well, it can work against you very fast if standards drop. Not to mention that you'll be competing with a group of other artists with very similar styles, all "branded" in some way.

If need be, take the advice of people and artists that you respect to get an unbiased view of things. Remember, the publicity may make the course appealing, but like anything in life you need to look beneath the surface a bit and do some investigation.

Learning Using DVDs, Books, and Online Tutorials

Since I make a living writing and producing tutorial DVDs, articles, and books, my outlook is a bit biased. However, I've been on both sides of the issue as someone who has used these materials when I started out learning and now I am making and writing them for others to learn from. I'd like to think it gives me a pretty unique viewpoint on the subject.

DVDs

Not too many years ago being able to find a DVD on ZBrush was a rare novelty that was anticipated with relish by nearly the whole community. Since then, there has been a proliferation of new companies producing tutorial DVDs and we now have a wealth of material to choose from. As a result, the quality is not always as high as it could be and the content can sometimes be patchy.

But this isn't to say that DVDs produced by small companies are less good than those made by larger, more established companies. Companies that are smaller can sometimes produce a DVD that is a nugget of gold just as the bigger ones can produce a few turkeys each year. So how do you make the choice as to which are good and which are bad? If you only read what people say online you get a mixture of unbiased user reviews as well as what is known as "stealth marketing," which is information posted by paid (or sometimes unpaid) people whose job is to talk up a release as much as they can and talk down those of competitors.

One way to find a good tutorial DVD is by soliciting recommendations from people you know and trust. This is especially helpful if the person is at about the same level as yourself in ZBrush and digital sculpting. What is "great" for a person at one point in the learning process is worthless to someone more or less advanced. Try to find out what is actually being taught on the DVD and whether it is basically a recorded modeling session or if the techniques and theory are being explained. Some DVDs are showcases for a particular modeler's style, while others are oriented toward how and why things are done. There is a place for both.

The adage "never judge a book by its cover" is one that we've all heard and used that also applies to tutorial DVDs. Just because you like the model on a DVD does not mean that you will learn what you need as an artist. Even the best DVD will never be perfect because there simply isn't enough time to include it all. So in short, take the advice of those you know well and respect and try to go for DVDs that can teach you what you need to learn.

I'll leave you with a closing story about one of my own DVDs that may illustrate some of what we've discussed. On release of my first DVD some time ago, I saw a thread discussing it online. Now as a rule I avoid them like the plague unless they are posts about clarification of something on the DVDs, as reading people's reviews on your work can soon drive you insane. But for whatever reason, in this case I decided to have a read to see how it had been received, and was surprised at a conversation that was in the thread. It had started with a guy saying that he couldn't understand a word I'd said on the DVD, with a few people adding that they had no problem. Toward the end it turned out that this person had not only "borrowed" the DVD (illegal in most countries), but didn't speak a word of English and his posts were going through Babelfish. As you can imagine, I couldn't understand why a person who had watched a DVD in a language he didn't understand and who didn't pay for it would then complain about it. So I guess the moral of that (true) story is that you should never take any review at face value, and instead should trust opinions and reviews from those with no vested interest either way.

Online Tutorials and Magazine Articles

Although there are a huge number of articles and tutorials available free online and in magazines, like much in the world the quality of the information within them depends largely on the person passing their knowledge on to others. There are two categories of tutorial writers as far as I'm concerned: those who write to help other users with something they have learned themselves, and those who get paid to write. (There are also those who release free articles for fame or to up the number of hits to their sites, but let's be kind and categorize them with the "helping other users" group, eh?)

If you are reading an article or tutorial written by a paid professional (and hence is held accountable), you can expect it to be of high quality; however, those written for free are in more of a gray area. Some who writes about ZBrush are not really advanced enough to be called "experts," but their articles do explain a certain workflow or part of the process that they've worked out. This is great and an excellent contribution to the ZBrush community and one that is appreciated by everyone.

What I suppose I am trying to get at without it coming across as nasty is that it can be easy for someone very new to ZBrush to take every written word as the gospel truth regardless of the source and experience of the writer. My suggestion is to try out new methods you read about and if it works for you, then add it to your list of good workflows. Workflows evolve as people discover new ways of doing things and approaching problems, and we can all benefit from sharing our good ideas.

Many amazing new workflows have been devised by relative new-comers, so discount nothing and keep your options open. Check out the amazing articles in the ZBrush wiki by people at Pixologic such as Ryan Kingslien. I also recommend Ryan's blog on the Pixologic site as an essential way to keep in touch with "up and coming" workflows. ZBrushCentral is also a site that every ZBrush user should check on a regular basis as the vast and friendly user base has produced many use-ful workflows and workarounds over the years. Of course there are many other web sites that contain tutorials on ZBrush of all types and it would take forever to list them all. I'm obviously far too modest to men-tion that my own site (www.DashDotSlash.net) has some as well.

One-on-One Tutoring

One-on-one tutoring by someone who knows both ZBrush and digital sculpting inside and out is without doubt the best option for many peo-ple. Although rare, there are a few who teach on an individual level. There are even some workplaces that offer unofficial tutoring in the form of in-house mentors, but again it is rare and you have to already be up to a certain standard anyway. Where a personal tutor is available, you are of course looking at paying some pretty hefty money for the privi-lege as personal tutoring takes up a lot of time.

The Combination Approach

For many people, a mixture of the above methods is deemed the best way to go as it provides the strengths of each method with fewer draw-backs. On the plus side, you are able to decide what you need and which methods work best for you. But on the negative side, it is far easier to get sidetracked and end up studying things that were not your intention initially. So it would certainly be a good idea to set out a list of things that you wish to learn and achieve before diving in headfirst. Just like digital sculpting itself, preparation is the key.

One thing I would say is to make sure that you do not push yourself beyond your physical limits. Sometimes it can appear to people new to the world of 3D that there is something "macho" about long hours and lack of sleep. I recommend that you limit your hours to a level that does not cause burnout because you may have to maintain that pace for quite some time. I spent about two years of between 14 and 20 hours a day of constant study when I started out, but since I'm a clinical insomniac that was within my personal limits. Well, truthfully it was maybe a little extreme and not something I'd recommend, but there does come a time when you have to slow down a bit. It may be hard to remember to take breaks when things are going well, but breaks are important. Not just on a physical level so that your hands get a rest, but also to give your brain time to process what you are trying to learn.

The Written Word

This section is what I'd like to call a "future proof," because when I started writing this book there were no books about ZBrush at all. When choosing any textbook it's best to keep in mind things such as recommendations from instructors, friends in the industry whose advice you trust, and of course any reviews.

Although reviews may be helpful, try to read the table of contents for a book and make sure that it contains what you need. You can usually read a few pages of a book to get an idea of the author's style of writing and philosophy. Obviously, the books you choose will be well-written and by an authority on the subject.

Form and Replication

The study of form and the ability to replicate it are fundamental digital sculpting skills. To an artist who has never sculpted, either traditionally or digitally, these can be rather difficult concepts. So what is form? Put simply, *form* is the shape and overall lines of an object. A more complex explanation is that form is the interaction of objects.

We must also remember to take into account the type of model we are sculpting. Sculpting a human being will be approached differently formwise from the methods used to sculpt an animal or a hard surface object. So how do we learn about form? Let's look at some of the basic concepts to get you on your way.

The overall outline or silhouette is the first thing we want to look at. This gives some basic information about the shapes that make up whatever it is we are sculpting. Those of you with a traditional background in drawing will probably already do this without thinking, but the ability to use negative space to work out the shape of the object is a core concept for people new to art.

If we take, for example, the human head, there are a number of common mistakes that we see new digital sculptors make. The most common of these is to make the front of the face flat instead of curved. (This is due to a phenomenon known as "iconography," which we will discuss further in a bit.) When studying the form of a human face, we need to look at it from a number of angles and concentrate not on the details but rather on the very big shapes.

You can break the head down into a number of primitive shapes such as circles, rectangles, and triangles. We can then refine these further by taking into account negative space (the area around a model) to give us the information we need regarding the actual shape of the features. When we look at the human head from above, you'll notice that the front of the face is not flat but rather a curved "V" shape. You will see that the features and the spaces between them make patterns that are easy to remember. Memorizing how things are put together and combining that with a knowledge of anatomy allows you to take your artwork to a higher level.

Breaking a model down into shapes and curves allows us to start looking at it less as a complex object and more as a series of simple shapes. This is the key to understanding form and is something that you will find yourself refining over time.

Studying the form and interpreting it correctly can be made easier with good lighting and made a whole lot more difficult with bad lighting or complex textures. For a beginner it is best to start your journey into the study of form by looking at traditional sculptures by the old masters. Since these are usually carved from a single material such as marble and often well lit in museums, working out the major shapes and curves is a lot easier. While we can learn a lot from the old masters, we should keep in mind that the sculpted piece was often meant to be seen under specific lighting, in a specific place, and from a certain angle. A classic example of this would be Michelangelo's *David*. If you could look at it from the floor level, you would find some of the proportions are "off" because it was meant to be seen raised on its plinth.

This was a conscious decision made by Michelangelo, and in fact is one of the geniuses of the work itself. So be aware that if you want to replicate a classical sculpture, the lighting, placement, and viewing angle are very important if you wish it to look the same as the original.

Many traditional sculpting techniques can translate very well indeed in ZBrush, and may be important to remember as you progress. The keys to learning digital sculpting are knowing what each tool will do, choosing and using the correct tool, and interpreting form correctly.

Iconography and Why It's Bad News

Iconography is best explained as a bad habit that all humans learn to use to represent forms. If you ask a young toddler to draw a tree, he'll probably draw a mess of branch-like lines sprouting from a central trunk; however, if you ask the same child when he is older, he will probably draw a classic "lollipop" tree shape. So why is that, and why and where does this change take place?

Children are born with no preconceived notions. As they learn and develop, society imprints on them what things "look like." So a big tree suddenly becomes a large stick with a circle on the top, and a face is a circle with two eyes, a nose, and smiley lips like the face you see in standard icon sets. Incidentally, the reason that these icons are designed as they are is to further use our built-in iconography.

As artists, though, is important for us to avoid the use of symbols and icons as it impedes our application of true form. If you start to draw a face and automatically draw the lips in a smile, you know this is incorrect. This is the difference between looking and seeing. Looking can be best thought of as iconography, whereas seeing can be thought of as a study and interpretation of form. So as you can see, iconography is bad.

In the words of a very famous green movie character, "You must unlearn what you have learned." You must forget what you think is there and see what is actually there. Three-quarters of all drawing and sculpting problems are caused by artists trying to reproduce what they "think" is there as opposed to what actually is. Learning to override our natural iconography instincts is not an easy process, and I'm not about to pretend that it is. In fact, it's a process that every artist never really finishes and continues to refine over a lifetime. But like many things in life, the more you practice the better you will get.

It is also worth remembering that even the best artists get into bad habits from time to time. Someone who sculpts the same shape over and over, such as the human male head, will end up with a lot of shortcuts and ways to make the human male head quickly and effectively. But unfortunately, unless you actively continue to learn about form and correct interpretation, it's very easy to get into a rut and do things the same way each time. That is the reason why criticism is of such importance to any artist regardless of their skill level, as we can all get into these bad habits from time to time.

If part of a sculpture is giving you problems, you may need to go back and break the forms down to see where the problem area is. Concentrate on and practice sculpting the area giving you problems until you feel comfortable reproducing that particular form. For example, if you're having problems sculpting the human nose, you may wish to do a number of separate nose sculptures.

If you find yourself stuck in your comfort zone too much you will find that the quality of your work suffers. It can end up stale, uninteresting, or downright bland. Artists who only do the things they are good at don't get a chance to sharpen their skills or learn and upgrade their skill sets, so it is essential to keep pushing into new areas and broaden your skills.

Form and Replication Part 2

Sculpting in Planes

Up to now I've been trying to explain how to "think" about form and get information that we can then use and interpret in a digital sculpture in ZBrush. In this section, however, we are going to outline how we can take this information and use it in a practical way. So the discussions here will be used later in our main project, "The Guardian," to interpret the anatomical information.

There are a number of ways to approach translating theoretical information we've gleaned from observation into a practical digital sculpt. Some artists prefer to analyze lines, negative space, curves, horizontals, and verticals to get the information they need and use traditional 2D skills to create their sculpts. Others like me prefer to incorporate traditional methods such as clay sculpting more directly into the digital form.

So while I do obviously make use of some of the aforementioned techniques that are based more in the 2D world to observe the form I am wanting to replicate digitally, I also add to these a whole host of more traditional sculpting skills. I find that this gives me the best of both worlds and the ability to translate the information faster and more accurately into a digital sculpture in ZBrush.

Earlier, we covered such things as the importance of looking not at the item itself that you are trying to replicate but at its silhouette. We can be the victims of optical illusion at times, but through analysis we can often see objects more accurately. I also use traditional sculpting skills like studying the planes of the human face and body to help me in the sculpting process.

If you take a look at the section on sculpting the Guardian's body in Chapter 18, you will see that I break the body down into flat areas (planes) before using these to create the final complex body sculpture. An easy way to think of planes is to visualize a 1,000-polygon model of a male in its untextured and unsmoothed state. In wireframe mode we would be able to see many areas that have been simplified down to flat planes. So by breaking this simplification of planes into smaller chunks, we can make the job of modeling the major forms fairly easy.

As an example let's take a photo of a human mouth and analyze the number of planes for the upper lip area running up to the nose. Many artists with little or no formal traditional sculpting experience would find it hard to interpret what they see and take for granted each day.

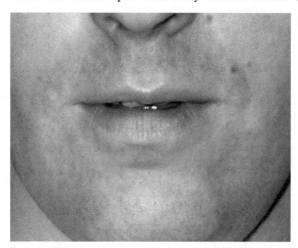

FIGURE 1-2

However, if we look at the image with some lines drawn in to show the major planes of that area, we can now see that there are in fact six distinct flat planes that can be used to interpret this area quickly and correctly. You will find that this series of flat areas of the human mouth is constant across ethnic, age, and gender barriers and only changes due

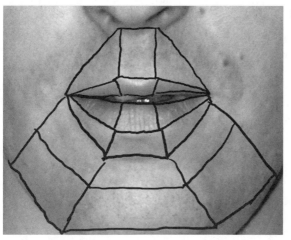

FIGURE 1-3

to expression. In the example here, I've extended the planes beyond the mouth to help show how they would integrate into the face

If we examined the nose we would find six distinct planes for that as well: one running from the top of the bridge of the nose to the tip, one down each side of the nose, and three for the bottom part of it. Obviously, these simplifications make it far easier to sculpt them in ZBrush. The more clearly you can understand and interpret a form as a series of planes and angles, the more technically adept at digital sculpting you will become. The rest is down to learning the tools of your trade and your own personal artistic ability. Learning to see your reference as a series of planes and angles means you are much more able to use this technique to create totally new models and designs with no reference whatsoever.

The study of planes as a way of modeling forms is not something new to ZBrush or digital sculpting; traditional sculptors have used this technique for a very long time. So how do you get your geometry to the stage where you can use these planes? My personal favorite workflow is to first add some mass for the area I'll be sculpting (in this case the mouth), and then break this into planes using the Flatten brush before smoothing them off and adding some finishing touches to the forms. Other brushes such as the Clay brush also work great with this sort of workflow as it already has a bit of a flattening effect.

If you are used to sculpting the old-fashioned way of adding a form and then making it look the way you want, you will certainly see a vast improvement in your speed and accuracy by using this method of sculpting. But I also want to point out that although I love sculpting this way, I do break it up and use it for certain parts of a model and use other methods for other parts. So while for a body I will certainly make heavy use of planes, I rarely use them for a face and only for areas that may be more complex to block in, and go "by feel" for the rest of it.

Form and its translation into a 3D sculpture is basically the same whether you are using clay or polygons in ZBrush. It comes down to the ability to see a form as a three-dimensional object in your head before you sculpt it. So while I can look at the mouth and see it as a mouth, I can also see this disembodied mouth as a separate entity that is made up of a series of flat surfaces. I cannot overstate the importance of planes in sculpting, be it digital or traditional.

The Use of Shapes to Sculpt Anatomical Detail

The use of basic shapes is something that those of you who draw will know well by now. If you were to draw a television set, chances are you would start with a rectangular shape, taking perspective into account. Now using this technique in a different way we can add the anatomical detail that we have already learned (or are learning). If you break the body down not only into its series of planes but also into a number of shapes that indicate each muscle "mass," you start to see how easy it can be to translate that anatomy knowledge into something you can start to use immediately.

If you use this knowledge of muscle shapes along with planes and negative space, you can interpret and reproduce the anatomical structure of the human body a lot easier. A sound knowledge of muscle insertion points, muscle types, and how they all fit together as an organic machine is a must if you are going to be serious about digitally sculpting the human form.

There is no "one size fits all" solution that can guarantee you will produce a great sculpt each time. Like all artists, you will have both strong and weak areas. It is up to you to try to correct those things you consider yourself to be weak on, and improve them where you can. To expand yourself as an artist you must tackle the hard things that drive you crazy trying to get right. But remember that the technical side of digital sculpting is the easy part. Adding the "art" to a digital sculpt is much harder.

Words of Caution

As I've already mentioned, the methods I've outlined are intended to be used in addition to knowing anatomy. Without proper structures, your model may look fine in its standard pose, but other poses will suddenly go wrong.

I would also advise treating each model you create as a separate entity that requires its own interpretation and not as a number of pieces that you can mark off on a checklist of things you have already done. While you can certainly use what you have learned from previous sculpts, always remember that each person or animal is different and as such you will need to adapt what you already know to be able to sculpt it in a way you are finally satisfied with. What I'm trying to say is there are no shortcuts, and you do have to put some work in — sometimes a lot of work — to get to the level that you wish to. But again, if it was easy to learn it wouldn't be fun, would it?

Another cautionary note is that after spending time learning human anatomy, if you do not keep using the knowledge you will find that you forget it. So try to do some regular sculpts that are as anatomically correct as possible every few weeks to keep your skills current.

Mental Approaches to ZBrush

One of the most common mistakes in the whole of 3D and art in general is one so simple it often gets overlooked. Your state of mind and how you mentally approach something can be the difference between sculpting something amazing and producing a piece of visual crud that offends the eyes of even the least artistic people. As artists, especially when starting out, we can often get far too caught up in *how* to do a thing. Technique can become all encompassing to the detriment of the art itself sometimes. It's important to think about the simple fact that for 99.9 percent of artists on planet Earth, their state of mind affects the quality of the art they produce.

The most common problem is the lack of self-confidence and taking the whole thing far too seriously. Many times we see people so anxious of making any wrong move in case they suddenly turn a promising model into a piece of rubbish they become overly cautious. Suddenly every single move and brushstroke (or move of a polygon in traditional polygon modeling) becomes a point of intense focus to make sure no mistakes are made. But as artists we learn from our mistakes. Surprising as it seems, the more you make early on in your sculpting life, the more lessons you will learn.

Now at the risk of alienating the entire readership of this book, let me outline something that hopefully may help put the whole thing into perspective. No one is going to drop dead or hit you with a baseball bat if your sculpt looks less than perfect. It's not like being an armed soldier in a combat situation where one mistake can cost him his life. I suppose what I'm trying to say is that this is *art*, not *war*! Take a look around ZBrushCentral (Pixologic's ZBrush forum) and you will very soon realize that the very best ZBrush artists are the ones who are obviously confident in how and why they are doing a model. They know they can do it and it's a much more relaxed and enjoyable process for them than stressing out over every brushstroke. This isn't to say that they don't take it seriously as an art form — far from it, in fact. Just that they have learned a very valuable lesson early on that their state of mind and knowing how and why to make a sculpt affects how well it turns out.

I am not advocating becoming a know-it-all, as even the greatest artist has plenty to learn. It's often said that being an expert at anything isn't about what you know but about realizing what you don't know.

When you sculpt it's a good idea to approach it with confidence, believing you can do it before you ever even open up ZBrush to sculpt. Keep plenty of backup copies, so that if you do indeed mess up you haven't lost the whole model and have learned something from the process of getting something wrong. This is why I personally see mistakes as a good thing, because they give me the most important thing in the world — information. If you know what areas you are having problems with, you can make a decision to concentrate on those until you improve.

A small character from a well-known film series once said, "Fear is the path to the dark side." He was right when it comes to art too. The moment that you are scared you will mess up is the moment your sculpt starts to take on a negative aspect. From then onward it is a one-way trip to the land of "bad sculpts."

Breaking what you are about to sculpt into a series of small steps also makes it much easier to feel confident. Adding the upper nose is a lot less scary than saying "I'm going to sculpt the upper face." But with experience comes another kind of confidence, one that can't be learned. It comes with having done enough digital sculpts to know that you can tackle any one of a number of types of models fairly easily. Once at this stage (which is the hardest to achieve), you stop thinking about technique altogether most times and concentrate on what your art "says." My opinion is that this moment — when it's about what your art is saying to others and how it affects their emotions — is when you truly become an artist.

Another impediment and one that is much harder to work around than a lack of confidence is working while under extreme stress. Let's face it, life can be stressful at times. Even if we totally ignore art or work-related stress we still have the stress of everyday life to contend with, which can put us in the wrong mood or mental "place" to sculpt.

If you are the sort of artist like myself, who when stressed manages to produce a sculpture that is total lifeless crud, you will know it can be a source of even more stress and can begin to affect your self-confidence as an artist. There are two basic ways to handle it: Either sculpt only when you're not stressed, or work through the stress and learn to use it to help your brain focus on the art when you need to. When working in an environment where you are paid to model, you obviously can't tell your boss "Sorry, I can't work today as I'm under stress." So sometimes you have no choice but to work through it or find another way to be productive.

Almost anyone can learn to sculpt given enough time, but only certain people have the mindset or learn the right mental approaches to become "artists." So the very fact that you are reading this book tells me that you are taking steps to learn.

I should point out that this section is a guideline only and not a set of "Wayne's golden rules," because everyone is different and each must find his own way. So use these guidelines in a way that suits you best. Overall, be confident that you can indeed do the job set out before you, and try to keep yourself from getting stressed out over any mistakes.

Let me illustrate with a little story to show you how I learned that stress and lack of confidence are not useful things for an artist. Some time back I had a model to do for a client that was well outside my area of expertise. As a result I wasn't confident about doing it, and I was worried I'd mess up and get a bad reputation, so stress set in. This of course turned into a self-fulfilling prophecy, and I did indeed produce a work of "non art" that no one has ever seen. When I sat and broke down why I had messed up so badly at something well within my technical skill level, I realized that my approach was wrong. My next attempt was approached with confidence that I knew I could do it. Additionally, I kept many backups (about 100!) so that any stress caused by potential mistakes ups was kept to a minimum. The result was a model I was proud of and money in the bank.

Have fun while you sculpt, as you're supposed to be enjoying it, and do not make every sculpting session your own personal version of 3D hell. Stay positive and realize that even from our mistakes we learn something new.

2 Finding Your Way Around ZBrush

Explanation of 2D, 2.5D, and 3D

With ZBrush you can work in 2D, 2.5D, and 3D. While best known as a 3D digital sculpting tool, it is capable of a lot more. It can also be used to produce 2D and 2.5D art, and has a number of specialized tools to help with this. The 2D tools can be used for creating concept art, and the 3D tools are commonly used for producing digital sculpts. However, many users have problems comprehending what the 2.5D tools are for and actually do.

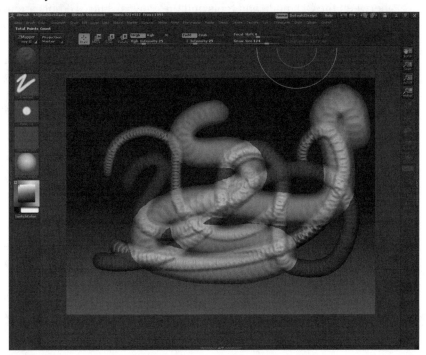

FIGURE 2-1

So what is 2.5D and how does it work? Put simply, 2.5D is like a standard 2D drawing or painting on steroids because it allows us to add elements of 3D into the drawing or painting. This is fast becoming a workflow for environment concept art, incidentally. ZBrush makes use of the technology called "pixols." Unlike standard pixels that record only the color, pixols also record depth and material information. So it really is a halfway point between 2D and 3D.

It's worth remembering that when you are working in Projection Master mode in ZBrush and drop your model onto the canvas, you are in fact working in 2.5D and can use all of the 2D and 2.5D tools. The 2.5D state lets you use tools that allow you to get effects that otherwise would be impossible to achieve.

The Difference between the Canvas and 3D Mode

In ZBrush it is important to realize that there is a very big difference between the 3D mode and tools and the canvas. The 3D tools are used to create our digital sculpts and can be rotated and generally messed around with until we are happy with them. The *canvas*, also known as the document, contains the lighting, depth, and shading information. For example, say you have made a model of a face in ZBrush you're happy with and have it textured and detailed just the way you want it. You can then uncheck Edit mode and drop it to the canvas. The model is now part of the canvas and is no longer 3D.

When we came out of 3D mode the model ceased to be a piece of actual 3D geometry. ZBrush automatically removed all the geometry that is hidden from the camera, such as the back of the head. Now you are free to use the 2.5D tools to get a number of effects in the viewport without having to drop the model into Projection Master.

For example, you can change the materials, lights, and color information, and even add some sculpting details. So you can see there are times when 2.5D is very handy indeed and is a very versatile part of ZBrush.

If you find that you've forgotten to save your 3D model, there is a very easy way to get it back again, providing you have not reinitialized ZBrush. Simply go to your Tool palette, find your model there, and then save it.

The easiest way to understand the concept behind pixol technology is to think of it as a long, narrow room with one of the walls at the short end as your viewport. So the back of any geometry that may be on the

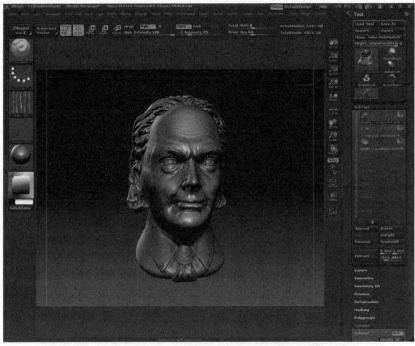

FIGURE 2-2

canvas is culled and thus removed from the memory used for the canvas.

So because we have depth, color, and material information in our canvas, we can change things such as the lighting. It also gives us the option to add different materials to different parts of a model. For example, if we have a model of a head on the canvas, we can paint the skin using a number of different materials with different specularity to better simulate human skin.

You can, of course, use more than one layer, and each layer can be moved in the Layer palette, which we will cover later on in the book. You can also completely ignore painting with depth and materials and just use ZBrush as a standard 2D painting tool.

Navigating Around ZBrush

When you first open ZBrush and begin sculpting, you are obviously going to need to know how to move around inside of the canvas. Although ZBrush sometimes gets a bad rap about its style of navigation, this is usually due to not understanding the reason why it works the way it does. It is important to remember that ZBrush was designed with the use of a tablet in mind, and as such its navigation makes minimal use of modifier keys (hotkeys) where possible.

Let's start our discussion of navigation by opening one of the default models on the splash screen. Now I'll outline the basics for you so that while you are reading you can mess around in ZBrush to get used to a few things as they are described.

Rotating the Model

A model in ZBrush can be rotated by dragging with the left mouse button (or pen if you have a tablet) anywhere in empty space around your model. You can rotate your model in any way that you wish.

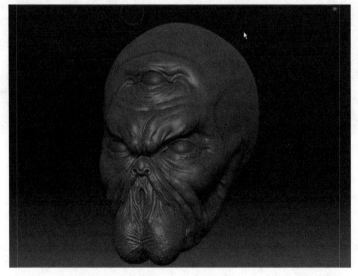

FIGURE 2-3

Take a look at a few of the options on the bar down the right side of the default interface. (This bar is called the "right shelf.") If you choose the **Local** button, the model will rotate around the last point of the model that you touched with a brush. This is actually very handy if you are working on a specific area on a large model as it will let you get a better look at things without having to navigate to that section of your model again and again.

Further down you will see the **Move** button. With this button active you can click and hold your left mouse button (or pen) to move your model up and down and from side to side in the viewport. You can also do this by pressing the **Alt** key and clicking and holding anywhere outside of the model in your viewport. You will notice that if you have a model containing subtools, all the tools move together at the same time.

The **Scale** button requires a bit more work. To zoom your model in and out (which is technically scaling your model up and down), simply left-click and hold down the **Alt** key as before, but then release the Alt key and move your mouse to scale your model. Again, you'll notice that this works on a model with subtools by moving them all together at the same time.

There are three buttons below the Rotate button that control the rotational axis used by ZBrush when you are rotating your model. **XYZ** mode, best thought of as the standard default mode in ZBrush, allows free rotation in any direction you wish. The **Y** button and the **Z** button constrain the rotation to the selected axis.

The **Frame** button turns on wireframe mode for the selected subtool. (It is also accessed with the hotkey combination of **Shift+F**.) Worth noting is that if you turn on your wireframe with a sculpt at its lowest subdivision level, you will have that low-res wireframe over the high-resolution mesh as you step up the subdivision levels of the sculpt. But if you switch it on while at your highest subdivision level and start to step down, it will automatically update.

The **Transp** button simply turns the selected subtool's view type to transparent. This allows you to see how it interacts with your other subtools should you have any and check alignments, etc.

At the bottom of the right shelf is the selection type. By default, ZBrush is set up to work using the rectangular marquee selection type. This is like dragging a rectangle over your model to select certain parts of it. If you switch to the Lasso selection type you can draw around the selection that you require.

This should give you enough of an idea to progress with the rest of the book and explore everything in ZBrush.

Hiding and Showing Geometry

Knowing how to not only sculpt your model but also how to hide and reveal certain parts are skills that no ZBrush user can really do without. There are a number of reasons why you may want to hide part of your model while you are working on it. For one, it simply makes it a bit easier to concentrate on the part of the model that you are working on. It also increases performance a bit to make the experience of sculpting a little easier and less taxing on your computer.

I'll start by outlining how to both hide and show certain polygons based on a single mesh, before moving on to polygrouped models and finally subtools.

Hiding Geometry on a Single Mesh

Before we start, it is important to realize that there are two ways that you can select geometry in ZBrush. You can use a mask and then hide the unmasked area, or you can drag a selection area over your model. The default drag selection type is set to a rectangular shape (or Marquee selection), but if you prefer you can switch to the Lasso.

Lasso selection is very useful for times when the shape you want to hide or show is irregular. This allows you to draw a custom shape around the areas that you wish to affect on your sculpt. If you have used ZBrush since version 1.4 or 2, you may be used to just having a rectangular selection and not really want to switch, and that's fine. The whole point is to find a way of working that is the most comfortable to you.

To hide a section of your geometry, simply hold down the **Ctrl** and **Shift** keys at the same time and **drag a selection** (or lasso) over the part of the model you wish to show. This should show up as shaded green within the marquee so that you can easily tell what is going to be hidden and what's not.

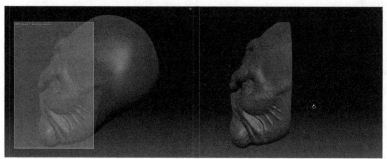

FIGURE 2-4

To remove a section of your geometry and add it to the hidden area, start by holding down the **Ctrl** and **Shift** keys as before and drag your area over the model. But before releasing your selection, **lift the Shift key only**. The selection will now be a red color and will add this area to your hidden selection. It's interesting to note that you can use this method to hide your model even with nothing currently hidden (see Figure 2-5).

If you want to invert your hidden area (as sometimes you will find it much easier to hide the parts that you actually need rather than the parts that you don't), simply hold down **Ctrl** and **Shift** and **left-click on the mesh itself.** You will find that this keypress and click combination performed on an empty area of the canvas causes your entire model to be shown again.

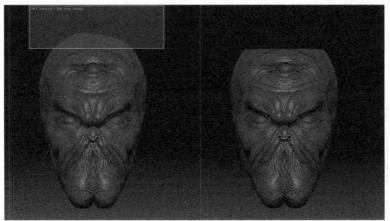

FIGURE 2-5

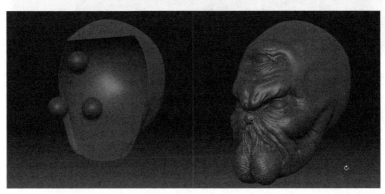

FIGURE 2-6

Hiding by Polygon Groups

You will probably find that it is a rather good idea to split your model up into separate polygon groups early on. A model containing polygroups is still one complete mesh; polygroups are just a simple way to help you manage your model. Polygroups can be used to hide and show the mesh, and also allow you to export each section and set up multiple UVs covering more than the traditional UV space.

To split a single model into groups, simply hide parts of your mesh as mentioned above and then go to the **Polygroups** section of your **Tool** palette and press the **Group Visible** button. This will add all the currently visible polygons to a polygon group. To see your polygon groups as you progress, click the **Frame** button on the main interface or press **Shift + F.** (You can also find Frame under the Transform palette.)

With your polygroups created, you can now unhide the whole model by pressing **Shift + Ctrl** and clicking outside of the mesh. Another option is to invert your visible selection as mentioned above, and simply group that section as well. If you need to set up rather complex polygon groups, you can hide all the polygons within a group by simply hovering over that group and **Shift+Ctrl+clicking** on it. This will automatically select the polygons within that group and hide all other groups and polygons.

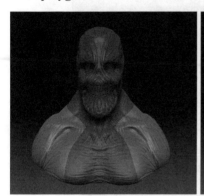 

FIGURE 2-7

So for a complex selection of groups, it is a simple matter of selecting a group, hiding more polygons from this selection, and making another group from those left. You can make as many groups as you need.

Tip: If I'm working on a humanoid type model, I set up groups for each limb and the head. Sometimes if I know the polygon count is going to get heavy I may also split the back and front of the torso as well.

When working on a human head I will often set up certain key features in separate groups. I usually have one for the eye area, one for the ears, the nose in another along with the mouth area, and maybe another for the back of the head. This allows me much more control of what to hide or show when I'm working and can vastly increase performance if working on a slower machine.

It is usually a good idea to only group things at their lowest subdivision level. The logic behind this is that if you need to export a section to be UV mapped in an external application at some point, there is no chance of polygons going missing due to having set up a polygon group in a higher level. It's a good habit to do as much of the "housekeeping" such as this in the first subdivision level.

Hiding Using Masks

Right above the Polygroups section in the right tray you will see the Masking section. Hiding and showing parts of your model using masks is really as easy as falling off a log.

FIGURE 2-8

To paint a mask onto your model, simply hold down the **Ctrl** key and paint. You can remove areas from your mask by holding **Ctrl+Alt** and painting as well. If you are working from outside of your model on the canvas, you can also drag a marquee mask over it to get a perfect straight edge.

Once you have the area you want selected with your mask (which should appear considerably darker than the rest of your model), just go to the **Masking** section of the **Tool** palette and press the **HidePt** button. This will hide every part of your model that does not have a mask painted on it at that time. If you wish to show your geometry again, either press **Ctrl+Shift** and click in the empty canvas, or use the **ShowPt** button.

Tip: If there is a part of your geometry that you wish to delete permanently, you can do this by hiding the part you wish to remove, and then pressing the DelHidden button located in the Geometry section of the Tool palette. Be aware that this will remove these polygons forever and there is no way back short of pressing Ctrl+Z to undo.

Showing and Hiding Using Subtools

Although the use of subtools will be covered elsewhere in this book, this section wouldn't be complete without mentioning hiding and showing geometry that is split into subtools. If your model has a number of parts, each split into its own tool (or subtool), life gets much easier when it comes to hiding or showing parts of your sculpt.

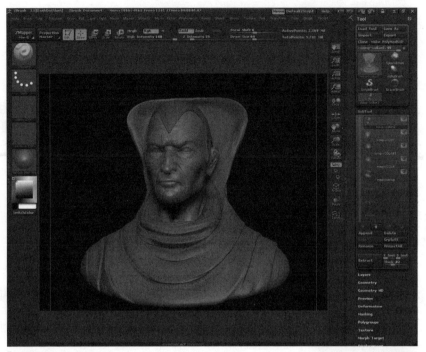

FIGURE 2-9

You may, for example, have each article of clothing or each accessory split into a separate tool. That way you can concentrate on a character's hat or jacket without the distraction or RAM overhead created by having all your tools visible at the same time. Or maybe you just want to be able to quickly center the area you're working on. But whatever the reason, there will be cases when you will want to work on a section of your model in isolation from the rest of the sculpture.

Notice that next to each subtool there is an icon shaped like a eye. Click on the subtool's eye icon to make that layer invisible until it is switched back on. If you have a large number of subtools for a complex project, you can isolate the currently selected subtool by clicking on its eye icon and then making all the others invisible.

To switch all the subtools back on, it is a simple matter of clicking on the icon again. It is important to remember that whenever you switch to another subtool, that subtool will then be isolated, and all the

FIGURE 2-10

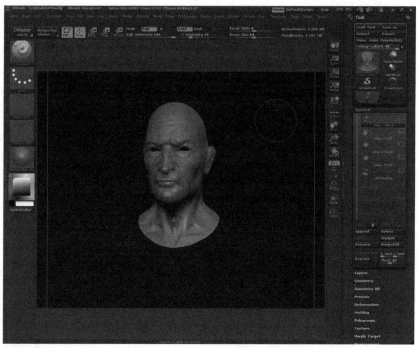

FIGURE 2-11

others will be invisible. As you can see, this is a very powerful workflow when you are working on a digital sculpt with many parts.

Tip: If you are going to be rendering out your final image in another application and are using multiple UV sets, this also means you can paint the texture for the selected subtool. For more information on splitting your model into separate subtools as part of a multi-UV set, see Chapter 11.

At the moment ZBrush does not support multiple UV sets on a sculpt being shown at the same time, so this is a very good workaround for occasions when your model has more than one set of UVs, or even for occasions where your UV set goes beyond the usual 0,1 range.

Hardware Requirements

Without a computer to run it on, ZBrush would be as much use as a chocolate tea cozy, so the choice of hardware you run it on is very important. I must first of all point out that inside of a few months any hardware information in this section will be out of date, so I'll just outline the concepts of what to look for as best I can.

If you have previously only been running a couple of spreadsheets and your email client, then you haven't needed a powerful PC. (In fact, something about five years old could do the job well.) But an application such as ZBrush needs more power behind it to make your experience as pleasant as possible. Although ZBrush is optimized to use fewer system resources than any similar application, you may still need to upgrade your computer a little to get it in the right "fighting shape" for sculpting.

Something that may surprise you is that ZBrush makes very little use of your graphics card. So an über fast card with amounts of RAM that would let you run the very latest PC game on its highest setting won't make a whole lot of difference. The only part of ZBrush that does make use of your graphics card is ZMapper. I do recommend using a name-brand card, though, because it will have fewer problems and you'll be able to find updated drivers for it more easily than for something made by two blokes in a shed in Norway.

It's a simple and rather harsh fact that software makers are always at the mercy of the drivers for hardware, so you really want to make sure that the company who designed your graphics card releases updates regularly.

What ZBrush does need is RAM. At the time of writing, 2 GB of DDR2 is the minimum you'd want. It will run and work with less, but you won't be able to go as high with your poly counts without slowing down. Bear in mind that your operating system may have limits imposed on what actual RAM it will allow to be used on any single application. Windows XP 32-bit will not allow any application to use more than 2 GB even if you have more in your machine. But what more RAM will do is allow you some breathing room for opening and using other applications at the same time, such as when using Photoshop with ZAppLink.

Windows Vista has both 32- and 64-bit versions that allow you to use more RAM and offer features such as "ReadyBoost" that allow you to use USB memory sticks as a type of additional RAM.

At the time of this writing the version for the Mac was not yet available, so please refer to the Pixologic site for those hardware requirements.

Another very important part of your hardware setup is your processor. ZBrush is very CPU oriented, so the bigger and better your CPU when used in conjunction with a decent amount of RAM, the higher you will be able to go in complete comfort polygon count wise. ZBrush supports a higher CPU core technology than is currently available, so as a rough guide, the more powerful and more cores your CPU has, the better performance you will get out of ZBrush. Without getting into a very long, drawn-out discussion about front side bus speeds, etc., you want to go for the fastest you can afford, along with a name you recognize that is aimed at a high-performance user. Don't be tempted to economize by choosing a CPU that is not intended for CGI or heavy use.

The monitor is often overlooked on a setup for ZBrush, but as it's our visual interface with the computer and allows us to actually see what we are sculpting, don't skimp here either. Always try to use a calibrated monitor so that you see what is actually there and not what is influenced by any characteristics your monitor may have. This is especially important for painting color texture maps for sculpts that may be seen in film or TV or those models you intend to print out.

You'll also want a resolution of at least 1280 or better so you will have enough space to see your sculpt. But be aware that the higher the screen resolution, the more of your memory Windows will require before any is handed over for ZBrush to use. You need at least a 17-inch monitor, but you'll be happiest with the largest screen you can afford that will fit in your workspace.

Other things you are going to want to look at but are optional are things such as external drives and a DVD writer. The files used to store your models take up a lot of space, so look for a good sized external drive that can store all your current projects at one time. Make sure it's fast, big, and robust as it's no good having a massive external drive that will blow up in a shower of sparks as soon as you blow on it.

For similar reasons you will want to pick up a fast, reliable DVD writer so you can regularly back up your models just on the off chance that one or more of your drives crashes and burns.

Lastly, you'll want to set up a comfortable environment in which to work. The more comfortable you feel while working, the better chance there is of you doing a stellar job. Once your work area is set up properly, take care of the "extras" such as headphones and an MP3 player so that valuable resources aren't going to your PC just to play some tunes. Look for optimizations online to eliminate all non-essential services in Windows, too. This extra headroom will help things run well and may even help stave off an upgrade. And don't forget creature comforts like a good chair and a conveniently located coffeemaker.

Once you have your ZBrush mega machine, you're ready to roll!

Graphics Tablet vs. Mouse

While it is possible, and many artists actually do use a mouse for sculpting in ZBrush, a graphics tablet does make things easier in that it allows you more control over your brushes and tools.

The adult human hand has been trained to draw and write with pen type instruments, whereas the mouse is a relatively recent addition. A graphics tablet is made purely for the reasons of allowing you artistic control in an application, and a mouse is a "jack-of-all-trades." A mouse exists purely to let you navigate around your operating system on your computer, open things up, and do "stuff." A mouse was never designed for art use and will never give you the level of control you can get from a graphics tablet and stylus. So a mouse is not something you would want to use over the long term in ZBrush. ZBrush was designed with the use of a tablet in mind, so if you intend on taking it seriously, then investing in a tablet is a good move. It will allow you to use the pressure sensitivity features to fade strokes in or out, and use more or less pressure on your brush or tool as needed. (And as artists we need as much control as possible over each and every one of our tools in our quest to get our ideas from our brain and onto the canvas.)

Which Tablet Should You Choose?

It may surprise you to find out that there is indeed a difference in the expensive brand-name tablets. They usually have a much superior "feel" and just seem to allow the artist a more intuitive control of ZBrush and other artistic applications. It is actually false economy to not buy a good brand (if you can afford it) as it will be less of a barrier between your ideas and ZBrush.

If you cannot afford to buy a brand-name tablet, such as a Wacom, pick up a cheap one to use until either you are sure that digital sculpting in ZBrush is your "thing" or you have enough money to upgrade. Even a cheap tablet is better than no tablet in my opinion.

The size of your tablet is a personal choice, but I'll explain the differences and hopefully it will give you a rough guide to which sizes to look at. The basic concept is that the bigger the tablet, the larger arc your arm will have to travel to create a line on your screen. So if you prefer to draw with long, exaggerated strokes, you may need a truly huge tablet, but otherwise, either an A4 or A5 size should suffice.

The main drawing area on any tablet relates to your screen, so if you have a wide-screen or dual monitor setup, you may wish to go for one of the wide-screen variations. (There are even new Wacom tablet monitors, but since they can be costly it may be wise to do some research yourself on this.) Try them out first if you can, and ask questions of other ZBrush users who seem to have a similar way of working as yourself to find out what size they use. This should give you at least an educated guide to which will be best for you.

Please remember that a tablet is not a magic wand and you still have to work hard. If your early sculpts are complete crud, don't worry as this is usually normal for the first couple of months. Learning anything new takes time, and while Pixologic can produce the best digital sculpting application on the market, they cannot instill the experience you will need in the long term. The more time and dedication you put in, the shorter this time will be.

Digital Sculpting and the Importance of Reference

I cannot overstate the importance of using good reference when modeling. Whether it is an organic piece such as a human, animal, or monster, or even a hard surface model, you will need to have some reference photos or images handy to help you make sure that you are getting things correct.

It's also worth pointing out that if you are sculpting humanoid models, use more than one set of references for your sculptures so that they won't end up looking too similar. In fact, it's also a good idea to have a "faces" folder that just contains interesting faces with features you like. Maybe one person has an interesting nose or eyes, and another has some wonderful wrinkles.

I would strongly advise against using another person's digital sculpt (no matter how wonderful) as a reference. Why is that? Each time something is interpreted it loses a little of the reality of the original reference. So inevitably you will end up with a digital sculpture that looks a little less realistic than you wanted.

While it's great if you have a decent camera and can take your own reference photos, there are a great many places on the Internet where you can get images, both free and those that are fee based.

Once you have a good number of images in your reference library, it's often a very good idea to sort them out into sets. So have a folder for heads, one for full body shots, etc. This will make it a lot faster to find images you need in a hurry without wasting time searching through a whole load of uncategorized images. You can select those images for your sculpture that are going to help in the session you are about to do and place them in a single document by using Photoshop. This allows you to use it as a background in ZBrush (with your model on a separate layer, of course).

Another option if you are using a dual monitor setup is to simply have your reference document open on one screen, with ZBrush open on the other. This has advantages in that you won't end up with possibly important parts of your references covered by the model you are sculpting.

Reference photos are all well and good if you are sculpting things that actually exist, but what about when doing fantasy creatures or monsters? In that case you simply choose images for each part of your design. If your monster has the head of a bull crossed with a frog, you would have bull and frog head references handy for those parts. You may also want to have references with color or texture on them that may have nothing to do with the design of your sculpture, but rather as inspiration to use when it comes time to detail and texture your monster.

As well as personality, texture, and color references, also make sure you have a set of "expression" references. You can actually make your own with any digital camera just by takeing some photos of yourself with different emotions and expressions on your face. You will want to take a photo of each expression from not just the front but also the side and a three-quarter view.

If you are going to be using photos to help texture a digital sculpt, make sure that you also round these up and put them in a folder where you can find them later. There are two schools of thought on using photos (or a combination of photos and painting) on a model. To some people this is bad and may (to them at least) mean the user has less talent, while others see it as an essential workflow technique that is needed to help beat deadlines. The truth is somewhere in the middle. I personally do not see the point in banging my head agains a brick wall creating a human skin texture if I can use a combination of photos and painting. There are many times I paint a texture from scratch, and other times when I use photos. It's a matter for you as an artist to decide. But remember when it comes time to get a job, you won't get any brownie points for producing an amazing texture two weeks after the deadline.

My tip is to never wall yourself into just one way of working, but do what is best for the particular sculpture that you are working on — not what is "easy" or what "usually works."

3 Main Concepts

What Are UV Maps and Why Do I Need Them?

A UV map is a bit difficult to describe. Imagine for a moment that we have sculpted a head in traditional clay. We're very happy with it and it's time to add some color to it to bring it truly alive. So out come our paints and we start to get on with the job when a problem arises... we are blindfolded and can't actually see where to apply the paint! Added to this we aren't allowed to touch the sculpture to find out where anything is located. So how can we color our fantasy clay sculpture if in fact we have no idea where to put the paint?

This is a very basic idea of why UV maps are needed; they tell the model where each pixel of our 2D texture goes. While ZBrush can handle raw polygon painting within the application, if you wish to use this color elsewhere you are going to have to export a texture map, and without a set of UVs you cannot create a reliable texture map to export.

If your sculpt is for use entirely in ZBrush it is possible to get away without having any UVs; however, in most production pipelines this is not of much use.

There are two ways to generate a set of UVs for your model. First, you can make your UV map in an external program and import it to ZBrush. Or you can use the built-in tools in ZBrush to make a UV map very quickly and easily.

Making UVs in ZBrush

Making UVs for your digital sculpt in ZBrush is very easy, although the resultant set may not be suitable for a complex pipeline where additional painting may be required afterward. But for home projects or personal things that you wish to get done quickly, they are perfect.

Simply step down to your lowest subdivision level and go down the **Tool** palette until you get to the **Texture** section (see Figure 3-1). You will see six buttons at the bottom (each button makes a different type of UV map that will wrap around your model in a different way) and a number of sliders. This is where you make your UV map in ZBrush. By hovering over each of the buttons that denote the type of UV mapping used, you'll see a short description that will let you know what each is and how it will affect your model.

The most interesting to most ZBrush users are **GUVTiles** and **AUVTiles**. GUV stands for Group UVs, and gives a different portion of the map to each UV group on the mesh. AUV stands for Adaptive UVs, and gives you the option of taking each polygon and mapping it in its own space. This can be set so each polygon gets exactly the same amount of space on the texture map/UV map, or so that the larger areas get more texture. To control how much area the larger polygons get, you can use the **AUVRatio** slider, which ranges from 1 to 5. A setting of 1 means that each polygon gets the same amount of space on the UV map, while a setting of 5 would give the largest polygons no more than five times the space of the smallest ones.

If we wanted to set a tileable texture for something like a wall, we could assign a map type and then use the **Hrepeat** and **Vrepeat** sliders to set how many times in each direction we would like it to repeat when a map is applied. You can check your UVs for any seams or overlapping by clicking on the **Uv>Txr** button to see a visual representation of what the UV map will look like.

To fix any seams you can simply click the **Fix Seam** button once you have made any adjustments

FIGURE 3-1

using the **AdjU** and **AdjV** sliders. These two sliders allow you to move your UV mapping either vertically or horizontally to get the UV map that you wish.

External Applications and UV Generation

There will be times when you need more control over your UV map, such as when it will be used in a game engine and other artists will be required to paint the model, or simply so that you can add some post-ZBrush work on your texture maps. Game engines require that every texture be optimized to the highest degree in order to conserve resources.

Some game companies may even have a "house style" that necessitates using an external application for UV maps. One thing to bear in mind when making your UVs in another application is to make sure that you use the lowest subdivision level of your sculpt. There are two reasons for this: First because it's easier, and second because ZBrush will only let you import models with the same number of vertices into your sculpt. If you have UVs on your models, they will only be used if you are importing into the lowest subdivision level.

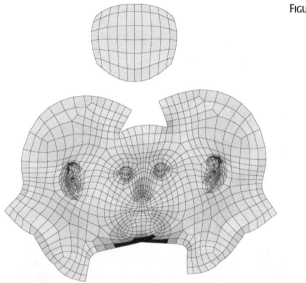

FIGURE 3-2

Make sure that you do not put each UV island of polygons too close to each other or to the edges of your texture. While it is understandable to try to get the most space you can out of your texture, especially for game models, you do not want to cut things too fine and produce problems further down a pipeline. Make sure that ZBrush has room to "breathe" a bit.

You'll also want to make sure that you do not have any overlapping polygons or vertices. Using any "relax UVs" options that your application may have can sometimes help, although there will be times when you will have to go in by hand and move vertices into the right positions. Always double-check for problems before you export your UV mapped model, as this saves a world of hair pulling later on.

ZBrush will only recognize UVs within the default 0,1 UV space. In most applications this square is clearly marked and highlighted for convenience.

So why do we have all this UV space if we can't use it? Actually you can, and multiple UV set models are often used, especially in the film industry. While ZBrush will not allow you to see every map used on a multiple UV set model (as there is currently only one slot for the texture and so it tries to apply that to every UV set), it does allow you to generate a displacement map for a multiple UV model. However, grouping your model by UVs (using the UV Groups button) will make a polygon group for each UV set on your model. So if your model went from 0,1 to 0,3 (horizontally), then you would end up with three groups. It is then a simple matter of hiding the groups not needed, painting a texture for each one, and exporting.

Tip: If you want to paint maps for a multi-UV model, my tip is to polypaint the whole model first to a certain level, as this will help with any problems with seams you may get when using this method.

What Are Subtools?

A subtool is a designated area of a model that is created by appending, splitting, or extracting polygons.

In previous versions of ZBrush you were only allowed one polygon mesh to sculpt on at any one time. Version 3 introduced the new subtools concept, which allows you to split your sculpture into many different parts.

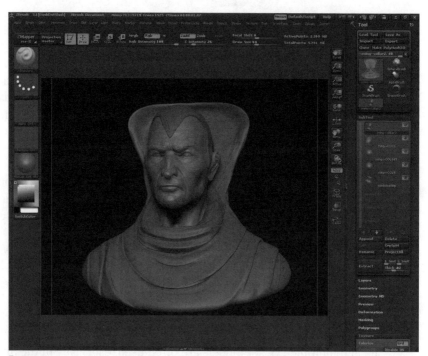

FIGURE 3-3

Now you can, for example, extract as a subtool each item of clothing a character has on, as well as specific elements such as eyeballs. What this does is separate each part so that if we are sculpting on one subtool and go near the edge where it intersects another subtool, we are prevented from making changes on the other one. This means the dangers of geometry running into each other are minimal if you take care.

There are a few ways to create subtools. You can import an entire model as a subtool. For example, you may have been working on a male anatomy study and have also been sculpting a pair of boots. You can open both tools and import the boots as a subtool to your main anatomy study. The SubTool section of the Tool palette also allows you to extract geometry from a painted mask as a brand-new part that is automatically set as a subtool.

The use of subtools also gives us the ability to hide and show the parts that we need so we don't need to have everything visible all the time while sculpting in ZBrush. Subtools also give you a way to get past your computer's maximum number of polygons. In ZBrush you can have a number of subtools with a polygon count near your maximum. This means that from a workflow perspective we have a lot of room to maneuver and can come up with interesting workflows.

There is no reason why we should use subtools only for accessories and clothes, either. Use them on any mesh where our polygon count is as high as we can really take it without going into HD geometry. This way, depending on the capabilities of your machine, you can go up to 1 billion polygons. We could also assign a different UV set to each part so that we could increase the amount of detail we could get at render time in an external renderer.

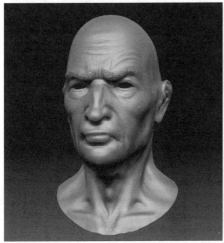

FIGURE 3-4: THE MODEL IN ITS ORIGINAL STATE

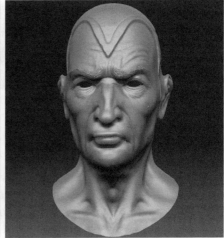

FIGURE 3-5: THE MODEL WITH PROJECTED SUBTOOLS

Subtools also give us the ability to project the details and form of one tool onto another tool. This allows a user to put together a library of parts that can then be projected onto a base mesh (a workflow that has a lot of possibilities in a game environment), or just sculpt one part as a separate thing without worrying about the rest of the model.

You will want to be completely familiar with how to use polygon groups and masks, and know a fair bit about UVs and their use in ZBrush to really get the very best out of subtools. Like a lot of things in ZBrush, you'll find that the more you explore it, the more possibilities you will find workflow wise. With the recent release of the SubTool Master plug-in by Pixologic, subtools are even more versatile than they were before.

FIGURE 3-6: A MESH WITH MULTIPLE SUBTOOLS

Appending vs. Inserting Tools

There are two ways you may wish to work with multiple tools. The first way, as mentioned above, is to use subtools as a multi-part sculpture. The other possibility is to insert other tools and sculpts into an existing model. An example of this type of workflow would be if you had a crea-ture that you wished to add another head to. If you had a suitable head that was already sculpted, you could insert this into your main mesh as opposed to using it as a separate subtool.

You append a mesh to your existing sculpt by clicking on the **InsertMesh** button in the Geometry section of the Tool palette. But to use it you must first have another tool loaded into ZBrush (as well as the one you are inserting into), and follow a few basic rules.

One very big thing to bear in mind before attempting this is that _each tool must have the same number of subdivision levels_ (either more than one, which is ideal because it allows you to continue to step up and down subdivision levels, or only one subdivision level). When you add another mesh in this way you are most likely to have a clear line where they join together. But luckily ZBrush has a special type of brush that allows you to melt these areas together so it is not noticeable.

The Clay family of brushes (**Clay** and **Clay Tube**) will let you melt your geometry together where two previously separate meshes meet. You can also use the **MeshInsert Dot** and **MeshInsert Fit** brushes to insert a piece of geometry, but these are usually more suited to a repeating theme, such as adding bullets to an ammunition belt. Inserting a mesh using the Geometry section of the Tool palette is best in my view for single items where multiple copies are not needed or required.

Appending an External Model to Your Sculpt

To add a subtool to an existing sculpture you must first load both tools into ZBrush. Please make sure that you use the **Load Tool** button in the Tool palette. If you import another OBJ over an existing model, some nasty things can happen. If you used the same base mesh (which is naughty as your models will look pretty similar if you aren't careful) and you are at subdivision level 1, it will overwrite the existing level one of your sculpture. If you are using a base mesh with the same number of points, then it will truly mess up your model in new and interesting ways. The reason for this is that it changes the point order so ZBrush doesn't know where to put the information for the other levels. And if you try to import an OBJ with a different number of points (or to a different subdivision level), you will simply get an error. So make sure that you load both your tools into ZBrush by using the Load Tool button.

Now select your main sculpture, which will make it active in the viewport, open the SubTool section of your Tool palette, and go down to **Append**. This will open a box that shows your next tool. Click on it to add this tool as a subtool to your main sculpture.

Rolling Your Own Subtools

I use the phrase "roll your own subtool" to describe taking one of the ZBrush primitives and using it as a subtool in your currently selected mesh. A typical example is the use of sphere primitives for eyes in a sculpture. In older versions of ZBrush you had to have them as part of your main mesh, which meant that not only were nearby areas more tricky to model, but also the eyeball spheres would get subdivided much more often than they needed to be.

But luckily, subtools eliminate this problem. We can use a sphere for each eye and subdivide only as much as needed, while still having total control over the main mesh we are sculpting on. Plus we can also use traditional sculpting techniques to improve the look of the eyeballs themselves.

The steps are simple for using a primitive sphere for an eye on an existing head model. However, instead of simply appending the tool into your SubTool section, this time you will need to click on your main mesh's icon in the Tool palette and scroll down to the sphere to make it active. Then, to make it a polygon mesh and ready for import as a subtool, simply press the **Make PolyMesh3D** button on the Tool palette. This will do the work for you of converting it to a polygon sphere from the special type used for primitives in ZBrush.

You can now repeat the same steps as above for the rest of the workflow.

Mask to Subtool

I could drone on and on about how cool this feature is and why you should use it. Lucky for you, I'll contain myself by saying there are a number of reasons why you would want to make a subtool from a masked area on your current tool. The most common reason, however, is so that you can create clothes or accessories for a model.

Achieving this is a simple matter of painting a mask on the part you wish to extract as a subtool and hitting the **Extract** button at the bottom of the SubTool section. It is worth knowing that you can get different types of extraction effects by using the controls found near it: E Smt, S Smt, and Thick.

E Smt

This controls how smooth you want your edges to be when extracted. The higher the number is, the smoother they will be. Put simply, it rounds the edges a bit, preventing any sharp edges; however, if this is exactly what you need, you may want to set it to its lowest setting of 1.

S Smt

This setting controls the smoothness of the surface that is extracted. So if you had a highly detailed sculpt and you only wanted to extract one of the major forms of your sculpt for use as a subtool, you would set this to a high level. If you want to extract an area with the same detail, you would set it to a low setting. Be aware that at the maximum setting it can cause interpenetration of any wrinkles, folds, and current detail into your newly created subtool.

Thick

This controls how thick you want your extracted mesh to be. For example, the default settings would be great for cloth, but you may want to increase them for leather clothing and armor. Bear in mind that not only does it work in conjunction with the other extraction settings mentioned above, but it can also be very sensitive at the lower settings, so trial and error is usually needed to find the very best setting for the type of extraction you need from it. Also remember that the current subdivision level will define the polygon count of your extracted piece, so it is rare that you will need to be at your highest subdivision level. It's usually best to work and extract at lower levels and sculpt things into place before subdividing further.

Projecting One Subtool onto Another

This often-overlooked feature of ZBrush enables you to take the details of one tool and project it onto your main (or selected) mesh. It will not only project details from one subtool onto another, but from all of the visible ones you currently have in your SubTool section.

They do not even have to be "full meshes," but can be parts you've extracted and further sculpted to your liking. An example use would be for embossed armor. Note that if the distance between the selected mesh and the other subtools is too great, you may want to use the Move brush (not Move Transform) to help lessen that distance. The closer together the surfaces, the more predictable the results.

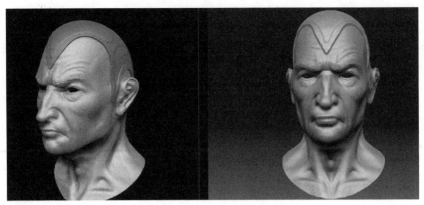

FIGURE 3-7

To project the details of all your visible subtools onto your currently selected mesh, simply scroll down in the SubTool section until you come to the **ProjectAll** button and press it. Remember that your selected mesh will only project within the limits of its currently selected subdivision level. Also, you need to remember that ZBrush will need some memory overhead to calculate what is actually a very complex set of instructions.

Hopefully now you feel completely at home with all the features of the SubTool section and everything it is capable of, and are able to add this to your workflow.

Tip: When projecting subtools onto another subtool, always store a morph target first so that you can then use the Morph brush to clean up the projection.

Low-Res vs. High-Res Base Meshes

There is one question that is common to those new to digital sculpting in ZBrush: "Is it best to start from a high-resolution base mesh or a low-resolution one?" It's not an easy question to answer and probably has as many answers as there are points of view.

You could choose a resolution based on what other artists use. The problem with this approach is that your skill levels might not match. Each approach has positive and negative aspects.

So what is considered a low-resolution base mesh? I use low poly count base meshes all the time as it fits best into my way of working, so I rarely go above 1,000 polygons for a base mesh and sometimes as low as 32 polygons for a model.

Points for Using a Low-Resolution Base Mesh

A low-resolution mesh could be considered to be as few as 32 polygons to as many as 1,000 polygons. The idea of a low-resolution base mesh is to make sure that you have just enough geometry to give the most basic idea of its form (such as two arms, two legs, and a head using the fewest polygons possible).

Making a low-resolution base mesh is faster than making a higher polygon version. You can easily make a low-polygon mesh by using ZSpheres. A ZSphere is a special tool in ZBrush that lets you create 3D objects by starting with a simple sphere shape and adding additional spheres with an easy click and drag technique. Other modeling applications have their own tools for making simple low-poly models.

In an industry such as ours where time is indeed money, this can give a great advantage. A low-resolution base mesh may also be used to create a large number of other models since the mesh itself contains very little information that may influence the direction in which the model is going. It has an added advantage in that a base mesh can be knocked out by anyone with a reasonable amount of traditional poly modeling skill and in just about any poly modeling package.

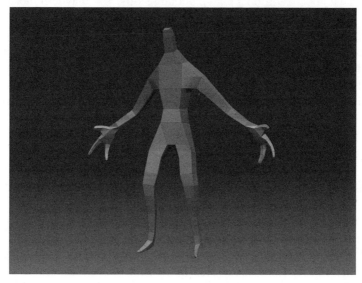

FIGURE 3-8

Points Against Using a Low-Resolution Base Mesh

So far there is a pretty good case for using low-resolution geometry for a sculpting base in ZBrush, I think you'll admit. However, it would be a little one-sided if I didn't also mention the points against using one.

Sculpting over a low-resolution mesh is hard for those starting out as it requires a good understanding of form and anatomy; arguably more so than using a high-resolution mesh. It can be very daunting for a new user to have just a handful of polygons to give any sort of hint where the forms and detail should go.

It could be said that if you can sculpt a "good" model using very low-resolution geometry, then you can easily sculpt using higher-resolution geometry. So it is a skill that users naturally drift into as they get more advanced in ZBrush.

Finally, although the chances are that any final sculpt will need to be retopologized so that it will be ready for the other stages in the process, such as animation, a low-resolution mesh is more likely to need it.

Points for Using a High-Resolution Base Mesh

If you have good traditional poly modeling skills, you may feel more comfortable using a higher-resolution base mesh in ZBrush and simply adding the finer details as opposed to sculpting from a very low-polygon base mesh. It is sometimes easy to forget that although both traditional modeling and digital sculpting in ZBrush make use of polygons, they use an entirely different skill set. A good traditional poly modeler may have a hard job adjusting to the digital sculpting workflow as it can be said to be less "logical" and more "artistic." So as a rule, many decide to continue to model to a pretty high resolution and just use ZBrush for the details, tweaking, and texturing.

It also doesn't take as much effort to learn to add those details in ZBrush over a high-res base mesh as opposed to a low one. Some may even prefer to create the majority of the form in an external package. Remember that in art there are no rules, so a production artist does whatever is needed to meet the deadline and produce good work.

There will always be issues between those who favor the low-res, more "artistic" approach and those who prefer to use high-res meshes. Just remember to work the way that feels comfortable to you at the time. Many artists find that when they reach a certain level they instinctively move from high-res meshes to low-res ones both for the challenge and because they allow more leeway to be creative. And we can usually avoid retopologizing the final sculpt because as a rule the topology will be good from our initial high-res base.

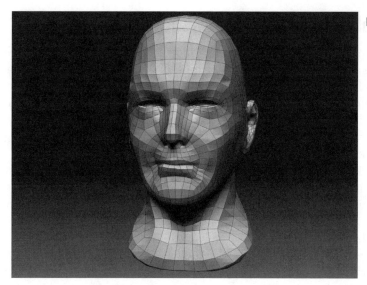

FIGURE 3-9

Points Against Using a High-Resolution Base Mesh

If you do not have a good level of traditional poly modeling skills, then using a higher-resolution base mesh may in fact require you to learn to polygon model as well as learn to use ZBrush.

Also, making a base mesh with a higher poly count is going to take a significantly longer amount of time than a low-res one. While it usually produces a model with excellent topology, that is a subject that needs to be studied all on its own. Once we have a high-res base we have sort of "walled ourselves in" to some degree artistically, as we now have a set form and polygon flow to stick to. So while it may be easy to turn a low-res mesh of a humanoid into a monster, it is a much harder process with a high-res mesh, so you are less likely to produce more than one model from it.

I also must at least touch on the uncomfortable subject of originality and artistry. If you are sculpting over high-res meshes you may be judged by other users as taking "the easy way out." It is much harder to be original if you are starting from a high-res mesh. When you get right down to basics, though, all we do as artists is make pretty pictures (which sometimes move, sometimes not), so there are no "rules." All that really matters is the final product. Providing you haven't cheated and used someone else's model as your own or claim to have done work that you haven't on a sculpture, then if it looks good that's fine. It's the differences in our workflows as artists that make the world of digital art so interesting. It would be very boring if we all produced digital sculpts in an identical style, wouldn't it?

Final Thoughts on Base Meshes

There are a few last things on this subject that I want to touch on. New users can be tempted to use base meshes such as models from applications like Poser or mesh generation programs. This sort of thing is frowned upon as a rule in the industry because not all of the work you have done is actually yours. So it is expected that either you make your own base meshes or you credit the source of the mesh you are using as a base.

I know that when you are starting out it is tempting to jump straight into the deep end by finding a head base mesh and posting your progress online. But be aware that those of us who have been around a while can spot a generic, widely available base mesh from 400 yards. So yes, people will know. If you absolutely *must* use a produced base mesh, please acknowledge the fact that you have used it and explain why. You can probably still expect people to tell you to go and learn to make your own, though, as it will make you a better artist. As I have said many times (and no doubt will say many more times), there are no shortcuts to learning to be a good digital sculptor. But providing you have the will and dedication to keep learning, you have a good chance of becoming a brilliant digital artist.

High-Definition Geometry in ZBrush

With the addition of high-definition geometry in the latest version of ZBrush we are no longer as limited in polygon counts. High-definition (HD) geometry allows us to massively increase the detail on each sculpture. There are a few things to bear in mind when using high-definition geometry, though. At the time of publication, version 3.1 does not support the use of normal or displacement maps from high-definition geometry details, although that is expected to change very soon in a future version. But for the moment, you should not expect to capture any details from within your HD geometry.

It is also worth remembering that certain commands and features are not available once a sculpture has been taken to the high-definition level.

There are still many uses that we can put it to. What sculpting in high-definition geometry allows us to do is to sculpt with our normal subdivision levels and then continue with further subdivision levels of high-definition geometry. This doesn't overtax our system for a number of reasons. First, when we sculpt using high-definition geometry, only a portion of the model is visible (which ZBrush makes sure our system

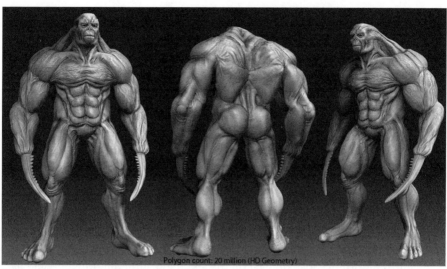

Polygon count: 20 million (HD Geometry)

FIGURE 3-10

can comfortably handle). Second, as long as we make sure that we do not overtax our system with standard subdivision levels, we can climb into some very high poly counts.

When word first got out that ZBrush version 3 could handle polygon counts up to one billion, many people did not believe it possible. Apart from the fact that it basically won the "poly count war" hands down, it also seemed impossible from a technology standpoint.

So why do we need that many polygons? While it may seem that one billion polygons is more than anyone will ever need, it does open up the ability to disregard topology altogether while sculpting. We can now do things that up to now we only dreamed of, such as sculpting a photorealistic character head.

You may be surprised at exactly how much geometry you will need to make something photorealistic in ZBrush. This is due to the fact that we are not using standard edge loops. Since we don't have them set up as in a standard base mesh, we sometimes have too little geometry in some areas and too much in others. A simple way around this, though, is to use the Retopology tools.

So let's have a deeper look at how to sculpt using high-definition geometry in ZBrush, and how to achieve those highly detailed characters that were never possible before.

Adding HD Geometry to Your Sculpture

To enable HD geometry on the current sculpture, you will need to take the following steps. First, you need to go to the Geometry HD section of the Tool palette. We only do this, of course, after we have finished with our standard subdivision levels.

To add HD subdivision levels to the current sculpture, just press the **DivideHD** button. Each press of this button adds another HD level. As with standard subdivision levels, we will want to add only the levels that we need, though. There is no point in maxing out your system if you do not need to.

The **SculptHD Subdiv** slider lets us step up and down between levels; sometimes we may only want to sculpt at level 1 of our HD geometry, and other times at level 2. To start sculpting on the high-definition level, you can press either the **A** hotkey or the **Sculpt HD** button. Both of those do exactly the same job, although most people use the hotkey.

There is also a button labeled **RadialRgn** that, when selected, causes a circular section of your model to be displayed. The region displayed depends upon the location of your mouse. If this button is not selected, a square region will be displayed.

When you are finished sculpting at the HD level, place your mouse cursor outside of your model (make sure it is not touching any part of your model) and press the A hotkey again. ZBrush will try to convert as much of the HD geometry to standard subdivision levels as it can. Obviously, it cannot capture every detail from the HD levels, but it can often maintain the silhouette of the HD sculpts. You are now free to hover your mouse over a new area, press the Sculpt HD button, and sculpt that area. You can continue in this way until you have finished sculpting your model.

To display your entire model in HD, simply press the A key with your mouse away from the model. You'll notice that ZBrush works its way over the entire model, including the back of the model that you will not be able to see. This is actually really interesting to watch. If you see any holes in your model, you will need to go down to the Display Properties section of the Tool palette and choose the **Double** option. Usually these holes are due to ZBrush only showing the front faces of polygons, but we can see them by turning Double on, which shows us both sides of any polygons that may be back facing.

It is also worth mentioning a couple of ZScripts that may be of use to you when you're using HD levels on your model. The first script is one by Marcus Civis called **HD render all**; the second is one I wrote called **HD turntable**. The HD render all plug-in allows you to see the

HD levels that are active on every subtool in your model. The HD turntable plug-in that I wrote allows you to render out a turntable for your model that displays it as an HD model (should your model have HD levels).

4 Important Palettes

The Brush Palette

Inside ZBrush there are two main types of brushes: those that are used for sculpting and those that are used for 2.5D/Projection Master. In this section I'll describe each of the most commonly used brushes, and why they behave like they do.

To become proficient in any application (and especially ZBrush), you must know what a tool will do and how it will behave before you even touch it. The coolest tool or brush is of very little use if the user does not understand why and how it is used and what to expect out of it. Feel free to use this section as a reference while you sculpt until what each brush does becomes second nature to you. Only then will you see your sculpting and 2.5D techniques truly improve.

All of these brushes make use of the stroke and alpha, both of which are explained separately and in depth.

FIGURE 4-1

53

Standard Brush

The Standard brush is one of the most commonly used brushes to sculpt with, mainly as it is selected by default when you open ZBrush. In fact, entire complex models have been done using just the Standard, Smooth, and Move brushes. The Standard brush moves the geometry inward or outward in the direction of the normal of the polygon at the center of the brush. (For more information about what a normal is, see Chapter 7.)

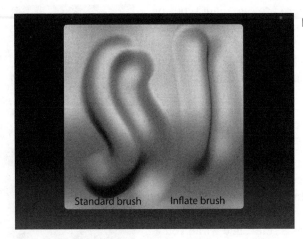

FIGURE 4-2

Standard brush   Inflate brush

If you imagine a flat 3D poly plane in ZBrush, a Standard brush would either push the geometry straight inward (if Zsub is selected) or straight outward (if Zadd is selected). This makes it a very predictable brush for users when they are first learning the application. It makes sense because it is similar to how an actual paintbrush would behave.

If you cross a stroke over itself with the Standard brush with Zadd selected, you will notice that you get a buildup at the crossover point where they intersect. It gives an effect that is similar to adding clay to traditional clay sculptures.

Like all the brushes, when a tablet such as a Wacom is used with ZBrush, you can vary the stroke by varying the pressure you use with your pen. Applying very little pressure will give a thinner stroke and affect the geometry less than a hard stroke. You can also vary the pressure on your pen during a stroke to get some interesting effects. Used in conjunction with different stroke types and alphas, it can give many different effects. Remember also that the Standard brush can be used to paint color onto your model, paint texture on your model using the texture currently selected in the Texture palette, or apply either of these and sculpt at the same time. Texturing is dealt with in depth later on in this book when we texture the Guardian creature in Chapter 19.

All brushes within ZBrush use modifier keys to switch the behavior of the brush. For a moment let's suppose that you have your Standard brush set to a Zadd setting of 10. Pressing the **Alt** key and using the brush will invert this so that you will be sculpting with the equivalent of a setting of Zsub 10. If you hold down the **Shift** key and use the Standard brush, you will switch to the Smooth brush while the key is held down. This is a massive time-saver when you are sculpting, as it means having to switch brushes a little less often.

Displace Brush

The Displace brush is a much overlooked but very powerful brush. At first glance it appears to most users to basically be another "standard brush," but it is a vastly powerful and useful brush that you'll need at some point. While *the Displace brush pushes the polygons in the direction of the normals* like the Standard brush, it has one vast difference — it maintains the details of the surface.

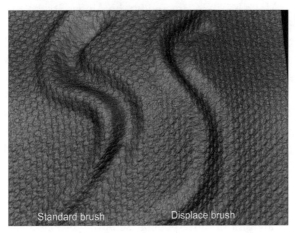

FIGURE 4-3

Standard brush   Displace brush

As you can see above, we have a simple sculpt that's had a cloth texture applied. So if we wanted to add some wrinkles to the cloth and tried to use the Standard brush, we would end up losing the detail in places we have sculpted. This is due to the Standard brush pushing the polygons together and making a bit of a mess of our detail.

As you can see, this really isn't acceptable and we would have to redo our cloth texture. But if we use the Displace brush, it will still push our geometry inward or outward while keeping our surface detail intact.

If we take this a step further into workflow land, we could have our cloth textured and detailed and then add the cloth folds later. This would mean we could speed up our workflow for a pipeline and indeed take several passes at sculpting the folds on the cloth using ZBrush layers to get a result we are truly happy with. The Displace brush can be useful for changes to a detailed organic model such as a face that you've added all your nice wrinkles and pores to and need to change some things near the end.

Move Brush

The Move brush is very different from the Move functions in ZBrush. Whereas the Transpose Move function uses action lines and can be useful for posing (more on this later), the Move brush allows you to physically move parts of your sculpture about like warm clay. As an example, think about getting your proportions correct on a model. If you noticed that the mouth was a little too low, you could step down a few subdivisions and move it into place using the Move brush.

I find setting the brush to between 20 and 30 gives me a feel that I like, although this is personal preference. Experiment to find out what works for you. The Move brush is affected by the Alpha, Stroke, and Falloff settings. For example, if the falloff is set to –100, it would have no falloff and would move as a rigid square. If your falloff is set to 0 and you use a small alpha, such as 51, it would affect a small area even when using a large brush size.

When using the Move brush always try to restrict its use to lower subdivisions of your model. Using it at lower levels makes the move behave in a smoother way. Moving at high subdivision levels can also slow the brush down (remember you can deal with some very high polygon counts in ZBrush!).

Inflate Brush

The Inflate brush is another of those popular sculpting brushes that just about everyone uses as part of their main set of favorites. While the Standard brush moves the geometry based on the *center of the brush area and in the direction of that polygon's normal,* the Inflate brush moves each polygon under the brush in the direction of its own normal.

An easy way to imagine this is to take the 3D plane we've used so far and imagine that the polygons under the brush are inflated like a balloon. This means you can bulk up part of a mesh with just a couple of strokes. As this brush uses alphas and strokes, it opens up a whole new world of possibilities.

Magnify Brush

The Magnify brush is sort of an inverse Pinch brush. While the Pinch brush moves the vertices toward the brush and "pinches them together," *the Magnify brush pushes them away from the brush center.* Changing the Magnify setting will give a whole host of effects from just inflating without moving the geometry "sideways" to a full-blown magnify effect.

When combined with the gravity controls, you can get some really useful effects for sculpting things such as massive folds of fat. It can also be used on a masked area that's been inverted to bulk up muscles like the pectorals and biceps.

Blob Brush

This brush is like a one-stop shop for getting distorted alien or monster skin effects. It is affected by the irregularities below the brush on the surface of the model, thus giving a unique or slightly different effect with each stroke. When a very small alpha is used with a scatter stroke type, you can detail areas of this sort very fast indeed. Beware of overusing it, though, as it can be far too easy to get carried away with it — and before you know it your great model has turned into blob city. So my advice is to use it in an understated way unless a particular effect is called for in your model.

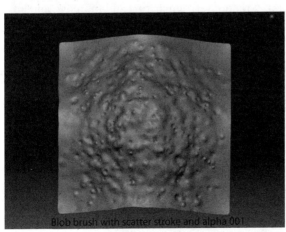

Figure 4-4

Blob brush with scatter stroke and alpha 001

Pinch Brush

So what does the Pinch brush do then? Well, putting it simply and at the risk of insulting the reader's intelligence…it pinches geometry together. The way it works is it takes the geometry below the brush area and pulls it toward the center. That really is it, to be honest. It does the job well and different Zadd settings will make the brush more or less "angry" in its response to your touch. Find a setting you like for the detail you want to pinch together (such as a wrinkle) and give it a go. It is also great for giving edges a harder, crisper look.

For edges that you really need to keep crisp and regular, it is best to use this in conjunction with the Lazy Mouse feature. This gives you a great result without the headache of having to worry about a sudden attack of shaky hands halfway through a stroke.

Flatten Brush

The Flatten brush is another one whose description I'm afraid I have to risk insulting your intelligence describing. The flatten brush "flattens"! Well, it is a little more complex that, but in essence that it what it does. It is very sensitive to not only the alpha used but the current irregularity of the surface under the brush. For a total flattening effect, you would use the default of a completely white alpha. To make an area like the side of a nose a bit more flat you would first use your Smooth brush on it to smooth out any random irregularities and then use an alpha such as 02. You can also control the amount of flattening with the ZIntensity controls.

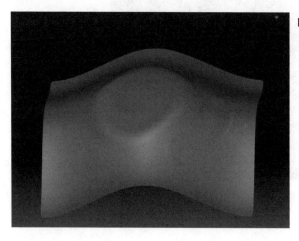

FIGURE 4-5

Gouge Brush

This brush does a very simple job — it gouges out areas of your model. Yep, it's that simple really, and very useful for removing large areas from a high-poly model. I would recommend using it at one subdivision level below the one that is your highest, and then smoothing it out on that level. This allows you to then add finer detail on your highest level.

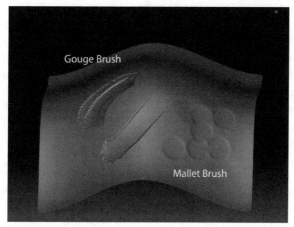

FIGURE 4-6

Mallet Brush

Use the Mallet brush to, well, hammer areas. The brush leaves behind round tool marks, which can be useful for creating metallic surfaces that require a hand-forged look.

Morph Brush

The Morph brush uses a morph target set by the user to change or revert the geometry. Let's say, for example, that you are about to redo the nose on a model and you have a feeling you may get it really wrong. Before you start to work on this area it would be a great idea to store a morph target (using **StoreMT** found in the Morph Target section of the Tool palette).

You do the sculpting on the nose and if it does indeed go badly wrong, you pick the Morph brush and paint the area back to its original state that you stored as a morph target. You can also use the brush to make complex facial poses by taking one expression and storing a morph target, then making another and using the Morph brush on one side of the face. The Morph brush has many uses that no doubt you will find through use.

Nudge Brush

The Nudge brush will nudge (or slide) the geometry in the direction of your brushstroke. If you had the above mentioned "bad nose" and you realized it was a bit too far to the left of center, you could use the Nudge brush to push it back to the right a little. It responds to the ZIntensity setting, which you can change depending on what sort of nudge effect you want and how aggressive you want to be.

Used along with the Gravity controls in your Brush palette, it can give, as Austin Powers would say, "Some wild and groovy effects, man!" It doesn't, however, respond well to Cavity Masking, as this means the brush cannot do its job correctly. If you're curious about what will happen, give it a go and see; just make sure you are using a backup copy of your model as it will be a right old mess afterward.

Rake Brush

This brush is another favorite, especially for those coming from a traditional sculpting background. It mimics the behavior of a rake tool used in sculpting. It allows you to add or take away clay from a surface using a special alpha. It can be used for quick, medium-resolution blocking and gives a great organic surface when crossed strokes are smoothed out.

Traditional sculptors often have a favorite set of rake tools that "feel right" to them, so it's worth experimenting with making your own rake alphas so that you get a rake that you like. This is a great way to make a tool your own and feel comfortable with it faster.

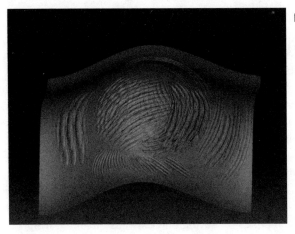

FIGURE 4-7

SnakeHook Brush

Imagine for a moment that your model is made of rubber or elastic. Then imagine that you are going to take a hook-shaped tool, grab a spot, and pull it outward. What the SnakeHook brush does is allow you to pull geometry outward from your mesh. It's great for adding spikes, horns, and many other things, although remember that it is "geometry dependent." That is to say that you must have enough subdivision levels on your model to keep the polygon distribution looking okay.

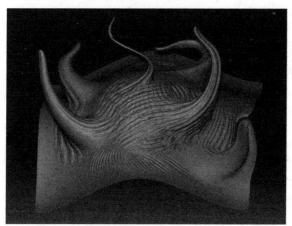

FIGURE 4-8

As it can be used in conjunction with an alpha and stroke type, you can vary the effect it gives in many ways. With a "dot" stroke type and a nice round alpha, you will pull out a single "horn." With an alpha with many "dots" on it, you would be pulling many "horns" out at the same time.

A good tip is to locally subdivide the area you are going to use the SnakeHook brush on to give you more geometry in those areas. First, step down to your lowest subdivision level and mask off an area before subdividing.

The SnakeHook control slider provides control over the type of snakehook effect you will get when using this brush. It controls the angle at which the geometry will be pulled outward.
be perpendicular, while a setting that is a positive va
mouse in a circle) will give a spiraling effect.

ZProject Brush

The ZProject brush is pretty useful, and very powerful in the right hands. It allows you to get color and sculpting data from another sculpted mesh and transfer this to your current model. For example, a while back I spent about two weeks making heads from spheres, which meant I had a stockpile of heads that I could bring into my models to speed up my sculpting time.

The ZProject brush can transfer the color data, the sculpture data, or both at the same time. When you are about to use this brush, it's always best to give it a bit of a helping hand by moving the polygons on the model you wish to transfer the data onto so they are as close as possible to the mesh you are transferring from.

When using the brush to transfer details from a photo to use for photo projection texturing, you will need to make sure that your action line is set to off. You can do this by going into Scale, Rotate, or Move mode and clicking in your model until the action line disappears. If you do not do this, it will offset the data. Sometimes offsetting the data is exactly what you want, as you may have an image plane you're working from that isn't an exact match to your model. This would mean you could set action lines to the eyes and paint those in, then the mouth and paint that, etc.

Smooth Brush

This brush does exactly what its name implies: It smoothes your geometry out for you. How much it smoothes is controlled by your ZIntensity, so high values will smooth very aggressively, whereas lower ones will be a bit more subdued and need a few more passes of the Smooth brush. This brush can also be accessed while using most other brushes by holding the Shift key down. The settings you have in the Smooth brush itself are important, as these will also be used for it when holding down the quick access key in other brushes.

The best way to smooth out large areas of geometry when you are dealing with a lot of polygons is to first step to a lower subdivision level, smooth out, then step up. This way ZBrush doesn't have to work as hard and you'll get a better result quicker. You may have some small amount of smoothing left to do at higher levels, but nowhere near what you would have if you'd tried to do it all on your highest level. This also gives the added bonus that if you smooth out at a lower level, your higher level detail will be preserved. (For example, you could smooth a wrinkle at a lower subdivision level, while still keeping the skin etc., on your highest one.)

MeshInsert Brushes

There are two brushes that can be used for inserting one mesh into
another one: **MeshInsert Dot** and **MeshInsert Standard**. Both do the
same job but in slightly different ways. So why would you want to insert
one mesh into another? Maybe you are adding accessories that you wish
to be on the same normal map for a game model, or have them controlled by the same subdivision levels. You could also add a second head
to a monster you are sculpting. You are limited only by your
imagination.

FIGURE 4-9:
MESHINSERT
STANDARD BRUSH

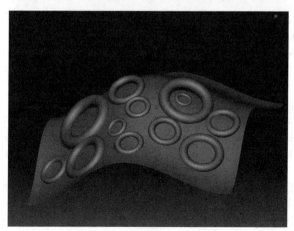

FIGURE 4-10:
MESHINSERT DOT
BRUSH

Only polygon meshes can be inserted; ZBrush primitives will not
work unless converted to polymeshes. To use the mesh insert feature,
load up your two meshes: the one you are inserting *into* and the mesh to
be inserted. With your MeshInsert brush selected, choose **MeshInsert
Preview** and select the mesh you wish to insert.

The Clay Brush Subset

Clay Brush

These brushes without a shadow of a doubt have fast become the favorites of probably every ZBrush user. They have many unique features that no other brushes have and give a sculpting experience that is immediately recognizable to people coming from a traditional sculpting background. All the brushes in the clay set have some similar features, so I'll cover those here, but they also apply to other clay brushes.

Common features

- The clay brushes are the only ones you can use to merge two separate pieces of geometry together seamlessly.
- It is the only brush set specifically made for use with alphas. (Many very cool effects can be created by using some of the different alphas both inside ZBrush and ones you've made yourself. This makes this brush set very powerful to the digital sculptor.)
- The clay brushes behave like clay itself would. With Zadd switched on, it is the same as adding a lump of clay on a traditional sculpture. With Zsub turned on, it is like scooping or taking clay off the sculpture.

Example of clay brush usage

Let's imagine that we have a body of one sculpt that we really like, but the head is not as good as it could be. But we do have another head that would make the sculpt look great; the trouble is they are separate models and you don't want a seam between them. Before the advent of the clay brushes this would cause a whole world of problems.

To merge these two models together you first import the head as a subtool and correct its position and size as needed. You then clone this head model to a separate tool and delete its lower subdivision levels, and also go back to the original tool and delete its lower subdivision levels (this is a very important step).

Now import the model into the geometry using the Insert Mesh button in the Tool palette. The head will not be part of the same mesh but in its own polygroup. This means we can use a mask to mask areas that are not going to be seen, and then use Delete Hidden (from the Tool palette) on the main body mesh. This means we aren't going to be wasting polygons in areas we aren't going to see. Now simply take your Clay brush and run it around the intersection of both meshes. (Be aware that if you use the Smooth brush it will open the edge back up again and make it visible.) After a little work you will have one mesh that has no seams.

Now at this stage you would probably want to go in and retopologize it in ZBrush to get some lower subdivisions back and some good topology. If you don't do this, the mesh can get unwieldy with very high poly counts, depending on your machine.

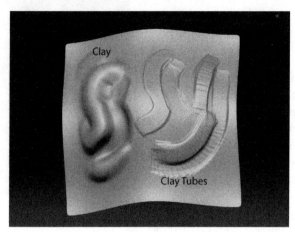

FIGURE 4-11

Clay Tubes Brush

I won't be going over the ground already covered for the clay brush set on this or the other clay brushes, as you can simply refer to that information above. Using the Clay Tubes brush is like adding a tube of clay when doing traditional sculpture. It can also be used along with Zsub to take a scoop of clay away from the model. It is very good for roughing out form and bulking up areas, as it responds very well to the Smooth brush.

The Document Palette

Most of the buttons at the top of the Document palette are pretty self-explanatory, as I'm sure by now you all know what open, export, and save, etc., do.

Briefly, **ZAppLink** allows you to integrate your favorite photo editing program into ZBrush.

Below the New Document button you will see a small color chip with the word **Back** on it. By clicking on this color chip you can change the background color of your main document to the currently selected color. You can also eliminate the fading effect by turning the range down to 0. This simply controls the way that the gradient of the background is viewed.

The **Border** color chips behave in the same way and do a similar job. The **Range** slider controls the color of the background, and the **Center** slider controls the midpoint of the color gradation. **Rate** controls the hardness or softness of the transition for the gradation.

FIGURE 4-12

The **Half** button will halve the size of your current document; this has the effect of doubling the resolution of the image, which can be useful when you want to print your renders at a higher resolution. (Another way of halving the size would be to use the **AAHalf** button.) The **Double** button will double the size of your document, which is useful if you want a bigger canvas for your final render to display online or on your desktop. The **Pro** button constrains the proportions of the document so that if you resize it, it will maintain its shape. If you need to stretch or squash it for any reason, simply press this button to deselect it and enter the values you need with the sliders for width and height.

Both **Crop** and **Resize** are fairly obvious in their use. **StoreDepthHistory** is used to record the current depth information of the document; this means that color brushes respond to this depth and not the actual depth later on. **DeleteDepthHistory** will eliminate all the previously stored information.

The Alpha Palette

In the Alpha palette you will find a number of black and white images that are used to affect your brush. You can load alphas in one of two ways: by clicking on the thumbnail visible in the interface or through the Alpha palette. Let's work our way through the controls in the Alpha palette.

By clicking on the **Import** button you can import an alpha that you have made yourself or one you have downloaded. ZBrush can import the following file types: JPEG, Windows bitmap, Photoshop PSD, and Mac PICT. You can also import several alphas at the same time by Shift+clicking on the alphas in the Open dialog. Any color images that you try to import will be converted to grayscale images.

The **Export** button allows you to export alphas as one of three main formats: 8-bit bitmap, Photoshop PSD, or Mac PICT.

The middle section of the pane shows the alpha you can select for your brush.

Use the **R** button to reset the palette if it gets overcrowded with thumbnails of alpha images.

FIGURE 4-13

The **Blur** slider lets you blur or sharpen an alpha. Negative values will sharpen the alpha, and positive values will blur the alpha. Some alphas blur better than others, so you'll need to experiment with the Blur control.

The **Noise** slider simply adds noise to the black and white image.

By pressing the **Max** button you can set an alpha to its maximum tonal range. What it does is make the lightest parts white and the darkest parts black; it's a bit like an auto contrast setting in Photoshop.

The **MidValue** slider is used to adjust the midpoint tone, or neutral intensity, of a displacement map.

You can use the **Rf** slider to adjust the radial fade values of an alpha. This could come in handy if you're using a tileable alpha that you wish to fade off around the edges.

The **Intensity** and **Contrast** settings allow you to control the strength and tonal range.

The **AlphaAdjust** curve lets you get different effects with the same alpha. Once opened, you can change the profile of the curve or add points and shape as required.

The **Flip H** and **Flip V** controls allow you to flip your image either horizontally or vertically.

The **Rotate** button will rotate your alpha in 90° steps. If you are using an alpha with a set direction, you may need to use this button to reorient your alpha so that your brush and alpha behave as you wish.

Inverse swaps the darkness and lightness range.

The **MRes** slider and the others in this section of the Alpha palette affect the polymesh made from the alpha. This particular slider sets the resolution of the polymesh that is made; the higher the number, the more polygons you get.

The **MDep** slider is used to set the depth of the polymesh created from the alpha. The higher the number, the thicker it is; smaller numbers will make it thinner.

If you need to set the smoothness of the polymesh created from your alpha, use the **MSm** slider. The higher the number, the smoother it will be, while a setting of 0 will create something called "cubic skinning" and make the alpha look as if it is made of very tiny cubes.

If you imagine that the alpha you're using is a line along the Z axis, then pressing the **DblS** button will automatically mirror your polymesh along the Z axis.

The **Make 3D** button is the one that does all the magic. It makes the polymesh using the settings from above. The polymesh will be symmetrical along the Z axis and use adaptive UV coordinates by default (so you don't have to go to the bother of setting your UVs).

The **Make Tx** button allows you to take a selected alpha and convert it into a texture, which then becomes the default texture in the Texture palette.

The **Make St** button converts the currently selected alpha into a stencil and activates the stencil for your use. Note that you cannot activate a stencil without first converting the alpha to a stencil.

You use the **Make Modified Alpha** button to save the changes you have made to an alpha in this palette. This can save you time if you find you need the same effect often.

Cc stands for clear color. When this button is active and the currently selected alpha is the same size as the drawing area, the CropAndFill button will clear the color information but not any depth information. When it is off, the CropAndFill action changes to retain the depth information, and the new color is overlaid on top of it.

The **CropAndFill** button resizes the canvas to the size of the currently selected alpha. This works along with the Cc button as described above.

The **GrabDoc** button creates a canvas-sized alpha from your document that includes the depth information.

The **Alpha Depth Factor** option has a couple of uses. If you are generating a 16-bit displacement map, you will need to record the number shown here. It also affects the intensity with which the CropAndFill function operates by mapping the depth displacements.

The Color Palette

At some point you will want to texture your model, which means you're going to paint various colors onto your digital sculpture. The Color palette controls are rather simple to understand. The color chips, which are similar to those in other palettes, are located at the top. The larger of the two is the active color; to switch between them you can click on them or use the **V** hotkey.

FIGURE 4-14

ZBrush allows you to set a color by eye and by using RGB values. If you prefer the standard Windows color interface, simply press the **SysPalette** button and this will give you the interface that you are used to. Click on the **Modifiers** button to open a panel that lets you select from other color selection palettes. You can even use a combination of different palettes.

The **FillObject** button will fill your currently selected object or tool with the currently selected color. If you are using layers, you can fill an entire layer with the same color by hitting the **FillLayer** button. You can also remove the color on your layer by hitting the **Clear** button.

The Layer Palette

Those of you who are familiar with Photoshop will find that layers within ZBrush are somewhat similar. Since layers are used to contain data in 2.5D as pixols, once a model is dropped to a layer it cannot be rotated anymore. The controls at the top of the Layer palette are pretty self-explanatory — they let you clear, fill, delete, create, duplicate, move the active layer up or down, or merge layers.

Press the **Bake** button to take the information from the current layer and bake this to your 2D image. Information such as the shading, material, and depth are all baked and a flat shader is applied to this layer. We can blend the amount of baking for a layer by using the **B Blend** slider. This will allow us to get any happy medium that we need between fully baked and not baked.

FIGURE 4-15

The layer can also be flipped horizontally or vertically by using the **Flip H** and **Flip V** buttons. This means that should we have a scene where one layer contains a house that is on the right side of a document, we could flip this to the left side of the document as if using a mirror. You could also flip the house upside down (although the people inside might be unhappy).

Although we cannot rotate our models once they are on a layer, we do have some freedom to move them about. The large button with a letter **W** controls the wrap mode and means that if we move the document horizontally or vertically using the Displace H or V sliders, information from the bottom of the document is wrapped around to the top. A good way to think of this is a bit like a dodgy old TV with a picture that spins around when the signal is poor.

Displace Z lets us move the layer forward or backward in space, bringing it closer to us or farther away.

3D Sculpting Layers

What Are 3D Layers?

Layers in ZBrush allow the artist to work on different versions of the same sculpt. Each layer contains its own "version" of the model that you sculpted on while on that particular layer. This enables the artist to keep a number of different versions of his sculpt within the same ZBrush tool. So you may use it for making "blend shapes" for export to Maya or 3ds Max, fading out detail, etc. In fact, there are a vast number of things that layers can help you with.

Each layer stores the data from the sculpting done while on that layer. For example, we could change our mind about a nose while sculpting on level 5 and later switch it off and make a new one to try a new nose design. In this way we can use layers to test different looks and forms for our model without actually having to commit to any of them at this stage. In fact, right up until you proclaim your sculpt "final" you can continue to tweak your layers, meaning that you have the best chance possible to get everything you need out of your digital sculpture.

Creating a Layer

Creating a layer to use to store sculpting information is actually pretty easy. Simply go to your **Tool** palette and scroll down to the **Layers** section. There you will see a number of controls pertaining to layers in ZBrush, but the one we are interested in at the moment is the **New** button. As you've probably correctly surmised, this makes a new layer. We can create as many layers as we like, but remember that the subdivision level you use to create your layer is the one you will use to control it. If you are at any level other than the one at which you created your layer, the controls will be grayed out. So it is important that you choose the level carefully.

In some cases you may be trying out facial shapes and may want your layers at a lower level; other times you may be trying out different medium-resolution or high-resolution forms and need your levels at a higher subdivision level. So if possible, work out in advance where you need them and for what purpose they will be needed.

Changing the Layer

Once you've sculpted something on a layer, you may feel the need to tweak it in some way. Luckily, ZBrush has a number of controls to enable you to change the sculpture based on the layer data. So you may decide that, for example, the skin pores that you have done aren't deep enough. By turning up the Intensity slider you will see the details painted on your layer become more pronounced. Also, if you turn the intensity down, the details contained within this layer will affect the sculpture less and less the more you turn it down. This means you are never stuck with a decision in the digital sculpting process. This allows for a more fluid workflow in that if you change your mind about an aspect of your sculpture, it's easy to make those changes with your layers.

Layers also give you the confidence to experiment, because you can simply turn off that layer and start again if you don't like your work.

Erasing an Area from a Layer

There will be occasions where everything on a layer is perfect except for one area that is giving you problems. You can easily remove the data from just that part of the layer so that you don't have to resculpt the whole thing again. Maybe you didn't realize that you accidentally hit part of the model with your Move brush while sculpting, so while the front of the face looks fine and dandy, the back of the head looks terrible. Rather than deleting the layer and starting over, or even trying to put it right, ZBrush allows us to remove the sculpting from any area we like.

To remove an area of a layer, simply turn off the layer, go to your **Tool** palette, scroll down to the **Morph Target** section, and create a morph target. (If you already have one stored you may wish to delete it and create a new one, or you may get unpredictable results as this morph target is probably based on a part of your sculpting session previous to the use of the current layer.)

After doing this, turn your layer back on and simply take the **Morph** brush and paint over the area you wish to remove, making sure your ZIntensity is set to 100 first, of course. But feel free to lower this for special effects, such as carving out damage to a wall.

5 Monster Head from a Sphere Project

About This Project

The whole idea behind this particular project is to take something that requires no prior experience on your part and create a simple but interesting digital sculpt of a monster head. I wanted to avoid using a prepared base mesh of any type as not everyone would be able to jump straight in at this stage and make the base mesh. This way everyone is able to start and follow along with this project every step of the way.

If you are new to ZBrush and digital sculpting, don't feel bad if your final sculpt bears little resemblance to the final one shown in this chapter. Digital sculpting is all about practice; no one ever starts digital sculpting and does amazing the first time around. It is important to remember that every artist who uses ZBrush had to start somewhere, and we all made a great many dodgy looking models before things started to mentally "click." So if your first attempt looks more like a potato than a monster, don't be too hard on yourself. Just keep practicing, and eventually with time and dedication you'll start making digital sculpts that you are proud of.

The reason I want you to follow along with the projects in this book as opposed to letting you come up with your own designs is actually two-fold. First, it puts everyone at the same advantage or disadvantage design wise, and second, by working through the projects you will learn what you need to know much faster and more thoroughly. If you do not have a good grounding in the basic skills, then later on you may hit an artistic brick wall.

Some Preparatory Theory

Okay, so chances are the title of this section is a bit scary to new users, but really it's just a section explaining the polysphere that we use for this project and how it differs from a normal sphere. The polysphere can be accessed from the initial splash screen you see when you open up ZBrush or as an option in the Tool palette.

What is so special about this sphere and why don't we just use the sphere primitive in ZBrush? First, because the polygon sphere that we are going to use is actually a subdivided cube, which has the advantage of better polygon flow. It also doesn't have a nasty pole at the north and south ends of the sphere. It's important to remember that the ZBrush primitives are very special geometrical tools and not simply "polygon primitives." They aren't actually polygons at all. You can think of them as something that enables you to generate a mesh with the required parameters. So a cube primitive, for example, would have options to control how many divisions there would be horizontally and vertically on each face of the cube. This way we can get the exact flow that we need.

Plus the PolySphere tool is much better suited. I can promise you that after sketching out hundreds of "sphereheads" over the last 12 months alone, it is more than up to the job. So start up ZBrush and load up the PolySphere tool, and we'll get started.

Starting the Sculpting

Now that you have the polysphere loaded into ZBrush and active in the workspace, make sure that you are in Edit mode by pressing the **T** key or hitting the **Edit** button on the toolbar.

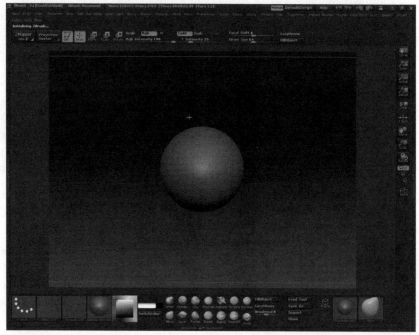

FIGURE 5-1

Before we get started, sit back for a moment while I outline what we'll be doing and my approach to writing. While I will discuss every step made on this particular digital sculpt, I will also keep the instructions general enough so that you can apply this workflow to many *sphereheads* of your own design. This will not be a "connect-the-dots" exercise, as many of you may already know from my ZBrush DVDs that I find that sort of tutorial worse than useless for teaching purposes. So I will explain *why* things are being done and the thought process behind them. Just showing you what tools to use where and when isn't really going to teach you much. But explaining why as well as how something is being done means you then take in the information better and you will feel much more confident about using these techniques in your own models.

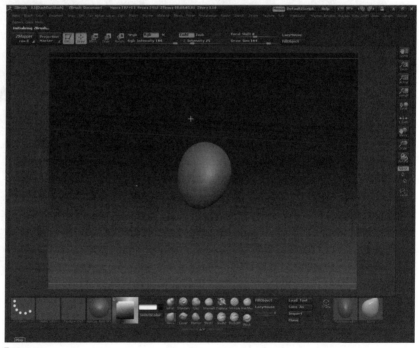

FIGURE 5-2

Okay, so let's get started. First, open the **Tool** palette, go to the **Geometry** section, and make sure you step this down to the lowest level. (The default is at level 3, so you will need to step down to level 1.) What I would like you to do is to make the head shape you see in Figures 5-2 to 5-7 using only the Move brush. Remember that this is *not* the Move transform tool; the Move brush behaves as if you were pulling and moving the geometry like clay. Start by making it a little longer, as shown in Figure 5-3, and continue using the Move brush until it looks as much like Figure 5-7 as you can make it.

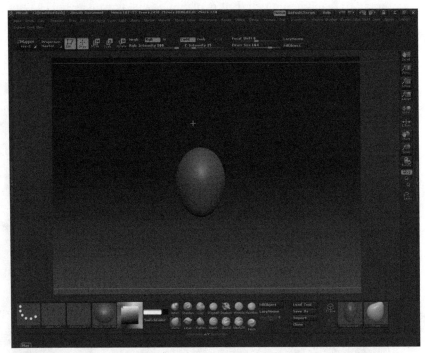

FIGURE 5-3

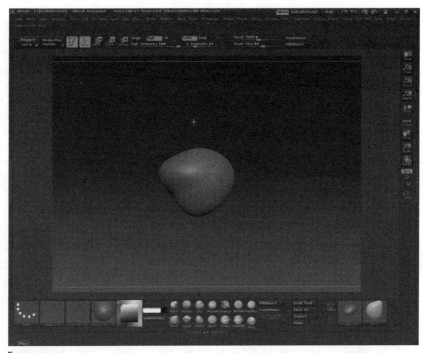

FIGURE 5-4

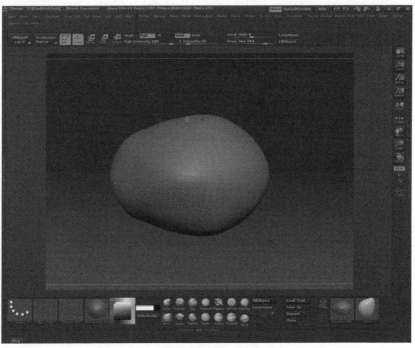

FIGURE 5-5

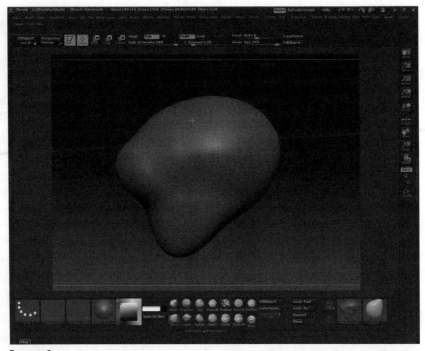

FIGURE 5-6

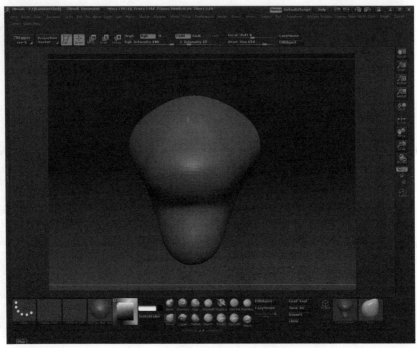

FIGURE 5-7

When inventing a character head, I try to find an interesting head shape to start with. It doesn't have to be "spot on the money" shape wise, but rather just interesting enough to make you want to continue with it and spark some ideas. So take as much time as you need to replicate the shape above as best as you can, and remember no one expects you to be an amazing digital sculptor overnight. *(Also feel free to repeat the projects within this book as many times as you feel you need to, as each time you attempt them you will learn something new from the process.)* Once you have done this, step back up to your highest subdivision level by going back to the Geometry section of the **Tool** palette.

Now, taking the **Standard** brush with a **ZIntensity** setting of about **12** to **15** and a smallish size, make the holes that you see in Figures 5-8 and 5-9. These will eventually become the eyes of the creature, but right now they are placeholders to make sure we get our positioning right.

Next, hold down the **Ctrl** key and paint a circular area around each eye as shown in Figure 5-10. This would be in the shape of the eye sockets in the skull, but we do not need to be too correct as we are going to adjust things as we go along. I find it is important to keep the vitality and energy of a digital sculpt at this stage.

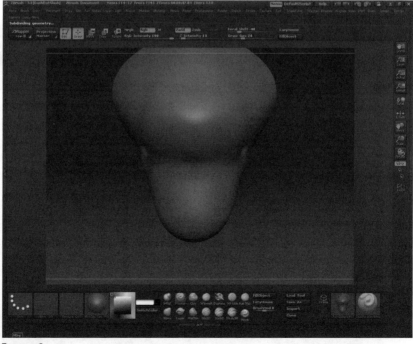

FIGURE 5-8

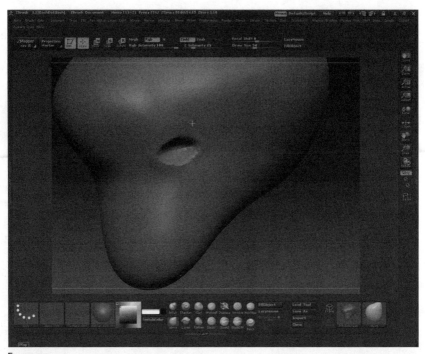

FIGURE 5-9

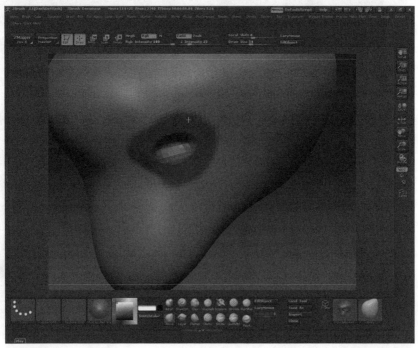

FIGURE 5-10

Once you have the circular areas painted, hold down the **Ctrl** key and click outside of the model on your workspace to invert the mask. Another way to do this is by opening the Tool palette and choosing **Invert Mask** from the Masking section.

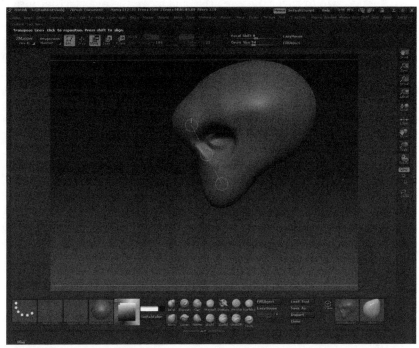

FIGURE 5-11

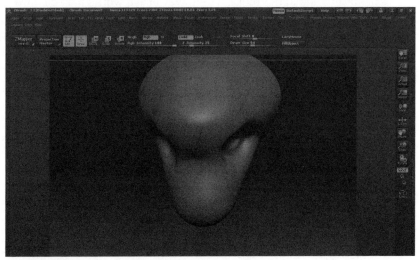

FIGURE 5-12

With this mask inverted, we now will only affect the unmasked areas and not the darker masked ones. Think of a mask a bit like a force field that is protecting things you do not wish to change. Now again choose your **Move** brush from the Brush palette, set it to a large enough size to cover the eye area, and move the eyes farther into the head. If we do not recess the eyes a bit, it will end up looking very "bug eyed" and not at all like a living thing.

Choose the **Inflate** brush and set the **ZIntensity** to about **10** with a brush size just big enough to help us build up a few areas. You will need to use a light touch with this; if you are too heavy handed the brush will react more aggressively than we need it to. You will find that much of digital sculpting is about having a good understanding and control of both your tools and your strokes. Slowly start to build up a very small amount under the eyes and around them on the side of the head. This helps us to start blocking out the boney parts of the head. Many artists like myself have an "inside to out" approach to sculpting and start with the bones, then build up the major muscle groups, the smaller muscles, and finally the skin and wrinkles. By treating your sculpt in this way, it will look more believable and it will be anatomically correct to at least some degree.

Note: The study of anatomy is something that all digital artists who work with organic forms must undertake to take their work to the next level. There are ways of faking it, but that is not advised as it will eventually let you down.

Now activate the **Layer** brush with a **ZIntensity** of about **2** to **4** so we can start to add in the teeth. The Layer brush works in such a way that it will add only one layer of the amount set by your ZIntensity, so no matter how many times you cross over your stroke there will be no buildup. You must not let go of your stroke until that part is finished or another layer will be added as you brush, so you must add each tooth in one continuous stroke. Paint in each tooth as shown in Figures 5-13 and 5-14. As this is just an early sculpt we do not need to worry about the accuracy of the teeth. You can, of course, look up references if you'd like, but for the purposes of this tutorial let's keep things simple.

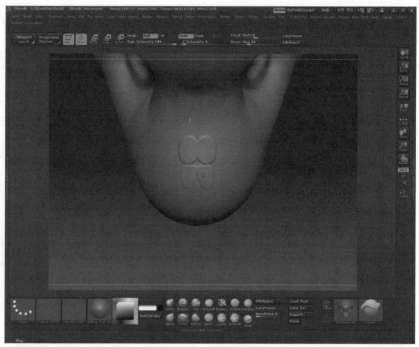

FIGURE 5-13

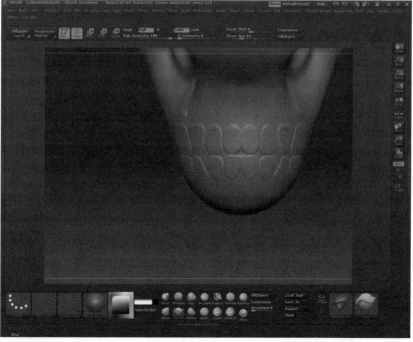

FIGURE 5-14

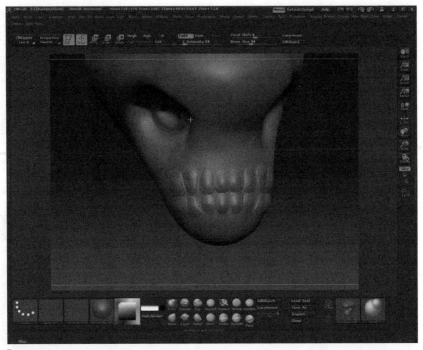

FIGURE 5-15

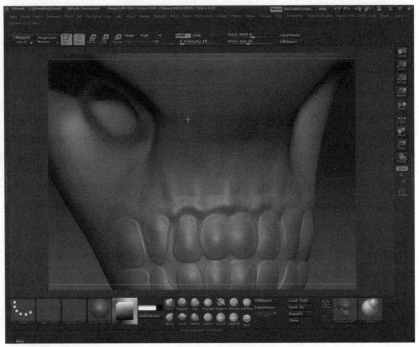

FIGURE 5-16

Once the teeth have been added using the Layer brush, switch to the **Inflate** brush again (which should still be set to about 10 ZIntensity) and slowly do a vertical stroke down the center of each tooth to give it a more "rounded" look and less like a sticker stuck onto the mesh. Once you have done this (remembering to take as much time as you need), take your brush size down a little and inflate along the gumline as shown in Figures 5-16 to 5-19. This not only helps the model to look more believable but also adds an area of interest for the viewer.

Note: It is important to think about how your art will be viewed and which parts may need more attention. The human eye and brain react to faces in very specific ways. If you are interested in finding out more about the psychology, do a Google search on the subject.

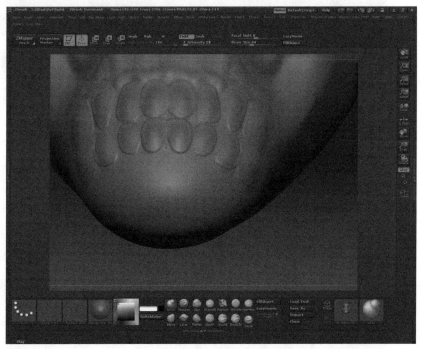

FIGURE 5-17

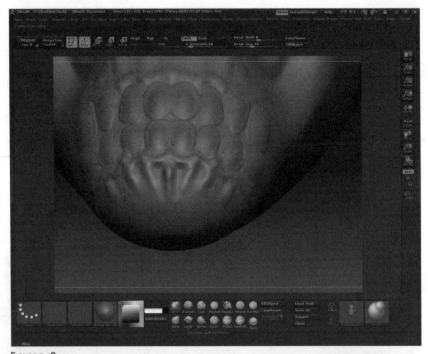

FIGURE 5-18

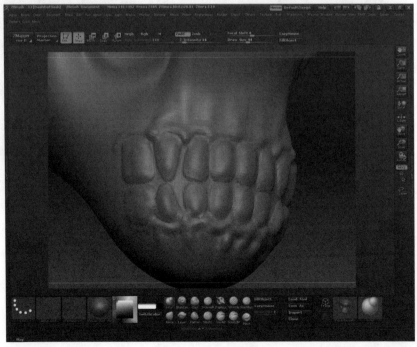

FIGURE 5-19

The next part is tricky, although it will give you practice in improving your quality of line and stroke. Keep your brush set to the **Inflate** brush, go to the **Brush** palette, and set the Cavity Masking to **–100**. You are going to mask off the areas between the teeth, but chances are you will not get a perfect mask using cavity masking alone. So you will need to switch it off once it's done as much as it can and do some cleanup by hand (See Figures 5-20 and 5-21). It's a dirty job, but someone has to do it. This will take you a good while at first if you're a new user because the tool is a bit difficult to control, but you'll soon get the hang of it.

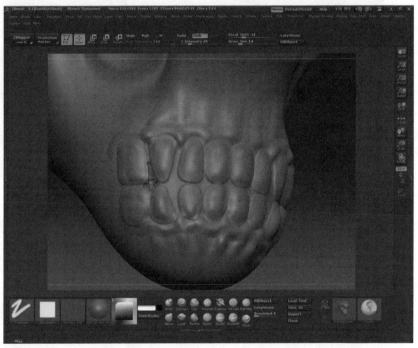

FIGURE 5-20

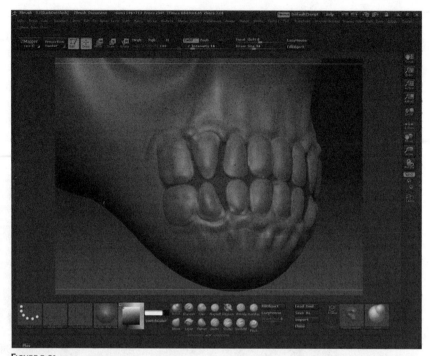

FIGURE 5-21

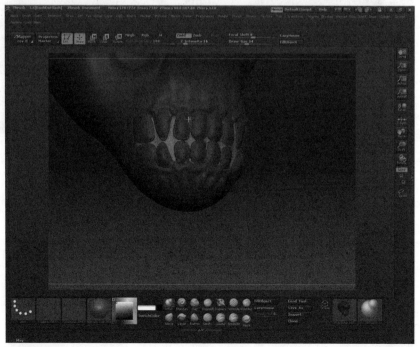

FIGURE 5-22

Once this is done, invert the mask by using the controls in the **Masking** section of the **Tool** palette, or by holding down the **Ctrl** key and left-clicking on an empty bit of the viewport. Now hold down the **Alt** key to invert your brush's action so that now it will press inward instead of inflate outward. Keeping that Alt key held down, brush the area between the teeth inward. This helps to give more separation to the teeth. This is what I like to call sculpting with light and shade. By pushing this area inward we are making sure that the light doesn't hit it very much, if at all. So we are really just sculpting a shadowed area. Plus you have to agree that saying you are a "shadow sculptor" sounds a lot cooler than a guy who sculpts polygons.

Now that we have our very basic shape sorted out as a guide, we can start to put right any problem area before moving onward to the medium-resolution sculpting. The first thing that we need to sort out is the jaw area, as it is not currently correct. So take your Move brush and pull the jaw back a bit from the side of model. You can snap to a side view by holding down the **Shift** key and moving your model in the correct direction. With the side view displayed we can make sure that it is the right shape from beneath the model.

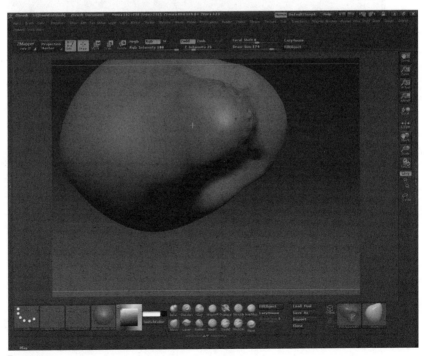

FIGURE 5-23

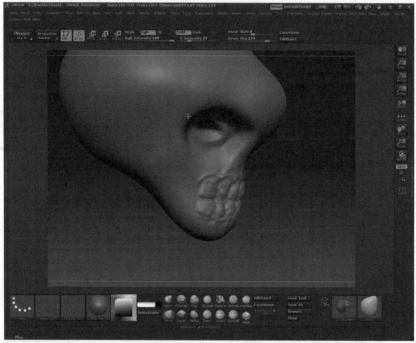

FIGURE 5-24

The shape of the jaw is especially important on human models, as it is one of the main "shape cues" that let us know a face is a face. So make sure that the jaw is arc-shaped as shown in Figures 5-25 to 5-27. If it isn't, use your Move tool to gently move it into place. It is vitally important that the shapes that define the head are as correct as possible in this low-level base mesh. You will find over time that form is more important than detail, because to be blunt, any monkey can be taught to apply a few alphas. The study of form is an entirely different matter indeed and requires more study, dedication, and skill. I realize that may sound harsh, but it's a very easy trap to fall into early on and one best avoided. Taking the time to study form properly will improve you immeasurably as an artist.

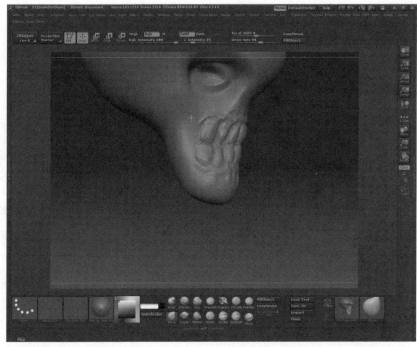

FIGURE 5-25

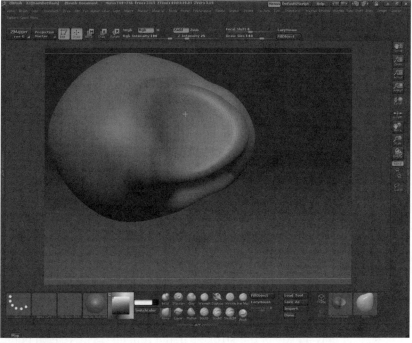

FIGURE 5-26

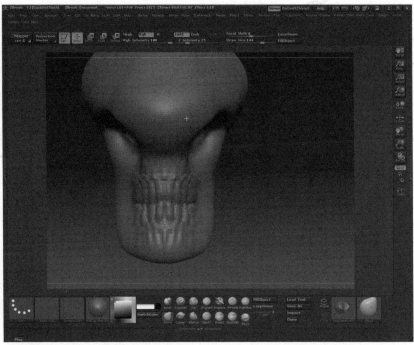

FIGURE 5-27

Medium-Resolution Details

This is the stage where we will start to do some "proper" sculpting and make the model look a bit more pleasing. So start off by taking your **Standard** brush with a low size and low ZIntensity and "cleaning up" the teeth area to give them more defined, crisp edges and make it look a bit more presentable. Don't go too mad with the crisp edges, as we are still at a fairly low subdivision level and you will not be able to carve in all the detail at this stage. Just keep your mind on cleaning things up a bit in the teeth.

We are now going to start using some new brushes, starting with the **Slash2** brush. The area between the brows currently has no definition at all, so to give this area a bit of interest I want you to drag your **Slash2** brush from the top of the brow line downward, as shown in Figure 5-28. The direction is important because the Slash2 brush gives a different effect depending on the stroke direction. So to get the effect that we require, we need to effectively "sculpt backward" in direction. Once you have done this, then the next step may seem rather pointless at first glance. Holding down the **Shift** key, smooth over this area a little so that only a little of the stroke's detail remains. The reason behind this is that at this stage we are only sculpting the medium-resolution details, so we need to set those areas up before we even start thinking of adding any higher-resolution or sharper detailing.

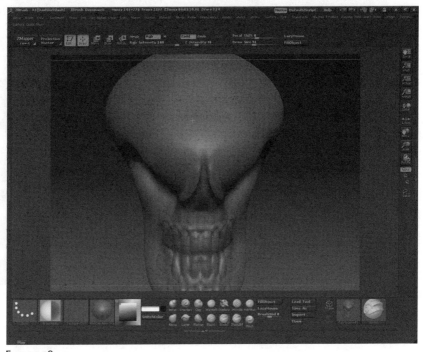

FIGURE 5-28

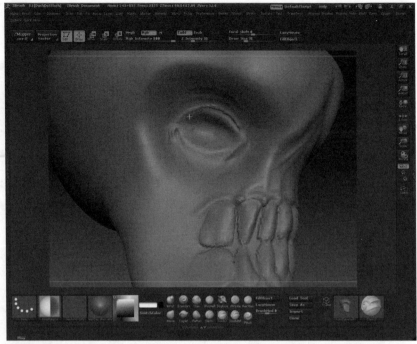

At this point we'll start to add a little more interest in the eye area by adding a few light strokes with our **Slash2** brush from the outer edge of each eye. We also add a secondary slash under the first on the brow area, as shown in Figures 5-29 and 5-30, to add interest and to give us something to develop later.

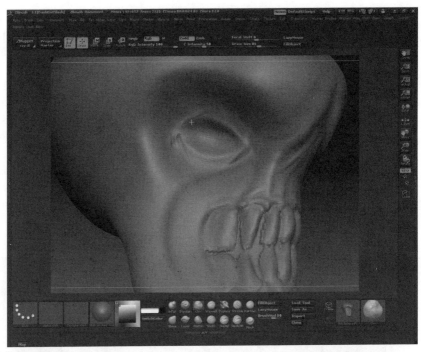

FIGURE 5-30

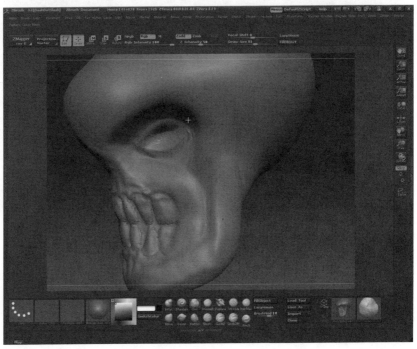

FIGURE 5-31

It is now time to bring in yet another brush — the **Clay** brush. We talked about the Clay brushes in Chapter 4, so feel free to consult that section to get an idea of what they do and how they work. As I've said before, learning to use the tools comes with practice and repetition, and there's no short way of learning it outside of doing a lot of models until you start to feel comfortable. Using the Clay brush, make a stroke from under the eye area where it intersects with (for want of a better description) the bridge of the nose area and down the sides of the outer edge of the teeth to bulk up this area a bit. We aren't using any alphas at the moment, and this gives us a wonderful soft falloff that I find is very organic and pleasing to work with. Now do another stroke that runs over the cheekbone areas to the sides of the head. This will help give our head a little more shape and make it look just a little more "alive." Although to be fair we still have a good way to go yet.

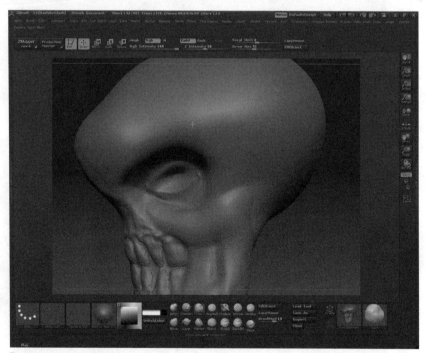

FIGURE 5-32

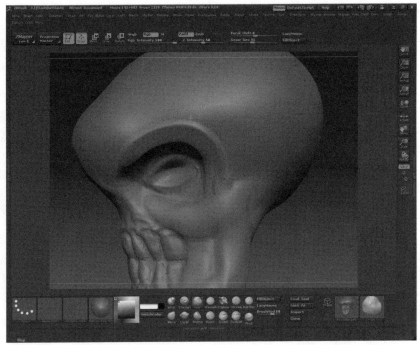

FIGURE 5-33

We can also bulk up the jaw and over the tops of where the ears will eventually go as well while we have this brush active and are working in the area. Next, we are going to use the Clay brush again, this time on the brow area to help give it a bit more mass and weight. These details will help focus the interest of the eye area and make the face a bit more believable, so bulk up the innermost area of the brows in the center. Then, while pressing the **Alt** key to invert the effect, push in with the Clay brush the areas just above the brow area.

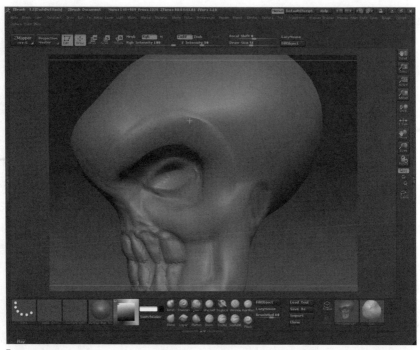

FIGURE 5-34

FIGURE 5-35

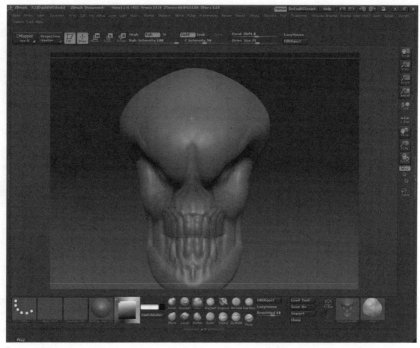

FIGURE 5-36

Switch for a few moments to the **Inflate** brush and increase its size substantially, inflate the top of this skull area a little, then switch back to the Clay brush again.

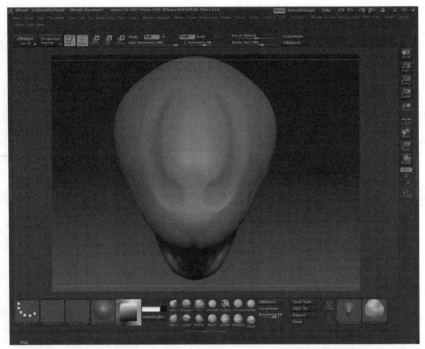

FIGURE 5-37

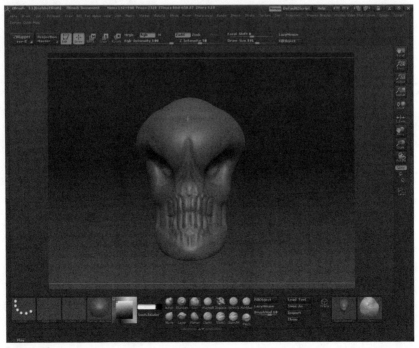

FIGURE 5-38

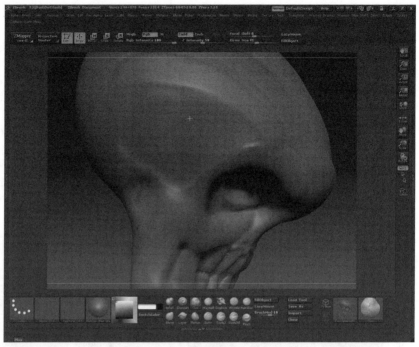

FIGURE 5-39

FIGURE 5-40

The sides of the skull as yet hold very little in terms of interest for the viewer. Let's make two strokes with the Clay brush that run in an arc the length of the side of the head, from the brow area's outer edge almost to the back of the head, as shown in Figures 5-39 and 5-40.

Switch now to the **Slash1** brush. This brush behaves slightly different from the Slash2 brush as it does not push an edge outward on each stroke but simply lets us cut in some detail. A common fault in many beginners' sculpts is the lack of both hard and soft details. Often the sculpt is either totally sharp detail wise, or the edges have a slightly soft look like a half used bar of soap. While organic forms are indeed soft, there are also hard-edged areas that catch light and shadow and help to further define the form. So adding a few harder areas is a very important step that will help us bring this creature alive. Run this brush along the top and bottom parts of the stroke you have just made and also use it along the edge of the ridge of bone near the outer eye.

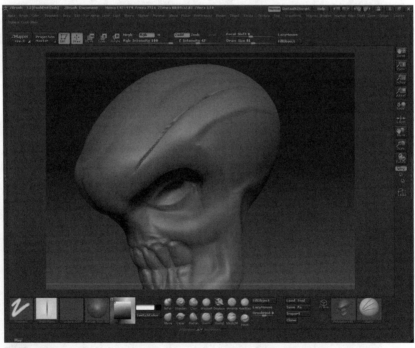

FIGURE 5-41

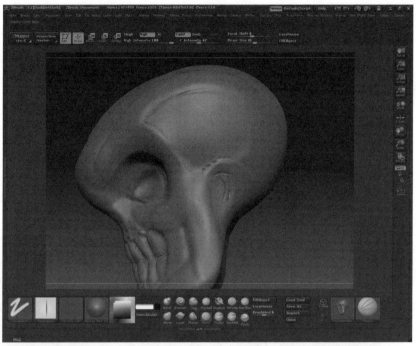

FIGURE 5-42

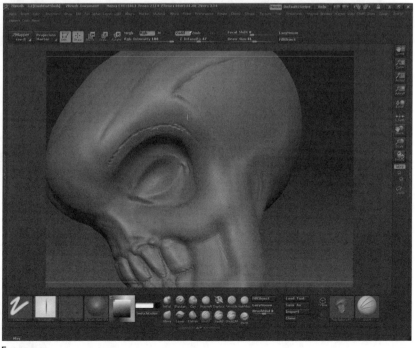

FIGURE 5-43

We will also add a few strokes in what will be our ear area to mark off where it will be and help to give us a visual cue where things are going to go later. Lightly smooth over these strokes you have added. (And I do mean *very* lightly — we only want to slightly soften them. If you smooth too much they will end up totally washed out.) See Figures 5-42 and 5-43.

Using the **Slash1** brush again, try to liven up the brow/eye intersection area a bit as at the moment it really is a bit boring with very little to look at. Do a stroke on the inner area of the brow as shown and follow the arc around the eye socket area. Again, slightly smooth it to get rid of any jagged edges. Many of these strokes we have done with the Slash brushes will be sharpened up later as we further subdivide the model and progress with the sculpting.

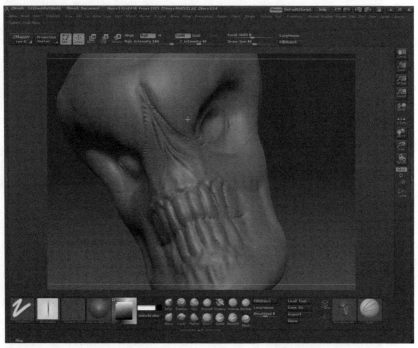

FIGURE 5-44

Now it's time to do the first pass at sharpening up the large slashes we made between the two brows with our **Slash1** brush. Also add very light slashes down the sides of the face as shown to further define the area a little. When smoothed (which I'd like you to do now), this will be almost imperceptible, but it adds some imperfections to the area that help show musculature beneath the skin. It is often the small details that we can barely see that give the eyes a visual cue that something looks either "real" or artificial. Add another light slash over the top of the outer edge of the upper eyelid for similar reasons, and again smooth it out very slightly.

We can now add a bit of tension in the skin of the upper brow area by using the **Slash1** brush to make some brow wrinkles. I have kept these pretty simple on purpose as this is a beginner's project, although as a rule I would make these more complex and lifelike. Smooth them out again, as at the moment they are just placeholders to remind us to add more detail there later.

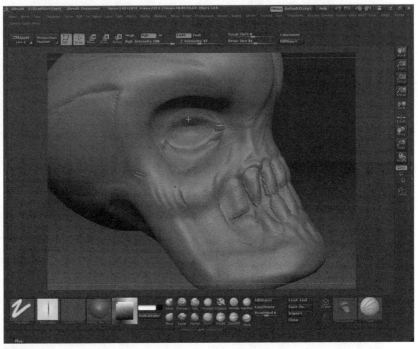

FIGURE 5-45

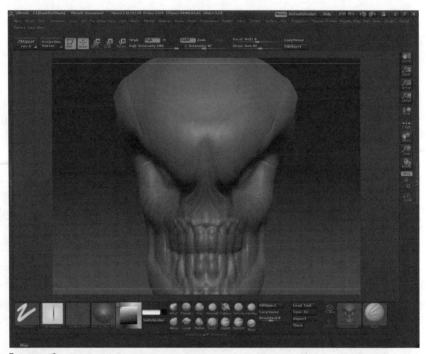

FIGURE 5-46

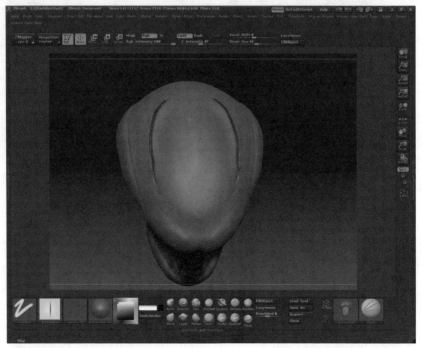

FIGURE 5-47

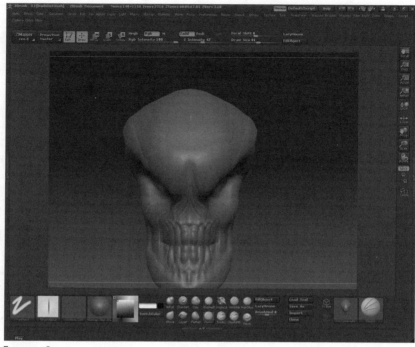

FIGURE 5-48

Next, with the **Inflate** brush selected and set to a ZIntensity of
about **10**, choose **Alpha 01** (which is the first circular alpha and one of
my favorites for sculpting). Add a few strokes around the bulged area of
the skull, then decrease your brush size slightly and press the **Alt** key
to push the area between these strokes inward a bit. Now we can start
to inflate the areas between some of the slashes created earlier. At the
moment they are simply lines and have no mass or weight at all, so by
inflating between them we can create the impression of folded skin. Do
the same for the slashes on either side of the nose area and the ones on
the eye and brow area. You will need to be much gentler with some
strokes than others and use slightly different pressures in order to keep
every stroke and skin fold from appearing identical. Add a few strokes
with your Inflate brush (without the Alt key pressed) over the cheekbones to begin to add the look of skin over bone. We'll refine them more
later on.

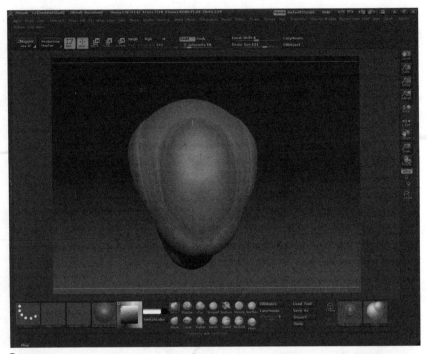

FIGURE 5-49

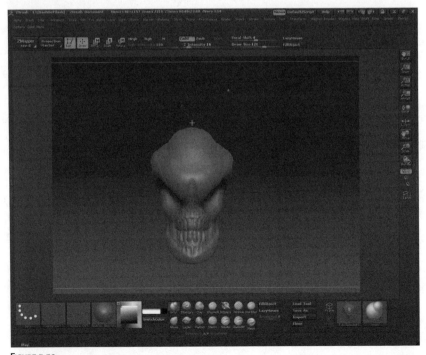

FIGURE 5-50

Continue to inflate areas such as the brow (above the line that we cut into it) and between the lines that we cut into the skull earlier to add a little more detail and medium-resolution form to the digital sculpture.

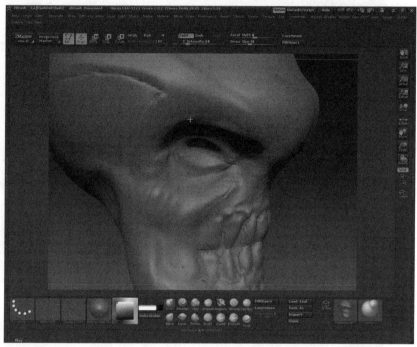

FIGURE 5-51

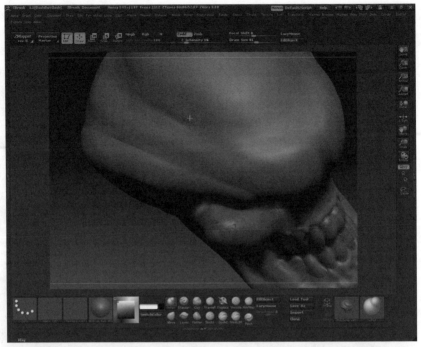

FIGURE 5-52

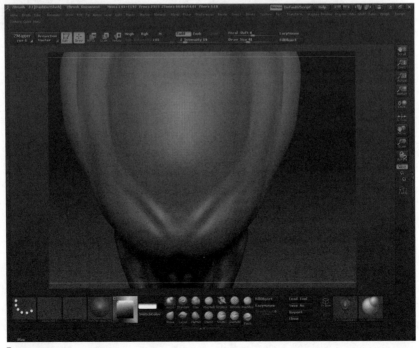

FIGURE 5-53

Adding the Eyes

We have taken this model about as far as we can in the eye area without the eyeballs being there, so it's time we added some. These will not only help when it comes to making sure that the proportions of the eye area are correct, but also will help us sculpt the upper and lower eyelids correctly. To add our eyeballs we are going to use the default ZBrush **Sphere primitive**, which can be accessed by left-clicking on your current tool to open a pane that contains many other primitives and tools. Select the Sphere primitive, and it will load into a viewport of its own. At this time we can't use this sphere as it is because it is still a "primitive" and not a polymesh that we can sculpt. The primitives within ZBrush are special tools that allow us to make sure we have the correct number of polygons and edge flow that we need before generating the polymesh.

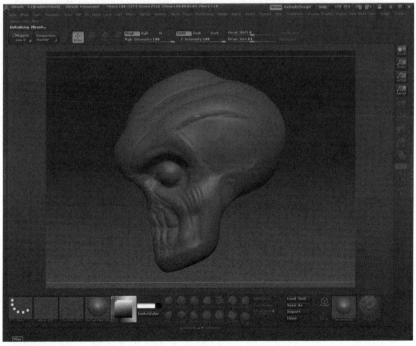

FIGURE 5-54

In this case we can use the default settings for the number of polygons. If you need different settings, you can go to the **Initialize** section of the Tool palette. Remember that many palettes are "dynamic" and only show some options when a specific tool is active. For example, there are options that you can only see when you are working with a primitive, such as the masking options, which are normally grayed out when you are working with polygon meshes.

To make this primitive into a polymesh, simply press the **Make PolyMesh3D** button. This will generate your polymesh from the primitive sphere and load it into the viewport in exactly the same position as the primitive. Although it looks as if nothing has happened, you will now notice that the **Initialize** section of the Tool palette is no longer present, which tells us that this is now indeed no longer a ZBrush primitive and is now a polymesh ready to use and sculpt.

So now we have a sphere that we are going to make into not one eye but two eyes. You may have noticed that the demon head model we are working on is also visible in the Tool palette. If you click on this now, it will once again become active in the viewport and we can position the sphere as one of the eyes.

First of all, go to the **Tool** palette and open up the section labeled **SubTool**. This is where we will store each eye so that it will not only save us resources (ZBrush can store many subtools at a polygon count at or near your maximum for a single tool), but it will also make it easier to hide and show parts as we work on the model. Click on the **Append** button at the bottom of the SubTool section. This once again brings up a pane with other ZBrush tools in it. You should see on the very top line your sphere polymesh loaded, so select that and it will be added to your current model as a subtool. You will notice that the size and position is all wrong at the moment, but don't worry as we'll be sorting that out next.

Our next big job is to resize and position the eye correctly. We can then mirror it for the other eye using a well-known workflow that saves steps.

Before we continue, let's recap how the transpose lines work for our transformation tools such as Move, Scale, and Rotate. At each end of the transpose line as well as at the center you will see a circle. By left-clicking and holding, we can move the transform line into position by dragging the edges of any of the circles. If you drag by an end circle, then that end will move with the other end acting as a pivot point. Dragging by the edge of the center circle moves the whole action line. Clicking in the center of each circle works in a similar way, except that the transformation is made in a uniform way (depending on the whether the Move, Scale, or Rotate tool is currently active). For example, if you have the Scale transform active with the action line vertically on the center line of your model and drag in the center of the circle at either end, it will scale the entire model up or down uniformly, while dragging using the center circle would scale the model horizontally but not vertically.

Make sure you have the sphere polymesh as the active subtool (by highlighting it in the **SubTool** section of the **Tool** palette). Then select the Scale transform tool and left-click and drag an action line out from the center of the sphere. *(If you hold down the Shift key at the same time, you can constrain it to the nearest surface and stop it from whizzing off backward in the Z direction in the viewport.)* You can now left-click and drag in the center of the outermost circle and scale the sphere up or down as needed to an approximate size that looks right to you.

Try and get it in the right "ballpark" so that there isn't too much resizing to do later on once it's moved into place. We now switch to the Move transform tool. Notice that the action line stays in the same place it was in for the Scale transform tool. You may feel that you would be more comfortable making this action line smaller or in a different place before moving it into place as our eyeball.

Feel free to move your action line as needed. Now it is a simple matter of moving the sphere into place as our eye. It may take you a while to learn to use the action lines and the transform tools, so don't feel dismayed if they feel awkward at first. Once you have your sphere in the right place you may need to resize it again slightly to make it fit.

Please bear in mind that we haven't sculpted the eyelids yet, so a certain amount of "eyeballing" the position and scale is necessary. (Yes, the pun was intended… I must get my fun where I can, I'm afraid.)

Two Eyes from One

To duplicate the eye we'll use a very simple and rather well-known workflow trick that less experienced users of ZBrush may not be aware of. As we have been sculpting with X symmetry enabled, both sides of our model along the vertical axis are simply mirror images of each other. (Later on we can add some asymmetry if needed.) So with your sphere polymesh selected in the **SubTool** section of the **Tool** palette, go to the top of the Tool palette and press the **Clone** button. What this does is it makes an exact duplicate of your sphere polymesh and places it among the tools in the Tool palette (which can be accessed by left-clicking on the currently active tool). We don't want to use the sphere we imported because it has been moved (and most probably resized) and we'd have to do all that work over again.

What we are going to do now is not change to that tool but stay exactly where we are with our demon head the active tool in the viewport. We go to the **Append** button and select the clone of the sphere polymesh that we just created to add it as a second subtool. This appears to have done nothing at all at first glance, but in fact we have added the same piece of geometry twice as two separate tools. As they also currently share the same space, we can't see that there are two of them. To mirror one of them over to the other side of the head in the correct position, simply select the last added sphere polymesh and open the **Deformation** section of the **Tool** palette. There you will see a function called **Mirror** that has three options labeled X, Y, and Z corresponding to the different axes we can mirror in. In this case we wish to mirror in the **X** axis, so make sure it is selected.

With the X active and making sure we have the last of our two sphere polymeshes selected, press the Mirror button. You should now have an eye in the other socket where we need it to be.

If for some reason you have disabled X symmetry, you can still mask off the "good" half of your model and press the **Smart ReSym** button to make both sides of your model symmetrical again. Be aware though that the more polygons you have in your digital sculpture, the more time it will take ZBrush to work out the position of every vertex in your model and create a symmetrical partner for it in your mesh. Remember that ZBrush may be dealing with millions of polygons.

Back to the Sculpting Again

Make sure that you once again have the main demon head subtool selected and active so you can sculpt on it without fear of affecting the eye subtools. With the **Standard** brush selected, hold down the **Ctrl** key and paint a mask that covers the eye area as shown in Figure 5-56. We then can invert this mask either by using the button in the Masking section of the Tool palette or by simply holding down the **Ctrl** key and clicking on an empty area of the workspace. The reason we are masking off the rest of the head in this way is because it is very easy to affect other parts of the mesh that we don't want to by mistake. To make sure this doesn't happen, we simply mask off areas.

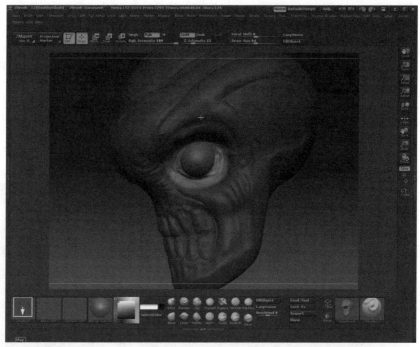

FIGURE 5-55

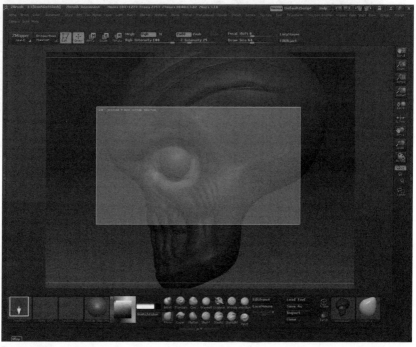

FIGURE 5-56

Hold down the **Shift** and **Ctrl** keys at the same time, and drag a selection over the area around the eyes as shown in Figure 5-57. We are going to need to move the eyelids into place to fit around each eyeball, and this is best done from "inside" the model. As such, we are going to need access to it and also be able to see both sides of our mesh. By default Double sided polygon mode is switched off, so to enable it go down to the **Display Properties** section of the Tool palette and press the **Double** button. This means we can now see both sides of each and every polygon visible in the viewport. We can also rotate as needed to get a good angle to work from.

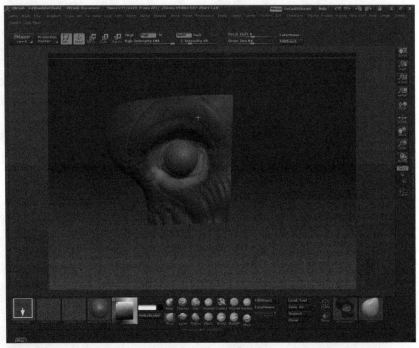

FIGURE 5-57

Switch to the Move brush and start to move the eyelids into place from the inside. Try to make sure that your brush size isn't too big or too small. I realize that sounds a bit obtuse, but the brush size and its effect on the model has a lot to do with a person's touch. Too big a brush and heavy pressure will give crude results, and too small a brush and light pressure will give uneven and tentative-looking results.

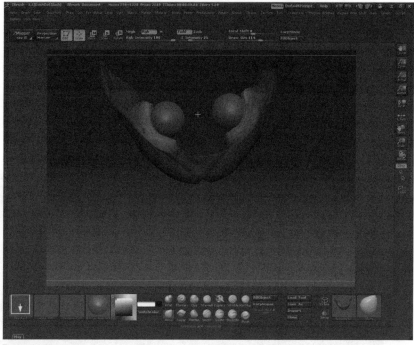

FIGURE 5-58

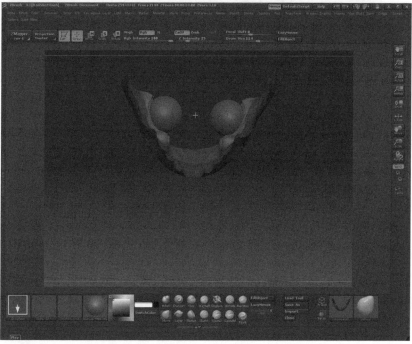

FIGURE 5-59

For some areas you may need to add more mesh back to the mask by again holding down the Ctrl key and painting an area, such as when dealing with the eyelids from the front and at the edges of each eye so that you don't accidentally move another part of the eye in a way you don't want to.

Tip: Remember that if you need to remove an area from the mask, simply paint over the area you wish to remove with the Ctrl and Alt keys pressed down. To add to a mask, press and hold Ctrl while painting the area.

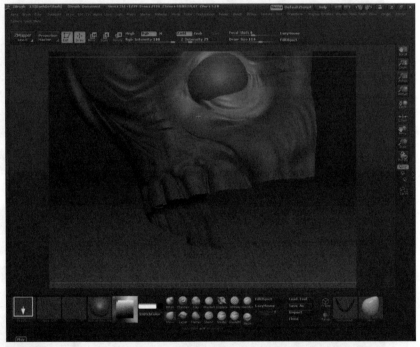

FIGURE 5-60

Once the eyelids are in pretty much the right place and are hugging the eyeball itself, work as slowly as you need to until you are happy with the result. Remember that with time and practice come speed and confidence.

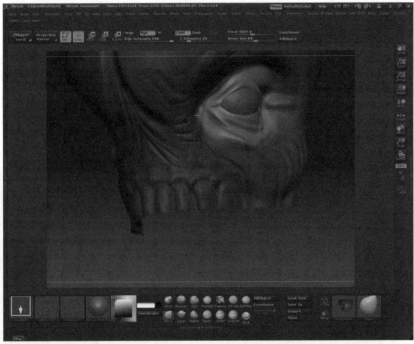

FIGURE 5-61

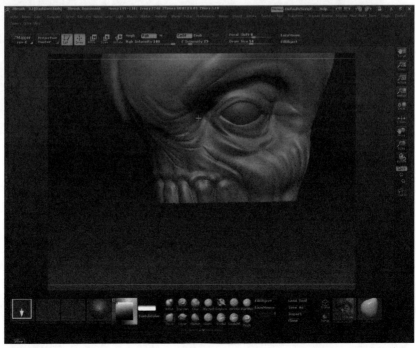

FIGURE 5-62

Cleaning Up the Eye and Moving On

Now that we have the eyelids nice and tight to the eye spheres, we will need to do a little tidying up on the eye and upper face area. At this point I feel a small change is needed to the muscle running from the side of the nose area under the eye and toward the sides of the mouth. So change to your **Clay Tubes** brush with a ZIntensity of about **10** to **12** and make a stroke on the upper part of that area. This gives us a little more of the muscle bulk that I want.

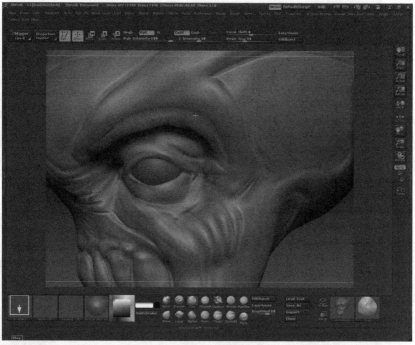

FIGURE 5-63

Figure 5-64

Now, back to the eye area where we will start to clean things up a bit and make it look more presentable. Start off by holding down the **Shift** key and smoothing over the lower lid area. I do this because all the moving about with the Move brush left it a little untidy looking. So rather than try to fix it, you can instead wash it out and resculpt that detail. You will often find that it is much quicker to resculpt a problem area because you have the benefit of your previous attempt, so a second pass will look much better.

Once you've done this and you have something similar to the image shown, let's switch to a brush we haven't used yet: the **Displace** brush. As discussed in Chapter 4, the Displace brush, unlike other brushes, allows you to sculpt on your geometry while maintaining any existing surface detail. So if, for example, you wanted to add more wrinkles to a face after creating the skin's pores, you can displace the geometry you need to (depending on brush size, alpha selected, and ZIntensity) without affecting the higher-resolution detail.

Select **Alpha 42** as active along with your Displace brush and set your ZIntensity to around **10** to **14**. We are now going to sculpt in a few of the wrinkles in the eye area by holding down the **Alt** key and carefully carving into our virtual clay. Notice the wrinkles originate from the corners of each side of the eye; your wrinkles will look a lot more realistic if they make anatomical sense. Again I have simplified them a little on this sculpt as this is your first big project in ZBrush. We will cover a more complex example later in the book. Once you have the wrinkles carved in, making sure they are not too evenly spaced, or too deep, or too "regular" looking, we can move on.

Now smooth these out just a small amount to take away some of the hard edges. Add and then smooth out a few on the line on the brow area and some running from the lower lid over the cheekbones.

If you look at the muscles of a human face, you will find that 90 percent of the wrinkle patterns run in the opposite direction of the muscle flow and not with them, as many beginners assume. Good references are also very helpful when starting to digitally sculpt in ZBrush.

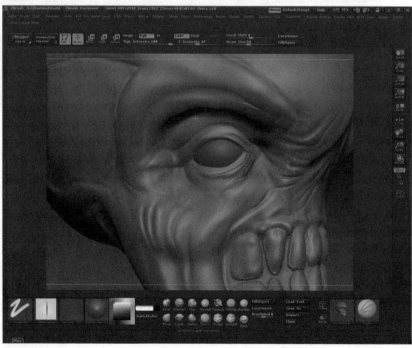

Figure 5-65

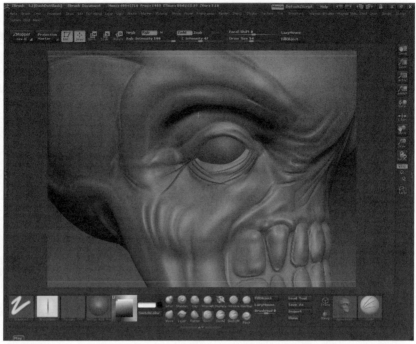

FIGURE 5-66

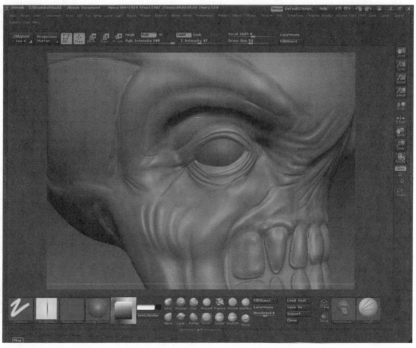

FIGURE 5-67

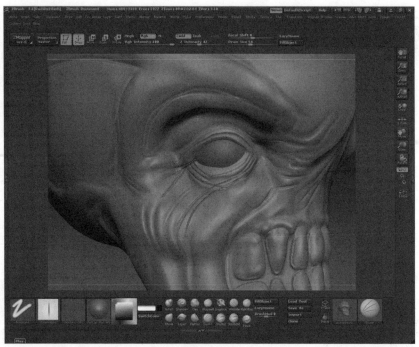

FIGURE 5-68

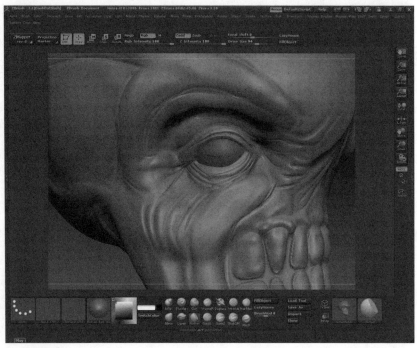

FIGURE 5-69

My advice is to use real life or good quality photographs where possible rather than relying on models created by other artists. If you copy another artist, you may also pick up his or her bad habits. I'm a big believer that each artist should strive to be unique, which will develop naturally over time and with practice.

With all the previous wrinkles created and softly smoothed out, add a very small amount of mass in the area running from the side of the nasal area and over the cheekbones. Use the **Inflate** brush at a very low ZIntensity, add a tiny bit more bulk, and then smooth the area very slightly.

Time for Some Changes

Now that we have a basic idea blocked out and some medium-resolution detailing added, this is the point where I usually rethink the design and change the shapes and forms I feel could be better. So first of all, step down a few subdivision levels and, using the **Move** brush, pull the back of the skull outward a little and the top of the skull upward a little. Use this time to look for any problems with the form and design of your digital sculpture and change them accordingly.

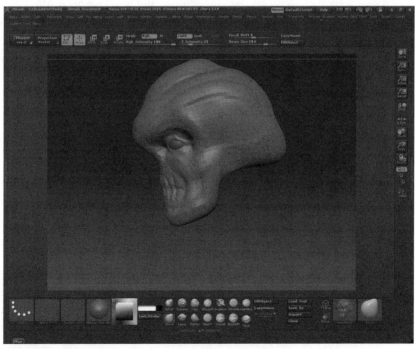

FIGURE 5-70

At this stage we are not expecting to have a monster head that looks like it is ready for a Hollywood film or the latest next-generation computer game. This is a stage where we are nailing down the most important part of the creature's character — its design and form. Although this is only a practice sculpture to help refine your skills, it is always a good idea to try to make the best of each design that you can for every model that you do. Being able to sculpt is no longer seen as enough to make a name for yourself in the industry; you must have a good eye for design as well. Even though at first you may be working from other people's ideas, there will hopefully come a time when you are higher up the food chain and it will be your designs that others will be working on.

The Importance of a "Back Story"

This section is a slight digression from the sculpting side, but a rather important topic to cover at this stage. So save your model (as I hope you have been doing regularly and under sequential names, such as head 1, head 2, etc.). Something I caught on to early on when starting out as a digital artist is the importance of knowing who the character you are designing "is" — where he comes from and what he does. Basically, the more you know about this fantasy creature's "life," the more believable you can make him.

So sit down and work out things like why he looks the way he does, what sort of job he would do, and how this would affect not only his physiology but also his mood and mental state. So if our creature were a mass murdering accountant, he would appear vastly different from a warrior creature. This would affect not only how the muscles on his body developed, but also how the wrinkles on his face would form to some degree. What I am really trying to get over to you is that you must "know" the character you are designing as if it is real. If you simply sculpt away with no regard to this, your sculpture may seem lifeless when you are done, even if the sculpting itself is done very well indeed. You can either make up the back story as you design him (as I often do), or have a detailed idea about the character before you even switch on your computer.

Some people find it helpful to work from sketches, while others such as myself prefer to freestyle designs as they find it produces more interesting ideas more often than not. But there really is no right or wrong way to approach the design of your character. It's up to you and something you will decide for yourself.

Okay, now it's time we opened up our model again and got on with the sculpting.

Continuing Onward with the Model

Using our **Clay Tubes** brush, we are going to add some mass and medium forms that are currently missing on the jaw area of the model. First of all, while holding down the **Shift** key, gouge out the area under the jaw as shown. Although this won't be seen very much (if at all), it affects the way that the design will progress. So even in areas that will remain unseen it is worth adding at least some rudimentary forms and details. Once the area is gouged out, be sure to smooth it over a bit to help the forms interact better later. We also need to add more mass to the sides of the jaw and the front of the jaw, and again smooth things out enough to help them look like one organic believable form as much as possible.

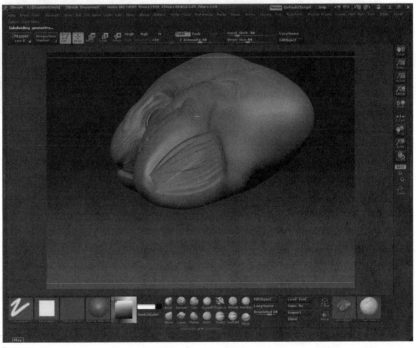

FIGURE 5-71

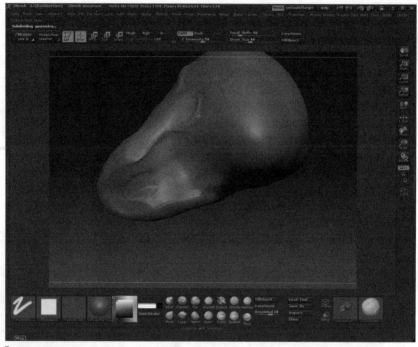

FIGURE 5-72

Finer Details

This is the stage that I know a lot of you look forward to, the stage where we start to add some finer details to our digital sculpture. In this section, I'll show you some standard techniques I use so that you will be able to apply them to your own models and designs within ZBrush. Now that we have the main forms nailed down for this simple project, we can move on to the things that give the creature a bit of realism. Although we are dealing with a creature rather than a human, and we are pretty much free to add anything we think looks good, remember that all models must have some sort of basis in realistic anatomy. You can see that although this particular design looks in no way human (if you know anyone who looks like this guy, my sympathies are with you), he has a very strong basis in human anatomy.

FIGURE 5-73

We are going to be changing brushes a fair bit now that we are at the detailing stage, but as you have obviously gotten this far with your model, I'm assuming that you're fairly comfortable with brushes. The main brushes we will be using are the **Displace** brush with a small alpha for cutting in some details, and the **Inflate** and **Clay** brushes for adding some mass between the wrinkles. You will see as you go through this section that I rarely make wrinkles as straight lines, but rather as either jagged or staggered lines drawn in with multiple strokes. Wrinkles in real life do not form in straight lines and the skin on either side of them often gives the appearance of a jagged line. I would suggest once you have finished this project to search online for more reference images to get a better idea of how wrinkles are formed on certain facial features.

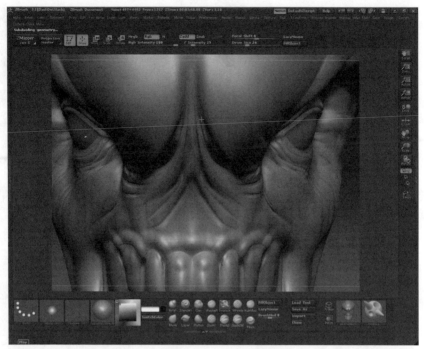

FIGURE 5-74

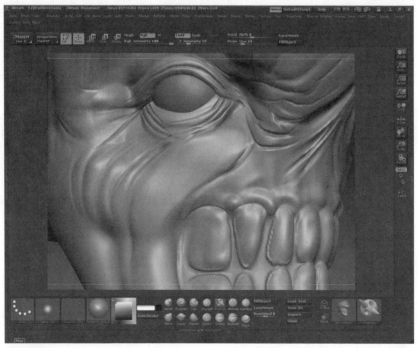

FIGURE 5-75

I don't expect you to copy every wrinkle I cut in but rather understand the basic idea I am trying to achieve. This means that you will be learning more as an artist. Remember that when you are carving in details to use the Displace brush with either the **Alt** key pressed or with **Zsub** switched on to reverse the effect. I prefer to use the Alt key. Generally speaking, to add mass you should use the Inflate brush for larger to medium areas and the Clay brush to help meld wrinkles together, and use the Displace brush (without the Alt key pressed) to add mass between very small wrinkles. Remember not to go too high on the polygon level when working as it's never a good idea to push beyond the capabilities of your machine.

If you reach your polygon limit and cannot reach the subdivision levels I use in this project, you can use HD geometry, which we covered in Chapter 3, or you may be better off using a local subdivision method instead, which we also discussed earlier.

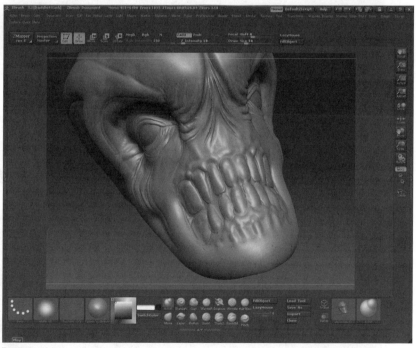

FIGURE 5-76

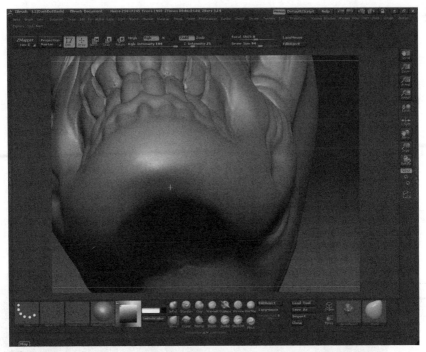

FIGURE 5-77

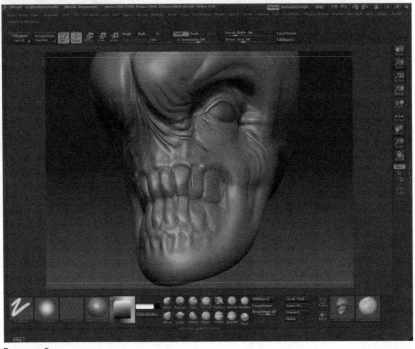

FIGURE 5-78

Let's start our high-resolution detailing in the nose area by adding a few very fine folds with the Displace brush set to a small round alpha and a ZIntensity of about **10** to **15**. Make sure the folds have a similar origin point and not only follow the flow of the forms but also behave in a way that is believable in normal gravity. Then while pressing the **Alt** key to cut inward, put some lines on the brow area around the center. Make sure that your strokes are not too straight and even; a slightly jagged stroke will work much better for regions such as these. Make sure that one of the lines running toward the center of the brow leads from the edge of the eye, as this helps our design to gel a bit better. Remember that the goal is for the viewer's eye to be led around the model in a fairly predictable way. Composition isn't just applicable to 2D; it can also be used in a three-dimensional digital sculpt.

Note: The WayneRoundClay brush used here is simply the standard Clay brush with Alpha 01 selected and the FreeHand stroke type set as your active stroke type.

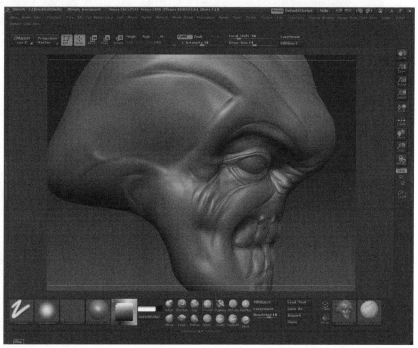

FIGURE 5-79

Next, start to cut some nice lines between the teeth and gums; these will help to create a nice line of shadow and a highlight on our model that will help to delineate the forms of the teeth and gums as well as the jaw. This may help you to see why I think of digital sculpting as "sculpting with shadows." In my mind I am not sculpting with polygons (as these are effectively a mathematically produced representation of what I want the digital sculpture to look like) but rather where the shadows and highlights will fall.

After carving in these lines around the area between the teeth and gums, feel free to inflate the gums a bit if needed (adding some gravity using the Gravity setting in the Brush palette may also help, depending on what your sculpt looks like at this stage). Cut a few larger lines over the upper eyelid area and inflate a very *slight* amount. Remember that the human eye is very sensitive and can detect the differences in "planes" between two very finely inflated areas. This all helps the believability of our model.

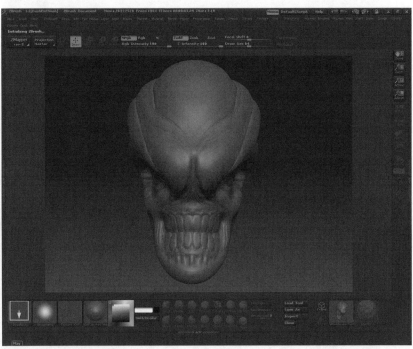

Figure 5-80

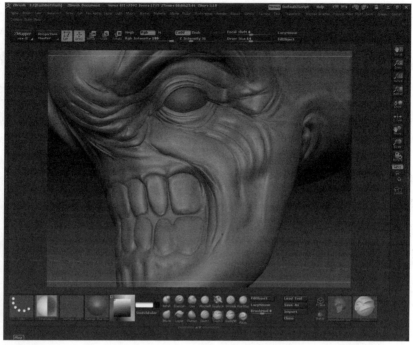

FIGURE 5-81

Use the **Flatten** brush with a ZIntensity of about **20** very lightly over each tooth to help eliminate anything that looks too rounded. You can also mask over the tooth next to the one you are working on and use the **Move** brush to adjust them so that the gap between each tooth is smaller. The folds on the brow that we put in and then washed out for placeholders at the beginning of this model can now be detailed a bit by cutting some lines in. Once this is done, inflate with a broad stroke between the two main lines of wrinkles. If you have time, feel free to go over the areas between even the smaller ones as well.

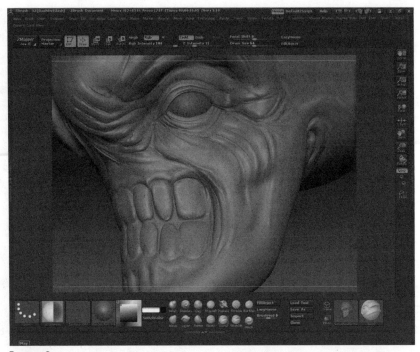

Figure 5-82

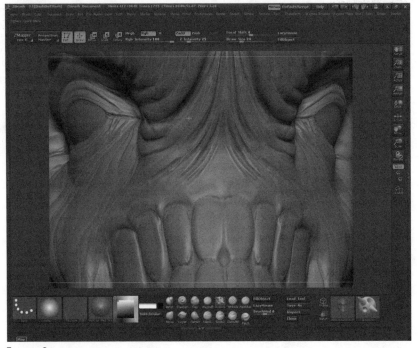

Figure 5-83

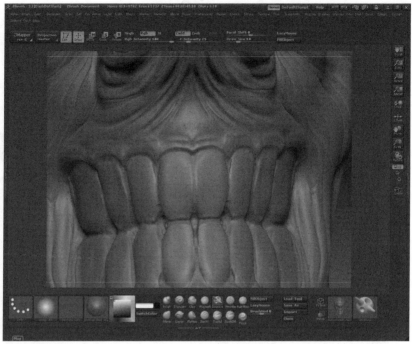

Cut some more lines on the outer edge of the brow area along the diagonal placeholder that we put in earlier and add some much finer ones at the bottom of the wrinkles between the brow areas above the nasal zone. The deeper these lines are, the more they will catch shadows and help to delineate form, but be careful not to go too deep or they will look unnatural. Cut another jagged overlaid line at the side of the mouth and smooth it lightly before carefully inflating on either side of it. We also need to cut some more lines at the corner of the eyes, again inflating between and smoothing the edges. If this were a more complex sculpture that I wanted to take to final, I would do this with symmetry switched off to help give it a more interesting look, but for this tutorial let's keep things symmetrical.

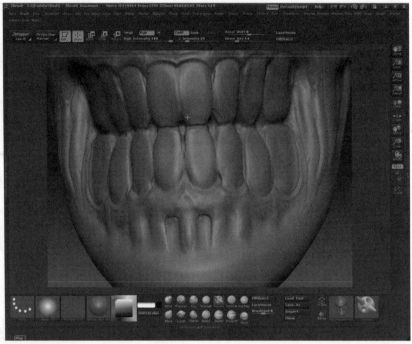

FIGURE 5-85

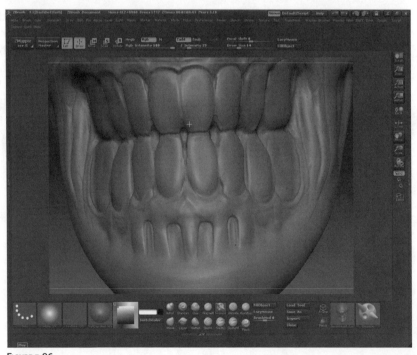

FIGURE 5-86

Adding an Ear

One of the last jobs that we need to do is to make an ear, or at least an "ear-like" part. As this particular creature is going to need some sort of hearing, carve in some lines and a hollow area that will be the ear hole. If you feel the need (or find that the ear area is giving you some trouble), look online for reference photos or just use a mirror to see your own ear. Inflate the areas as needed and then switch to the Slash1 brush and use a light stroke and a very small size to help bring back some of those sharp edges where needed.

Finishing Off

The creature's head is now done. If this is your first model and you've ended up with a decent-looking figure, then you have done amazingly well. Take a break from it for a while, then in a few hours or a day later, start to clean up and polish off the model. Look for the "bad" areas, work out what needs to be improved, and inflate between any wrinkles that you may have missed, such as the eyes and inner brow area. Take as much time as you need to make this first digital sculpt in ZBrush something you are proud of. Art can be thought of as work that is never "released" but "escapes." Knowing when to stop is a skill in itself, so don't let this drag on too long or you will find it begins to look overworked.

Some Final Thoughts

I thought it may prove useful to add a few comments about this model that may help explain my modeling methods and ways this model could be improved. You may have noticed that I changed materials partway through modeling sessions. The reason for this is simple: As an artist I sometimes am uninspired with the way a material looks, so doing something as simple as changing the material can give me a whole host of new ideas. If you are wondering why I didn't use alphas to create groups of wrinkles, the answer is I personally find the use of alphas for mean features to be a bit predictable and it can give a "production line" look to ZBrush models. Alphas are great things to use, but overuse can kill a great model stone dead if not used with extreme care. I prefer to create as much detail as possible by hand because it gives a far great level of control and arguably quality (although that is obviously open to debate).

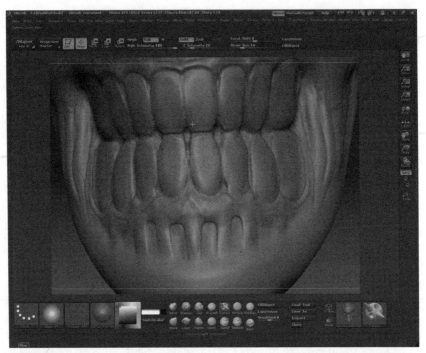

FIGURE 5-87

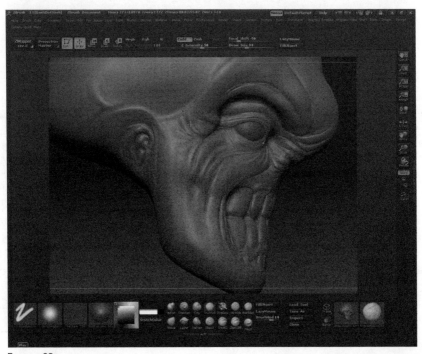

FIGURE 5-88

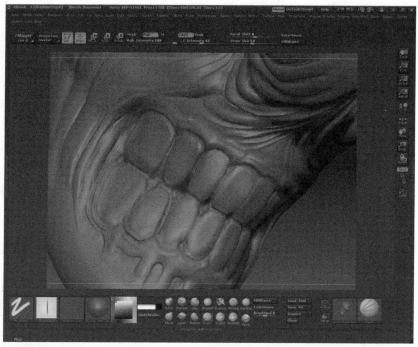

FIGURE 5-89

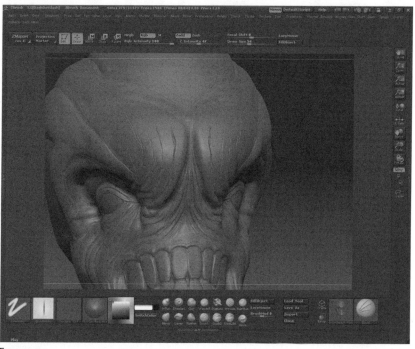

FIGURE 5-90

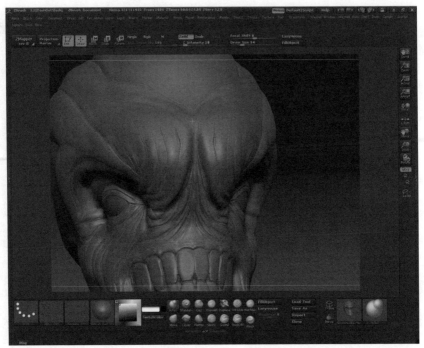

FIGURE 5-91

In life you sometimes have a choice between what is "easy" and what is "right." When we think about that in an artistic way, it comes down to the judgment of the artist. The way I work may not be what you would find is best. *I would still urge new users to avoid using alphas for the main features — at least for a while.* It's a good idea to get your core sculpting skill set down first before using the things that can make life easier. This gives you more tools in your creative toolbox and can help make your digital sculpts more lifelike and organic.

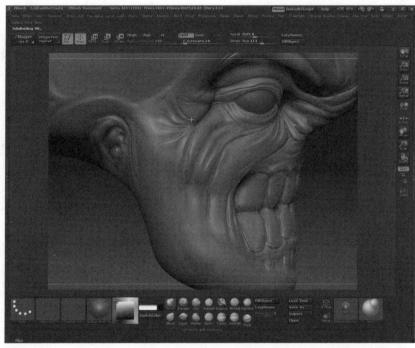

FIGURE 5-92

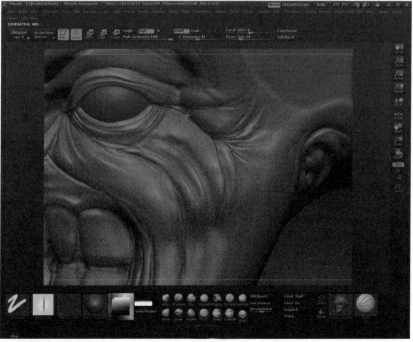

FIGURE 5-93

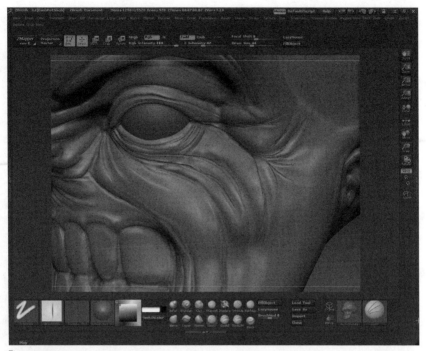

FIGURE 5-94

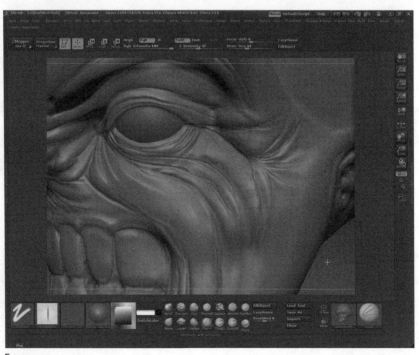

FIGURE 5-95

The model we created was not textured or even taken to the skin pores level for a reason. It is always a good idea to make sure that a model's design is as perfect as possible before you get to those stages. Although a bad model can be made to look a whole lot better with good textures and lighting, a good model will look amazing when textured, lit, and rendered. So you may want to keep this model once you've gotten it to this stage and use it for practice for skin pores, map generation, and even texturing. I've tried to give you a first project that is not only interesting but also challenging. Hopefully, I've also given you enough information that you will be able to start sculpting your own models in ZBrush while we work through this book.

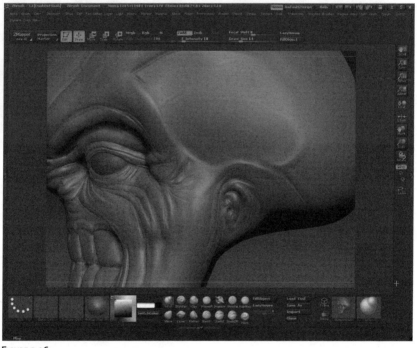

FIGURE 5-96

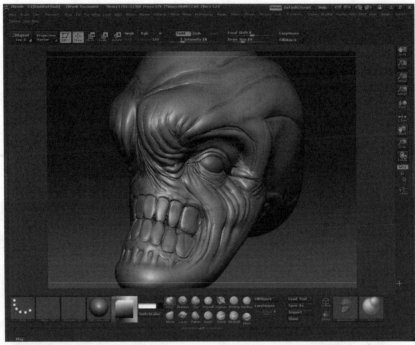

FIGURE 5-97

The skills you've learned from this project can be applied to a great many other model types and are pretty portable across different digital sculpting genres. In this project we started sculpting from a sphere, which helped to speed things up. This particular "spherehead" was roughed out in less than 30 minutes. I don't say that to brag but rather to illustrate that the more you practice, the faster you get.

The following images show a number of close-ups of the final sculpting stages for this model. They'll give you a good idea of exactly what is going on in each area so you can do the same for your model.

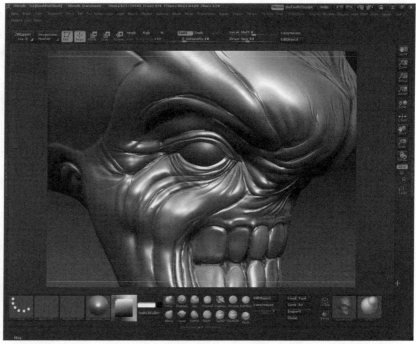

FIGURE 5-98

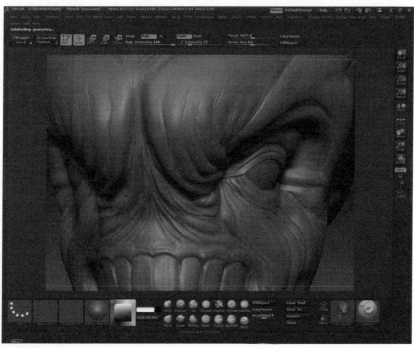

FIGURE 5-99

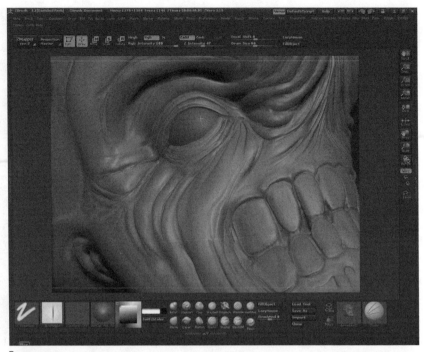

FIGURE 5-100

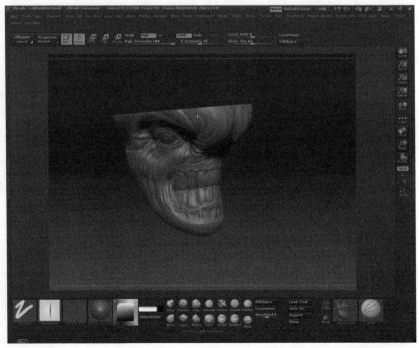

FIGURE 5-101

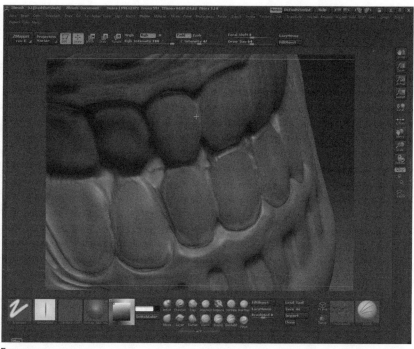

FIGURE 5-102

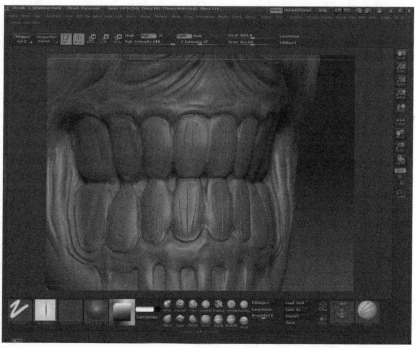

FIGURE 5-103

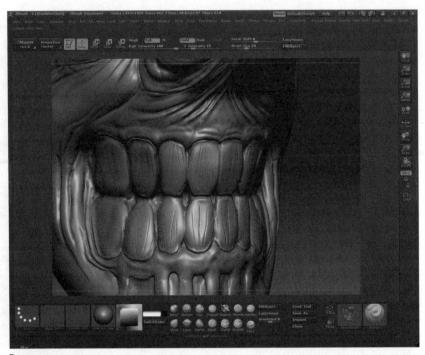

FIGURE 5-104

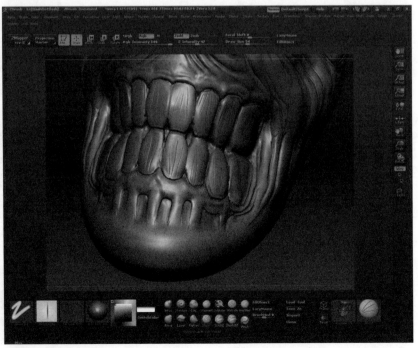

FIGURE 5-105

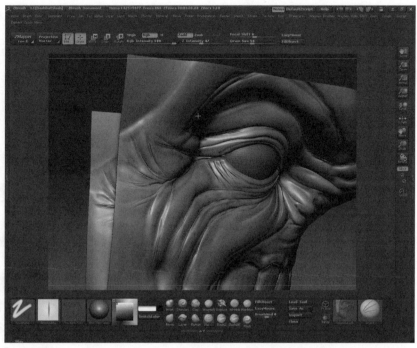

FIGURE 5-106

FIGURE 5-107

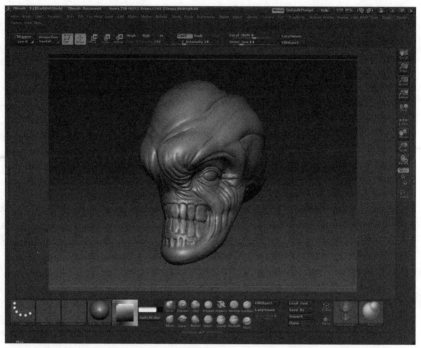

FIGURE 5-108

In our next project we'll tackle something a bit different and more challenging. Congratulations on finishing your first ZBrush digital sculpture.

6 ZSpheres

What Are ZSpheres?

ZSpheres are a revolutionary invention by Pixologic that simplify a whole host of tasks inside ZBrush. To get the very most out of ZBrush you'll want to learn all you can about ZSpheres, as they are an integral part of the program. They are capable of being used for jobs ranging from base mesh creation to retopologizing and posing your mesh.

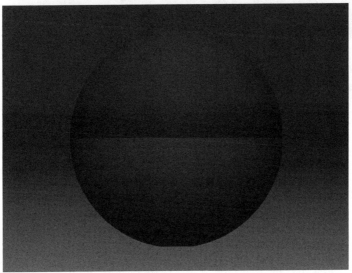

FIGURE 6-1

Basic ZSphere Creation

There are a number of basics that we need to cover before we dive into actually working with ZSpheres so that you'll feel comfortable using them. Many users give up on ZSpheres because they think they're too complex, or simply assume that if they can already poly model to a high standard there is no need to learn about them. The truth is that even those who are very proficient polygon modelers also use ZSpheres for basic mesh creation to improve their productivity.

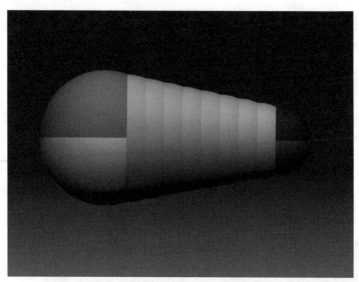

FIGURE 6-2

To start us on our journey into the ZSpheres, we must first select one as our active tool. If you click with your left mouse on your active tool slot, you will see a panel of tool options. Simply select the two-toned sphere that you see among them, which is the ZSphere. Before you draw anything, be sure to press either the **Edit** button or the **T** key to make sure you are in Edit mode. If you do not enter Edit mode, the tool will be dropped to the canvas and cannot be manipulated. Remember that like other tools, ZSpheres can make use of symmetry, so you may want to press the **X** key to make your model symmetrical along the X axis. Now draw a ZSphere onto the canvas by dragging with the left mouse button.

Congratulations! You have just made your first ZSphere. While I'll agree that at first glance it looks rather underwhelming, it is in fact probably the most powerful tool in the whole of ZBrush. To add another ZSphere, you simply click on the existing one and drag.

Tip: Make sure that you keep the size of your brush very small indeed, as a large brush size may affect more than the ZSphere that you wish it to. So consider using a small brush size as a good standard practice to get into very early on.

To move, scale, or rotate a ZSphere or a ZSphere chain (more on these later), you use the transform tools and not the Move brush as many new users assume. The reason for this is a logical one that may also help you understand a bit better. The ZSphere, like other ZBrush primitives, is a special type of tool unlike those used for digital sculpture. I like to think of the ZBrush primitives as "internal" tools and rather special because the transform tools such as Move, Scale, and Rotate act directly on the tool itself. With "regular" tools such as digital sculptures you would use the Move brush to move parts of your model's polygons and use the transform tools and their associated action lines. However, the special internal tools do not use action lines, which is why I say they act on the tools "directly." This also makes for a faster workflow than if we had to use action lines to transform our ZSpheres.

A ZSphere may be moved, scaled, or rotated using the transforms in a couple of important ways. You can rotate a ZSphere itself using the Rotate tool, and you can also rotate an entire chain of ZSpheres by hovering the mouse over the *join* between the ZSpheres. Joins are shaded a different color for easy recognition, as you've probably already noticed. To get a very basic feel for how they behave when drawn in the workspace, just take a few minutes to mess around with them.

Making and Adding ZSpheres

You can add a ZSphere to an existing one by simple hovering your mouse over it, left-clicking with your mouse, and dragging one out. The more you drag, the larger the ZSphere will be, which gives us great control over our ZSphere rig. You can also click between two ZSpheres on the chain and add a ZSphere here as well. In fact, many people start their mesh for a human figure with just the body and a single ZSphere at the end of each limb, then add more spheres as they refine the rig.

You can add a ZSphere of exactly the same size as the one you are adding to by holding down the **Shift** key while left-clicking. This is a quick way to create a chain of ZSpheres of identical size. Later, as we work through some of the example projects in this chapter, you will see a few examples where this is used to help block out the basic shape and form quickly.

Symmetry and ZSpheres

Using symmetry while creating your ZSphere rigs will halve the time required. You will find that more times than not you will be creating a ZSphere rig that needs to be symmetrical in some way. Usually, this will be along the X axis, as most animals and humans are to a large degree symmetrical.

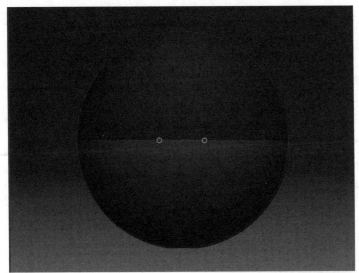

FIGURE 6-3

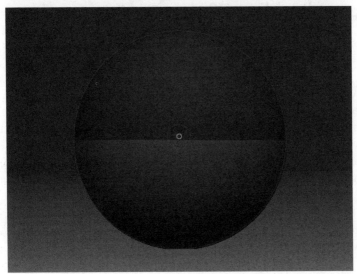

FIGURE 6-4

Remember, though, that you are not restricted to X symmetry; you can also use symmetry on the Y or Z axis or indeed combinations of them. This by itself gives an amazing degree of control, although we're still only scratching the surface of ZSpheres. Use the Radial Symmetry feature of ZSpheres by first activating symmetry on either the X, Y, or Z axis, then go to the **Transform** palette's ZSpheres section. Choose the **Activate Symmetry** button to switch your symmetry on and off, and the X, Y, and Z buttons to control the axis of symmetry. The **M** button tells ZBrush that you wish your actions to be mirrored across the selected axis.

Choose the **R** button to turn on Radial Symmetry, which allows you to create many ZSpheres with a single dragged stroke. For example, if we had to create an octopus we could create eight identical legs with this instead of having to create each one separately. The number of ZSpheres created each time is controlled by the RadialCount slider. The slider ranges from 2 copies to 100 copies, which should be more than enough for everybody I think, as not many creatures (even fantasy ones) have more than 100 limbs.

It can take a little while at first to get used to the different axes and how they affect ZSphere creation, but it is well worth learning for the times when you need to create a multi-limbed creature or two.

Adaptive Skin

Now that you understand the basics of ZSpheres we can learn how they affect the modeling side of things. While ZSpheres can be used for many things inside ZBrush, one of their more important functions is to make the creation of base meshes a lot faster and easier. So how do these two-tone spheres translate into a base mesh?

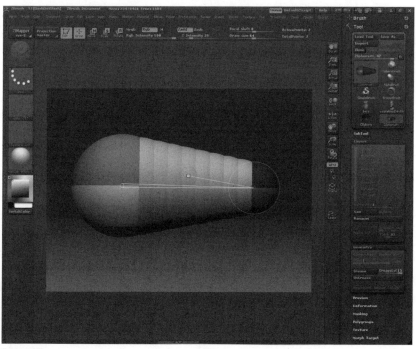

FIGURE 6-5

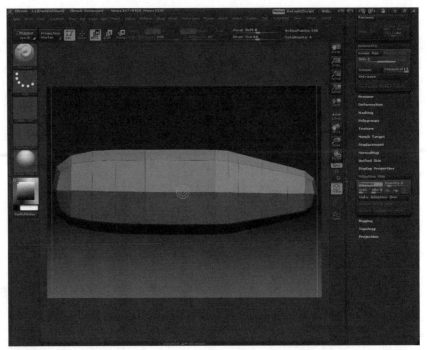

Figure 6-6

Let me outline my personal workflow by taking you through the steps I use when making a base mesh with ZSpheres. My first step is to study the number of limbs and any joints the model may require, along with the head (or heads). Assuming this is a humanoid type creature with paired limbs, it will probably be symmetrical. So I start by creating a basic shape out of ZSpheres with X symmetry switched on, making sure to keep the ZSphere count as low as I can at first. I keep previewing the eventual base mesh by hitting the **A** key to show me the adaptive skin (which is what will be our base mesh). Once I am happy that I have the very basic shapes blocked out and feel I am ready for the next stage, I then hit the **Create Adaptive Skin** button to create the base mesh before continuing with the sculpting side of things.

Let's digress from the mesh creation process for a minute to talk about adaptive skin. The way that the adaptive skin is generated can be controlled by a number of settings that used in different combinations can give very different results from exactly the same ZSphere rig. The **Adaptive Skin** section at the bottom of the Tool palette contains a number of controls. Some, such as the **Preview** button, are pretty self-explanatory, while others such as the **Ires** and **Mbr** sliders are a bit more confusing.

The slider labeled **Density** controls the number of subdivision levels that will be used when the mesh is generated. So if you set this slider to 1, you will be able to preview your mesh as an undivided "raw" mesh. I find it helpful to use the mesh generated by ZSpheres at this particular level because the unsmoothed polygons make it easier to judge proportions and basic layout of form. As you up the density slider a notch, it will subdivide your model one more time, and make the mesh a bit smoother looking and rounder with fewer sharp edges.

It is always considered to be good working practice to work at the lowest subdivision level that you can each time and get the very most out of this level before you move on to the next. So with meshes made from ZSpheres we want to get a rough estimation of the form only, and not by any stretch of the imagination a finished sculpture.

Something I must point out is that if you have tweaked the polygons on your previewed adaptive skin mesh and then change the ZSphere rig itself by adding or removing one, those changes will be forgotten. It's important to keep this in mind as you work.

The two most mysterious settings for ZSpheres are the sliders labeled **Ires** and **Mbr.** The Ires slider simply affects the way that ZSpheres can intersect, meaning how many ZSpheres may be connected to one particular ZSphere. Say you have a hand made from ZSpheres and you find that the intersections at the base of the fingers do not look right. In a case like that, upping the Ires would help a lot.

The Mbr slider controls the membrane curvature and thus the way the adaptive skin is generated. Membranes can be generated from either T- or L-shaped intersections between ZSpheres. So the higher the slider's setting, the smoother the membrane will be. If the slider is set to 0, there will be no membrane at all.

Put simply, these two sliders control the way the joints and intersections of your ZSphere rig are translated into actual geometry.

Parents and Children with Minimal Skin

That heading got your attention, huh? Actually it was a simple mnemonic I came up with when first starting out in ZBrush long ago to remember what the **MC** and **MP** buttons are for. Minimal skin to child (the **MC** button) affects the way that the adaptive skin is generated at intersecting points where a ZSphere may have more than one child sphere. When there is more than one child sphere, the first is used to determine the connecting points for the mesh but doesn't contribute any actual polygons to it as it normally would do. This means that you can generate meshes with V-shaped intersections with comparative ease. You may also find that any curves on the mesh flow with a bit more ease and give the mesh a more "curved" look.

Minimal skin to parent (the **MP** button) works in a very similar way but from a different perspective. Instead of the child sphere being used to determine the connecting points, it is the parent sphere that is used. In this case the parent sphere contributes no extra polygons to the adaptive skin as it normally would. So it is yet another way to iron out any troublesome intersection points on your ZSphere rig.

By making full use of these controls, we can help to get a base mesh that we want from our rig much more easily. And there's no reason why you can't start a base mesh with ZSpheres and then export it to a traditional polygon modeling application to add a few loops if you want to.

Multiple-Resolution ZSpheres

The most commonly heard criticism of using ZSpheres to generate a low-resolution base mesh is that the geometric distribution is sometimes far too even and not concentrated in the places the digital sculptor needs it to be. This actually is a bit of a fallacy, because ZBrush allows control over the resolution of the geometry generated for each particular ZSphere through the correct usage of the Xres, Yres, and Zres controls. These controls allow us to vary the resolution as needed. For example, if you are making a bust of a character, you're probably going to want much more resolution in the face and head than in the neck, shoulders, and upper chest area. These controls allow us to do exactly that, and as such are really powerful tools in the right hands.

Each of these sliders ranges from 0 to 8 and must be set before the ZSphere is created in order for the resolution to be affected, so you must do a bit of planning. Increasing the resolution of a sphere means that the intersection with the next and previous ones in a chain (should it indeed be part of a chain and not at the end of it) also change. This also means that we can have more spheres connected to it and still have a good overall shape and form when we generate the adaptive skin.

The way the Xres, Yres, and Zres sliders work is to set the number of polygons for each face. If you'll follow along with me for a minute it'll all start to make sense. First, set your preview density level to 1 so you can see the individual mesh lines easier. Now, create a very simple chain of three ZSpheres, with the initial one in the center and then one above and one below it. These all have the same Xres, Yres, and Zres setting of 0, which is the default when starting up ZBrush.

Now go to your Transform palette, scroll down to the Symmetry section, and turn the Xres, Yres, and Zres sliders up to 3 for each. This means that instead of creating a box or cube for each sphere, the next sphere that we draw will create what amounts to a smoothed cube with three faces vertically and horizontally on each of the six faces of the cube. Now add a slightly larger ZSphere to each end of the chain that you created. If you now preview the adaptive skin by hitting the **A** key, you will notice that the geometry at each end (where we added the higher-resolution ZSpheres) have more geometry than the others.

As you can see, this method of controlling our mesh density gives us exactly the amount of geometry that we want in exactly the places we need it. When combined with retopologizing the mesh near the end, it means that there is no longer any good reason not to use ZBrush for the creation of your low-resolution base meshes.

Spheres of Influence (Attractor Spheres)

One of the things that first got me really interested in the usage of ZSpheres to generate base meshes was a thread over at ZBrushCentral in which a number of ZBrush 1 and 2 users showcased complex meshes made using only ZSpheres. As a new user, this sparked my interest since polygon modeling isn't as immediate as digital sculpting and is usually (at least to me) the slowest part of the overall process.

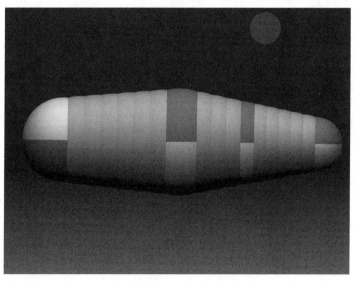

FIGURE 6-7

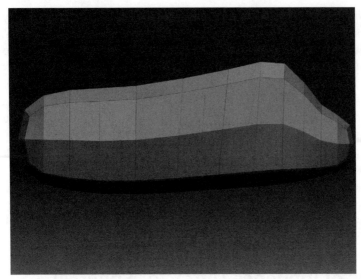

FIGURE 6-8

Probably the biggest revelation to me at the time is that important but overlooked features of ZBrush can save a lot of time.

An example of something that is often overlooked is attractor spheres. Put in simple terms, an attractor sphere is a bit like a magnet. You just draw out a ZSphere in the direction you feel your base is lacking "bulk" and then hold down the **Alt** key while left-clicking on the connecting part of the ZSphere chain (not the ZSphere itself). This will shade the sphere red and make it partially transparent so that you now know that it is not a normal ZSphere but instead is an attractor sphere.

Wherever you move this attractor sphere, your base mesh will be pulled in that direction. Also, the bigger you make this attractor sphere, the bigger your virtual "magnet" and the more pull it will exert on the base mesh at that point. You can use as many of these as you like and end up with a very complex base mesh that would take a much longer time to create in a traditional polygon modeling application.

If you search the threads at ZBrushCentral you will notice that a lot of the best and most complex base meshes made from ZSpheres use this very method. Since the advent of massive polygon counts, fewer users bother to learn about this rather simple but very effective technique to get the best out of a base mesh, but I can assure you it's still worth learning. Suddenly you will be able to make base meshes that you never thought possible inside of ZBrush, and that's got to be useful from a timesaving point of view alone.

One thing I must point out is that you should never use a multi-resolution ZSphere as your attractor. Although it will work, you will often end up with a disembodied sphere floating near your model. Hopefully after reading this section you now have a good understanding of basic ZSphere usage. Later on, when we are using ZSpheres to retopologize a model, there should be less confusion and you'll see just how important these little two-tone spheres in ZBrush really are.

Inverted Spheres

An inverted sphere is one that when it is about halfway into an existing ZSphere appears as a semi-spherical "hole" (or to be more correct, an indentation). These can be used to add things such as eye sockets to your base, and as a result will add some extra resolution where you need it. They also have the added advantage that, like other ZSpheres in your rig, they will be assigned a polygroup. This makes it easy to isolate them at different stages in the digital sculpting process.

FIGURE 6-9

In addition to eye sockets, inverted ZSpheres can be used for any sort of hole or indentation. The case can even be made for adding inverted spheres when there is no hole at all in your model. By this I mean that you may know that a certain area of your model is going to need more resolution, but you are hesitant to up a ZSphere's resolution for any one of a variety of reasons. So in a case like that you could add some resolution by adding an inverted sphere and then simply smoothing the area out. This is a powerful way to up the poly count in certain areas in cases where different intersecting resolutions that could be

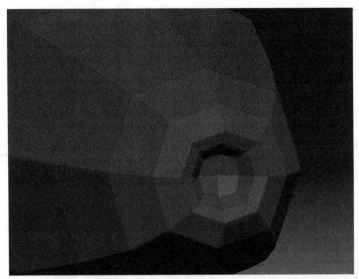

Figure 6-10

caused by different ZSphere resolutions would be inadvisable. This inverted ZSpheres technique is just one more way to solve a problem.

At this point I'd like to show some practical examples of using ZSpheres. The idea behind this is to enable you to feel confident enough to explore their use further. While it would be impractical to cover every possible type of base mesh and retopology situation, I hope these examples will give you enough knowledge to be able to easily work out anything you wish to know on your own.

ZSphere Project: Guardian Body Base Mesh

In this section we will be building the ZSphere rig used to create our base mesh for the Guardian, which is our main project that will also be used later on in the book. I should point out that the way I approach this ZSphere rig can be tweaked to be used for any human or nonhuman bipedal character.

Make a base mesh that has enough geometry in areas that need them and gives us the fullest amount of control for our later sculpting. Although you could retopologize the base mesh to improve edge flow to make it more animator friendly, this mesh is to be used for a still image of the character, so that will not be necessary. Don't worry if you are still a bit unsure about ZSpheres, as this project should help to show you how easy they are to use.

The Guardian Biped Base Rig

Okay, so let's get right down to making the base mesh we are going to need for our main project! Load a ZSphere as your active tool from the Tool palette, and then center it in your viewport. Press **X** to activate symmetry across the X axis so that everything we create on one side of the model's body is mirrored on the other side as well.

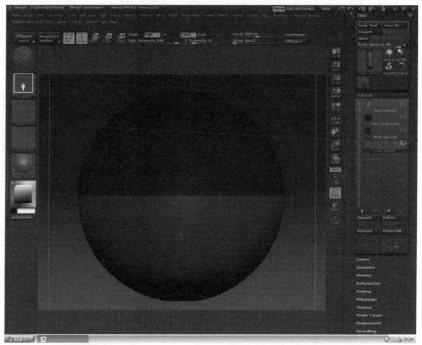

FIGURE 6-11

Like many other modelers who use ZSpheres, I'll start the base mesh with a sausage shape. Once we have our basic "sausage," we'll then add limbs to it. After this we will add a neck, then further refine our ZSphere setup and generate our base mesh.

Making the Base Mesh ZSphere Setup

I'd like you to first look from the top downward onto your initial ZSphere and, making sure that you have a very small brush size (between 1 and 5 should do), hold down the **Shift** key and left-click in the center of your initial ZSphere. This will add a second one of exactly the same size. If you now switch to Scale transform, you can very slightly increase its size and add more segments, and we now have our sausage shape as shown in Figure 6-12. To see your generated mesh at any point in the process, simply press the A key to activate and deactivate the preview. What you have now is the very start of the torso, although we are going to be adding to it as we progress.

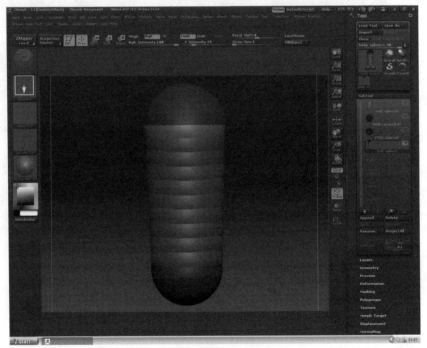

Figure 6-12

We now need to add the shoulder joints where the arms go, and the hips where the legs will originate from. So start by left-clicking and dragging out another ZSphere on one side of the bottom ZSphere as shown in Figure 6-13. Repeat this action to make the ones for the shoulders. Feel free to increase or decrease the size of any of your spheres as needed while you progress through the rig. You will find that small changes can make a world of difference in the way your mesh is

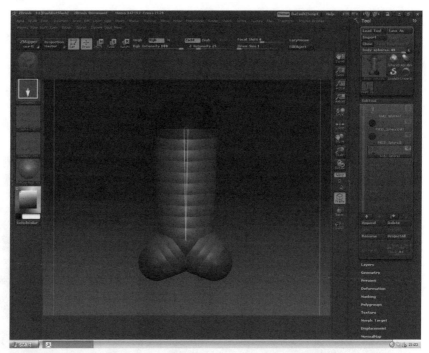

FIGURE 6-13

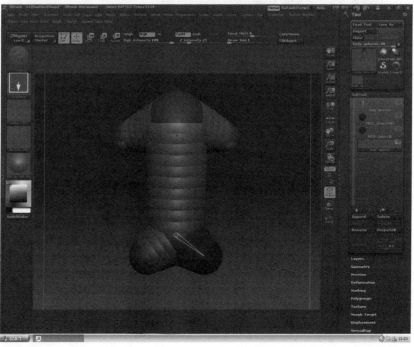

FIGURE 6-14

generated. (We will talk about this more toward the end of this section.) Although it may not look like it at the moment, you are only a very short step away from a basic body shape.

Now we simply **Shift** and **left-click** on the shoulder ZSpheres to add another one of the same size, then by switching to the Move transform, pull them outward toward where the arms will meet the hands, and do the same for the legs as shown in Figure 6-15. Make them a bit smaller using your Scale transform to keep things in proportion.

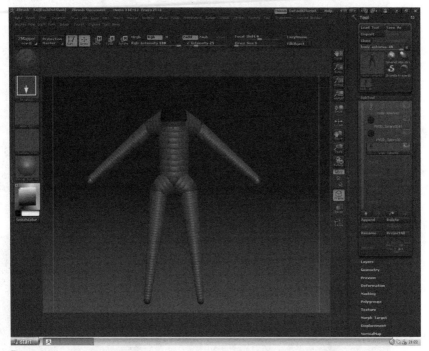

FIGURE 6-15

Approaching a ZSphere setup for a base mesh in this way — by pulling out to the ends of the limbs before adding the joints — is fairly standard practice as it allows you to see the overall proportions of your model better as you progress. This means you are able to change and adapt the rig as needed.

All we need to do before we start to refine and add to our rig is to add a neck, so on the ZSphere that represents the top of your torso, draw a ZSphere as shown in Figure 6-16. Then add another of the same size and, using your Move transform, pull it into place. The neck in this model is a bit longer as we are treating the head as a separate item, but there is no reason (especially if you are going to retopologize anyway) why you couldn't make the last ZSphere for the head a bit larger. But for the purposes of the Guardian project, we are going to simply leave ours with a rather longer neck than a human would have, as this will make our job easier later on.

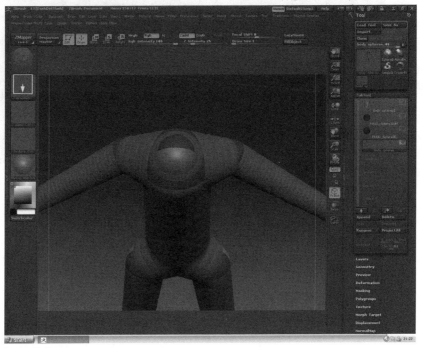

FIGURE 6-16

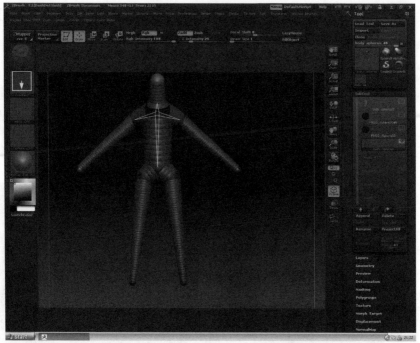

FIGURE 6-17

At the moment the torso area is rather bland and it doesn't have enough information or polygons to help us to sculpt it later on. So add a ZSphere where the bottom of the ribcage would be and adjust its size to make it smaller, then add another at about stomach height.

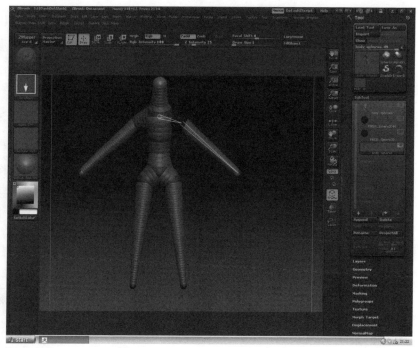

FIGURE 6-18

Position and resize them as needed, using the final image of the ZSphere rig (Figure 6-33) for reference. Now comes the time to add some joints to our body base, as right now it's not going to win us any awards and would be rather unwieldy to sculpt upon. To add a ZSphere for a joint you just need to left-click (making sure you are in Edit mode) in the place in the ZSphere chain where you want the new one to be. Once you've got some arm and leg joints, go ahead and rotate them into a fairly neutral pose as shown in Figure 6-19.

Add a joint just above where you wish the feet to be and add some smaller ZSpheres to make the feet themselves. The feet on this character are not incredibly detailed, so we do not need to worry about making actual toes.

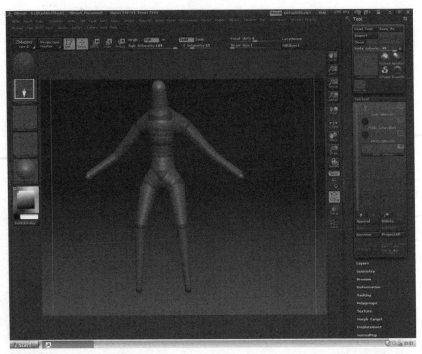

FIGURE 6-19

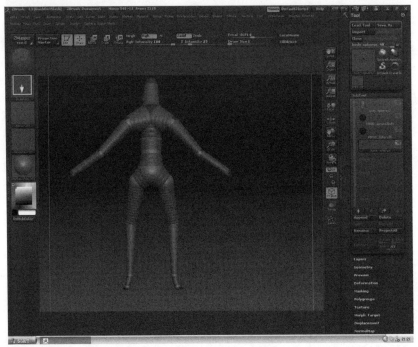

FIGURE 6-20

Turn your model so that the back is facing you and draw a sphere on the back of the pelvis to make the stub of the tail area. You can draw another sphere on this and pull it into place with your Move transform, then scale the end of the tail to size, add a couple more spheres, and give them a bit of a position change as shown in Figure 6-22.

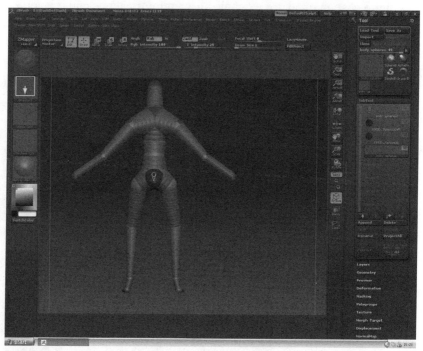

FIGURE 6-21

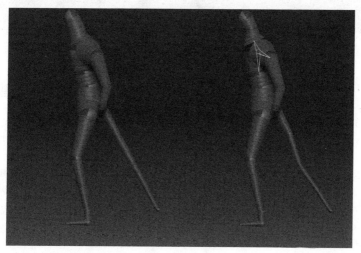

FIGURE 6-22

There is no hard-and-fast rule about whether your mesh should be in a T or relaxed T pose. This depends not only on how your model is to be used (animation or a still), but also on your pipeline itself. In this case I'll use a relaxed T pose as I find it gives a good balance for sculpting and allows me to easily adjust it using action lines. But if you have a definite pose in mind, for example an asymmetrical one and it is for a still or personal use, you could also set the pose at this stage. Just remember that this may limit your options later on should you change your mind.

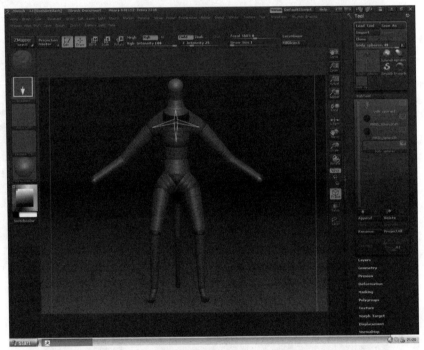

FIGURE 6-23

If you preview the base mesh at this point, you will notice that the joints look curved and not "joint like" enough. The reason for this is that we do not have enough supporting geometry for ZBrush to generate the base mesh that we need. So to help it out a little, add a ZSphere in the chain just above and below each joint as shown in Figure 6-24. Now when you preview your sculpt you will notice a distinct improvement, but you will also see that some areas in the limbs are a bit sparse polygon wise. Add another ZSphere into each chain in those sparse areas and preview again, and you will find that the polygon distribution is a lot better.

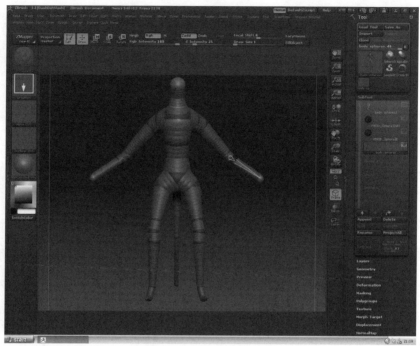

FIGURE 6-24

It's now time to get to the one thing I know a lot of ZBrushers hate doing with ZSpheres — hands! Our character's design calls for a hand with one thumb and two fingers, but it is quite easy to add more fingers to make a more human-looking hand. Although there are a number of ways of making hands using ZSpheres in ZBrush, the method outlined here provides a good balance between getting the form of the hands correct and having a decent polygon count.

Another method uses a ZSphere for the palm of the hand with an X, Y, Z Ires of 3, and an Ires of 1 for the rest of the model (including the fingers). This method allows you to have the fingers coming from the hand in the "proper" manner, but as a side effect you end up with a large number of wasted polygons in the hand area that use up a terrific amount of your final polygon count.

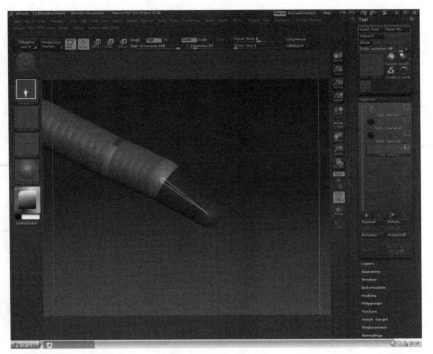

FIGURE 6-25

I would strongly advise you to keep a library of hands and feet that you've made so that when time is short on a project you can simply export your base mesh without hands and feet and add them later using a traditional polygon modeling package. This can also give you further control and allow you to add edge loops where you need them.

To make your hand, start by adding a ZSphere to the end of the wrist area to help with joint deformation (should you not have already done so), then add another to it as shown in Figure 6-26.

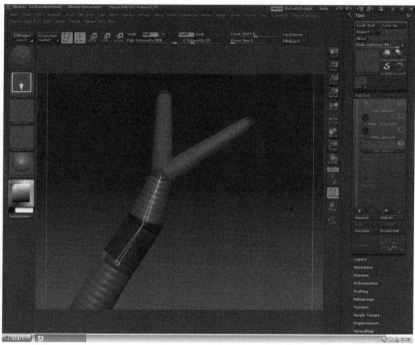

FIGURE 6-26

This new ZSphere will eventually be the palm of the hand and where the fingers are going to come from. The thumb, oddly enough, will be coming from the wrist as it is easier to move this into place later when sculpting than to attempt to get all the fingers and the thumb in exactly the right places at this stage. Some may feel that this is a waste of time, but I believe that if there is an easy way and a hard way to do something, you should opt for the easy way where possible.

Once we have the palm ready, we need to add the two fingers as shown, and then the thumb. Then we just need to add a few more spheres to get things pulled into place so that the base mesh previews correctly. The first is added to the base of one of the fingers as shown in Figure 6-28, which is then pulled sideways a little to make sure the fingers spread correctly. A second is added in this area near the joint of the base of the finger. We can then add some finger joints, although in this case do not add the supporting spheres near the joints. If we add them on the fingers, we will end up with higher polygon counts than we need to, and it's much easier to position the fingers at subdivision level 3 and upward than at level 1 or 2 (which are generated with the base mesh).

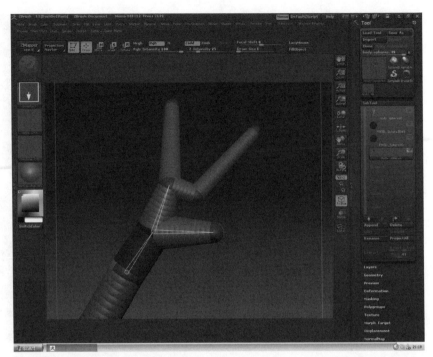

FIGURE 6-27

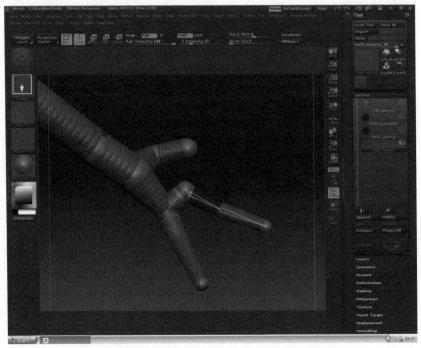

FIGURE 6-28

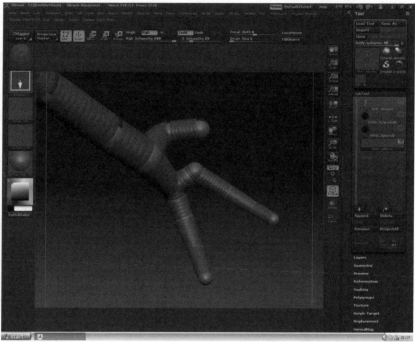

FIGURE 6-29

If you look at the final rig you'll notice I also added a couple more supporting spheres in the shoulders to help correct any deformations. So with our rig done, it's now time to resize and tweak everything until you are happy with the preview. The Adaptive Skin settings I used are **Ires 6**, **Mbr 60**, and **Minimal Skin to Parent** activated.

These give us the base mesh we are looking for, so once you're happy with it, press the **Make Adaptive Skin** button and save it out. I would also advise saving out your actual ZSphere rig as well. This can either be reused and tweaked for another model, or used as a ZSphere posing rig if you wish. Now that you have everything saved out and ready, you can set it aside for use later as the body mesh for the Guardian in our main project later on in this book.

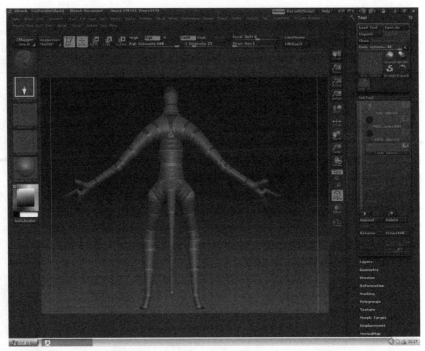

FIGURE 6-30

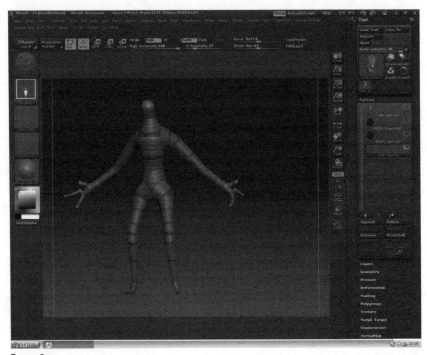

FIGURE 6-31

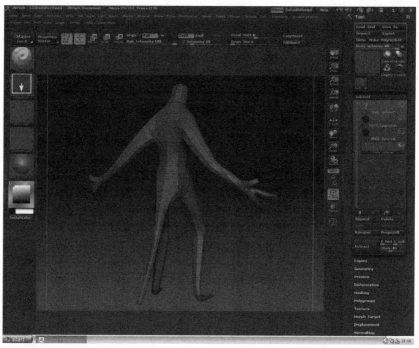

FIGURE 6-32

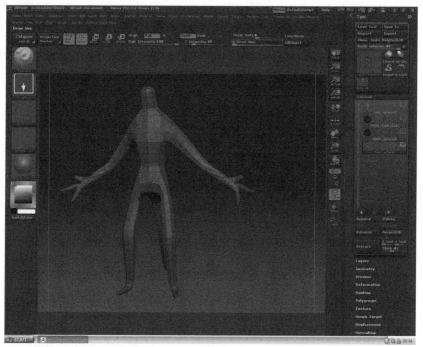

FIGURE 6-33

7 Displacement and Normal Maps

The Importance of Texture Size

When generating maps of any type, it is very important that the map is the correct size. If it is much larger than is needed we are wasting resources, and if it is not large enough we won't get the quality that we need at render time. So to a large degree it is a balancing act. If the model you are working on is for a game, the map requirements for the game engine will determine the size of the texture or map. If you are working on a personal project or a model for a film, you may have a lot more leeway.

So why do we need to make a map that is the perfect size and not just use a really large one or one that is some "one size fits all" default size? The short answer is because it will slow down the render times and portability of the models. Knowing how to lay out a good optimized set of UVs and make the best usage of the available texture space is of utmost importance, especially if you are modeling for computer games. The simple rule is that the more polygons and the larger the texture (keep in mind more than one is usually required), the slower performance will be whether it is on a next-generation platform or for a feature film. The adage "time is money" is still quite true, especially when it comes to renders. Although each field has its own requirements, the basics covered here will stand you in good stead whichever direction your career takes you.

The size of our texture will to a very large degree be dictated by the number of polygons we are working with. The more polygons you have, the larger the texture size you will need in order to capture every single detail onto a texture. The number of polygons that each texture size will capture is calculated by some very simple math. Our aim is to make sure that every polygon has at least one pixel allocated to it; however, you must bear in mind that the way your model is UV mapped may mean that you require a larger texture. For a perfect usage of your texture space you will find that ZBrush's AUV tiles UV method works very well, although its downside is that any post work or touching up by hand is almost impossible to do.

Texture Size	Pixel Count	Max Polygon Count
1024 x 1024	1,048,576	1,048,576
2048 x 2048	4,194,304	4,194,304
4096 x 4096	16,777,216	16,777,216

As you can see from the table above, if we assume that one pixel is equal to one polygon, we have the maximum polygon count for each of the most commonly used texture sizes. Most often, though, it isn't quite that simple. There are many other things that can affect our choice of texture size to be taken into consideration, such as UV distribution and the amount of detail in our model.

If we had a model with detail that really pushes our polygon count to its limit, then obviously we will need at least a pixel per polygon for the main areas of the model. You also should calculate the texture size based on the amount of space of the most "active" polygons. By "active" I mean the polygons that actually have some detail or color information in the most used area of a model. You do not want to waste texture/UV space on areas of your model that contain little or no sculpting or color information. So if you were working out the texture size for a bust, you would want to make sure that more UV space is given to the front of the face with particular attention to features with dense amounts of sculpting or color data. Areas such as the back of the head and neck would not need as much space as they often contain less information that needs to be captured to a texture map.

So we will need to work out the polygon count of our finished model and make sure that areas with lots of detail have enough texture space in our UV layout. From that information we can determine the correct size of the texture map. Don't cut it too fine if you are using a solution for UV'ing such as pelt mapping. The reason for this is that you may be giving the important areas lots of space but at the expense of the less used areas. This is fine if your detail isn't too "heavy," but if you have a model that is submerged in dense detail, you may need to up your texture size. My suggestion is that you generate your maps at twice the size you think you'll need, even though it may take a few minutes more of render time. If you've made a mistake with your calculations, you'll still have plenty of space, and if you find that you do not need it, then you can simply delete the file.

If you like to subdivide your models to a high level just so they will look nice and smooth in the viewport at render time, be sure you calculate the texture size based on the active subdivision level and polygon count — your higher "smoothed" polygon count. Otherwise, you'll end up with a texture size much bigger than you actually need. For example, you have a bust with a final render time polygon count in ZBrush of 6 million; however, the last subdivision level is only to make it look nice and smooth for the work in progress renders. In this case, simply step down a subdivision level and you should have a polygon count of around 1.5 million that needs to be captured. So you would probably only need a texture of 2048 x 2048 (2K), which would save valuable resources and speed up render times.

Hopefully this has given you an understanding of texture map size and why it's important not to just go for a large size out of habit, but rather to take a few minutes to work out the size that is needed. If you have a number of objects in a scene, each with a normal, color, and spec map, then the time and resources you'll save by using a 2K map for each rather than a 4K map will really add up. An additional point is that if you have painted a specular map, it may not need to be as large as your main color map if it does not contain as much detail "per pixel." Good map usage and UV'ing is very important and isn't something you will get away with not knowing about.

A final but important point to consider is whether there are set limits you must work within. For example, if you are working on a model for a game engine for which your art or technical director has set the maximum map size as 2K (2048 x 2048), then you should know that there is absolutely no point in sculpting a mesh with a count of over 4.1 million polygons — not only because it wouldn't be captured in your target map size, but also because your resulting maps may look "muddy" and not as crisp as they need to be. If you'll keep this in mind, you will notice your models will look better once they leave your hands and your speed will improve because you won't be sculpting detail and adding color that cannot be captured. There is nothing more heartbreaking than to produce a great model and find it doesn't meet the requirements you were given. (It's a damn good way to displease your boss, too!)

Displacement Maps

What Is a Displacement Map?

A *displacement map* is a special type of texture map that is often used to render a low-polygon version of a finished model in another application while keeping the look of the high-polygon version. This saves time and system resources as rendering out a model with an extremely high polygon count can be slow or in some cases impossible. Hence displacement maps are often used in production environments.

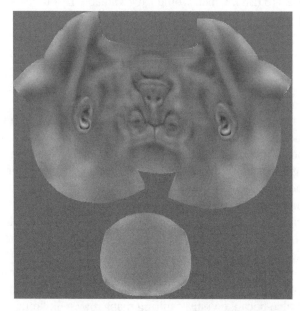

FIGURE 7-1

A standard workflow for taking a high-resolution ZBrush digital sculpture and rendering it out in an external render engine such as Mental Ray or Renderman would be to first take your sculpt to its lowest subdivision level and generate a map of the correct size. You would then import your level 1 subdivided model, apply your displacement map to that, and tell the render engine how to interpret the information. At render time you would get an almost identical copy of your multi-million poly sculpt rendered faster and with fewer resources.

The Difference between Displacement, Bump, and Normal Maps

New users can sometimes get confused as to how the different maps are used and what they actually do. A displacement map when rendered out changes the geometry or silhouette of your model, and makes it look like the original sculpture. A bump or normal map does not change the geometry or silhouette of your model, but simply tries to make it look like changes have been made, with light areas raised and dark areas lowered on the surface.

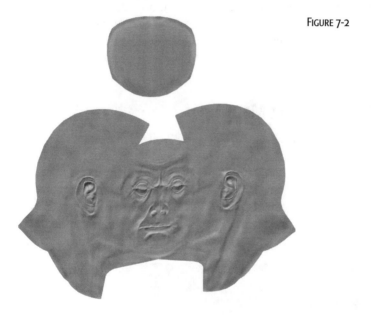

FIGURE 7-2

So to cut a long story short, while bump and normal maps do not change the geometry in any way at render time, a displacement map does. As a result, displacement maps are currently not used in the computer game industry because the actual changes to the geometry of a model cause them to be much too resource intensive. Displacement maps are more commonly used in models for movies and in still images, while normal and bump maps are preferred for computer games. This may change at some point as hardware gets more and more powerful and more able to take a resource "hit" when they are used, but until that time, displacement maps are not "game friendly."

Bump and normal maps do a similar job of making the model look more detailed than the geometry may actually be. A bump map is a grayscale image that is basically a shader effect that gives the illusion of more detail by pulling the information from this grayscale texture. A normal map is sort of like a bump map on steroids, because instead of just grayscale information, we have all three color channels, it is inexpensive to use resource wise, and it gives a much better result more often than not. Thus normal maps are currently the hot favorites for use in computer games since with correct usage they give a very high-polygon look while using a low-polygon model.

To generate a displacement map in ZBrush we can use the Multi Displacement 3 plug-in that comes with ZBrush 3.1, which gives us tremendous control over how the displacement map is generated. For normal maps the ZMapper plug-in is commonly used. ZMapper also gives the user very high quality controls so that maps can be generated to suit any occasion and requirement needed. We'll discuss the use of each plug-in briefly in this chapter, and Chapter 8 covers ZMapper in detail.

8-, 16- and 32-bit Map Types

ZBrush can generate 8-bit, 16-bit, and 32-bit (also called "floating point") maps. The difference between them is the size of the file produced. So 8-bit maps are far smaller in file size than 32-bit maps, and also are of lower quality and contain less information. The maps are limited in the amount of information they can hold by the color space that they work in. So while a 16-bit map may give you most of the details from your model, a 32-bit map would contain all the details because it

FIGURE 7-3

32-bit displacement map (with increased exposure and gamma)

uses a floating-point color space and hence has more space to store information.

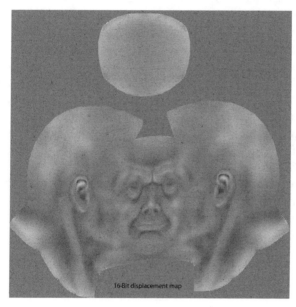

FIGURE 7-4

16-Bit displacement map

These days 8-bit maps are rarely used because the quality that they give at render time is fairly low, and these days we can render out floating-point displacement maps with ease. In a realistic environment you would choose either a 16-bit grayscale displacement map or a floating-point 32-bit displacement map; however, there are still a few render engines that do not support 32-bit.

While a 32-bit map undoubtedly is the best choice for quality, there is also the issue of file size to take into account. A floating-point map file size is much larger than a 16-bit one as the 32-bit map contains much more data. You also need to keep in mind how much of the detail in your model will actually be seen and how far it is from the camera. A "hero" model, which is the highly detailed version of a model that is often used for close-ups, may use several 32-bit maps, while for a version used farther from the camera we may be able to use a single 16-bit map.

A good guideline to what size map to use is an old one but still relevant today. Find out the closest point that your model is to the screen, and if the closest point is where the camera closes in on the head of a figure, you would want to use a map 1½ to 2 times the size of the screen resolution. This would let you know how many maps of what size you would require. There is a certain amount of judgment needed as well, as you should remember that the color and specular maps, and maybe many other types as well, will also need to be increased in size in a similar relation, which will slow down render times.

With the advent of HD screen resolutions, major feature films these days use a great many maps on CG characters. As a result, it takes longer to render, and more and more powerful machine are needed in render farms to produce them. This is also the reason why usually only the big-name FX houses are able to produce realistic CG characters in feature films. They are the only ones with enough sheer computer muscle to render out a complex character in time to meet a deadline.

So as you can see, the choice of map type and even how many maps are used in your model depend on a great many things indeed, and there isn't a "one size fits all" solution. In production environments your choices will be subject to limitations that you will need to work within. When doing something for personal enjoyment, though, you only have to worry about the final look and whether your hardware can actually render it out. Learning to get the best look you can within a set of given limitations is part of what being a good 3D artist is about.

Generating Displacement Maps

To generate displacement maps we make use of ZBrush's built-in Multi Displacement plug-in (hereafter referred to as MD3). MD3 gives the user the ability to generate 8-bit, 16-bit, and 32-bit maps. Since 8-bit maps are rarely used these days as the quality is far too low for a quality render, your choice is between 16-bit and 32-bit displacement maps. Now I should point out that just about every one of the major render engines and big 3D applications requires a different setting when you

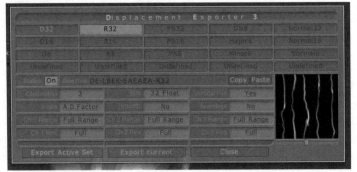

FIGURE 7-5

generate your maps. For the purposes of covering as many readers as possible, we will concentrate on using Mental Ray inside 3ds Max and Maya.

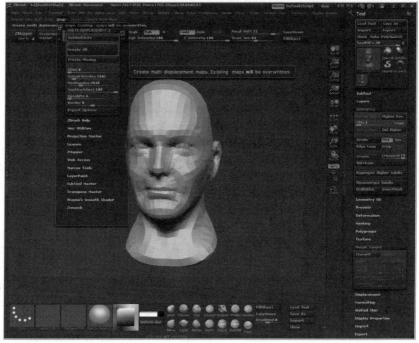

FIGURE 7-6

The versions I'll be using for this are **Maya 2008** and **Max 2008**. You will find that once you know how to make displacement maps work in one application that runs Mental Ray, others that run it are no problem at all to set up. Each of the main applications has its own "quick code" that you can enter into MD3 to get a map that will work both easily and effectively with a minimum of fuss. I use and get great results with DE-LBEK-EAEAEA-R32 for both Maya and 3ds Max, although you will find many others on the ZBrush wiki and on the ZBrushCentral forum.

To set up your quick codes in MD3 let's start it up and get things moving along. It is important to remember that you will need to be at your lowest subdivision level, as ZBrush will try to work out the difference between your low-resolution mesh and the highest subdivision level of your digital sculpture.

I should also point out that a good set of UVs are needed on your model. A model without UV coordinates cannot have a map generated for it because the displacement map needs to know where on the model each pixel needs to be. You can UV your model either within ZBrush using one of the built-in UV types or with an external program if you like. Using the UV types within ZBrush is faster to set up, but making your UV layout in an external program gives you more control over the layout and makes it easier to do any post work you require in Photoshop. So either way, your model must have a set of UVs.

Also be very careful to check that there are no overlapping vertices or faces on your map. If you do, at best you will get an unusable map, and at worst you can get a crash or an error and the map will crash on generation.

You can access the settings for MD3 from your Alpha palette and there you can pick one of the predefined map types or paste in a quick code that works for the render engine or application that you are going to use. The actual map generation is done within the **ZPlugin** palette under **Multi Displacement**, where you set everything from the size of the map to the number of "tiles" of UV space your model needs to use (should you have set up a model with UV coordinates in multiple UVs). To control the number of tiles your multi-UVs model requires MD3 to generate, simply use the **UDim** slider. Remember that your first UV space is 0, the next one to the right is 1, and so on, so you must start counting from zero and not one. The **InitialFileIndex** setting is simply a way for us to choose the number that is added after the map name to represent UV set 0. Unless you have a special requirement or an in-house map name style, you won't really need to change this.

All the map types are outlined very well in the ZBrush wiki, so I strongly urge you to read through it for more information. It is kept up to date and contains reference material that is beyond the scope of this book.

To generate the map itself once your settings are correct for the render engine or application you are using and you are at the subdivision level you wish to use to generate your map from, first export an OBJ of this level and keep it in a safe place. This is the base mesh you will be using to apply your maps to. Make sure that you have **Qud** and **Mrg** turned on and **Grp** switched off in the Export section of the Tool palette. This will ensure that you do not export your model as a series of separate parts (with one for each polygroup), and that the mesh you export is quads and not triangulated.

Now go to the **Multi Displacement** section of your ZPlugin palette and set the size of map you require. If you need help with this, see the earlier section called "8-, 16-, and 32-bit Map Types." If you model has a multiple set of UVs, set the **UDim** slider to the correct number; otherwise leave it set to 0. All you need to do then is to click on the **Create**

All button and tell ZBrush the name and location for the map. If you have generated a 16-bit displacement map, write down the **Alpha Depth Factor** number that you will find at the very bottom of the Alpha palette. You will need this number for 16-bit maps to work out some settings later on. If you are generating a 32-bit map, you don't need to bother writing it down as the Alpha depth factor is baked into the 32-bit map.

Normal Maps

What Are Normal Maps?

Put simply, a normal map is a way of making your model appear to be much more detailed than it really is. While a displacement map affects the actual geometry of your model by subdividing and displacing the polygons of your model, a normal map does not affect the silhouette of your model at all. It simply maps the normal from a texture that contains the details of the higher-resolution model. So to put it simply, think of normal maps as a "shading trick" way of replicating your model without displacing anything.

One of the biggest advantages of a normal map is that it doesn't have to calculate the positions of millions of subdivided vertexes so it is far faster to render. That's the reason why it sees so much usage in next-gen game pipelines, where every polygon and pixel of a texture is at a premium. Since the use of a normal map is far cheaper computationally, you can have many normal mapped characters in a game as opposed to maybe one if you were using a displacement map.

Normal maps come in two main types: tangent space normal maps and object space normal maps. (There are others, but chances are you won't be using them much if at all right now.) So what is the difference between tangent space and object space normal maps? One difference that is obvious is that they look different. While a tangent space normal map is primarily a blue color, an object space map is much more colorful. From a technical point of view, an object space normal map is usually used on non-animated, static items such as walls, floors, and objects, and a tangent space map can be used on animated characters. So as a ZBrush user you will use tangent space normal maps much more often unless you are creating environmental pieces or props.

Modeling with Normal Maps in Mind

The silhouette of a model that you are applying a normal map to is of prime importance because the map must follow the actual silhouette as closely as the polygon count will allow. If your normal mapped model is to be believable you must not only try to maintain a good silhouette at all times, but also make it topologically correct so that riggers and animators can actually use it. (Try to give a bad topology mesh to a rigger and see his reaction; it makes his job harder if not impossible in some cases.)

As normal maps are great at replicating structure that is indented, this is where the majority of the detail on your model must be. The more the shape protrudes on your high-resolution mesh, the harder it will be to replicate a good silhouette. So when you are making a character that will be normal mapped for a next-gen game or for use in a game engine, try to avoid areas that extend outward or are going to use up a lot of polygon count. This will not only make for a more believable model "in game" but also help to avoid a lot of problems when you hand over your asset further down the pipeline.

Some common things to try to avoid unless you have the polygon count available to support them are things like horns (especially curved ones, as they are polygon "black holes" to get looking good), sci-fi type armor with lot of protruding detail, and spikes. So if you are in charge of designing a character for a game, try to keep these things in mind and how they affect the polygon count you are going to need.

I've mentioned working to a polygon budget before, but I want to stress how important that is when you are working as a modeler for a computer game. You are not given carte blanche to use as many polygons as you need on a model for a game because game resources are expensive computationally. Often a very fine balance has to be made to keep the game both on budget (or as near to it as can be) and within the allowed system resources. So you will be given a maximum polygon count that you can use for each character, prop, environmental piece, etc., that will appear in a game. You will be given maximum texture sizes for each type of prop depending on its importance and whether it is a main character or simply a background filler character.

The texture size you are allowed will also affect the amount of detail that you can put into a character. If you are working to a maximum texture size of 1K or 2K (1024 x 1024 and 2048 x 2048), that will dramatically affect the amount of detail that can be captured even on a very well laid out (or even theoretically perfect UV layout, such as AUV tiles) model.

Texture Size	Maximum Polygon Count
512 x 512	512 x 512 = 262,144 polygons
1K (1024 x 1024)	1024 x 1024 = 1,048,576 polygons
2K (2048 x 2048)	2048 x 2048 = 4,194,304 polygons

So as you can see from the table above, there is a massive difference in the number of polygons you can theoretically capture details from depending on the texture size you have to use. So if you are limited to a 1K map, it is pointless going into über detailing heaven as most of the details will not be captured and it can even make your model look worse once normal mapped.

Producing Normal Maps Using ZMapper

In this section we'll briefly cover the steps needed to create a normal map in ZMapper. For a detailed explanation of ZMapper's tools and usage, please read Chapter 8, "ZMapper." I'll explain some workflows for generating normal maps in ZBrush. I should also add that ZMapper has the ability to generate cavity maps, which is also covered in Chapter 8. Let's start with a simple, single subtool model that you wish to normal map.

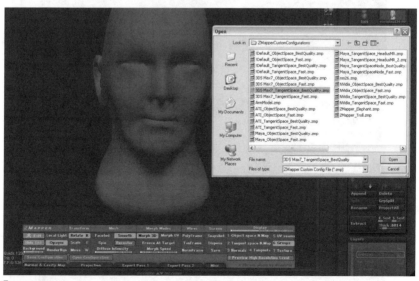

FIGURE 7-7

Basic Workflow for Single Subtools

You must have a set of UVs applied to your model before you continue. If you do not, you cannot generate a map as the texture will not know where each pixel is supposed to go in relation to your model. You can generate your UV map either in ZBrush or in an external program with UV capabilities.

Note: For more information about making UVs, see the section in Chapter 3 called "What Are UV Maps and Why Do I Need Them?"

Once you have UVs for your model, step down to the level you wish to make your normal map for. (This will probably be level 1, but could be 2 or 3 depending on the use for your normal mapped model.) Then press the ZMapper button at the top-left corner of the interface to open the ZMapper panel of options. Pressing the **Normal & Cavity Map** tab will display options for creating normal and cavity maps. Use the **Open Configuration** button to choose the preset that matches the external application or engine you are using, and then press the **Create NormalMap** button.

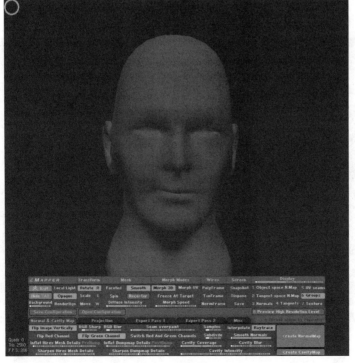

FIGURE 7-8

You can then sit back and watch the map being generated for you. Once it's done, you'll see your normal mapped model previewed in the ZMapper interface.

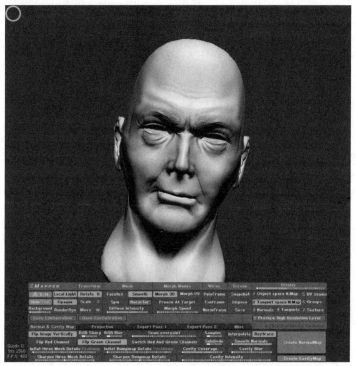

FIGURE 7-9

Baking a Normal Map from an Arbitrary Mesh

Many people forget that ZMapper has been able to bake normal and cavity maps from arbitrary geometry since its first inception. *Arbitrary geometry* means that the topology of your base mesh can be totally different from your high-resolution sculpture. What this means is that you can sculpt first and retopologize and UV map later. Before we start, you will need both a high-polygon mesh you wish to capture details from and a base mesh with different topology with its own UV map loaded into ZBrush.

You'll need both your meshes to be an identical size, so first clone your high-resolution model and delete all but level 1 of it. Then import your new OBJ with different topology to check its scale. If your models are of different scales, the different positions of pivot points are going to cause problems down the line. So be sure that all of these match as well as the scale.

With your high-resolution model active at its lowest subdivision level, enter ZMapper and click on the **Projection** tab. You will see a button labeled **Capture Current Mesh**. Click on this button and then exit ZMapper. Now switch to your model with different topology and UVs and once again open ZMapper. All you have to do is press the **Create Projected Normal Map** button and ZMapper will bake a normal map from your high-resolution model onto the base mesh with different topology.

If the new model you are baking to has not been sculpted, it will be smoother if it were subdivided and may miss some of the details on your model. If this is the case after baking a test normal map, use the Raycasting Max Scan Distance slider to up the distance and try again.

By default ZMapper will create a 2K normal map if a texture of your own is not active. Should you need a larger size, create the blank texture before entering ZMapper.

Using Normal Maps and Displacement Maps

Using Normal Maps in 3ds Max

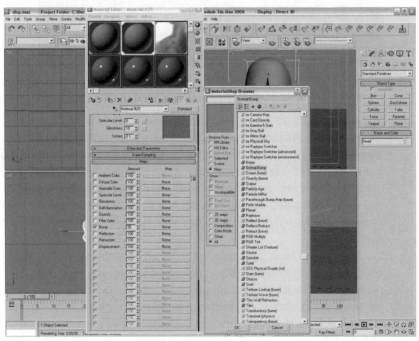

FIGURE 7-10

To use a normal map on your model in 3ds Max, first import your base mesh OBJ file, making sure that you keep the current texture and UV coordinates on import. Then right-click your model and convert it to a polygon mesh.

In the Material Editor, make a new standard material and apply it to the model, then scroll down to the Maps section and click to open it. As you have made sure to generate your normal map with 3ds Max in mind, you won't have to do any major tweaking with the settings. In the Bump section, click on the button to the right and from the Material/Map Browser list select **Normal Bump**. This will get connected into your material as a control for your normal map. Then browse to your normal map and step back through to the main part of your material.

FIGURE 7-11

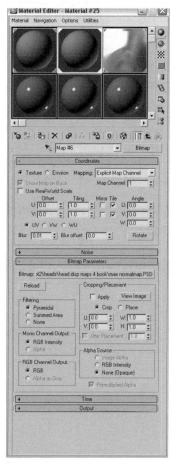

FIGURE 7-12

You can at this point render out your model with a couple of nice lights added if you wish. Or you could scroll a little further down the material's main panel and activate the real-time preview (providing you have DirectX as your display type). This will allow you to see your normal mapped model in real time in the viewport and it will react to all the lights the same way it would when rendered out.

Using Normal Maps in Maya

The workflow for using normal maps in Maya is pretty straightforward. First of all, import your base mesh (using **File > Import** and then clicking on the small square option box next to it) and make sure that you set **Create Multiple Objects** to **false** in the OBJ options. If you wish to use your model in the same way as it would appear "in game," you will first need to soften the normals. To do so, choose **Polygons** mode from the drop-down box, then look under the **Normals** menu and click on **Soften Edge**. This will take your model from a hard-edged look to a smoother set of normals.

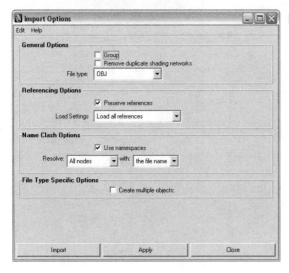

FIGURE 7-13

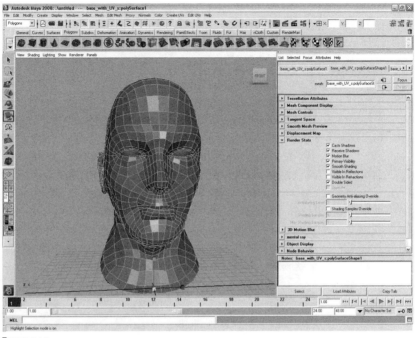

FIGURE 7-14

Now open up Hypershade (**Window > Rendering Editors > Hypershade**) and create a new material (a Blinn will do fine). With your model selected, hold down the right mouse button over your Blinn material in Hypershade and choose **Assign Material to Selection**. Open up your attribute editor and click on the checkered button next to the Bump Mapping slot. When the **Create Render Node** dialog box opens, choose **File**. You will then have some options in the attribute editor to control your map. First of all we need to change the Use As type for Bump to **Tangent Space Normals** (providing of course that you are indeed using a tangent space normal map and not an object space normal map). Then simply click on the **File1** tab and browse to your normal map.

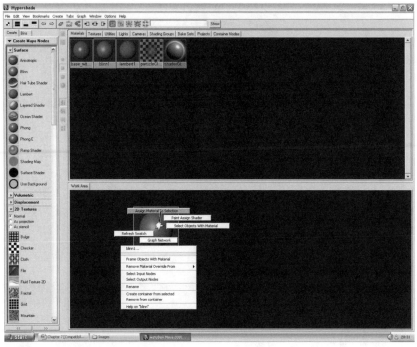

FIGURE 7-15

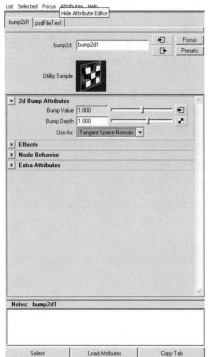

FIGURE 7-16

You are now free to light your model and render it out. If you find that your normal map is too aggressive, try turning it down a little from the bump map node. You can find it through your attribute editor by stepping through from the Bump section of your Blinn shader. You can also access it by viewing all its import and output connections from the Graph in Hypershade. This also allows you to make more complex changes to your shading network.

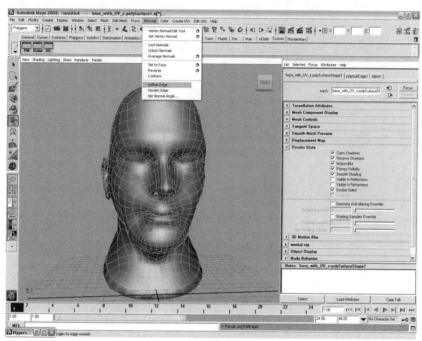

FIGURE 7-17

Using Your Displacement Map in 3ds Max Using Mental Ray

Let's look at how to get your displacement map working in 3ds Max using Mental Ray as your render engine. First, import the OBJ that you exported earlier from the File menu, making sure you import it as a single mesh and keeping the normals and UV coordinates. If you are using a 32-bit map (as we will for the first example), then

FIGURE 7-18

do not change its size as the displacement information is baked according to the model's size.

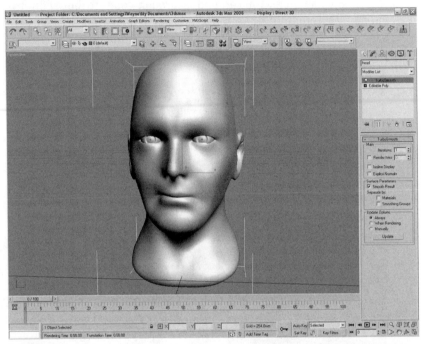

FIGURE 7-19

Right-click on your model and change it to a polygon mesh, then from the modifier stack add a TurboSmooth modifier to smooth the rough look of your model a bit. (If your base mesh is too low, you may need to set the number of iterations to 2 instead of 1.) Once you have lit your model as needed, open up your render settings panel and change the render engine to **Mental Ray**. Now go to your Material Editor. For this example, let's use the default Blinn material, so open up the Mental Ray section near the bottom and click on the small padlock icon next to **Displacement** to unlock it.

FIGURE 7-20

Click on the button next to Displacement and choose **3D Displacement** from the list provided, then set the extrusion strength to **2.2** before adding a bitmap section and browsing for your displacement map. (Should you be using a multi-UV set, you will need to use a multi-layered shader with one for each set of polygons that are contained within each set of UVs.)

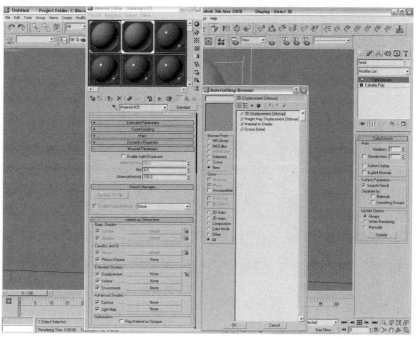

FIGURE 7-21

With your map now open, change the Blur setting from 1 to **0.01** so that you do not get any seams when you render. Chances are if you are using the codes I've provided your map will not need to be flipped vertically, so we can move right on to one of the very important parts. Go to the Output section at the bottom of the panel and change the RGB Offset to **–0.5**. Finally, apply the material to your model.

Now we can choose the render settings for Mental Ray. If you look in the Renderer tab's Shadow & Displacement section, you will see a setting for edge length. The smaller this number, the more accurate the render will be. *BUT* the smaller the number, the longer it will take to render out your model. I find a good setting for most renders is an edge length of 1 and a maximum displace of 30. The maximum displace simply tells Mental Ray what to use as a maximum distance. So if you see on your render that some areas are cut off, simply increase this number.

Set the maximum subdivisions to **64K**. Once all of this is done and you have set the size of the render, render out your image. You should have a great working displaced model.

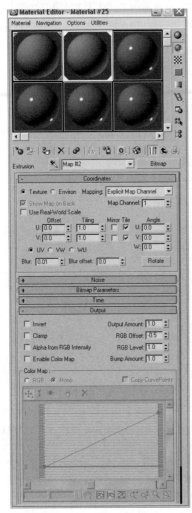

FIGURE 7-22

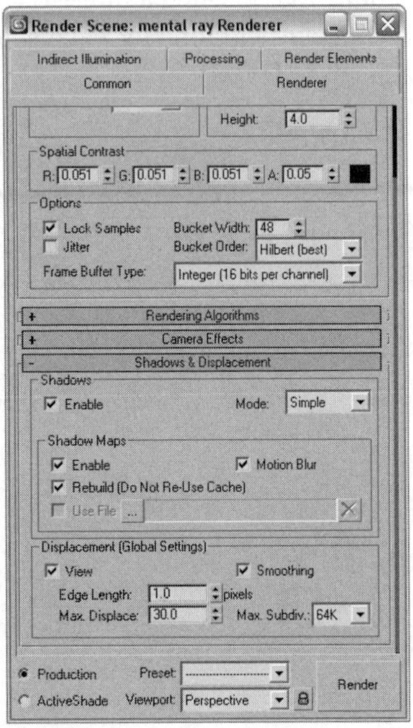

FIGURE 7-23

I should add that using a displacement map takes much more time than using a normal map because it actually changes the geometry, whereas a normal map does not. So as you add more complex lighting and shaders, the render time will go up accordingly. If you can optimize your scene, such as if at some point your model is not very close to the camera, you can increase the edge length to speed up your render. With our displacement map working now in 3ds Max, let's now move on to Maya.

FIGURE 7-24

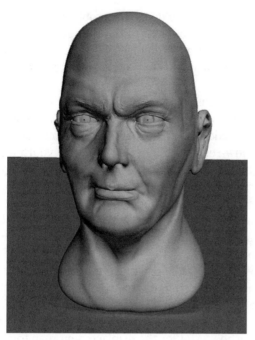

Using Your Displacement Map in Maya

When getting your displacement map into Mental Ray using Maya, you will notice that although there are some differences from the procedure for 3ds Max, many things stay the same. The beauty of using Mental Ray is that if you move to another application, much of your knowledge moves with you. If you are coming to this section "cold," I recommend that you go back and read the section called "Generating Displacement Maps" so we don't have to repeat that information here. That said, be sure that you used the correct quick code; if you generate a map with the wrong quick code it may be unusable in Maya. In fact, many (if not most) problems with getting displacement maps to work are due to generating a 32-bit map using the wrong quick code.

If you do not use a quick code, you will have to research how the render engine treats and reads displacement maps and 32-bit maps. (Note that some engines can't read them at all.) Otherwise you are in uncharted territory for the settings and are reduced to trial and error (or begging the settings from a previous explorer). Although Mental Ray can read a 32-bit TIFF file perfectly well, Maya cannot and often complains about it. This may throw off new users because they then assume incorrectly that this is the source of their problem.

Not to worry you unduly, but if you do have a problem my first suggestion would be to check the obvious things first, then recheck them. It is rarely the unusual things that go wrong but often the simple things that get overlooked, and the simpler it is to do, the bigger chance there is of it not getting done right.

So with your low-resolution model inside Maya (when you import it, be sure that in the import options **Multiple Objects** is set to **false**), let's open **Hypershade** and add a test material to use as an example. Apply a new Blinn to the low-resolution mesh by selecting your model and then with the Blinn material highlighted inside Hypershade, right-click and choose **Assign Material to Selection**. If you do a very quick render now you should have your gray Blinn applied to your low-resolution model with no displacement at all (as we haven't added it yet). Be sure that Mental Ray is set as your active render engine from the render options controls before continuing.

Now with your model highlighted, open up your attribute editor by pressing **Ctrl+A** or by using the icon in the top right-hand corner of your interface. Go to the Blinn material tab and then click on one of the two small box-shaped buttons that shows a triangle pointing into or out of the box. You should now see a slot for the displacement map to go, so click on the checkered box next to it, choose File, and then browse to your displacement map.

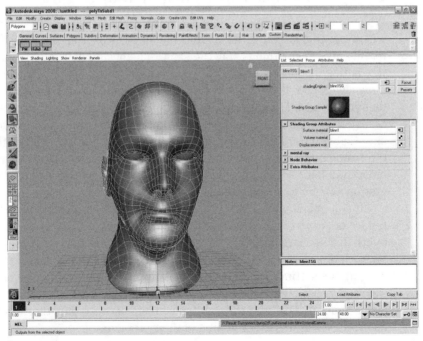

FIGURE 7-25

As ZBrush creates a displacement map in which gray is the "no displacement" point, and Maya and most other applications treat black as "no displacement," we need to alter this for our displacement map. For the 32-bit map we are using, set the Alpha Gain to **2.2** and the Alpha Offset to **–1.1**. Now that our displacement map is set to treat middle gray as "no displacement," we can move onward.

Open the **Shape** tab for your model and go to the Displacement section, then uncheck **Feature Displacement**. (If you don't, all sorts of hell breaks loose that can drive you crazy as a beginner, such as vastly bloated displaced models.) We now need to add a subdivision approximation to our model so that Mental Ray can interpret our displacement correctly. (If you're using Maya 2008, please read the next section, "Note for Maya 2008 Users," as there have been changes that affect the workflow for it.) So with your model selected in the viewport, go to **Window > Rendering Editors > Mental Ray > Approximation editor.**

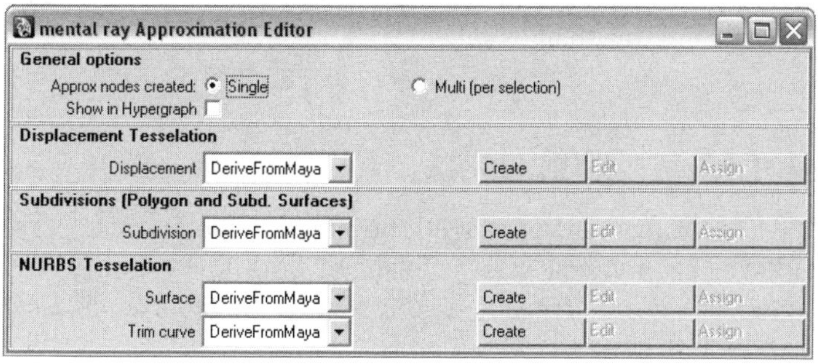

FIGURE 7-26

Click on the **Create** button to the side of **Subdivisions** and once the **Edit** button is active, click it. This is where the quality of your displacement is sorted out. Set the Approximation method to **Spatial** and the min and max settings to **3** and **5**. Set your length to **0.1** for now. (This is what controls how sharp your render will be in regard to your displacement. You can lower this once you have your initial tests done.) What this subdivision approximation actually does is subdivide the model at render time only. So the edge length that you set here is telling it the maximum length that any triangle edge can be. The smaller the size, the more exact the displacement will be, but the slower your render will be as well. (All displacement map rendering techniques have to have the model subdivided at render time or the process simply would not work. Unlike normal mapping, it is actually changing the geometry in relation to your displacement texture map.) Also click the **Fine** and **View Dependent** check boxes.

So render this out now and see what it looks like. If it is too rough, lower the edge length a bit at a time until you find the sweet spot. If you find that your computer simply cannot handle the amount of polygons in Maya that you need to accurately reproduce your model when being displaced, another option is to get the silhouette as close as you can using displacement and then apply a normal map (set to about 0.5 and –0.7) in your bump map slot as well. In this way the normal map brings out the detail that displacement cannot, and the displacement helps by altering the silhouette of the model, which makes the normal map look much better than usual.

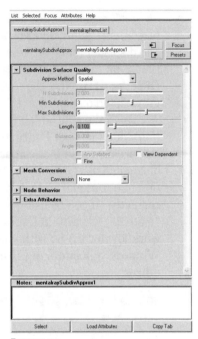

FIGURE 7-27

Note for Maya 2008 Users

With Maya 2008, Autodesk changed the way the subdivision approximation works; as such, if you follow the above workflow you may end up with some nasty seam artifacts in your render. To get around this you need to force it to use the old method.

Note: If you have the very recent (days old at the time of this writing) extension 1 update for Maya 2008 or Maya 2008 ext 2, then you can continue to work as above.

The workaround (thanks go to "Aurick" for this, by the way) is to type the following into your script editor:

addAttr –ln "miExportCCMesh" –at bool mentalraySubDivApprox1

Highlight this text in your script editor and press Ctrl+Enter to execute; your mode will now use the old subdivision algorithm. The name of the node is mentalraySubDivApprox1, so if yours is different change the line accordingly.

8 ZMapper

What Is ZMapper?

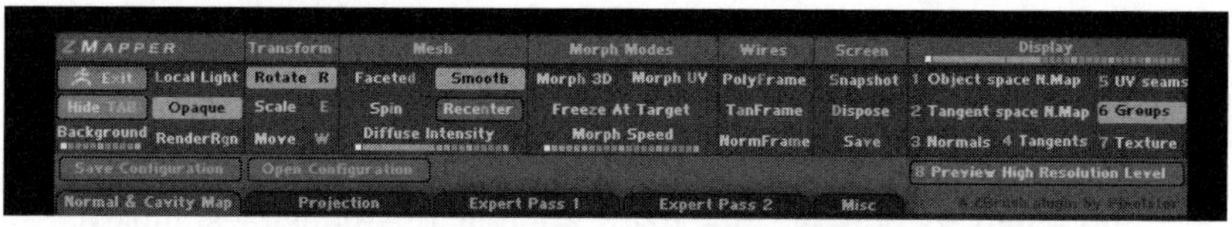

FIGURE 8-1

ZMapper started its life as a Pixologic plug-in for ZBrush 2 that allows the creation of normal and cavity maps for a model. The maps can be created from your lowest level of subdivision or from a mesh with totally different topology. So it is perfectly feasible to not only sculpt from a very low-res base mesh and then retopologize, but to import a retopologized mesh from elsewhere in your 3D creation pipeline and bake a normal map to it.

ZMapper is capable of creating all types of normal maps and is very versatile, fast, and reliable. It allows you to dig deep (should you need to) into the creation process to get a map that works perfectly in your pipeline. This is a very important feature to those in the computer game field because the requirements for normal maps can vary from game engine to game engine. And since you can project the high-resolution details of one model onto a pre-rigged and skinned base mesh that is already in the pipeline, you can see that production speed can be improved.

What Is a Normal Map?

Although we discussed normal maps in Chapter 7, let's delve a little deeper here. You can think of a normal map as three maps in one: the red channel, the blue channel, and the green channel. When combined together as one normal map and used either in a render engine or a game engine capable of rendering these out, it gives the impression of your lower-resolution base mesh actually looking like your high-resolution digital sculpt. It does this by mapping the normals of your high-resolution sculpt from three different directions onto the three channels.

These three channels are then interpreted in the engine rendering them out by mapping these normals from your high-resolution model onto your lower-resolution one. A normal map does not affect the silhouette of your model, so you must make sure that you have enough geometry to avoid any obvious hard edges. Normal maps are used in game engines mainly because of their speed in rendering and because they give the illusion that much higher detailed models are being used.

A normal map is often described as a bump map on steroids, and that is actually pretty accurate. A bump map uses a range of shades of black and white to create the illusion of detail, while a normal map uses more information. Normal maps are now the industry standard.

Normal maps generally come in two different types: tangent space normal maps and world space normal maps. The world space normal map, which is brightly colored, is usually used on items that are not going to move or be animated within the game engine. A tangent space normal map, which is primarily blue in color, is more suited to characters and props that are going to move around inside the game engine so that they will react to the light within the scene in a realistic way.

So if you have an animated character in a game, you would use a tangent space normal map, whereas for something such as a wall, the world space normal map will be much more suitable.

There are a few things to bear in mind when it comes to modeling if you plan to use normal maps. While a normal map will try to map every single detail of your high-resolution sculpt onto your low-resolution sculpt, you will find that some types of detail look much better than others. For example, detail that is inset such as the decoration on a door would look very good from most angles as the majority of the detail is below the main surface of the door frame. However, if you have a character wearing a lot of armor where the majority of the detail protrudes outward, you would find that from certain angles the illusion in detail would be broken. It is important to take this into account when designing and sculpting your character and models for game engines. Always make sure that you have enough supporting geometry and edge loops to believably block out the silhouette of a high-resolution sculpture.

With the improvements of game engines for both PC and console games, we find that every year the highest poly count allowed in games goes up. This means that it's easier to create believable silhouette models within a game engine, and the more believable the silhouette is, the more believable our normal mapped model will be.

So the difference between a normal or bump map and a displacement map can be explained very simply. A displacement map changes the actual geometry to replicate your high-resolution model while using a much lower resolution base mesh, and normal and bump maps do not change the geometry at all. This is why the silhouette is so important. Sometimes you may find it easier to paint a simple bump map for very high-resolution detail and then roll this into your normal map.

We'll discuss this in more detail a bit later, but I do feel the need to point out that a good set of UVs is very important for game related models. Because texture space is at a premium in game engines, the artist must make the most of the texture space that is available. This is also why the majority of game friendly models use what are called "mirrored UVs," as this saves on texture space and thus memory, and helps the game to run faster.

What Is a Surface Normal?

A *surface normal* can be best explained as the direction a single polygon is facing. Imagine an invisible line that projects from the center of a polygon and at a 90° angle to its surface. ZBrush, along with game and render engines and external applications, uses the information of the surface normal to determine what part of a model is the outside and what part is the inside. For example, if you have a simple six-sided polygon cube with the surface normals pointing outward from each face on this cube, this would be interpreted as a box structure with its main surface on the outside. If, however, these surface normals pointed inward, we would have the beginnings of a room.

When using the base mesh generated in an external application it is all-important to make sure that the surface normals are aligned in the same direction. If they are not, then there may appear to be holes in your mesh when you import it into ZBrush. Now there aren't really holes in your mesh; ZBrush has just read them as inverted normals and treats them as if they are facing in a different direction from the rest of your mesh. It is important to remember that it is actually doing its job correctly, and the fault lies not with the program but rather with the base mesh before it is exported.

How Normal Maps Are Used in Game and Render Engines

The reasons for using normal maps as opposed to displacement or standard bump maps are varied. The main one is that they are a great way to give the appearance of a lot of detail on a model that is actually only a low-polygon base mesh. The trick is that when modeling your base (or retopologizing your mesh for use as a game or animation-friendly model) you pay attention to the silhouette of the mesh so that it holds up well against the high-resolution sculpt.

By this I mean you must have enough edge loops in the right places not only to make it easy for the animation department to deal with but also so that areas do not look too blocky. Imagine that your base is being lit by a very bright light from behind so that the whole thing is in shadow. This is what I mean by the "silhouette." If you do not have enough geometry to support the details from the high-resolution version of the sculpture, then no matter how hard you try, the in-game model isn't going to hold up well.

So it is of the highest importance that your topology meets any in-game polygon maximum requirements, is easy for the animators to deal with, and holds the silhouette well. Of course normal maps are not the only maps used in game engines, and the list is expanding all the time. Most next-gen game engines can also handle specular and normal maps with ease, along with many others such as parallax maps.

It's also a good point to mention that your export settings in ZMapper will depend largely on which game engine you are using and its requirements. Each engine will need different settings, and the renderers that you find in big 3D applications also have a different set of requirements. For example, in 3ds Max, if the green channel is not flipped in your normal map, it will look bad... really bad. However, with the correct setting it can be used with an amazing quality in the viewport for real-time preview.

Since the setting requirements vary so widely, you'll have to research what works in the particular game engine that you are interested in getting your model into. If you can't find the information you need online, you may be able to find other modelers who will share their knowledge. Or if you are lucky enough to be able to get your hands on a working example, you can simply reverse engineer the normal map. We'll cover that next; although it's not really a ZBrush-specific subject, this knowledge will help you to get the most out of ZMapper.

Reverse Engineering an In-game Normal Map

For those times when you cannot find the requirements for a normal map in a game engine that you are interested in using, it is good to know how to reverse engineer a normal map. This also helps if you are moving to a new application. It's pretty easy to do and a no-brainer really.

The main thing is to find an example of a normal map that works in the engine you're using. If you're really lucky there may be official ones; if not, look for game modding sites for the engine you're working with. Open the map in Photoshop along with a normal map created in ZBrush. (For the normal map in ZBrush use one with the default settings, as it's far easier to change things from a default stage than from an application-specific preset.) You want to make sure that you look at the channels for each map, both the working one and the ZBrush one.

Look for any channels where the information has been inverted or flipped. Also keep a lookout for any sharpening that the engine you're working with may require. For example, one big-name game engine needs the normal maps to be very "aggressive" in their sharpness. While you're examining the map, write down everything that you learn and make your changes methodically. Then once you've adjusted the settings, save it as a preset in ZMapper so it can be tweaked as needed (as you can bet that it will).

From there it's a simple matter of testing a few times to get the best normal interpretation you can. ZBrush is easily capable of generating any normal map you may require for next-gen game use. Since the field changes so often, you can't expect to find a preset for everything. A number of very good starting points are installed in ZMapper that you can use or adjust as needed, but a certain amount of work is to be expected. (Although if you're very lucky, there may be someone on the ZBrushCentral forum that has exactly the knowledge you require.)

Starting ZMapper

In this section I'll cover some important points that you will need to know when using ZMapper. First of all, if you are using a smaller screen resolution such as 1024 x 768, you may need to make room on your ZBrush screen so ZMapper will show up when started. So close your side panels and pull the bottom area up a bit. Starting ZMapper is easy. All you need to do is drop to your lowest subdivision level and press the **ZMapper Rev E** button.

The following shortcut keys will help you out when you first start using ZMapper for creating your normal and cavity maps. You can find them all on the ZMapper interface, but it is good to know a few of them in advance.

Key	Description
X	Pressing X exits ZMapper and returns you to ZBrush.
Tab	Pressing Tab hides the entire ZMapper interface, although it will still be running.
1-7	The 1-7 keys allow you to choose different display modes.
R	Press R to return to the default Rotate mode.
E	Press E to switch to Scale mode.
W	Press W to switch to Move mode.
S	Press S to take a screenshot that you can use as a reference.
D	Press D to clear the screenshot from the work area.
I	Press I to switch to Spin mode, which allows the model to continue rotating after a drag operation.
N	Press N to center your model facing forward.
O	Press O to open the Configuration dialog.
C	Press C to start the normal map creation process using the current settings.

With these shortcuts handy you should be able to get normal maps out of ZMapper more easily.

Quick Start to Normal Mapping

I want to first show you the easy, no-frills way to generate your normal map before moving on to the more complex methods that allow you more control. As mentioned previously, make sure that you have a set of UVs created on your model. If you do not, then drop to the lowest subdivision level (where you should be already) and create a set of AUV tiles UVs from the **Texture** section of the **Tool** palette.

Now start up ZMapper by using the button in the top toolbar area (if you are using a small screen resolution, you may have to make room for it). You should now see your model in the default Rotate mode. In this mode, moving the model will make it rotate on a slightly changed axis, which doesn't matter at all but can be annoying. If you look toward the bottom of the interface of ZMapper you will note a button labeled **Open Configuration**. Press this button or use the **O** shortcut key and browse to a preset that best fits your render engine. I'll be using 3ds Max in this case, so I've picked the **3DS Max7_TangentSpace_BestQuality.zmp** preset. This allows me to make sure that all the relevant options are already selected and saves a fair bit of time.

You will want to now make sure that the **Normal & Cavity Map** tab is selected. This is where the rather important button to generate a cavity or normal map is located. It also contains a number of important options that we can use to tweak our normal maps to get exactly what we need. Go ahead and press the **Create NormalMap** button (or the shortcut key **C**) and ZMapper should now start to work through the process of creating your normal map. The amount of time this takes depends on how many subdivision levels you have and your system resources. As a general rule, the orange clock that you see in the upper left of the work area should be moving; this shows the process of the map generation. Once this is done and the normal map looks fine in the preview, press the **Exit** button.

Once finished you will have a 2048 x 2048 (2K) normal map that already has the green channel flipped and is ready to use in 3ds Max. If you need a larger map size than this, you would first create a blank texture of that size for your model in the Texture palette before starting ZMapper. Once you have your normal map, just export it from the Texture palette and save it where you can find it (along with an exported copy of your lowest subdivision level as this is the level that we used to generate the map).

Getting to Know ZMapper

So that you can find your way around the interface with ease as well as make use of its more advanced functions, I'm going to take you through all of the interface in detail. As we go through each button and slider I'll explain in detail what it is and what it can be used for, with examples where appropriate. When you open up ZMapper it can look a little daunting at first, but it makes more sense once you know what everything does.

When you first open ZMapper, the default interface shows a wealth of buttons and sliders, as well as a row of tabs at the bottom of the interface. Click on the orange tab labeled **Normal & Cavity Map** to open the additional controls for creating normal and cavity maps. Each tab along the bottom of the interface contains a whole new set of controls.

Main Control Block

For the moment let's just look at the top half of the interface and work our way around it. Notice that the top part of the interface groups the controls into columns labeled Transform, Mesh, Morph Modes, Wires, Screen, and Display. This isn't just for the benefit of making things look nice and pretty; you'll find that controls that are related or similar in some way are grouped together. The group on the far left under the word ZMAPPER that contains the Exit and Hide buttons contains controls that affect not the way the normal or cavity map is made but the look of the interface itself. For example, you can temporarily hide the interface if you're short of room by hitting the **Hide** button or pressing the **Tab** key and you can exit completely by hitting the **Exit** button or pressing the **X** key.

FIGURE 8-2: THE NORMAL & CAVITY MAP TAB

FIGURE 8-3: THE PROJECTION TAB

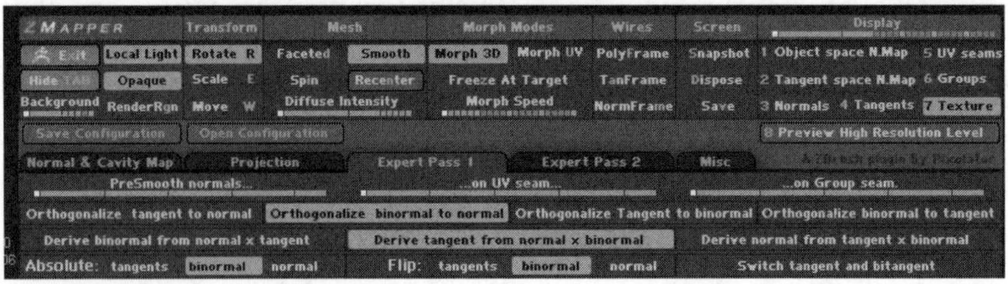

FIGURE 8-4: THE EXPERT PASS 1 TAB

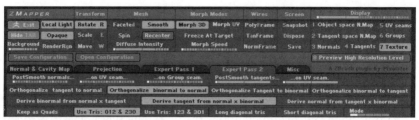

FIGURE 8-5: THE EXPERT PASS 2 TAB

Use the Local Light button to turn on or off a local light that will rotate around the model. This means that you will be able to preview how a normal map will look under different lighting conditions. The local light also works in conjunction with the **Diffuse Intensity** slider in the Mesh control block. If you drag the **Background** slider to the extreme right, you will notice that the viewport background darkens to black, and sliding it the other way makes it lighter. This setting doesn't change the map generation process in any way, but can make the model easier for you to see. The **Opaque** button simply toggles the opacity of the model on and off.

The RenderRgn button is used to render only a preselected region of the model. This allows you to quickly preview the settings, which means you can get the job done in less time than if you had to allow for the entire map to generate each time you make changes. To look right in use, some game engines or render engines need normal maps to be a bit over sharp or over inflated. The render region box can be resized as needed by holding down and dragging any of the four corners. To move it, simply drag it by one of the borders.

The Transform Block

The set of controls in the Transform column handle very basic transforms of your model. By this I mean scaling, rotating, and moving it around. If you've gotten to this stage in the book, then chances are you have already done each of these three things in ZBrush. These controls simply allow you to do the same in ZMapper. They are simple to use and each has a hotkey assigned so that you can quickly switch from one to another.

The Mesh Block

In this column you will find a number of controls that affect the basic ways you see your model. You can view your model using either a smoothed angled normal look (which basically makes the model look as smooth as possible in the viewport with its given polygon count) or a faceted view more like a basic poly modeling package. Most people will stick to the smoothed normal view for the simple reason that it is the way that the mesh is going to be used 99 percent of the time in a game engine.

You will have noticed by now that when you first start ZMapper your model spins around in the viewport, and that it's easy to get yourself into all sorts of strange rotational angles. The **Spin** button simply allows you to turn off Spin mode, which makes your model perfectly still and at rest in the viewport, and the Recenter button reorients the model to the original angle. You'll need to spin your model on different axes in order to see how the light is reacting to specific areas of your model when it is normal mapped to check for problem areas. Since not every model is symmetrical or oriented to the same axis, Recenter basically resets your model to its initial starting point when you first opened ZMapper in a particular session.

The **Diffuse Intensity** slider controls the intensity of the local light. Higher settings make the light stronger, and lower settings make the light weaker.

The Morph Modes Block

Morph UV is without doubt my favorite part of ZMapper, purely for eye candy reasons. What it does is cycle between the model itself and a 2D plane that represents your UV map. I have to say that it's rather addictive to watch and can give you an excellent understanding of how a UV map relates to your model. Its "real use" is to help you to see where any seams on your normal map may be so that you can fix any problem areas that occur at those points. A highly visible seam can ruin the illusion of a normal mapped model being a high-poly one.

Morph 3D is very similar to Morph UV except instead of showing you how your texture coordinates translate onto your model and where any seams may be, it cycles between any morph targets that you have set in advance. Use this if the base that you are using for your normal maps is already rigged and skinned in another application and you want to see if certain facial expressions are going to cause any problems with your normal map. This lets you check your map against the base mesh and against any poses that you wish, which is an excellent time-saver.

Freeze At Target can be used with either Morph 3D or Morph UV. Instead of having to wait for a visual morph between the model and its UV representation, or between the model and its morph target, this button lets you simply switch between them with no intermediate stages.

When you have finished with this and need to switch back to your model, simply switch off the morph action that you used.

Morph Speed simply controls the speed of the transition between the **Morph UV** and **Morph 3D** actions. The higher the slider setting, the faster the transition.

The Wires Block

The options in this section let you view overlaying lines over your model in a few different ways that can be of great use. These buttons are simple on/off toggles and you can have them on in any combination that you wish. **PolyFrame** will show the borders of your polygons, while **TanFrame** will show the tangent and bitangent vectors of each polygon that ZMapper will use to generate your normal map. **NormFrame** will show you the directions of the normals for each polygon on your model.

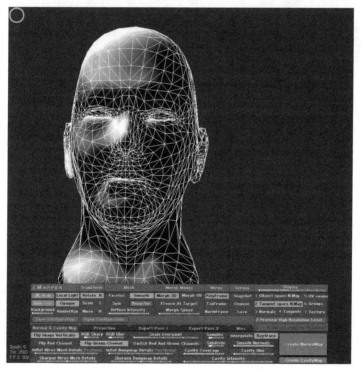

FIGURE 8-6:
POLYFRAME
VIEW

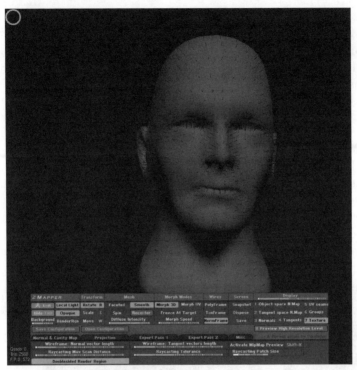

FIGURE 8-7:
NORMFRAME
VIEW

Viewing your model in different ways lets you hunt down why an area may be giving you problems.

The Screen Block

The options in the Screen column control the screenshots that you take within ZMapper. Screenshots can help when you are correcting problem areas on a normal map. You can also use different rendering options and even poses for your snapshots to use for reference.

To take a screenshot or a series of screenshots, first position your model as you wish in the viewport. Press the **Snapshot** button to place a copy of your model in the viewport background. Additional snapshots will be placed on top of the previous snapshot in the back of the viewport. If you want to save them, just hit the **Save** button and a dialog box will ask you where you wish to save them and under what names. To clear the viewport background, simply hit the **Dispose** button and it will leave just your model in the viewport. Do make sure that you do not build up so many snapshots that your video card is screaming for mercy, as this will slow down performance and it will take a bit longer to generate your maps.

The Display Block

At the top of this block is the **Display** slider, which controls the per-spective effect in ZMapper. If it's set very low, your object will look as if it is viewed through a telephoto lens; higher levels will look like a view through a wide angle lens.

The **Object space N.Map** and **Tangent space N.Map** options allow you to specify that type of normal map. Any texture on your model will be treated as if it is a normal map of the particular type selected.

Choose **Normals** to see the object space normals on your low-reso-lution mesh. **Tangents** shows the tangent vectors instead. **UV seams** is interesting as it shows how different areas of your model are going to map to different areas of your normal map. When you switch **Groups** on you will see a colored representation of any polygroups that your model has. Polygroups can also be useful for finding out why a particular area is giving you a problem. When **Texture** is pressed, it will show any nor-mal or cavity map as a simple texture. To show it as a normal map in the viewport you must switch back to either tangent or object view mode again.

Configuration and Preview Buttons

ZMapper comes with a number of handy presets that can help you to get a good quality normal map "straight out of the box." As mentioned ear-lier in this chapter, different render engines and game engines often have different requirements when it comes to normal maps. So one that would look really good in 3ds Max, for example, may look really bad in LightWave or Maya. To open up a preset that comes with ZMapper, sim-ply click on the **Open Configuration** button and click on the preset that best fits your requirements.

A preset can also be saved out for later use by using the **Save Con-figuration** button. This allows you to share a really good setup with others in your pipeline or others working in the same engine. This saves all the settings that are currently active in ZMapper for later use.

Preview High Resolution Level renders the high-resolution mesh over the top of the low-resolution one that you are using in the viewport. If the high-resolution model has a texture applied and you go to generate your normal map, ZMapper will overwrite the texture map with the normal map, unless you either make a blank texture or make sure no texture is active. This means that you can compare a normal mapped version of your low-resolution mesh with the high-resolution mesh. It will also help point out any problem areas that you may need to work on.

As you can see, ZMapper gives the user a large variety of ways to check a normal mapped base mesh for problems. This is one of the reasons it is the tool of choice for normal mapping at many large game firms.

The Subtabs

At the bottom of the interface are a number of tabs containing additional controls that allow you further settings for the generation of normal maps. You can switch from one tab to the next by simply clicking on it. A rather cool thing is that if you hold down the Shift key and click on one of the tabs, it will open without closing the tab you were previously viewing. So you could in theory have the contents of every tab visible at once should you wish to. I'm not quite sure why you would need all the tabs visible at once, but no doubt there are a few cases where it would indeed be handy.

The Normal & Cavity Map Tab

The Normal & Cavity Map tab is where most of the nitty-gritty work will be done when you are in ZMapper because this is where your map is generated from. Most of the time users rarely even need to visit the other panels. Since this tab contains the normal and cavity map creation options, when you open any preset you will see changes in this section.

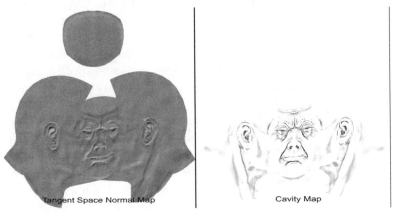

Tangent Space Normal Map

Cavity Map

FIGURE 8-8

Sometimes the normal or cavity map that you produce in ZMapper will need to be flipped vertically, and you can do this before exporting by simply choosing the **Flip Image Vertically** button. Next to this are a couple of important settings for your normal map generation. **Flip Red Channel** and **Flip Green Channel** are often used as some engines require these channels to be flipped to give the best results. What this actually does is to flip the channel of your map vertically. If you are curious you can check this out in Photoshop by viewing the channels both before and after these buttons are selected. **Switch Red And Green Channels** is used for similar reasons. What this button actually does is switch the x and y coordinates.

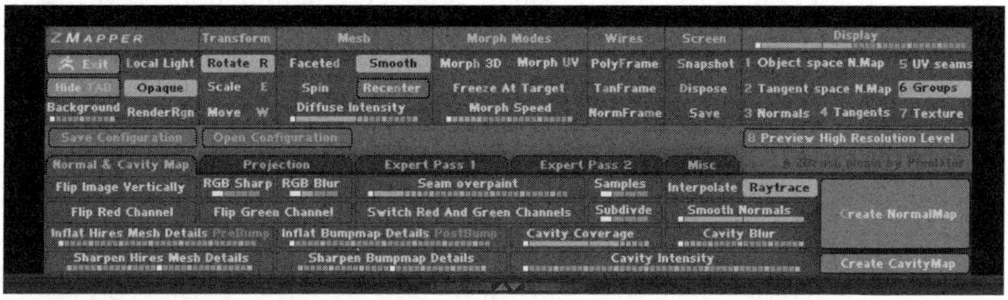

FIGURE 8-9: THE NORMAL & CAVITY MAP TAB

From time to time when generating a normal map in ZBrush using ZMapper you may see some artifacts that look like black speckles or dots. These are an inherent problem of all normal map generation programs and plug-ins because they are generated by mapping high-resolution detail onto a lower-resolution model. Other artifacts can be caused by bad UVs on your model or topology problems. The **RGB Blur** slider can be used to get rid of a number of these smaller artifacts. **RGB Sharp** can be used if you need to sharpen up your normal map to get a little bit more of the fine detail. For example, if you have a sculpt of a knight with lots of chain mail that you need to capture every nuance of, you may wish to use RGB Sharp. Be aware, though, that it is a bit of a trade-off at times. If you have planned your sculpt carefully and have your sculpts grouped according to different types of detail, you can render out two or three different normal maps, each one looking perfect for one particular surface type on your model. Then you simply add and erase areas for other maps in layers using Photoshop. This is actually a good way to get the perfect normal map for a digital sculpture when your low-resolution model is going into a game as it gives you total control at a level that would be almost impossible for just one map. Use this tip for a model with different surface types, concentrating on each surface type and generating a map for each and then compositing them together later.

To explain **Seam overpaint** it is first necessary to go into a bit of theory as to why we need this and why it is important to have control over it in ZMapper. When a render or engine is processing a map of any type (not just normal maps), it has to deal with seams. Areas next to each other on your model may not be next to each other on the UV map, and this can cause problems if not dealt with correctly. When calculating how the map relates to the model itself by looking at the UVs, it can sometimes have to look outside of the actual group or polygon area. So this control gives us the option to control how many pixels outside of the map that information may be written.

A good way to help get rid of any issues you may have at the seams of your UVs is to increase the Seam overpaint setting. You will find that a lot of normal map issues stem from how well your UVs are laid out, so it is worth taking the time to make sure — very sure — that your UVs are laid out as well as you can in the time you have available. Another important bit of information to keep in mind is that ZBrush cannot overpaint an area used by another group, so if the borders of your groups are too close together then you may not get any overpaint, no matter how high you take the slider. This can be a particular problem if you use AUV tiles as your UV option. So if you feel you may need to overpaint your seams at some point, make sure you use a different mapping type.

If you feel that no matter what you have tried so far, your normal map still is not looking good enough, the **Samples/Subdivide** sliders can be increased to give higher quality. But as you take either (or both) of these sliders higher, you will notice it takes longer to generate your map. The more information any application has to process, the slower it will run. So again you'll have to balance the decision based on the type and design of not only your model but also your UV layout. My tip would be to get your map looking as good as you can with the lower settings first before you even think about increasing either your samples or the subdivide level; otherwise it is going to take an eternity to fine-tune your map.

The **Inflate Hires Mesh Details** and **Inflate Bumpmap Details** sliders are both used to exaggerate the fine details on your mesh to make them a little more obvious. By using Inflate Hires Mesh Details, the model will be inflated using only geometric details before any bump details are applied, while Inflate Bumpmap Details inflates the details after they have been applied. If you use both sliders together, you can induce artifacts if you do not take care. This is a balancing act that vastly depends on the model being used and the detail that it has. Another option that can bring out some details is the **Sharpen Bumpmap Details** slider. This allows details to be shown sharper, but may result in a slightly pixelated effect in the final map depending on the model you are using it on. **Sharpen Hires Mesh Details** does basically the same thing, but works on the mesh itself instead of just the bump map.

Generating good cavity maps in ZMapper requires a bit of knowledge on the subject. So first off, what is a cavity map? Simply put, a *cavity map* is a way of simulating an ambient occlusion effect in ZMapper. Okay, so what is ambient occlusion then? This is a bit more difficult to explain. If a model is lit with only diffuse light without shadows, you will find that the recessed areas become a lot darker. Maps that simulate this effect are very useful in many ways in texturing and rendering. So to put it simply, a cavity map will make the details that are inset darker.

ZMapper gives a good amount of control over cavity maps using just a few controls, so let's quickly look at each one. **Cavity Intensity** controls how dark the cavity effect will be; the higher the value, the darker the cavities will be rendered out. If you set this to zero, you will get no cavity effect whatsoever.

Cavity Coverage is used to decide what ZBrush treats as a cavity and what it doesn't. Remember that a cavity is a detail that goes inward. As you increase this setting, it will include more and more of the finer and smoother wrinkles and details that will then be treated as cavities when it comes time to generate the map. So the higher you crank it up, the smoother and finer the wrinkles will be shaded in the cavity map.

If you find that the cavity map you generate is a little too sharp for either your tastes or usage, then use the **Cavity Blur** setting to soften the cavity map. The higher it is set, the more it will blur the map out, while if you set it to zero there will be no blur at all. It's also a great way to get rid of any areas that are causing problems in your cavity map.

Cavity maps are created using the **Create CavityMap** button in the same way that normal maps are created using the Create NormalMap button. (I'm guessing that everyone already worked this bit out, but I put it in for completeness only.)

When it comes to generating your normal map you have two options — Interpolate and Raytrace — each of which will generate the normal map in a different way with slightly different effects. The map is affected by how you have sculpted your high-resolution model, because some tools such as Pinch and Nudge can move vertices around in a way that makes the topology difficult. Most problems can be resolved by retopologizing your model if necessary, though.

My advice is to generate a test map with each setting type to see which one looks best. There can be a difference in generation times, but this is to be expected as they are generating the maps in different ways. Depending on how the model was sculpted, look at areas like the ears, eyes, and mouth to get an idea of which generation type works best for your model.

The Projection Tab

The options in the Projection tab allow you to do something rather cool that is of major interest to those of you working on computer games. Since the days of ZBrush 2, ZMapper has allowed the user to bake a normal or cavity map from one high-resolution mesh to a low-resolution mesh with totally different topology. Putting it simply, if your high-resolution digital sculpt does not have topology that is correct or easy to use for animation and you have a retopologized base that you can use, ZMapper allows you to bake the normal map onto this retopologized base mesh instead of the usual way. It's a feature that isn't as well known as it should be in my opinion and alone is probably worth the price of ZBrush to many in the game industry. In some game pipelines, the same base mesh may be used for a handful of different characters, each given different details and textures. A technical director may already have this mesh rigged and using good topology, so it saves a lot of time to be able to bake your maps to a common base mesh as opposed to a new one each time.

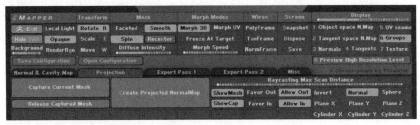

Figure 8-10: The Projection tab

Later on I'll walk you through the process of creating a set of maps for an "arbitrary mesh," but for the moment let's see what all the buttons and sliders are for and what they do.

Capture Current Mesh is used to take a sort of 3D snapshot of your high-resolution mesh that you wish to use with your base mesh with different topology. To do so you would load up your high-resolution digital sculpt and take it to its highest subdivision level. Then you would start ZMapper and press the **Capture Current Mesh** button before exiting ZMapper. You would then restart ZMapper with your new base mesh active in your viewport and click on the **Create Projected NormalMap** button to bake a normal map using the settings in the **Normal & Cavity Map** tab. This is a simple way to bake arbitrary meshes within ZMapper.

When you have done the above steps you may wish to press the **Release Captured Mesh** button to let you see the finished model in the viewport as opposed to the captured mesh. I would advise that you bake normal maps in different ZMapper sessions to give you the highest level of control and the best balance of speed and quality.

Due to the differences in shape between your high- and low-polygon meshes, you may occasionally find that some details are cut off and look flat. You may need to increase the **Raycasting Max Scan Distance** setting to allow ZMapper to capture all the details on your mesh. This works by allowing the user to set the maximum distance that ZBrush will look for your high-resolution digital sculpt when generating your normal map. It will try to find matching points where it can within the distance that you put in. So if your low-resolution base mesh does not follow the silhouette of your high-resolution mesh very well, you may need to increase this maximum distance a fair bit.

Sometimes you may find that even if your high-resolution mesh is working alongside your base mesh, it will still give you problems. ZMapper can capture detail from either upward or downward, so having surfaces close to a particular polygon that can capture detail from either side may well cause issues in your generated normal map. Thankfully, you can control this effect and prevent it from being a problem by using the **Allow In** and **Allow Out** buttons. When both are on (as they are by default for most presets), they allow ZMapper to capture data from either side of a polygon. However, if the Allow In button is switched off, it will only capture data above the level of any polygon and all data below it will be ignored. You can use a combination of these to try to sort out any problem areas, such as generating separate maps with each button active, along with one that has neither button active. This allows you to composite the two maps in post in Photoshop to get the best normal map that you can for your geometry. Keep in mind that if you have to change the default settings of these buttons, then chances are your geometry has become folded or is overlapping in a way that's not good.

Another way to help with problems is to use the **Favor In** and **Favor Out** buttons. If ZMapper is allowed to capture detail both from above and below the surface of a polygon, these buttons indicate which direction it must favor if two points are available. Think of it as a way to set the direction you wish ZMapper to use as a default in case it needs to make a decision. You will find that it is usually best to make your own decisions whenever possible. Rarely will a random CPU-generated decision be the correct one since computers only follow the instructions given to them.

The other controls you see in this tab affect how the normals are projected during the generation process. If you think of them in the same way you would a set of UVs for a model, you will find they are pretty easy to understand. But as a rule you won't need to touch these at all; in fact I've not needed to change these once since the first incarnation of ZMapper was released for ZBrush 2.

The Expert Pass 1 and Expert Pass 2 Tabs

The chances are that unless you need to get very deeply into the normal map creation process, 90 percent of the time you'll never need to touch the Expert Pass tabs. For those times when you do, though, you'll probably need to try things out first and make sure that they fit well within your pipeline and intended use.

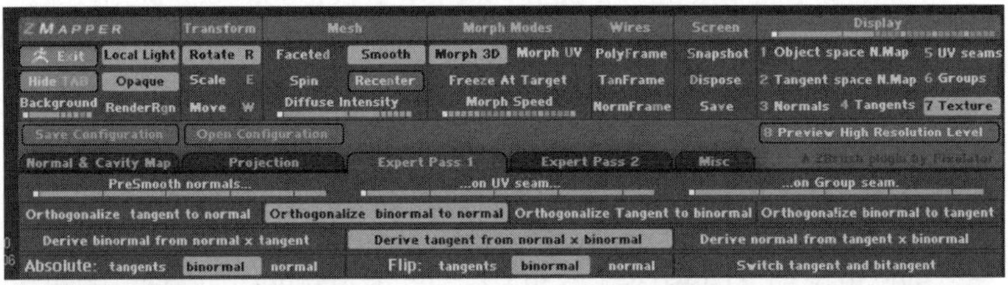

FIGURE 8-11: THE EXPERT PASS 1 TAB

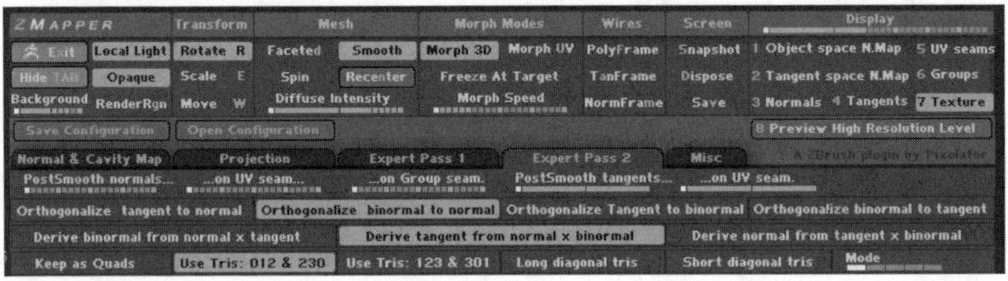

FIGURE 8-12: THE EXPERT PASS 2 TAB

Once you have the settings as needed, it's a good idea to save them into a ZMapper configuration file for use in a production environment. I suggest that you test out your settings in these two tabs and make sure they are producing a normal map that is usable in the engine that you need it to work within before saving it out as a settings file.

You will notice that some settings are available in both Expert Pass 1 and Expert Pass 2. This is because it is a two-stage process. Treat Expert Pass 1 as the first pass at things, so the settings within that tab will all be done in the first pass, and the settings in the Expert Pass 2 tab will be done during the second pass.

This means that you can make certain effects take place before one another, and even choose different settings should you need to. As mentioned previously, since there is no standard for normal maps, each engine can have totally different requirements. Having this level of control in ZMapper makes ZBrush a very powerful normal map creation tool. It allows control to a very fine and subtle level over the entire creation process to make sure that you get the map that you need to meet the requirements of the engine you are using.

We should look at the way that the surface normals are interpolated in ZMapper to understand how best to use these more expert settings. We might take for granted that we are using low-resolution and high-resolution models, and may assume that the rays to generate the normal map are cast perpendicularly. Although this may appear to be a sensible conclusion to those less experienced with the normal map creation process in ZBrush, it's actually incorrect. What actually happens is that ZMapper interpolates using either the surface normals or the vertex normals of the low-resolution mesh. This takes for granted that since you are generating a normal map, it is a model meant for a game engine of some kind and will therefore follow the silhouette of the smoothed version of the mesh. If ZMapper did in fact use perpendicular projection, this wouldn't be taking this fact into account and hence our map would not be of much use.

Unfortunately, the standard mesh formats used for import and export by ZBrush are not always interpreted throughout the industry to indicate which parts of a mesh should be genuinely "flat surfaces" and which should be interpreted as following a more rounded form in relation to the high-resolution mesh. So as a result, a solution is usually provided in the normal map generation program and ZMapper is no different in this regard.

So you may want ZMapper to consider when generating the map that any polygon borders with an angle above a certain number would be interpreted as sharp edges, and ones of less than that as smooth edges. You can also use polygroups or UV islands to indicate certain borders that are to be interpreted as hard edges. Options such as **PreSmooth**, **PostSmooth**, and the **UV**, **Group**, and **Seam** options are some of the ways you can control the final maps.

When generating a map for a low-resolution mesh to capture the details of the high-resolution mesh onto a normal map, you can sometimes end up with some stretching due to the sheer amount of translation being done from one type of space to another. Often the angles in one type of space do not translate perfectly into the other type. We can control and fix any stretching problems with the **Orthogonalize** and **Derive** options available in ZMapper. One thing that may make you a little crazy is that if you change one of these values, the other will change as well. This is due to the fact that the two interact with each other, so this is not only normal but desirable. Until there is some sort of industry-wide agreed standard for normal maps, we will all need these more advanced options though.

The Misc Tab

This tab contains all the settings that don't have a home anywhere else in the interface. Along with controls that cover the ray tracing scan distance, patch size, and tolerance, we also have others such as **Wireframe: Normal vector length** and **Wireframe: Tangent vector length** that basically control the length of the lines drawn when the corresponding controls are activated in the Wires column.

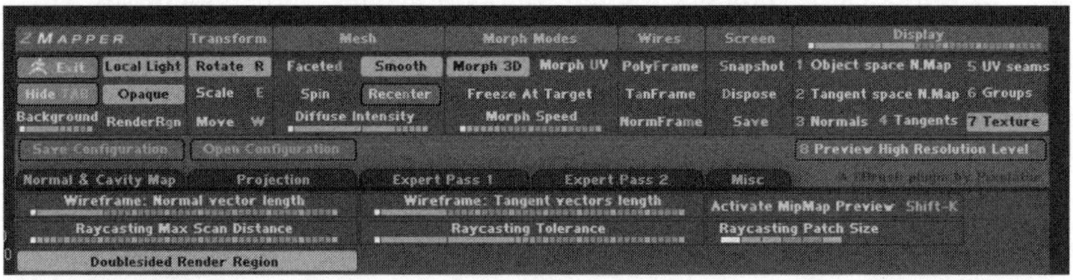

FIGURE 8-13: THE MISC TAB

When activated, ZMapper uses mipmaps for the previewing of your model. Those allow you to move, scale, and rotate your model when you are checking how the generated maps look and hunt for any issues or problems that will need to be resolved when switching between the mipmaps.

While the Misc tab is often neglected, there are a few things here that are quite useful.

Overview

So as you can see, ZMapper is quite powerful when it comes to normal map generation. Although the number of controls seems a little scary at first, you'll find with use that they make a lot of sense. While for many hobbyists the majority of the more advanced or exotic settings are probably never going to be touched, for those working in a production environment they are a godsend. It's sometimes hard to remember that ZBrush is a professional production tool with a very robust toolset. So like the rest of ZBrush itself, learning to use all the settings in ZMapper is worth the effort for anyone who uses normal maps in any capacity, be it as a hobbyist or as a professional. And the added feature of cavity map generation is worth learning for that feature alone.

9 Posing a Digital Sculpt in ZBrush

FIGURE 9-1

In this chapter we are going to look at the whole range of ways to pose our digital sculptures in ZBrush. As opposed to traditional applications where a model would need to be rigged and skinned before any posing can take place, ZBrush provides us with a few different ways that we can work. These range from action line posing and ZSphere rig systems to using the new **Transpose Master** plug-in, which allows you to pose a mesh comprised of multiple subtools.

If we take a step back in time to the days of ZBrush 2, we will see exactly how far the posing workflow has come. In those days most people modeled in a standard "T pose," also known as the Da Vinci pose. The reason for this was that if you wanted to pose your mesh after sculpting it, you would have to first export it to another application such as Maya, 3ds Max, LightWave, or XSI and rig and skin it there. You would then reimport your base mesh and do any necessary corrections before rendering it out. So in those days, modeling in a pose was pretty rare because most artists didn't really have much of a clue about the

233

rigging and skinning side of things. The only other option was to model a base in a pose and sculpt it asymmetrically, a more difficult job that took twice as long at best. So as you can see, the ability to pose our models from within ZBrush itself takes far less time than it would to rig and skin them in another application.

Why Is a Pose Important?

At its most basic level, a pose helps to give your digital sculpture life. A pose that is too static can often look more like a technical exercise than "art." How a model is posed depends on how it will be used and if it is for work or a personal project. If you are treating it as a personal project for a still or a turntable, then you would indeed be looking at a pose as you would in a traditional sculpture. (You don't see traditional marble sculpts in a T pose, do you?) However, if you are sculpting a high-resolution model that will be used to extract maps for a game or as a film animated model, then posing is not a good idea because you will be passing it off at some point to be rigged, skinned, and animated.

So as you can see, whether or not a model needs to be posed actually depends on what you are using the model for. Many artists still sculpt in a T pose of some type and pose later. This sort of workflow is a personal choice. I will assume for this chapter that you are planning on posing a model.

Where to Get Pose Ideas

Since earlier versions of ZBrush did not have a native system to enable posing, many users simply never needed to know much about poses. As our workflows have evolved, however, now the ability to pose a model in a convincing manner is just as important as any other modeling skill.

I often see artists at a bit of an impasse when it comes to the subject of the "artistic pose." Some seem to use a process of posing like this:

- Take model
- Randomly move limbs and head around using the preferred system
- Wonder why it looks stiff
- Try again…
- Still it looks too stiff and lifeless
- Give up and go back to T poses

This process is totally frustrating to most people and is what causes them to either give up or stick with it until good results are achieved either by practice or accident. Those who are trained or naturally talented at drawing using traditional media instead use something called a "gesture drawing." While it is outside of the scope of this book to give detailed instruction on gesture drawing, I will give a very quick overview here.

Gesture Drawing and Its Relation to ZBrush Posing

Gesture drawing is a skill that can be of immeasurable help to a ZBrush artist. Gesture drawing can be thought of as a way of drawing that concentrates on the pose and form as opposed to the technical aspects of proportion.

Using only a few simple lines, the artist gives the impression of the body in motion or in a convincing pose. The purpose of such a sketch is not to produce a work of art, or even in some cases a recognizable body, but rather to draw a few simple lines that tell us basically where everything is. After a while it is possible to quickly knock a tremendous number of these out and even archive them for later use. A good technique when learning gesture drawing is to go outside to capture poses in real life. For example, take a half hour every day just to sit somewhere and do some sketches. You want to concentrate and draw only the basic shapes and how they relate to each other.

This interrelation of forms is the key to any pose, particularly when gesture drawing. You'll be surprised how it helps with coming up with unique, believable poses.

Other Inspiration for Poses

Inspiration can be found in many places and themes as diverse as watching gymnastics on TV to observing works of the old masters. I'll outline a few of the more popular things you can look at to spark some ideas. This is by no means a comprehensive list, but it should give you a general idea of where you can go to get some really great ideas for poses.

At the top of my list of inspirations isn't works of the old masters, but YouTube. YouTube? In my opinion YouTube is a whole new world for artists in search of inspiration and poses because it is such a success and has such a massive user base that just about anything you require for a reference can be found on it. You can search for videos on anything from dance to sport and beyond and you are limited only by your own imagination. Some topics you may want to look at for poses would be any form of dance (ballet and modern being especially useful), sports (with martial arts being of interest to many ZBrushers), and short snippets of film, starring classic actors. These are only some very basic suggestions and there is so much more out there.

And since you can save any YouTube movies that you like, there is no reason why you can't keep a library of links to stuff that you can then use later. If you find a good pose, you can freeze frame or save it to your hard drive.

The traditional method of observing old masters' works should not be ignored. While it is always a good idea to see a work of art in person where you can fully appreciate it, this isn't always possible. So look for pictures online, on DVDs, and in art books. If you hunt around, you can even find DVD sets of collections of art such as the entire Vatican or selected sculptures from the Louvre. While not exactly Hollywood blockbuster material in terms of entertainment value to most people, they are amazing inspiration. Studying poses done by the old masters can be just what you need to help you pose your model in a convincing way.

Do not discount more modern works of art and even photos, as they can provide equally good reference. Just remember that the pose you give your character must fit. You wouldn't put a rigid looking "enforcer" type male digital sculpt in a pose from a ballet. (Unless of course humor is what you were aiming for.) If you know the character you are creating and his back story, that can help you make sure that you choose a pose that is fitting.

Some Tips Before We Move Onward

In this section I want to give a few more important tips before we move on to the different types of posing systems within ZBrush. These points apply to all the different systems.

Remember that the human body is not like a child's doll with fixed limbs rotating on a fixed body. The body is an organic thing and as such we have the movement of fat, muscle, and bones to take into account. For example, the spine is rarely in a pose that is perfectly ramrod straight — it bends and twists. Make sure that you have at the very least a basic idea of how the human skeleton moves and which bones move in which way so that you can create convincing poses.

It is also important to know where the bone is under the muscle, especially at the joints. Say for example you are using action lines and you place the hip bone in the wrong place. You'll spend all your time trying to keep the pose "right" when the actual problem could be solved easily. So what I am saying is at the very least, keeping some sort of basic anatomy reference handy will pay dividends. Knowledge of anatomy is something that cannot be avoided, especially if you are serious about wanting to be a good ZBrush digital artist.

Posing with Action Lines

Action lines are best thought of as sort of an unofficial "default posing system" in ZBrush because they are easy to use. We briefly mentioned action lines in our very first project in this book, but now let's look at how they work and how to get the best out of them. Action lines appear when using any of the default transform tools (such as Move, Scale, and Rotate), and can be thought of as having two parts. One part is the line itself, which helps us to line up our geometry along the axis needed. The other part is the three circles, which we use to move, scale, or rotate our geometry.

You may remember from the first project in this book that if you left-click and drag on the edge of one of the circles at either end you can move it anywhere on the model. If you do the same with the edge of the center circle, the whole line can be moved. If you left-click and drag inside either of the two end circles, you will be using the opposite one as a pivot point for your moving, scaling, or rotating.

Action lines affect any unmasked areas of your model, so if your entire model is unmasked the whole model will be affected. If you use either regular masking or the more commonly used option of topological masking, you can restrict changes to only the area that is unmasked, such as a lower leg. Before going any further, let's refresh our memories about topological masking.

Topological Masking

Topological masks follow the edge flow of your model and so are very dependent on the edge flow of your base mesh. You can mask smoothly if you have good enough topology to support it, and the better your edge flow is, the more control you will have. However, I should point out that even with a rough mesh made from ZSpheres with no optimized edge flow, you can still mask areas such as limbs well enough to pose a model easily.

To create a topological mask, simply switch to Move, Scale, or Rotate mode. Like most things in ZBrush, you can make a symmetrical topological mask by making sure that your selected symmetry is switched on. As a rule, this is going to be in your X axis, although there are exceptions depending on the model you are sculpting. We can now draw out an action line. For example, to add a line on the leg of our humanoid model from where the hip joint would be, we hold down the Shift key so that it snaps in a straight line below the foot. We are now ready to mask off the rest of the body. (Remember that we have X symmetry enabled, so we will be rotating both legs at the same time and also masking off our model in a symmetrical way.)

Holding down the Ctrl key, drag down close to the area you wish to mask until it meets the join between the hips and groin area. The reason that we mask starting quite close is that it is far easier to control than starting much farther away and dragging down to the same point. Notice that both legs are now the only areas left unmasked and that ZBrush has blurred the edges of the mask a bit for us. If you wish to blur the mask further, simply hold down the Ctrl key and left-click on the darker masked area. The more masked this transition is, the smoother and less harsh the transition will be after we rotate the leg. Although we are trying to emulate how a limb in real-life moves, we don't want it to be blurred too much or we will lose the very look that we need. You will find that the more you use the topological masking functions, the better you will get at predicting how sharp or blurred you need it to be.

Now that everything apart from our legs is masked off and will be unaffected by our use of the Rotate tool, left-click and drag in the center of the bottom circle (below the foot) and rotate the leg into position. You can also rotate the leg using the center circle to turn the legs inward or outward as the human leg does not twist from the knee or below. The legs can only twist from the hips similar to the way the arms twist from the shoulder joint and not the lower arm.

After doing this we can continue posing by adding a bend to the knee. Hold down the Ctrl key and left-drag downward toward the knee, realigning the action lines into place with the pivot on the knee joint. Make sure that you hold down the Shift key to constrain the action line so that the bottom part doesn't fly away into space. Again check that your action line is indeed aligned from both the front and side of the leg. If it isn't, you can use the outside of each action line to carefully move it into place. You can then rotate the lower leg into position.

Action lines can be used to pose the entire body as we will see later on in our examples. Once learned, they are easy to use. They also form an integral part of the Transpose Master plug-in that we cover next.

The Transpose Master Plug-in

Transpose Master is an official Pixologic plug-in for ZBrush that allows the user to pose a mesh that may contain many subtools. Before the advent of Transpose Master, it was impossible to pose a mesh with many subtools all at the same time without some complex (and rather confusing) workarounds. You no longer have to pose your model before extracting any subtools that you need. As it uses action lines that you're already familiar with, you'll find it easy to pick up and complementary to the posing workflow.

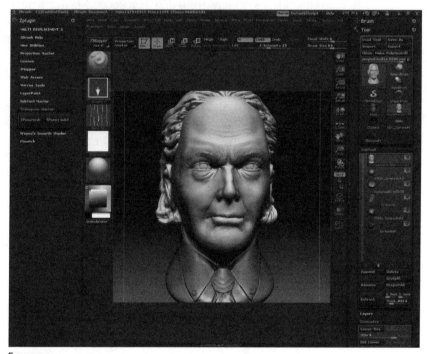

FIGURE 9-2

To use Transpose Master you first need your ZTool (a digital sculpt is referred to in ZBrush as a "tool") loaded into ZBrush. Then go to the ZPlugin palette and click on Transpose Master. Two buttons will appear. **TPoseMesh** takes your current model with all its subtools and stores a version with each subtool at its lowest subdivision level. Once we are finished and have the model posed to our satisfaction, simply press the **TPose > SubT** button to transfer each subtool from our posed mesh onto our high-res version of the model. It works in a similar way to the old workflow of posing a lowest level OBJ of a model in another application such as Maya, and then importing it back in over your level 1 model in ZBrush.

When using Transpose Master, it's not a good idea to cut things too fine with your computer resources and cause ZBrush to run out of memory. For example, if you are used to getting every ounce of power that you can out of ZBrush, and you try to pose a completed mesh that has been fully sculpted, you probably won't have enough resources to execute each command. Running out of memory by pushing your computer beyond the bounds of reality will cause problems in any application. This is something that is commonly overlooked by many users.

My recommended workflow for using Transpose Master would be to not make using it the last step before posing. Having each subtool subdivided to a high level will only increase the resources needed to pose your model, as all this information for each subdivision level on each subtool has to be stored. So posing earlier on in the sculpting process means things will be easier and go faster. Another reason you should pose early on is for artistic considerations. Sculpting a figure to a high level and then posing may produce many areas that are going to need to be resculpted due to changes in form. So it doesn't make a whole lot of sense to sculpt areas that will need to be redone anyway.

There is no reason why you could not use Transpose Master together with the more traditional action line method if you feel a particular subtool could be handled more easily separately from the group of subtools. Masking off in Transpose Master is just as important as in the action line method of posing. In addition to using topological masking, you can also use painted masks to refine the area you wish to mask off. This way you can get high-quality results in a short time.

If you are simply dying to try out posing using action lines, Transpose Master, or ZSphere rigs (which we'll get to in a minute), remember that the guys at Pixologic have included a number of models that ship with ZBrush. There is a good selection, including a couple of models that include subtools, that you can use for a test run with Transpose Master. These models can give newer users a great way to "get their feet wet" with ZBrush quickly.

So as you can see, posing using action lines and Transpose Master are rather similar. Now let's look at a different method of posing from within ZBrush.

An Overview of ZSphere Rigs

Using a ZSphere rig to help to pose your mesh is about as different from other methods as you can get. Like the other methods it has both strong and weak points. A ZSphere rig works by making a representation of the model using ZSpheres that closely follows the form of the original model. You then pose the model by rotating, moving, or scaling the ZSpheres, either at individual ZSphere level or using connecting chains. We discussed ZSpheres and how they work in Chapter 6. If they are still a bit of a mystery to you, you may wish to go back and read that chapter again before continuing.

One limitation of posing with ZSpheres is the fact that they cannot pose a multi-subtool model. So if you had a figure with clothes as subtools, while you could pose the body perfectly well, posing the clothes would not be possible with a ZSphere rig. Another problem with using ZSpheres is the difficulty of twisting a limb on its axis or bending it. ZSphere rigs are best used for simple poses in my opinion.

Posing with a ZSphere Rig

This method of posing digital sculptures within ZBrush debuted about 2004 in a preview video for ZBrush, and it impressed a lot of people. It allows you to take any mesh (even one not made from ZSpheres) and pose it within ZBrush using a ZSphere rig. It's a relatively simple matter to take something such as a scan of a figure and on import to pose it using a rig you have made that closely follows the form of the model. When combined with retopologizing using ZSpheres, it means that those of you who must clean up scan data from physical sculptures in clay can also pose a mesh as well as retopologize it.

A rough guide to the workflow would be to first take your mesh that you wish to pose using a ZSphere rig and either open it if it is a sculpture made in ZBrush or import it if it is something such as scan data like an OBJ. (One word about exporting something to the OBJ format for late import into ZBrush: Make sure you export each "part" as a single piece of geometry. For example, if you had a man wearing a pair of jeans, the jeans would be one "part" and the body another, so the jeans would be exported as a single-piece mesh and not a series of groups.) Then you would make a ZSphere rig that matches the figure so that the joints are all in the right place and the limbs are the right size. After this stage you would "bind" the rig to the mesh and pose it, creating an adaptive skin afterward.

There are a few things to keep in mind. First, do not make your ZSphere rig overly complex. Unlike a traditional rigging for animation system, there is no weighting, so if a rig is overly complex you would need some significant corrections to problem areas of the sculpt once it has been posed. Second, always start creating your ZSphere rig from the center of gravity of the figure that you are working on. If you do not do this and make the initial ZSphere somewhere like the top of the head or halfway down an arm, you are going to hit problems. Remember that once your ZSpheres are in place, you can store morph targets to enable you to store more than one pose or return to your initial "bind pose." Always create your adaptive skin at the level 1 posed mesh and export this lowest level as an OBJ. This will then mean that it has exactly the same poly count as your original unposed model. Most important of all, *always* work on a copy of your main model that you wish to pose, *never* work on the original, and keep plenty of backups. My motto is "the more backups I have, the safer my work is." Keep backups on your hard drive as well as on an external drive or a DVD so that should the nightmare scenario of a complete computer crash and data loss happen, your work is safe.

A final tip is to always save out your ZSphere rig once it's made so that you can reuse it later for another model. Of course if your model started out with ZSpheres, you have just saved yourself a lot of work, even if you have to tweak and simplify it a little bit for use as a posing rig. So to put that simply, the more simply made your ZSphere rig is, the better.

Posing with a ZSphere Rig Workflow

First of all, make sure that you are working on a copy of your main digital sculpture that you wish to pose and *not* the original. Consider working on your original mesh as a cardinal sin that is to be avoided at all costs. Step the subdivision levels of this model down to the lowest level (level 1). The reason for this is that posing at a higher subdivision level will slow things down a heck of a lot, and means there is more data for ZBrush to deal with in real time. You run the risk of maxing out your system resources, which is never good.

After making sure you are at your lowest subdivision level, left-click on the model's thumbnail in the Tool palette and select the ZSphere. By now you should be very familiar with this two-tone sphere. If you scroll down the Tool palette to the Rigging section and open it, you will see a button labeled **Select**. Click on this and select the mesh that you previously stepped down to subdivision level 1. You now have your mesh visible in the viewport along with a ZSphere.

Now you are going to take your Move transform tool and move it into position at the center of gravity. Scale it down a bit as we do not want it to be too large; remember, we are not generating a base mesh but simply adding a skeleton of sorts to act as a control for us to pose the model. Now go to the **Topology** section of the **Tool** palette and click on the **Edit Topology** button. This will allow us to start creating our skeleton. Use the image in Figure 9-3 as a reference to show you a rough guide to the low level of ZSpheres that we are going to use. Since we are not generating a base mesh, we are not going to need a ZSphere at each side of the joints such as the knees and elbows. This helps to simplify the rig and cut down on the ZSphere count. The more ZSpheres that you use, the more information ZBrush has to process. Each ZSphere can be thought of as a point of "influence" that must be processed, so we keep the ZSphere count as low as we can. Also worth noting is that you can create your ZSphere rig with symmetry enabled, which saves having to do everything twice.

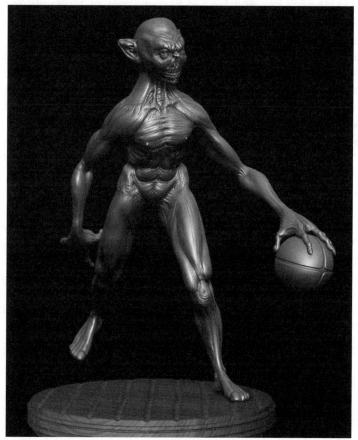

FIGURE 9-3

Once you have finished making your ZSphere rig, all joints are aligned to those on your model, and the limbs are all the right length, we are ready to proceed. Press the **Convert to Main** button in the Topology section of the Tool palette. This tells ZBrush that you are happy with the rig you have created. Next, deselect the Edit Topology button and we are all set to go. Should you need to at this stage you can use your Move, Scale, and Rotate tools to make sure this rig is "inside" the body and not on the surface of it. This is important in order to get the deformation that we want in a moment. Once you are happy that everything is correct and that the ZSphere rig is inside your model in the same way that a human skeleton is, go to the **Rigging** section of the Tool palette and press the **Bind** button. Just before doing this you may want to save out your ZSphere rig for later use. Be aware that the higher the number of subdivision levels that your character has and the more complex it is, the longer it will take to work out your bind pose.

We are now all set to pose our character. All we need to do now that the rig is bound to the model is add our pose. So now by simply using your Move and Rotate tools you can pose the mesh in any way you see fit. Once you have a pose that you are happy with, either set it as a morph target or generate an adaptive skin at level 1. You may also, as mentioned before, set a morph target of both your initial "bind pose" so that it can be returned to and a second pose done before generating another adaptive skin for it. In fact, you can do this as many times as you need to.

With your pose now saved out as an OBJ (by selecting the adaptive skin you made for your pose and exporting it at its lowest level), you can now open up your main unposed model. Step it down again to its lowest subdivision level and import your posed model. Your model can be stepped up to its highest subdivision level so you can check the pose for any areas you may feel need corrections. It's perfectly normal for a pose to need some work on the forms and muscle flow to make it more believable.

Another workflow for creating your ZSphere rig is to simply import a single ZSphere as a subtool and then create it from there. This means that with transparency switched on you can do all of your work in one panel. It also gives the advantage that you know the ZSphere rig is always somewhere you can find it when saved out prior to posing.

Closing Thoughts

As you can probably appreciate now after seeing three ways of posing your digital sculpture within ZBrush, each method has good points when creating certain types of poses. Which you use and when is up to you as an artist. Feel free to experiment as well with using ZSphere rigs as "surface rigs" to help with details like facial posing.

10 Customizing ZBrush

Overview

One of the great things about ZBrush is that it is customizable. You can do everything from changing the way the interface looks and behaves to scripting your own plug-ins using ZScript. In this chapter we will be covering basic and advanced interface customization, creating your own custom hotkeys, and making custom pop-up palettes containing your most commonly used tools and ZScripts.

If there's something you don't like about the ZBrush interface, or you want a more optimized workflow, no problem! It's not hard to change it around to just about any color and design that you wish to, even down to a custom set of hotkeys for your most commonly used actions. As you can see, ZBrush is to a large degree "whatever you want it to be" and that is part of its massive attraction to its ever-increasing user base.

The Custom Stuff Built In

ZBrush ships with a number of alternate interface layouts already installed that you are free to use as is, or you can change them until they are to your liking. Along with these different interfaces there are also a number of predefined color schemes that give you many possible combinations even before you think about either customizing the interface further or starting a new one from scratch. As a general rule, many users start with an interface that they like and then customize it until they are happy. You can store any custom interfaces that you make.

To access the different built-in layouts go to the top bar of the interface. On the right-hand side you will see buttons labeled **Menus** (which switches the menus on and off in the interface), **DefaultZScript** (which takes you back to the opening splash screen), **Help**, and then two pairs of buttons with arrows pointing left and right. The first pair is used to scroll between the different color schemes that ship with ZBrush.

The second pair of buttons with arrows pointing left and right is used to switch between the different interfaces that are built into ZBrush. Both the color schemes and the interface layouts can be used together, so you have many possible choices. Remember, though, that if you create a set of custom hotkeys, they will only work on the particular interface you have them set to and not all the others. If you have switched layouts, you will need to reload these hotkeys again.

Changing the interface design does not affect any models you may have in the main viewport, so you can safely switch between them without having to worry about saving your tool each time. Of the five predefined layouts, there is an "expert" one that shows no controls or menus at all but gives you more screen space to work in and several "user friendly" layouts. The final interface provides a selection of commonly used brushes along the bottom of the screen and is a favorite of many digital sculptors. I personally use a custom variation on the default startup layout.

Areas of the Interface

If you plan to customize the interface, you should have a good idea of what things are called and what they are for, so let's work our way around the interface.

Note: Not that it will happen to you, but if you go a little far with your experimentation and end up trashing files that are part of ZBrush's startup routine, knowing what the interface parts are called will help you understand the repair instructions you are given if you have to call tech support at Pixologic.

Along the very top of the interface is the title bar, which displays the ZBrush version number and your username. The title bar won't change with the different interface options. Below this are the menu bars; the upper row contains the standard out-of-the-box ZBrush menus, and the lower row contains any custom menus you may have made. Below these there is a small space and then we get to the "top shelf," where things such as our transform controls, the Projection Master and ZMapper buttons, and our main brush controls are. Shelves are expandable areas that can be used to store individual interface elements but not menu palettes.

Below the top shelf is the main viewport or workspace of ZBrush. This is where our models reside and we can sculpt, texture, and render them out. To the right and left of the viewport are additional shelves. One contains the larger things such as materials, alpha textures, strokes, and brush types. The other contains navigation type controls such as the Zoom and Scroll controls. These shelves can be customized as needed, but the areas themselves will still remain. Like the top shelf, the left and right shelves can only be used to store individual items and not menu palettes.

To both the left and right of the shelves are areas called the left tray and the right tray. You can open these by left-clicking on the arrowheads at the outer edges of the left and right shelves. Closing the left and right trays gives you more space for the viewport when you need it. Unlike shelves, the trays can be used to store palettes if desired. You can do this by first opening the tray, then left-clicking and dragging the circle-shaped icon in the upper-left corner of the palette into the tray. This way you can have all the menu options you need open in front of you at one time. You can also place custom palettes there as well. For example, I have a palette that gives me some fast basic controls over my turntable recording in the left tray.

Lastly we have the bottom shelf that is below the main viewport window. Due to its size many users prefer to keep some favorite brushes there.

The bottom tray, which is opened by clicking the down arrow below the bottom shelf, is one other area of the interface that we cannot customize without the usage of ZScript. This area is used by ZScript when an interface is required as a front end to the actual script (think of the way the ZMapper interface works and you'll get my drift). It is also used to play back recorded ZScripts.

If you want to eliminate an interface item from a layout, simply drag and drop it into the viewport. In this way you can keep only the things you need in your interface and save screen space. Hopefully you now have a basic idea of what everything is called on the interface and their default locations.

Moving Things Around

Important Things to Know

Before we get started moving things around in the interface, it is important to know a couple of things. These include how to get back to our default layout should we screw up, how to save our layout once finished, and how to load a layout for later use. To restore the default interface layout should you mess things up a bit, simply go to the Preferences menu and press the **Restore Standard UI** button. Saving and loading of interface layouts can also be done from the Preferences palette and the **Load** and **Save** buttons can be found in the Config section. Should you wish to change the UI on startup to the one you have designed, you can simply overwrite the **CustomUserInterface31.cfg** file, although it is wise to back this up first. Should your interface customizing go *really* badly wrong, you can delete the **CustomUserInterface.cfg** file and restore to your backup file to bring things back to normal again.

Enabling Customization

Before we can actually customize ZBrush's interface we must first tell it that we want to change things. This is a handy feature because you then know the chances of accidentally messing up your layout are virtually zero. So to enable customization, go to the **Preferences** palette's **Custom UI** section and click on the **Enable Customize** button, and you are all ready to go. It is important to remember once you are finished to deselect that button again. You must also save your interface after you work on it; otherwise, on closing ZBrush your interface will be lost.

The Actual Moving Stuff Around Bit

Now that we have customization enabled in ZBrush we can left-click and drag any interface item around that we like. Remember that menu palettes cannot be put on shelves but only in trays, whereas single buttons and interface items can be placed on either shelves or trays. Before going crazy moving things around it is important to have an idea of what you are trying to achieve with your layout. Are you making a layout for one

FIGURE 10-1

aspect of your work such as texturing or digital sculpting, or just one that holds the tools you use most often? I know this seems a bit obvious, but I have lost track of the number of times I've seen new users change the interface around with hardly any chance to use it in advance.

I would advise you to "live with" the standard layouts for a while to figure out what you would and would not change. Find out the things you really need on your interface and the things you aren't going to use, as this will help when it comes time to making an interface that you are going to find truly useful. You may also want to draw out a basic plan of what you are going for with your design. You can start from a quick sketch or even go so far as to using Photoshop with a few screenshots of the interface and make a mockup to use as a reference. This may seem over the top to some of you, but if you are serious about making a truly well designed interface, then it's time well spent.

Any items in the interface that you do not need can be dragged and dropped into the main viewport to remove them from your design. You can even save a few different versions and see what works best for you.

Custom Hotkeys

What Is a Hotkey?

A _hotkey_ is basically a key that can be used as a shortcut to perform a particular task. For example, you may have a hotkey to change to a certain brush that you use a lot. Custom hotkeys can be set for most of the ZBrush controls with the exception of navigation. Any button or menu item or even a certain favorite material you like to use when modeling can be set to a single keypress. Hotkeys can also be used to control a ZScript. Custom hotkeys let you avoid a lot of menu clicking, which speeds things up a lot. I find them indispensable.

Setting Custom Hotkeys

Setting a hotkey inside of ZBrush is as easy as falling off a log. Simply hold down the **Ctrl** key and left-click on the interface item, then press the key

FIGURE 10-2

you wish to use as a shortcut. You can set hotkeys for items such as brushes by Ctrl+clicking on the brush. For example, I always set my Move brush to "1" because I want very fast access to that one brush more than any other for tweaking forms and shapes on my mesh. You can also set a hotkey for an entire palette by Ctrl+clicking on it. I have one that contains my most used brushes.

To save your hotkey setup so it will be there the next time you open ZBrush, just go to the Hotkeys section of the Preferences palette and press the **Save** button. To load a set of hotkeys created by yourself or another user, use the **Load** button. To reset to the factory default hotkey setup, press the **Restore** button.

The Default Hotkeys

ZBrush ships with a number of very useful hotkeys that are ready to roll to save you the job of setting a hotkey for everything you need. In fact, the chances are that many will be things you will use all the time anyway, so here's a list of the default hotkeys available in ZBrush for your reference.

Hotkeys

Action	Hotkey
General	
Tool palette	F1
Brush palette	F2
Stroke palette	F3
Alpha palette	F4
Texture palette	F5
Material palette	F6
Show QuickMenu	Spacebar or right mouse click
Show/hide palettes	Tab
Projection Master	G
ZMapper	Ctrl+G
Assign a custom hotkey	Ctrl+click on item (store the hotkeys in the Preferences > Hotkeys section)
Color Palette	
Select color under cursor	C
Switch color	V
Fill layer	Ctrl+F
Document Palette	
Open document	Ctrl+O
Save document	Ctrl+S
Draw Palette	
Draw size	S
Focal shift	O
RGB intensity	I
ZIntensity	U

Action	Hotkey
Perspective	P
Increase draw size by 10 units	]
Decrease draw size by 10 units	[
Edit Palette	
Undo	Ctrl+Z
Redo	Shift+Ctrl+Z
Layer Palette	
Clear layer	Ctrl+N
Fill layer	Ctrl+F
Bake layer	Ctrl+B
Marker Palette	
Place marker	M
Remove marker	Ctrl+M
Movie Palette	
Snapshot	Ctrl+Shift+! (US) Shift+Ctrl+PgUp (UK)
Preferences Palette	
Store configuration file	Shift+Ctrl+I
Load user interface configuration file	Ctrl+L
Save user interface configuration file	Shift+Ctrl+Alt+I
Render Palette	
Render all	Shift+Ctrl+R
Cursor selective render	Ctrl+R
Stencil Palette	
Stencil on	Alt+H
Hide/show stencil	Ctrl+H
Coin controller	Spacebar
Stroke Palette	
Lazy Mouse	L
Replay last stroke	Ctrl+1
Record stroke	Ctrl+3
Replay all recorded strokes	Ctrl+2

Action	Hotkey
Texture Palette	
CropAndFill	Shift+Ctrl+F
Grab texture from document	Shift+Ctrl+G
Tool Palette	
Save tool	Shift+Ctrl+T
Divide	Ctrl+D
Lower res	Shift+D
Higher res	D
Edge loop	Ctrl+E (partially hidden mesh)
Toggle HD sculpting mode	A (cursor over mesh)
Render all HD geometry	A (cursor over background)
View mask	Ctrl+H
Invert mask	Ctrl+I
Clear mask	Shift+Ctrl+A
Mask all	Ctrl+A
Preview adaptive skin	A
Transform Palette	
Activate symmetry	X
Draw pointer	Q
Move	W
Scale	E
Rotate	R
Edit	T
Center mesh in viewport (in Edit mode)	F
Draw polyframe	Shift+F
Point Selection mode	Shift+Ctrl+P
Set pivot point	Ctrl+P
Clear pivot point	Shift+P
Snapshot	Shift+S
Lasso selection mode	Ctrl+Shift+M
Zoom Palette	
Actual size	0 (zero)

Action	Hotkey
Antialiased half size	Ctrl+0
Zoom in	+ (plus sign)
Zoom out	− (minus sign)
ZScript Palette	
Load ZScript	Shift+Ctrl+L
Reload ZScript	Ctrl+U
Hide ZScript	H

Edit Mode Hotkeys

Action	Hotkey
Transformations	
Free rotate	Click+drag background
Move	Alt+click+drag background
Constrain to 90-dregree rotation	Click+drag, press Shift
Scale	Alt+click, release Alt, drag background
Rotate around Z axis	Shift, click, release Shift, drag
Masking	
Paint mask on object	Ctrl (hold down)
Delete or paint reverse mask	Ctrl+Alt (hold down)
Reverse mask	Ctrl+click background
Clear mask	Ctrl+click+drag background
Constant-intensity mask	Ctrl+click, release Ctrl, drag (starting off mesh)
Alpha-intensity mask	Ctrl+click+drag (starting off mesh, Lasso off)
Blur mask	Ctrl+click on mesh
Stencil	
Create custom stencil	Shift+Ctrl+click, release Ctrl, drag (Lasso selection mode)
Partial Mesh Visibility	
Show mesh portion	Shift+Ctrl+click+drag
Hide mesh portion	Shift+Ctrl+click, release Shift, drag
Show entire mesh	Shift+Ctrl+click background

Action	Hotkey
Show only selected polygroup (on a fully visible mesh)	Shift+Ctrl+click
Hide selected polygroup (on a fully visible mesh)	Shift+Ctrl+click
Reverse visibility	Shift+Ctrl+click+drag background

ZSphere Hotkeys

Action	Hotkey
Draw Pointer	
Add a child ZSphere	Drag ZSphere
Delete ZSphere	Alt+click ZSphere
Add a child ZSphere at same size	Shift+click
Add a child ZSphere at draw size	Start drag, press Ctrl
Sphere define magnet/break mesh	Alt+click link-sphere
Insert ZSphere	Click link-sphere
Move Mode	
Move ZSphere	Drag ZSphere
Pose (natural-linked move)	Alt+drag link-sphere
Move chain drag	Link-sphere
Scale Mode	
Scale ZSphere	Drag ZSphere
Inflate/deflate chain	Alt+drag link-sphere
Scale chain	Drag link-sphere
Rotate Mode	
Spin chain	Drag ZSphere
Control twist	Alt+drag link-sphere
Rotate chain	Drag link-sphere

Mouse Action Hotkeys

Action	Hotkey
Toggle Zadd and Zsub	Hold down the Alt key
Toggle all layers on/off	Shift+click on Layer thumbnail
Select layer on which clicked pixol resides	~+click canvas (US) @+click canvas (UK)
Move layer content up/down/ sideways (X and Y)	~+drag (US) @+drag (UK)
Move layer content forward/ backward (Z)	~+Alt+drag (US) @+Alt+drag (UK)
Show item description (when Popup Info is switched on)	Ctrl+cursor over item
Move item to custom interface position	Ctrl+drag (Enable Customize must be switched on)
Remove item from custom interface position	Ctrl+drag to canvas (Enable Customize must be switched on)

Custom Startup Document

Sometimes you may find that you end up repeating the same set of actions in ZBrush to get things set up to your liking such as document size, lighting and default material, render settings, and even the background color of the document and the border around it. Well, the good news is there is a very easy way to sort all of this out when you first open up ZBrush. I'll illustrate by showing you how to create a default startup document.

Simple Change of Document Size and Color

To change the default document size, just start by creating one of the size you want and with your preferred background color, then use the SaveAs command in the Document palette and save the file as **StartupDocument.zbr** in the ZBrush3/Startup folder on your hard drive.

The next time you open ZBrush, your startup document will be the size you specified and have the background color that you set.

Note: If you prefer your startup doc to have a solid color background rather than a fade background, simply set this to zero in the Document palette.

Adding to Existing Materials, Alphas, and Textures

You may already know how to add custom alphas, materials, and textures to ZBrush's default palettes. If not, here is a very quick guide. I should warn you, though, not to overload your startup with hundreds of alphas and textures that you hardly ever use. Only add the most used and those that are most important to your workflow, and remember that you can change these as needed.

Place any custom alphas into the \ZBrush3\Startup\Alphas folder and they will start up with the default ones each time. In a similar way, custom brushes can be placed in the \ZBrush3\Startup\BrushPresets folder, and custom textures can be placed in the \ZBrush3\Startup\Textures folder. So you can guess where the materials go, right? (\ZBrush3\Startup\Materials)

Making a Custom Palette

I use a couple of custom pop-up palettes — one that appears under my brush to contain my favorite brushes and another for when I am ZSphere modeling. Having them appear under my brush is simply a matter of adding a hotkey to the palette. Let's look at how to add a custom menu palette or two.

FIGURE 10-3

Go to your Preferences palette and open the **Custom UI** section. To create our custom menu palette we must first click the **Enable Customize** button to tell ZBrush that we want do some work on the interface. With this switched on, we can now customize the interface in any way that we want, but for now we are only interested in making a menu of our very own. So click on the **Create New Menu** button and give your palette a name. (We can rename it later, but try to make it something descriptive.) I've called mine "Wayne's fav Alphas" and it will contain some of the alphas I use most often during sculpting.

You should now have your custom menu palette, but it will be empty until we add something inside it. So drag whatever tools, materials, or interface items that you wish to have inside of it. Remember that you can also add the orange buttons that are available in the Custom UI section of the Preferences palette to space things out a bit. Remember that you can change the contents at any time by activating Enable Customize again and adding or removing items from your palette.

Once you have added your items to the palette, uncheck **Enable Customize** and press **Save UI** from the Config section of the Preferences palette. If you save it as **CustomUserInterface31.cfg**, it will start by default each time. You can now add a custom hotkey (and remember to save it) to get this palette to pop up under your brush whenever you press your hotkey.

As you may have noticed from the list of the default hotkeys, some palettes can be accessed with the hotkeys F1 to F6 (Tool, Brush, Stroke, Alpha, Texture, and Material). So you can switch off just about all the interface items while you sculpt if you so wish.

11 Common Workflow Tips

This chapter is intended to answer a number of common questions about certain workflows and techniques in ZBrush. The idea behind it is to give newer or less experienced users of ZBrush information on how to do some simple but often confusing things. While these tips probably won't save your life, they may save you a heck of a lot of time if you are stuck. It is assumed that by this stage in the book you have a pretty good working knowledge of ZBrush, so I'll detail things that we haven't used much but skip over tools you're already familiar with, such as the Move brush.

UV'ing a Finished Sculpt with No UVs

This is a problem that is probably at the top of the list of things that less experienced ZBrush users ask about at some point. They will have taken a model to its final sculpting stage and it won't have any UVs, and they wish to export it with a painted texture for rendering in another

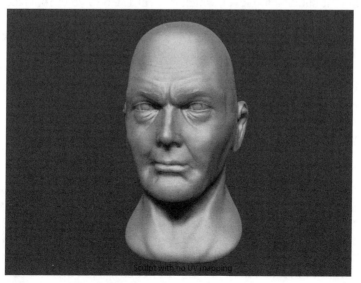

FIGURE 11-1

Sculpt with no UV mapping

application. As ZBrush allows you to paint a texture for your model with polypainting and thus without UVs, many people don't bother to UV a model until they are sure that their model is worth the effort.

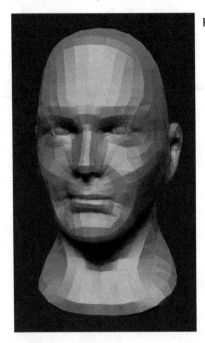

FIGURE 11-2

To UV a digital sculpt in an external program, first step down to your lowest subdivision level, which is level 1. Go to your Tool palette and look in the **Export** section. When you export this level, make sure that under your export options in the Tool palette the **Obj**, **Qud**, **Txr**, and **Mrg** buttons are the only ones enabled so that the polygon groups are not exported as separate meshes. With ZBrush still open (unless your UV'ing is going to take a long time of course, in which case save the file and close ZBrush for a moment), open the external program that you are using to UV your low-resolution model.

Once you are done, export as an OBJ and get ZBrush ready to import it. *But not just yet!* There is something rather important I want to explain before we take steps to import the UVs for this model and explain why we do not just import it over the top of our level 1 mesh. Some UV'ing programs use a baked scale system, meaning that they resize an OBJ on import to fit a standard size. So as a result, your OBJ may end up in ZBrush either very tiny or absolutely huge and unusable. To allow for this, we first need to store a morph target using the **StoreMT** button found in the Morph Target section of the Tool palette.

We store this morph target so that we can keep the geometry exactly the same as it is now, which is immensely important if you have a digital sculpture consisting of a number of subtools.

Tip: If you don't take this step and your OBJ is the wrong size, it's going to take a while to clean things up again.

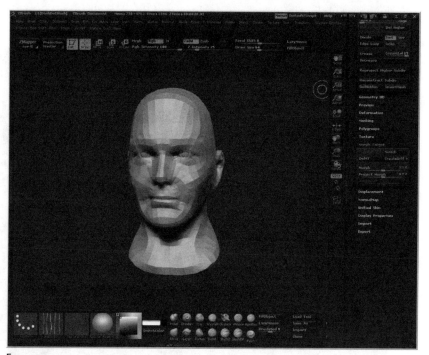

FIGURE 11-3

Now import your UV'ed level 1 base mesh and ignore any scale changes. Do not touch, move, or otherwise do anything but look at your model for the moment. My reason for this is simple: We have just imported a mesh that affects every vertex of our highest subdivision level, so as a result it's going to take a lot of processing for ZBrush to catch up if we rotate our model at all. Most of the time ZBrush can handle this, but it's best not to make any program work too hard if you don't need it to.

What we do next is a little bit of magic that is going to solve any scale issues that may be caused by resizing on export from your UV'ing application of choice. Simply go to the Morph Target section of the Tool palette again and press the **Switch** button and then the **DelMT** button. This will restore the morph target we made a few moments ago, but it will also keep the UVs from your previously imported model. Now using my "better safe than sorry" motto, save the file and then step up to your highest subdivision level and apply one of the default textures such as the checkered one to check your UVs.

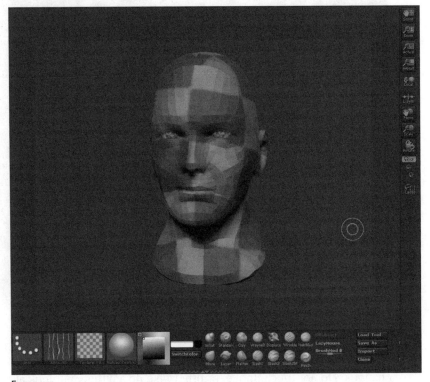

FIGURE 11-4

Another way to check that your UVs are working correctly is to open the **Texture** section of the Tool palette and press the **Uv > Txr** button. This will give you a texture that shows your UV layout complete with colors so you can judge where any seams are. That's the simple way to import some UVs on a completed digital sculpt in ZBrush. Easy, wasn't it?

Wayne's "ZBrush 2" Style Smooth Brush

With the advent of ZBrush 3.1, the Smooth brush now behaves differently than it did in version 2 and earlier. You may either like it or loathe it, but if you miss the "old style" Smooth brush and the way in which it worked, you can create a custom brush that works just like the old one.

Here is the simple way I changed the brush to make it behave how I wished it to.

Small Changes Can Affect Big Things

The change I made was minimal and rather embarrassingly easy, to be honest. I simply changed the **ZIntensity** of my custom smooth brush to **50** (sometimes I set it to 25 for fine work), and changed the **Edit Curve** to be a fair bit sharper. You can edit any curve in ZBrush by clicking on the curve itself. Points can be added by clicking anywhere on the curve and moved by clicking on a point and dragging it to the desired place. The Focal Shift setting will make a curve sharper the closer it gets to 100 and fatter the closer it gets to –100. Together, these changes produce a smooth effect as close as you're going to get to the "old style" Smooth brush. There are many other ways of doing something similar, such as using the Brush Mod controls, but I feel that the way I customized mine was faster and simpler to do and replicate.

FIGURE 11-5

Need More Polygons But Don't Want to Use HD?

This is probably one of my best tips for those of you who want the benefit of using the polygon counts that HD geometry provides in ZBrush but with the advantage of being able to generate maps from it. As of the time of writing, the HD geometry in ZBrush does not let you take this HD geometry and sculpting into account when you generate any map type in ZBrush.

So let's assume for a moment that the maximum polygon count that your PC is able to comfortably handle is 8 million or so. Your trouble is that you are sculpting a highly detailed humanoid type creature and you know you are going to need 20 million to 40 million polygons! It's a bit of a head scratcher, isn't it? But thankfully one with a rather simple solution that will enable you to do all the things such as map generation and retopology that you do for a non-HD digital sculpture.

The Process

Your first job for this workflow is to UV your model, making sure that the limbs, head, and body are each in a separate "island" of UVs and in a different UV space.

Note: For those who may be a bit hazy on these topics, an *island* is a group of unwrapped UVs (let's think of them as faces for the moment), so if for example you had a group of faces unwrapped for a leg into one section, this would be an "island." What is UV space? Put simply, it is the 2D representation of a three-dimensional object, where U is the left-right direction and V is the up-down direction.

If you look in the application you use for UV'ing, it allows for the creation of UVs in not just the "main UV square" but in other areas of the grid as well. So thinking of the "main UV grid" as 0,0, the next one to the right would be 0,1, and the one to the right of that 0,2.

Set your model out so that the joins are in sensible places on your low-resolution mesh for each limb. For the arms you may want to split them at the shoulder and use the hand and arm as one island of separate UVs in its own UV space. Work your way through your model until it is complete.

Note: Some more advanced ZBrush users may be thinking at this point, "but ZBrush can't handle a multi-UV mesh!" They are correct to a point, as although ZBrush itself can't, ZMapper can. (Although to further confound matters, we won't be touching ZMapper as part of this workflow.)

Reimport your multi-UV'ed level 1 mesh as outlined in the first section of this chapter and save it out for the moment before we do anything else. Since you have just done a fair amount of work, you want to avoid any possibility of ruining your model.

So at this moment we have your high-resolution digital sculpt in ZBrush with a polygon count of around 8 million, which is your maximum usable raw polygon count. We have a set of multiple UVs set up for it and are ready to roll with the "magic" bit. Let's examine what justifies this many polygons in a digital sculpt that would require maps. The answer is of course *extreme detail*, which is the tiny stuff you sculpt into your model once the major changes are done. So the reason that this workflow works so well is because we are going to be making what amounts to many tiny changes to the geometry.

In the SubTool section of the Tool palette you will notice a button labeled **GrpSplit**. This along with the **UV Groups** button in the Polygroups section are going to do most of the work for us. Go to the **UV Groups** button and press it; it will assign a polygon group to each of the UV islands in their own UV space. I should point out that if you have any trouble getting this to work then either your UVs are too close to the edges of the UV grid or you have some overlapping vertices in your UVs that you would need to go back and check.

Next, scroll back up to the SubTool section, press the **GrpSplit** button, and wait. It will split your model into separate subtools for each of the parts you initially set as a UV island in its own UV space. Now instead of one model that can have a maximum of 8 million polygons you have split it into a number of pieces (four limbs, one body, and one head for a total of six subtools).

So now each subtool can have up to 8 million polys for a total of 6 x 8 million. You can then continue to sculpt and extract maps from the 48 million polygons as needed. I think you'll agree that this is a fair number of raw non-HD polygons available to you! I should remind you though to make sure that you generate maps of only the required size and not any larger in order to minimize render time.

For those of you in a work environment, there is no reason why each part cannot be split off into a separate tool and handed out to different members of a team. You could even split tools such as limbs into even more separate subtools to enable film-quality polygon counts and map extraction. Although remember that for film-quality polygon counts, you are going to need a film-quality render farm for your animations! I've used this technique many times and it can give detail of astounding clarity when needed.

Tip: When working to the edges of your computer's capabilities, make sure you back up often and in different locations. Working on the edge of your machine's capabilities carries a certain amount of risk. You run the risk of pushing your machine past its breaking point in the search for the ultimate polygon count. But if something is truly worth striving for, then it's worth taking a risk now and again.

Rendering Out from ZBrush in Passes

Rendering out a number of passes in ZBrush for later compositing in either Photoshop or After Effects is a sometimes much misunderstood subject. Rather than using ZBrush's native render engine, some users export to another application such as Maya, XSI, or 3ds Max and try to create a "perfect render" there. Before we go into how to render out in passes, though, let's take a short journey into the land of the movies.

How It's Done in the Movies

Many times on forums I see users creating still images, seeking the perfect shader or material and trying to get a raw render that looks like something out of a movie. If your aim is to achieve the photo real or movie look, you need to know what it is you are trying to achieve and how the big FX houses do it. No effect house involved in making visual effects or scenes of models for the movies puts raw renders straight into a movie. It just isn't the way things are done and for good reason. The final render isn't the final product but has to be passed further down the line to compositors and others who help create the "final look" of a scene or movie.

A person responsible for texturing and sculpting a character may have a certain idea of how the scene "should look," but as a rule is not responsible for the final look of it. The director is the person who has final say and assigns jobs to the people who can best create the vision he wants for a movie or scene by creating a number of additional render passes. These can then be manipulated in different ways to accomplish the director's personal vision.

This gives scenes flexibility at the compositing stage that is especially important when trying to composite CG footage into an existing real-life shot. Breaking down a render into passes allows minute control over each render pass. So if, for example, the compositor is told that the colors need to be darkened a bit, as opposed to rerendering out the entire scene again, he or she can simply render out just the pass or passes that need to be changed. In short, it takes less time and gives a great many more options than using a simple raw render. Also keep in mind that excellent lighting is essential for a realistic scene of movie quality, and a lot of time and care is spent on getting the lighting for a scene just right for the movies. Lighting (when dealing with movie qualities) is a vast and complex subject all by itself. So you can see why a scene is broken up among many different people doing many different complex jobs to get the look you see on the big screen. (Indeed it could be said that the model itself is comparably unimportant if you look at what goes into the scene as a whole!) Once the shot is rendered out and composited into a scene, that's not the end of its journey. All films use "color grading" to get the final look. This is the reason that *The Lord of the Rings* looks far different from *The Matrix* or *Star Wars*. One director may want some colors boosted and others cut a little, or a vignette added to a scene in a subtle way, while another may use color grading to help denote the feeling of a scene.

This is obviously a rather simplistic explanation of a very complex subject, but it gives you a good overview. So the question is if the use of render passes and post effects and color grading are good enough for the film industry, then surely it is good enough for us, right? I would say "yes" and that anything that can be used in a film can be used in a still image from ZBrush. By rendering out in passes we can often get material and lighting effects that we cannot from a raw render straight out of ZBrush.

So is the use of rendering out in passes allowed and considered good practice? My answer is that since most anything you can do in post in Photoshop can be duplicated for moving footage, I see it as fair game. I actually encourage the use of passes because anything that lets you achieve your goal is worth it in my opinion.

Types of Passes

There are a great many types of render passes that you as an artist can use, although truthfully you may not need every single available type of pass. The most commonly used passes are listed below.

- Beauty pass
- Ambient occlusion (or dirt pass)
- Specular passes
- Shadow/lighting passes
- Matte passes

■ Color pass

■ Depth pass (ZDepth pass)

The list is not complete, but chances are that these are the ones that you will be using most in ZBrush. I'll outline what each pass type is before telling you how best to achieve it. Then I'll give a practical example of one of the easier setups for the usage of render passes.

Beauty Pass

This is essentially your main "normal" render that you would do as a matter of course in ZBrush. Some people use it as a base to work from and add other passes over the top, while others use it as a guideline. It's important to get this one as close to perfect as possible in the time you have available, though. I usually use it as a base to work from.

Ambient Occlusion (or Dirt Pass)

An ambient occlusion pass is one that attempts to emulate the way light is blocked (occluded) by objects. It uses an image that in traditional applications (such as Maya, 3ds Max, XSI, etc.) colors an area darker the nearer it is to another surface. So if for example you had a box sitting on a flat plane, the area where the box and the plane meet would be darker as the geometry is closer together. Another style of ambient occlusion pass is where global illumination lighting is baked into a texture to darken areas such as depressions and dips. This often helps to simulate the dirt and grime that gets caught in crevices.

This image can be used in post to darken these areas or even in some cases to mask off an area for another pass. They can also be colorized and manipulated like any other render pass to provide you with an excellent utility pass for a great many jobs at composite time.

Specular Passes

A specular pass is used to generate a layer that can be used later to add or modify the specular level on a render. A specular pass is usually black with only the highlights showing as white or colored lit areas. When used in combination they can simulate real life better than a single material ever could. Specular passes can be colorized and played with in the same way that a normal render can be to best get the look that you are after. As with all passes, they can be faded in and out as needed and truly can add the extra "something" to a render.

One tip is to make sure in ZBrush that you use a material with cavity shading turned on, as rarely does something have a specular effect in cavities and inset areas. Having specular that is white is another bad idea, as in real life the specular color is very rarely white.

There is an old saying in 3D that the specularity of a model can either make it or ruin it. There are plenty of times that we see fantastic models that look amazing with a simple shader that suddenly look terrible due to a bad specular pass or specular map. Along with lighting, it is probably the most important part of the whole rendering setup. So you should spend time on these passes at composite time to get things looking great. Some excellent effects can be achieved from a couple of specular passes, each with a different specular "width" and each with a different color.

Shadow/Lighting Passes

Put simply, these are used to add lighting to a render (usually when starting from a flat render setup as opposed to a beauty render setup). They are simple black and white images that are used to add the lighting information to a render, and you can render out a whole host of different lighting passes to effectively light your scene as desired at composite time. This means that you won't have to rerender the entire scene.

By increasing or decreasing the opacity level of a lighting layer, you can effectively turn the intensity of the light itself up or down. For example, if you are not sure what rim light would look best at composite time, then you can render out a few different versions of the rim light and pick the best one.

I rarely use lighting/shadow passes on my composites because I find I can get the lighting I want without them. The times when I do use them is to add a rim light, such as when using a MatCap material.

Note: MatCaps have built-in lighting information, and as such lighting them can lead to a ton of problems without experience and a large amount of luck.

Matte Pass

What is a matte pass and why do you need it? A matte pass allows you to isolate the geometry in your scene from the background. If approached correctly, you can even isolate each subtool so that you can treat each as a sort of mini-composite. This allows you a great degree of flexibility and can help with some more complex effects. A matte pass can be (in the case of rendering from ZBrush) a black and white image with the white being the actual geometry, or you can color each subtool a different color. This color can be totally unrelated to its actual color or texture and is used only to isolate the object in Photoshop using the Magic Wand tool.

This allows you to do what is called "non-destructive editing," using masks to show only the areas of a layer that you need to affect. The best part (and this is used extensively in matte paintings for movies) is that because nothing has been done that cannot be undone by altering the masks, you can change any part of your composite should you need to. To make a simple matte pass for a digital sculpt that has been textured using polypainting and is a single piece of geometry, simply turn off the colors for your model and change the render mode to Flat. This will give you a very simple and effective matte pass that will enable you to isolate your model from the background.

Color Pass (Diffuse Pass)

A color pass is simply the color information alone for your model with no shading, specular, lighting, shadow, or any other type of information. It's simple to do in ZBrush when not using an exotic material by switching the render mode to Flat with your texture active. If your material is a vital part of your texturing final color, however, there is another option; you just need a slightly more roundabout route to get what you want. This involves first exporting your polypainting to a texture, which by this point in the book you should be able to do with no problem. You then need to empty your canvas and use a Plane tool (which we convert to polygons), and subdivide to roughly the same poly count as our main model. We then apply the texture and also a 16-bit displacement map into the Alpha slot. (I hope you're still with me here as I realize this sounds complex, but actually it's rather easy if you follow along with it.) Go to the Displacement section of your Tool palette and turn the Displacement setting up.

You need to make sure that the polygon plane is aligned to totally fill the viewport and not go outside of it and that it faces the camera straight on. You can now render this out as a texture map with your material information baked in, and you can then reapply this to your model when it comes time to do your color pass. Now I'm not going to lie and say that aligning the polygon plane is "easy" and something you'll get good at with time, because it's a pain in the backside to do. But here's a tip I used to cut the time down.

Start ZBrush up from scratch and do nothing but align the polygon plane to the viewport and fill it totally without going outside of the viewport. Take your time over it as chances are it's the last time you are going to need to...*ever*! (Note: Make your viewport size 4096 x 4096 since this is likely going to be your maximum texture size in most cases; for anything smaller than this you can reduce the size in Photoshop.) Once you have it perfect, simply go to your **ZScript** palette and hit the **End Rec** button to stop the automatic recording of the ZScript and save it out safely. You can now use this ZScript by loading and playing it any time you need to create a texture with your material information baked in.

This is an old ZBrush 2 trick but one well worth knowing and using in a lot of cases, as it can bake in all the material information that can make your model look as good in another render engine as it does in ZBrush.

Depth Pass (ZDepth Pass)

A depth pass is a way of recording in a visual way how far back the model goes in the viewport. It can be used for a variety of effects such as depth of field effects to simulate macro photography or to add realistic fog to a scene. Another use is to help you select certain areas of your model. To do a depth pass in ZBrush you are going to want to wait until you have done every other pass before continuing. Then drop your model from 3D to 2.5D. By clicking the **Edit** button to deactivate it, your model is now no longer 3D but a 2.5D version of it that will allow us to generate our depth pass. From the list of tools pick the **MRGBZ Grabber.** This will grab a version of the render in the viewport, along with the ZDepth information that will appear in the Alpha palette. One big tip is to make sure you disable the **Crop** function under the modifiers for your MRGBZ Grabber or it will crop your image to just the parts with your model in them. For use for depth of field effects (especially when using plug-ins for that purpose), you must have your depth pass exactly the same size and dimensions as your main renders and passes or they simply will not work.

The Practical Application in ZBrush

Now that I've outlined the basics of the different types of these very basic render passes, it's time to give you a more practical example. As this is actually a two-stage process, we will be using ZBrush as well as Photoshop.

The model I'm going to use to illustrate this process is one done as a demo piece for a client. It is a fantasy design of a fish I called the "Numpty fish," and is some basic speed sculpting from a sphere in ZBrush, combined with some fairly easy texturing work by hand and a lot of work in post with the render passes. That's the main reason I chose this image as it is perfect for showing how render passes can be used to get the very best out of a model or render and achieve effects that would either take a lot longer to do or simply be impossible in ZBrush.

The PSD file with the final composite render layer set up is available on the companion DVD.

Passes Used

Beauty Pass

The beauty pass was made on the basic textured model using the white MatCap with some blue/green added in the Colorize section.

FIGURE 11-6

Cavity Shader Pass

This was produced using the white MatCap with slightly increased cavity shading. I was less bothered about getting a replication of the ambient occlusion shading effect than getting a good pass that would help pull the details out of the render.

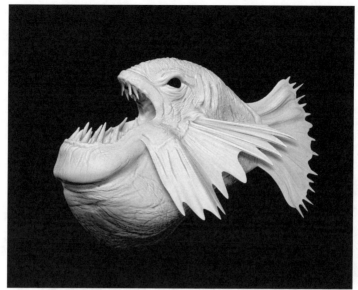

FIGURE 11-7

Flat Shade Pass

The simplest pass of all — just change your render mode to Flat.

FIGURE 11-8

Light Pass

The light pass was produced using the Basic material with the Ambient setting at 0 and the Diffuse turned up to 100. I then put a light into a place that brought out the nicest highlights, which as it turned out was above and to the right.

FIGURE 11-9

Wide Specular Pass 1

All the specular passes were produced using the Toy Plastic material with various specular curves to capture differing amounts of specularity. I also used pretty aggressive cavity shading along with turning the Cavity Specular setting down to –1. This made sure that the cavities were not given any specular highlights.

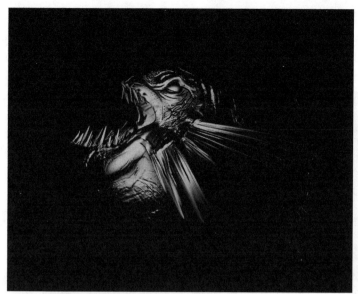

FIGURE 11-10

Wide Specular Pass 2

This pass was made the same way as the version above, but this time I used a slightly different specular curve and rendered it out using a blue light. (You could also colorize this in Photoshop later on in post.)

FIGURE 11-11

Thin Specular Pass

The tightest of all the specular passes was produced using a very tight specular curve very sparingly to bring out the brightest parts of the specularity in the image.

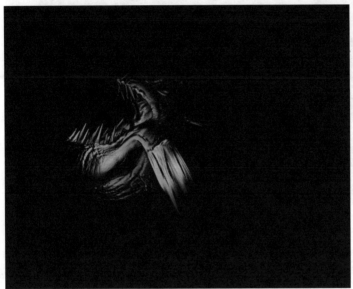

FIGURE 11-12

In this case I didn't need any depth passes because a depth of field effect wouldn't have worked well with the image.

The Process

The first job is to copy the passes into separate layers in a Photoshop document. The order from top to bottom is as listed below.

Layer	Blending mode	Opacity
Light pass	Screen	22%
Wide specular pass 1	Screen	16%
Wide specular pass 2	Screen	51%
Thin specular pass	Screen	74%
Beauty pass copy	Overlay	30%
Beauty pass	Normal	100%

If you're wondering what happened to the Cavity shader pass, I'll explain how I used this in a different way than normal in a moment. (As a rule, it would be set to a blend mode of Multiply and used to darken the cavity areas.)

For the Beauty pass, first of all I boosted the dark areas using the Levels control and duplicated the layer. This duplicate layer (Beauty pass copy) was then combined with the Flat render set to Overlay and faded back a little to lighten it. Then the Flat render and Beauty pass copy were merged.

The Thin specular layer was then overlaid on top of these and set to Screen. This lets only the white areas through, completely ignoring the black areas to give us a tight specular highlight.

Our Wide specular pass was a little unique. I used our Cavity shader pass (lightened a fair amount using the Level controls) as a mask on this layer. So as well as only the lightest areas being let through due to its blend mode being set to Screen, it also used any dark areas on the Cavity pass as masks as well. This gave me a much more complex specular wide pass than I otherwise would be able to get. (Sometimes thinking outside the box can produce an interesting effect.)

The second Wide specular pass I colored to a reddish-brown color by going to **Layer > Adjustments > Hue / Saturation** and switching on **Colorize**, then finding a nice reddish-brown color. As a direct result, for the lightest areas that pass through onto the layer below (due to the now reddish-brown specular pass being set to Screen mode), the highlights were a reddish hue instead of a pure white.

This along with the blue and white highlights was how I gave a bit of a mother of pearl effect to the render. In ZBrush it would have taken some considerable time to achieve the same thing. The lighting pass I colorized in the same way as the second Wide specular pass to help to reinforce the reddish specularity in places with a red lighting effect. A lighting pass acts like adding another light into the scene.

After setting up the layer as above and setting the opacities to something that looked good, all I did was play around with some levels and color correction. I first used the **Layer > Adjustments > Levels** controls and then **Curves** in the same place to boost the blues a little.

As you can see from this simple project, it is possible to render out a series of layers to get many effects. While neither the model nor the render shown in Figure 11-13 will win any awards, it does show how render passes work and how to come up with fresh ideas for renders.

FIGURE 11-13

12 Materials and MatCaps

Materials

Families and Types of Materials

There are five separate types of materials in ZBrush that I prefer to think of as residing in "families." The families are Standard, Special, MatCaps, Fiber, and the Flat shader (which isn't a true material as it contains no color or shading information at all and hence requires its own family). Let's go through these families one by one and outline which materials reside in which one and what they do. Once you have a basic understanding of this we can continue on to other concepts involving materials.

The Standard Material Family

The standard family of materials contains the basic materials such as the FastShader material, Toy Plastic, Double Shader, TriShader, and QuadShader. The FastShader contains only two settings: the Ambient and Diffuse controls. So of the standard material family, this is without doubt the most basic and contains no specularity. As it contains so little information for the user to control, it renders faster and consumes the least amount of your computer's performance capabilities.

The Double, TriShader, and QuadShader materials have more than one channel (2, 3, and 4, respectively), which allows you to create complex combinations of material effects. The Toy

FIGURE 12-1: THE QUADSHADER MATERIAL HAS FOUR SHADER CHANNELS: S1-S4.

Plastic material is a highly specular material that reminds me of a pool ball, and is often used as a material for eyeballs or surfaces that need a very high specularity.

The Special Material Family

I use "special" to round up all the materials and shaders that do not fit into any other group. As a rule they are materials with special jobs and properties that would not comfortably fit into another group. One special material is the Bump Viewer material, which allows the user to paint a bump map and view it in real time on a model. Although ZBrush 3 allows truly massive polygon counts, the Bump Viewer is still useful when you actually manage to use up every available polygon for a model and still need more detail. It is worth remembering though that the amount of detail a bump map will be able to show isn't dependent on the Bump Viewer material but rather on the texture that you convert it to. If it is not of sufficient size, the fine details will be lost. It can be combined in one of the channels of another material, such as the TriShader material.

The materials in the special family are materials that you may only use occasionally and won't be ones you will use every day.

MatCap Materials

The MatCap is one of the features of ZBrush 3 with the biggest "oooh" factor. A MatCap is a very special material type that allows high-quality real-time shadows and shading.

A MatCap is based on an image map that contains the shading and lighting information that ZBrush then uses to interpret into the real-time effect in the viewport. This means that the lighting is baked in, and when used alongside normal lighting can give unexpected results (and some pleasant surprises as well). Some users have found that a pleasing effect can be achieved by making the active light setup duplicate the lighting baked into the MatCap. This means that should you be using multiple materials in your scene along with a MatCap, the shading will remain constant throughout. Great care should be taken if you are using more than one MatCap in your scene, however, as the lighting information baked into each MatCap may be entirely different and make your scene look "off."

MatCaps can be made either with the built-in MatCap tool in ZBrush or by hand. Many users render out an image of a sphere using a render engine in another application such as Maya or 3ds Max and then use this as the MatCap image once cropped to size.

The greatest advantage to MatCap materials is that since the lighting is already effectively set up (baked into the material), you do not need to mess with all the numerical sliders as you do when using materials from the Standard family. And since you can capture the surface color and reflections into a MatCap, you can blend the model nicely into a background photo. We'll cover making your own MatCaps in a moment.

The Fiber Material

The Fiber Material is a special material used to simulate fibers/hairs, etc., and can only be used in 2.5D. These "hairs" are drawn along the surface normals by default, although this can be adjusted in the material's settings.

Rolling Your Own MatCaps in ZBrush

In this section I cover two different ways of making your own MatCap material, the first of which is the "traditional" way using just a photograph and the MatCap tool in ZBrush. So first of all before continuing I would advise you to go hunting for a photo of something you would like to duplicate as a MatCap. You can use a photo from an online site that provides royalty-free use or a photograph you've taken. My preference is to use my own photos because they give me far more control over both the image and the eventual MatCap.

The MatCap tool works by sampling a number of points that are then used to generate the MatCap image and hence the MatCap itself. The more samples we take, the more accurate the final MatCap will be. You will find by trial and error that the images that make the best sources for MatCaps have a few large round surfaces, as these are far easier to capture. Each sample we take will define a surface normal and color information, so by using a number of these we build up a complex (and hopefully accurate) copy of the surface we want to replicate from our photograph. How accurate it turns out depends on the complexity of the surface as well as how much time and practice you are prepared to put into making your MatCap.

Make sure that your reference photo captures the lighting from all angles (or as many as possible), as this also will give a much better effect in the end, and that the surface color is uniform and not patterned. Your source image can be lit in any way by any number of lights of various colors and this will all be captured into your final MatCap. So let's move onward and capture our first MatCap material.

Making Our First MatCap

First make sure that you have the Flat Shader material active and then import your source image. If you have any other material selected it will instead colorize and change the reference image, so this is a very important step. We are now going to load the MatCap tool and sample a number of surface points to gain the surface normal and color information before adding the specularity we need to our MatCap. So select the MatCap tool from the Tool palette and we are ready to roll.

With your MatCap tool active, select an existing MatCap material to modify such as Red Wax or MatCap White. You are now going to left-click and drag on the image in the direction the surface normal is facing. Remember that a surface normal is best imagined as a short line pointing perpendicularly from the center of an imaginary square outward. For every point you sample, make sure that the surface direction arrow is pointing in the right direction. How many samples you need depends on how complex the lighting and shading is on the surface you are trying to replicate. So make a number of points, making sure that all surface directions are covered. Notice that the light ball that appears each time you take a sample will start to build up. Keep doing this until you are happy with the initial shading result. Should you need to edit a sampled point, simply move your cursor over the marked normal and then click and drag it as needed.

Now at this stage it will not have any specularity at all and we will need to add this in. To add specular highlights, first decide from what direction the light is coming and where the specular highlight will be. Set a sample from this point out toward where the light would be coming from, but do not let go yet. If you hold down the Ctrl key and drag out and around, you will be able to easily set the specularity that you require. Remember to keep your eye on the light ball as you do this to get good visual feedback on what it is looking like.

To fine-tune your MatCap there are a number of special controls at the bottom of the Material palette that only work when making a MatCap. A good tip is to copy your source image into Photoshop so that you have two versions side by side. If you darken one, you can press the B button and define the secondary MatCap to make the surface you are copying even more believable. The other controls are pretty self-explanatory. Once you are finished and happy with your new MatCap, save it by clicking the Save button at the top of the Material palette and put it in a safe place for later use.

Making MatCaps Externally

There are many ways ways to make a MatCap image for use in a MatCap material. You can use any image of a sphere for your MatCap texture if it is correctly cropped. The most common workflow for producing a MatCap texture externally is to render out a sphere in the application of your choice with a good lighting setup. The sphere can then be cropped to size in Photoshop and imported as the texture. The advantage of this is that you can get some fantastic MatCaps very easily if you are familiar with your application and render engine. Yet another way is to hand paint (or modify) in Photoshop an image of a ball. You can even take an image from an external application and use the Dodge and Burn tools to add some highlights and shadows where you want them.

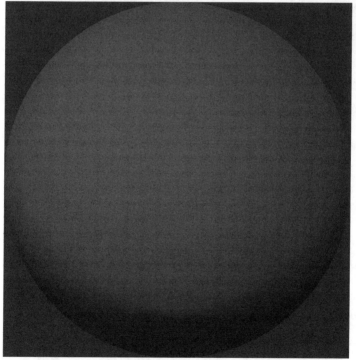

FIGURE 12-2

FIGURE 12-3

FIGURE 12-4

If using an external application to generate your MatCap images, it is best to make the renders/textures at least 1024 pixels to maintain quality and to save as a PSD or BMP and not as a JPEG, which is a lossy format and can produce noise in your MatCap that can ruin its look. Once you have your image, simply import it into ZBrush and, with a MatCap selected, click on the texture image and change it to the one you have just imported. You can now play around with the settings in your MatCap to get something interesting that you like. If you use two sphere images side by side, the one on the right will be used as the cavity shading information in your MatCap, as shown in Figure 12-5.

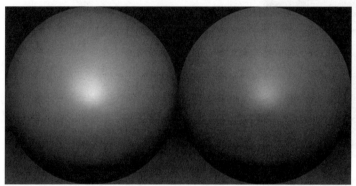

FIGURE 12-5

You can tweak any MatCap you have currently selected in ZBrush by opening the Modifiers section of your Material palette. As shown in Figure 12-6, you will see a number of options that enable you to modify how the MatCap is displayed in the viewport. Let's work through them one by one to get a feel for what they do.

FIGURE 12-6

Opacity

The Opacity setting controls the visibility of the MatCap shading effect itself. When turned up to 100, the MatCap shading effect is fully visible, and when turned to 0, no MatCap shading effect is shown at all. As a general rule, this is normally set to 100.

Cavity Detection

The Cavity Detection setting controls how mildly or aggressively the cavity shading effect is detected for later use by the MatCap. It uses the A and B settings along with the Cavity Transition setting to control the way in which the cavity shading effect is shown in the viewport for any object with the selected MatCap applied to it.

Cavity shading often helps to bring out the details in a digital sculpt, although you should not rely too heavily on the cavity effect to produce your texture because it is difficult to reproduce in other applications.

Cavity Transition

Cavity Transition controls how sharply or softly the actual cavity shading effect is. It can make a great deal of difference to the look of a MatCap and small changes can give quite different looks on some MatCaps.

Intensity A/B

The Intensity settings are basically brightness controls for the A and B channels, where channel A controls the non-cavity areas, and B is in charge of those areas that are detected as cavities for cavity shading. These settings allow you to get some great balances to reproduce a range of surfaces from the lighter cavity areas of marble to the darker areas of extremely coarse surfaces. The slider goes from 0 to 5, and small changes can have a big effect.

Monochromatic A/B

These settings desaturate the color of your A or B channel. When turned all the way up, it effectively turns that channel's color information into a black and white (or gray) version. This can be of use if you find, for example, that the cavity on your MatCap is a bit too brightly colored to be believable. These settings can be set from 0 to 100.

Depth A/B

In a similar way that the Intensity sliders control the A and B channels to determine how bright the surface is, the Depth sliders control depth information whether it is raised or recessed. Use Depth to make raised areas look higher or make recessed areas look lower.

These sliders can have a variety of effects depending on the MatCap in use at the time. It can affect not just the depth information but also the specular highlights, ambient occlusion, lighting direction, and much more.

Colorize

You can affect the coloring of a MatCap by using this slider along with the Col color chip below that you can use to add a color. This setting ranges from –1 to 1; when set to –1 it will colorize the surface facing toward you, and when set to 1 it will colorize the faces facing away from you. With a setting of 1 it is possible to approximate a rim lighting effect.

Base Color Chip

At the bottom of the panel are four color chips. The first one on the left is the base color. This acts as a color filter to offset the color. For example, if you have a green shader and you put a color of green into this color chip, it would turn your MatCap white.

To add a color to any color chip, use your color selector to pick a color, then simply left-click on the color chip that you wish to add this color to. Color chips can be used only for colors and not textures, and you can change or edit a color in a color chip by simply reselecting a color and adding it again.

A/B Color Chips

Use these chips to add a color to either of these two channels, with B being the cavity shading channel. This can then be balanced using the Intensity slider to fine-tune the effect that you want.

Col Color Chip

Use the Col color chip in conjunction with the Colorize slider, as described above.

Material Texture

If you are generating a MatCap using an external program, this is the place where we would select our custom texture to import for use as a MatCap. Two types of textures can be used in this slot depending on the type of effect needed. If you browse some of the existing MatCaps that ship with ZBrush, you will notice that while some use only one sphere texture, others use two. Those that use one sphere as a texture map create "normal" cavity shading. Those that use two spheres create a MatCap style cavity shading effect.

When making custom image maps for this use in an external application, I strongly suggest making a template in Photoshop to save you some work each time. Also make the spheres a tiny bit bigger than you think you will need to. If they are too small, it will affect the MatCap's shading effect in a negative way by adding some of the "non-sphere" part of the texture as part of the MatCap shading effect.

Capturing a MatCap Texture

In this section I'll show you how you can export the texture used by a MatCap so that you can change it or do post work in Photoshop on it. This is a wonderful workaround that I have to thank Ryan Kingslien for.

It enables you to not only export the materials for a MatCap but also export the combined double sphere images used in MatCaps as well.

First make your canvas size pretty big to help with antialiasing, then drop a nice smooth subdivided polysphere onto your canvas. (I subdivided mine about six times to get it lovely and smooth.) Center the sphere and make it as large as you can without letting it go off the edges of the viewport. Pick a MatCap for this smooth polysphere. Now we need to drop out of Edit mode to do the next parts of this workflow, so uncheck the Edit button. You now have access to the 2.5D tools that are hidden in 3D mode.

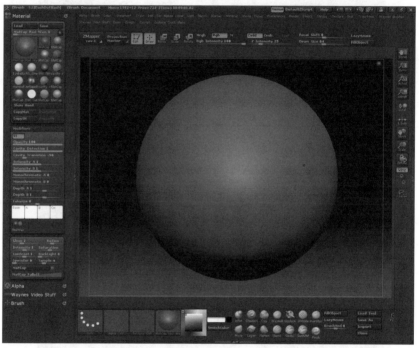

FIGURE 12-7

Choose the MRGBZ Grabber and drag it across the entire canvas. The tool's default setting will crop the canvas tightly around any object, so it will crop very tightly and perfectly around your sphere and produce a texture of it. (You can ignore the alpha it also produces.) If the MatCap only has a single sphere texture, you are done. If it has a twin sphere texture, then continue on.

FIGURE 12-8

FIGURE 12-9

For twin sphere MatCaps, repeat what you have just done, making sure that Intensity A is set to 1 and Intensity B is set to 0. Then adjust the settings so that Intensity A is now set to 0 and Intensity B is set to 1. Make sure that the first texture you just captured is active, hold down the **Ctrl** key, and capture this second version again. This will add it beside the first one to give you a perfect twin MatCap.

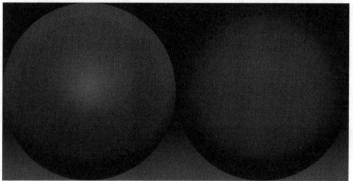

FIGURE 12-10

So apart from allowing you to do post work and even use compositing tricks on your MatCaps, what else can you use this for? Well, let's say that you have a MatCap that you always end up tweaking the same way and want to save yourself the bother of going through this time and time again. Simply capture the twin MatCaps as described above, only this time adjust the settings for the A and B channels accordingly.

Geometry Projection in ZBrush

In this section I will outline a few ways to project geometry onto another mesh within ZBrush. In addition to the ZProject brush, we also have a number of other options available to us, such as the ability to project one subtool onto another one within the SubTool section of the Tool palettte. This is without a doubt the easiest way to project geometry from a high-detail mesh on to another mesh. For example, if you wanted to sculpt a head separately from the rest of the model, you could then use that head on other models. Actually this workflow of sculpting a number of options for each body part frees up our pipeline and gives us a lot of options to be creative.

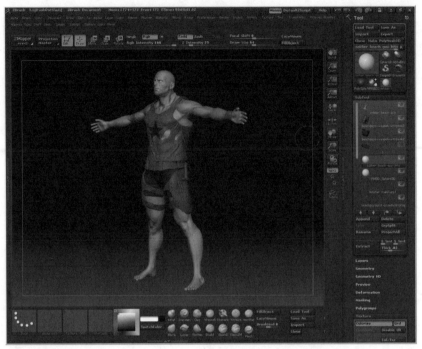

FIGURE 12-11

Sculpting in separate body parts also allows us to use much higher polygon counts than we otherwise could, and lets us sculpt in much more detail. So this is another method of optimizing your pipeline.

Using Subtools

Projecting geometry using subtools is rather simple. All you have to do is simply use mesh extraction on your main mesh as deeply as needed. Then if we press the **3D Project** button, this will combine both subtools into one mesh. This makes things much simpler when it comes to generating normal maps, as it is always easier dealing with one mesh as opposed to many. This allows us to use one UV set for all texturing for the entire model.

FIGURE 12-12

13 Hard Surface Sculpting: The Door of Secrets

Sculpting hard surface models in ZBrush has recently become quite popular, although people seem to think that it is much harder than it actually is. In fact, once you've finished sculpting the surface door in this chapter and the Guardian's weapon in Chapter 14, you may find it a little too easy. I've tried to cram in as many sculpting techniques as possible into this and the next chapter so that you can see how each works and decide which methods you prefer.

Sculpting hard surfaces is totally unlike organic modeling in just about every way. While organics are all about form and anatomy, hard surface sculpting is about hard edges and regularity. I'll also point out some common pitfalls for those wanting to use hard surface sculpts as the high-resolution model for a normal mapped, game-friendly version. While we will be using ZBrush for the entire sculpting stage and map generation, later on we will do the actual texture work in Photoshop over our UV layout. Although I won't be covering this in depth, I will explain what was done and why. I prefer to use Photoshop for hard surface texturing because it is simply a lot easier to line up textures to your hard surface UV map than it is to align the same thing in ZBrush. This isn't to say it can't be done, but this is the way that I prefer to work.

For this project we will use a very simple base mesh that I created in about three minutes in Silo 2. (Actually, it's just a thin rectangular box with a few edge loops added to it.) I'll explain in a moment why I added some edge loops but not others. You're probably quite capable of making your own base mesh, but feel free to use the one on the companion DVD.

The Door Base Mesh

This is probably the simplest base mesh ever put into a book on 3D. We don't actually need anything more complex because we want to add the detail ourselves in ZBrush. Let me explain why I added some edges onto the rectangle I used for the door and didn't approach it a different way.

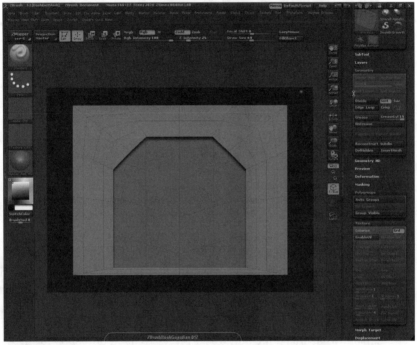

FIGURE 13-1

You will notice that while I have added some vertical edge loops for the door and have indeed kept it symmetrical, the horizontal actually come to a point in the center of each loop. The reason for this is that when doing hard surface sculpting in ZBrush, we can add details only where the flow leads. While you can sometimes get away with going against the polygon flow while sculpting a human, animal, or monster, if you try to go where the flow isn't heading when dealing with hard surfaces, you will end up with jagged edges and have to subdivide to crazy levels to keep it looking even remotely clean. If I had made all the edge loops simple horizontals and verticals, we would have been walled into a very simple, regimented design that wouldn't be terribly interesting. I wanted to make a design that would have a little more visual appeal so I

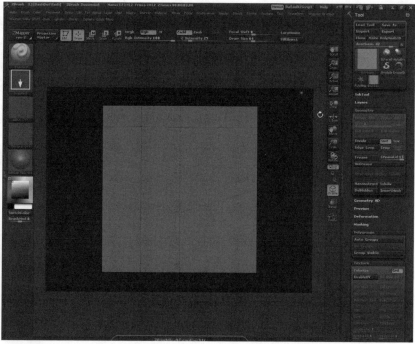

FIGURE 13-2

decided early on to make the horizontal edge loops come to a point in the center between where the left and right doors will eventually meet.

As we will not be using this base mesh for our low-resolution one but rather an even simpler one, I haven't UV'ed it at all. We may add some simple AUV tile UVs if we need to for texturing purposes, but those will be to help with our workflow and not to generate maps from.

Sculpting the Door

So the time has come to attempt what may well be your first hard surface sculpt. It's not as scary as you may expect, and the door you will see at the end took only about six or seven minutes to sculpt from the base mesh. (So if you include a couple of minutes to make the base mesh itself, the whole thing took less than 10 minutes.) For this example I wanted to use a simple design so we can concentrate more on the techniques used.

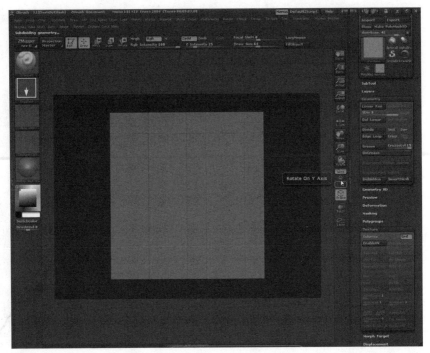

FIGURE 13-3

Before we do any sculpting we first need to subdivide our base
mesh, but if we simply start to subdivide now the mesh would become
rounded and end up looking nothing like we need it to. So how do we
get around this?

First, open up your Tool palette and go to the Geometry section.
This is where after importing your base mesh OBJ file (by using the
Import button at the top of the Tool palette), you would normally subdivide your model to give you enough polygons to work on. For this
project, though, before we subdivide I want you to uncheck the **SMT**
button. When SMT is switched on, it smoothes your model each time it
is subdivided. Since we don't want smoothing at a low level, we switch
it off. Now press the **Divide** button twice so that your base mesh is now
at subdivision level 3.

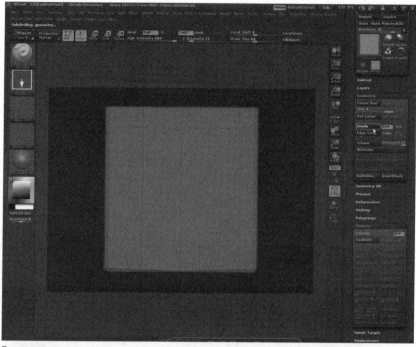

FIGURE 13-4

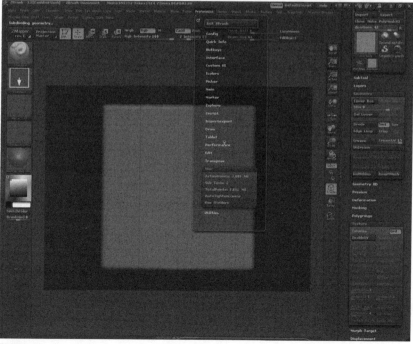

FIGURE 13-5

Now for the magic part, switch the **SMT** button back on and subdivide a few more times until your polygon count is between 1.5 million and 4 million. This will smooth off the geometry a bit and give us some nice rounded edges. We don't actually have to have them for this particular hard surface sculpt, but for most hard surface sculptures of your own you will. To be honest though, this isn't subdivision as we know it but rather tessellation. Now that we have enough polygons to sculpt with, we can start to work on things.

What we are going to do now is use ZAppLink to produce a very simple texture for our model that we will use to mask off certain areas. This will enable us to nail down our larger forms of hard surface sculpting before adding some smaller details. But before we exit to ZAppLink I would like you to ensure that Perspective mode is turned off from the Draw palette. I find that it makes more sense when dealing with hard surface mechanical things to deal with them in Orthographic mode, as an engineer would. Switch on your Polyframe as we are going to need this as a reference for our edge flow. Once you've done this, go to your Document palette and press the ZAppLink button, which will open your model in Photoshop with the screen print split into layers.

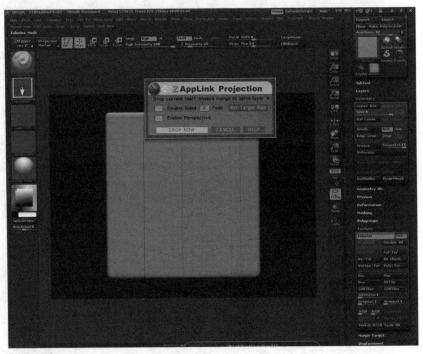

FIGURE 13-6

With Photoshop open I would like you to first create a new layer between Layer 1 and the top layer. Once we are done, we will merge this layer down onto Layer1 before saving and closing it.

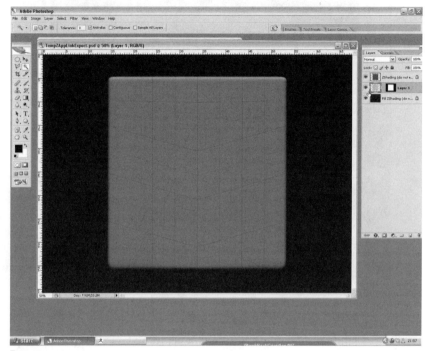

FIGURE 13-7

You should now have your layers set up from the bottom to top as follows. At the bottom is the Fill Shading layer, which we do not touch. Above this is Layer 1 where eventually all our texture color will be. Layer 2 is above this and where we are going to do our work before merging it down. Finally, at the top of the layer stack is the ZShading layer.

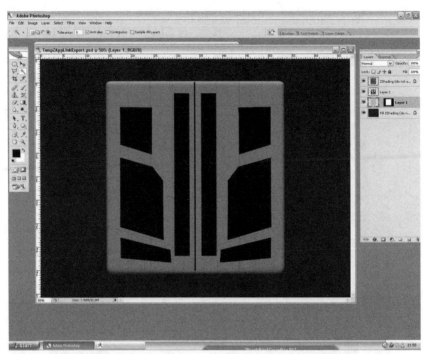

FIGURE 13-8

Using the Polygon Lasso tool, start to make some geometric patterns on the right-hand side of Layer 2. What we are painting now is the color that we will later use in ZBrush as a mask on the model. The golden rule for this, and the reason that we turned on Polyframe before using ZAppLink is that we need information about how the polygons flow so that we keep our detail as tight as possible to the flow. If you look at the pattern I made you'll notice it follows the polygon edge flow exactly, so I know that it will give us good deformations. We need to keep our design to large shapes for the moment as we will be adding the smaller parts of the hard surface design using ZBrush later.

When selecting an area using the Polygon Lasso tool, remember that you can add to a selection by holding the Shift key down, and remove an area by holding down Shift+Alt. Once you have your shapes, fill them on Layer 2 with a solid black color. Remember that since the design is symmetrical, you can duplicate the layer and mirror it over to save time. Notice that at this point these would work not very well as masks because the edges are simply too sharp. For ZBrush to mask the way we need it to we do need a very small amount of blurring on the edges to give us a slight bevel, as shown in Figure 13-9. Let me explain why.

When you are using a normal map, it cannot reflect a perfectly vertical surface change; you must have at least a slight bevel or slant to it for it to be able to work well visually. So as a result, all our details will have this slight bevel (some more than others) to help with our normal map later. Sculpting and designing with normal maps in mind is fairly easy once you know its rules. Another rule is that while a normal map can easily fake the look of protruding geometry, it is often best to restrict this for areas that are not going to be seen in profile. Our door will have lots of inset detail and only a small amount of protruding detail that we'll place toward the center where it won't be seen on an angle.

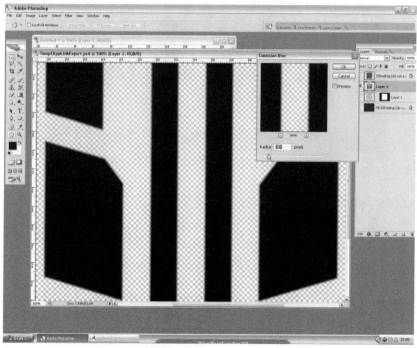

FIGURE 13-9

So now that you understand why we are going for a slightly blurred mask, go to **Filter > Gaussian Blur** and set the Radius to **2** pixels for Layer 2 where our black areas are. This slight blurring will be reflected in our mask in the same way and so the geometry will have a slight bevel as a result. Once you have done this, select Layer 2 and go to **Layer > Merge** to merge it downward to Layer 1. At this point Photoship will ask if you wish to apply the underlying layer's mask before merging. Reply yes to this, then save and close Photoshop and go back to ZBrush.

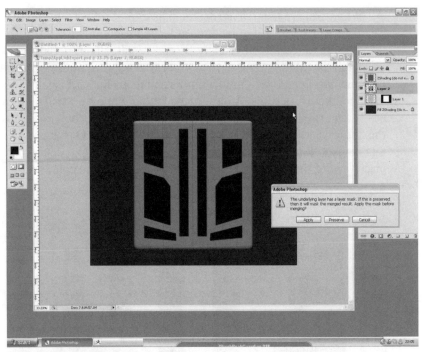

FIGURE 13-10

FIGURE 13-10

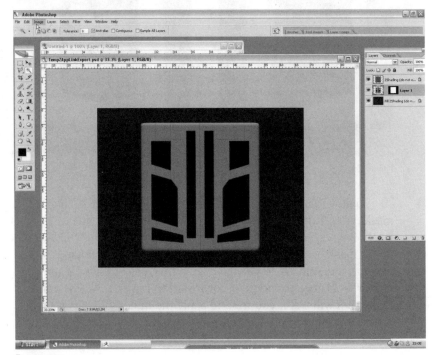

FIGURE 13-11

Back in ZBrush, accept the changes. Once you are done, you should have the black and white design on your model applied as polypaint. Go now to the **Masking** section of the **Tool** palette and press **Mask By Intensity**. This will take your polypainted design and convert the black areas into masked areas. Invert this using the **Inverse** button and then scroll down to the **Texture** section and disable the texture to see things better using the **Colorize** button.

FIGURE 13-12

FIGURE 13-13

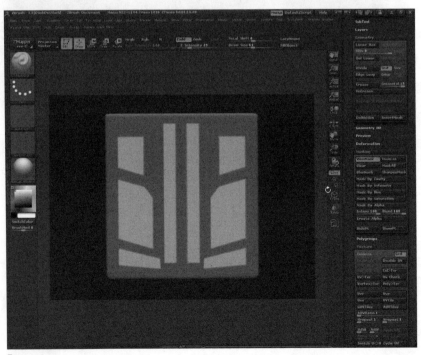

FIGURE 13-14

Now remove the unmasked areas in the center of the design by **Ctrl+dragging** a mask over the center sections, leaving us with just the designs at either side. We do this because we will treat each of the sections in a slightly different way. With just these three box shapes on either side left unmasked, open up the Deformation section of the Tool palette and set Inflate to –35. This will pull these sections backward a bit. If the edges look a little rough, simply take a very light Smooth brush at a small size and run it round those edges to smooth things out a little. Remove your mask again and then do another **Mask By Intensity** after temporarily enabling **Colorize** before you reapply the mask. This time add it over the two side designs of three panels each.

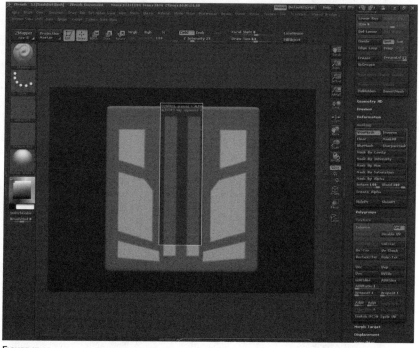

FIGURE 13-15

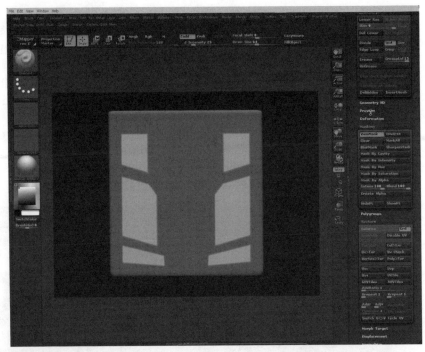

FIGURE 13-16

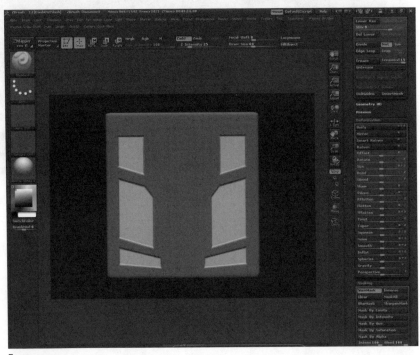

FIGURE 13-17

Now let's use a different technique in order to create some outset areas.

We create the two lines that protrude near the center by using our **Layer** brush set to a **ZIntensity** of **25** and make one continuous stroke until both sides that are unmasked are covered as shown. Then invert this mask and smooth off any jagged edges the same way you did before.

FIGURE 13-18

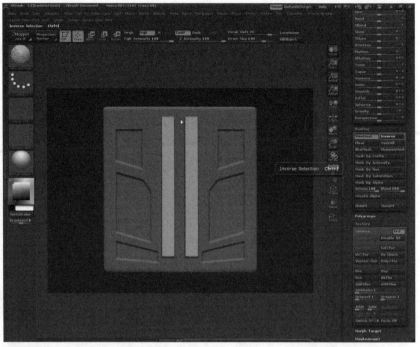

FIGURE 13-19

We still need to add the seam for the center where the two doors meet. So mask off the whole door first, then remove most of the mask from each side, leaving just a thin line in the center that is masked. Invert this mask before using your **Layer brush** set to **Zsub** with a **ZIntensity** of **13** to create a groove where the two doors meet.

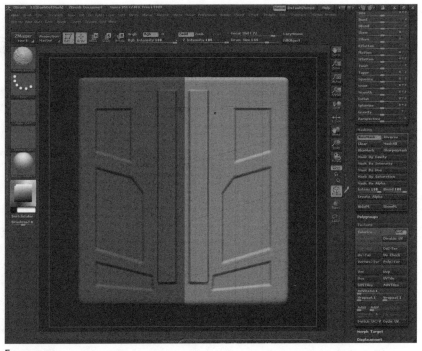

FIGURE 13-20

FIGURE 13-21

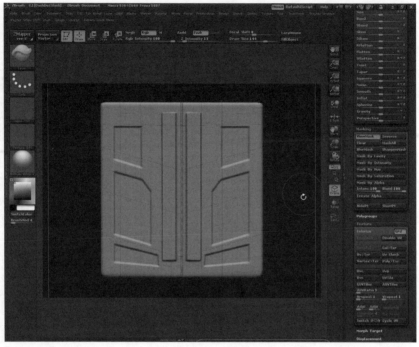

We now have the basic forms of our hard surface blocked in and ready to detail. Simple, wasn't it? Actually, these techniques make all hard surface sculpting just as simple. It's one of those things that just looks complex.

Adding the Small Details

When it comes time to add the small details, you can either approach it as I do here (if it's a simple design like this one), or use the Projection Master method outlined in Chapter 14 if it's more complex. The majority of the details will be added with a simple combination of the hard-edged circle Alpha (number 35), the Layer brush set to a **ZIntensity** of **13**, and the **DragDot** stroke type. As we are going for a very bold design and this door is supposed to look old and solid, I didn't want to go over the top with details.

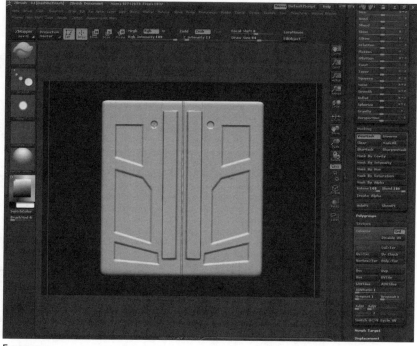

FIGURE 13-23

First we will add the four recessed circles near the top and center of the door by setting the Layer brush to **Zsub** and using the **DragDot** stroke to drag each one into position. (Symmetry is enabled of course, meaning we only have to work on one half.) While I did this by eye, feel free to use Projection Master for this and the other details if you have any problems.

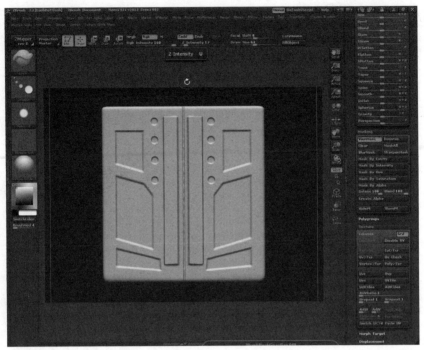

FIGURE 13-24

Set your Layer brush to **Zadd** and make the brush size a bit smaller before adding the rivets to each recessed panel on the door. Now keeping your brush size exactly the same, use your Zadd to add a rivet in the center of each of the four recessed circles we made near the top and center of the door to make them look a bit more special. Although this is a simple example to show you how to sculpt hard surfaces, this technique can also be used to make very complex designs.

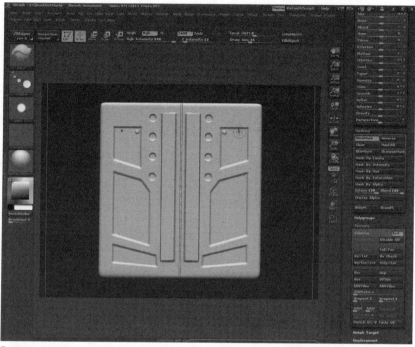

FIGURE 13-25

FIGURE 13-26

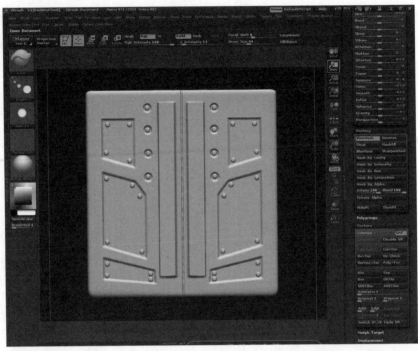

FIGURE 13-27

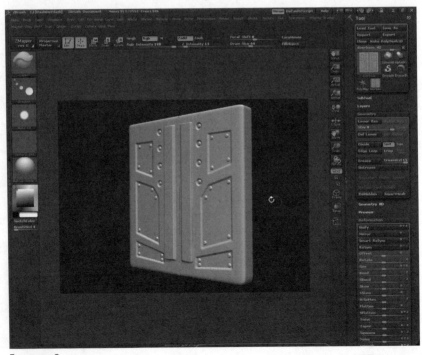

FIGURE 13-28

With that, our sculpting is done. Next, we'll apply the surface damage by using a bump map created from a texture and a specular map also created from the texture map mixed with a cavity map that we'll create in a moment.

Creating the Textures and Maps for the Door

Before we start, I must point out that creating a good set of UVs in an application outside of ZBrush is essential to the way I am going to work. We discussed UV generation in Chapter 3, so reread those sections if you need a refresher. Make sure, though, that you understand UVs and can paint over them in Photoshop where I do the majority of my hard surface texturing. I suggest that you avoid the automatically generated types of UVs in any program as there is a certain amount of control you gain by doing it yourself.

The Color/Diffuse Texture

For the doors I used a scratched metal texture I found on www.imageafter.com. In Photoshop make your metal texture fit your UV map as best you can. As only the front of the door will be seen, this is easy to do by just scaling it to size in the right position. Now find a grungy texture that you can overlay on top of this to add a bit more complexity to your texture. Set it on a layer above your metal texture and play around with the blending models for the layer. (Mine is set to Multiply and turned down to about 40%.)

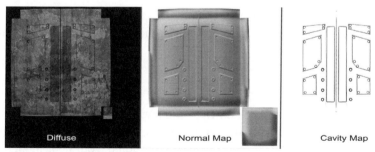

FIGURE 13-29

Now use ZMapper on your lowest subdivision level and generate a cavity map. You can then lay this over the top of the other layers in Photoshop with the layer blending mode set to **Multiply** and bring its opacity back to a point you like. You may also want to apply a Gaussian Blur filter (**Filter > Gaussian Blur**) to it to help the edges blend nicely into the rest of the texture. That's your diffuse texture done, so let's start to turn this into the other map types.

Specular Level Map

Merge all your layers in Photoshop and desaturate them. (On the PC this can be done by pressing **Shift+Ctrl+U** or by using the **Hue/Saturation** controls under the **Layer > Adjustments** menu.) Bring the brightness up or down using the Brightness/Contrast controls (found in the same menu as the Hue/Saturation controls) until the main shades of gray look like a "middle gray" you would get with an RGB setting of 127, 127, 127.

You can then use your Dodge and Burn tools to darken or brighten any areas that you feel need it before saving out your specular level map.

Specular Color Map

This time we will start with the specular level map you just made and turn it into a specular color map. While a specular level map tells a render engine how much specularity to give to each point of your texture, a specular color map tells it what color to reflect. Many people get confused about the two types and seem at a loss how to create a specular color map. For mine I simply chose two colors (a bluish color and a mustard) and painted them in a layer above the specular level with the Opacity turned down a bit and the layer type set to Multiply. Yes, it's as simple as that!

Use whatever colors you wish to be reflected on a surface. You can also map an image to use as a specular reflection for a great material effect at render time.

Normal Map

Back in ZBrush, step back down to the lowest subdivision level of your model, go to the **Morph Target** section of your **Tool** palette, and press **StoreMT**. Now import the UV mapped version of your door model, go back to the **Morph Target** section, press **Switch**, and then delete the morph target altogether. This will allow you to import your UVs without changing anything physically in your sculpt.

Open up **ZMapper** now and choose the preset for the software that you will be using to render out in. For me it was 3ds Max, so I opened up the best quality Tangent Space preset. Turn the samples up a notch to get a better quality map (although this will take a bit longer for map generation time as a result). Now press the **Normal Map** button to generate your normal map, then press the **Escape** key to exit back to ZBrush and export it.

We covered ZMapper in great detail in Chapter 8, so if any part of this workflow is giving you problems, feel free to consult it. You should now have all your map types ready for render for the Door of Secrets.

14 Hard Surface Sculpting: The Guardian's Weapon

About the Workflow

In our first hard surface sculpting project, the Door of Secrets, I showed you a workflow that involved painting textures for use as masks in Photoshop using ZAppLink to help with the hard surface detailing. This time I'm going to show you another way that only limits your hard surface sculpting detail to your polygon count. This time we'll be making use of Projection Master to give us some very sharp, hard surface details easily. As with the hard surface door for the Guardian project, this isn't as hard to do as it may appear to be when first looking at the image.

For this project I first did three rough versions, then I took the strongest points of each design and combined them into a final design for the hard surface sculpture. The polygon count I use for this weapon should be easily handled on most modern PCs, and should you feel the need to, it can be increased further by the use of HD geometry. Just remember that at the time of writing, there is no way to export a normal or displacement map for a sculpt that makes use of HD geometry.

As our final sculpt must be next-gen game friendly and look good when we render it out with normal maps, this will affect the way that we detail our model. So while some of my three rough versions had good details from a design point of view, other details would not be suitable for use with a normal mapped low-resolution model and had to be adjusted accordingly. Remember that if the silhouette of your model does not support the details, then it will not look right. To make the best use of normal maps, we need to restrict detail to be inset or raised only slightly above the surface.

I subdivided the base mesh I created in Silo before export to ZBrush because it is always good practice to have even distribution of polygons on your base mesh. Aim for each polygon to have a square shape as opposed to rectangular. Long rectangular-shaped polygons are much harder to sculpt on. So an easy way to do this is to simply subdivide it before export. This does multiply the polygon count by a factor of four as with any subdivision.

Sculpting the Weapon

Import the base mesh into ZBrush by using the **Import** button at the top of the Tool palette. The base mesh is available on the companion DVD. (It's already UV'ed and comes with all the support files needed to follow along with this project.) As the base mesh is composed of a number of separate pieces, we can use this to help us split the model into easy-to-handle parts. So scroll down the Tool palette to the **Polygroups** section and hit the **Auto Groups** button. This will place each separate part of the base mesh into its own polygon group.

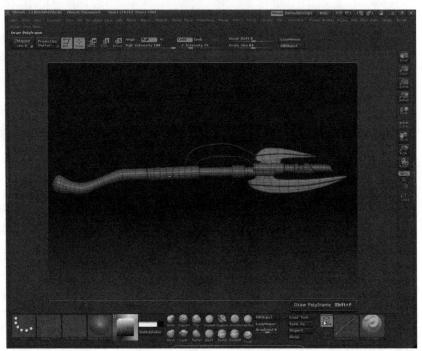

FIGURE 14-1

It's now time to add the subdivision levels that we need so we'll have enough geometry to comfortably sculpt the hard surface details on the model. So from the **Geometry** section of the Tool palette, press the **Divide** button until you reach level 6. (This will give us about 4.5 million polygons to work on.) Let's split the mesh into a different subtool for each polygroup on the model by first stepping down to level 1 and then opening the **SubTool** section. Pressing the **GrpSplit** button splits it into subtools with one subtool per polygroup.

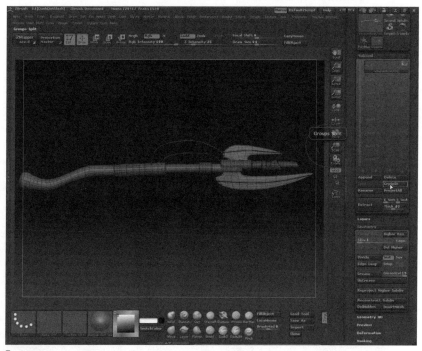

Figure 14-2

Now that your model is split into a separate subtool for each color of your polygroup, you can click on the eye next to the currently active subtool (part of the gun barrel) to make all the other subtools invisible. It helps to only have what we need visible in the viewport at any one time. It also allows us to concentrate on each part as a separate item design wise. So that everyone starts at the same level we will use only the default alphas that ship with ZBrush. This will give you confidence enough to later expand upon this workflow with custom alphas in your own hard surface sculptures.

With your first subtool active and all alone in the viewport, take it up to its highest subdivision level (level 6) so it's ready to start

326   Part III: Projects

sculpting. Make sure that it is centered and as large as you can make it without protruding past of the edges of the viewport, as you will need the whole model visible for the next part.

Press the **Projection Master** button to enter Projection Master, which allows us to do many things that are impossible, impractical, or just too hard in the standard 3D viewport. Set the following options on and all others off:

> **Double Sided: On**
> **Fade: On**
> **Deformation: On**
> **Normalized: On**

With these settings on, all detail will follow the normals of each polygon, the details will be automatically mirrored to the opposite side of the model, and added details will "fade out" when they reach an edge rather than stop abruptly. This fading effect will give us some really nice effects in a moment.

Figure 14-3

Now let's set up the brush we will use for the sculpting. Change to the **Layer** brush with **Alpha 36** selected (one of the hard-edged circular ones) and the **Line** stroke type. Apart from changes in size and stroke type, this is the only brush you'll use on this model. Changes to the stroke type, ZIntensity, and whether we use Zadd or Zsub will give us all the variety that we need.

First we want to create the ridged areas on the hand grip. Using a Draw Size of **32** and a ZIntensity setting of **25**, draw a line horizontally across the center of the longest part of the subtool. If you hold down the Shift key as well, the stroke will be restrained to horizontal or vertical. Take your Draw Size down to **15** now, and while holding down the **Alt** key, make another horizontal stroke down the center of the last one as shown in Figure 14-5. Now comes one of the things that makes Projection Master so appealing for hard surface sculpting. Go to the Transform menu and press the **Move** button so that you can reposition the last stroke. The move icon does not use action lines, but rather a circle with a cross in the center of it. By holding down the **Shift** key and dragging on an axis, you can restrict movement to that direction. If you click somewhere between the lines of the cross shape, you can freely move your last stroke about. Always remember to step back to Draw mode once you've finished your Move transform.

Note: If you have pressed the Alt key to reverse your stroke, it will be invisible because that is how the Zadd/Zsub buttons are set by default. If that is the case, simply switch to Zsub. In Projection Master the Layer brush's strokes are treated as continuous strokes and hence do not "build up" the geometry.

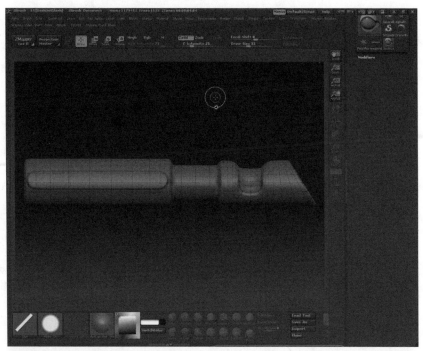

FIGURE 14-4

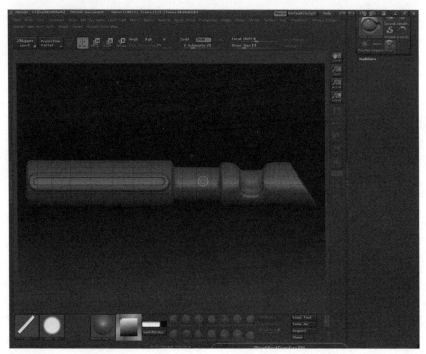

FIGURE 14-5

Move your last stroke if necessary to reposition it properly. We'll add some indentations to the middle section. With your brush set to **Zsub** and a Draw Size of **15**, draw a line across the center of the middle section of the subtool as shown in Figure 14-6 and move it into place using the Move transform tool.

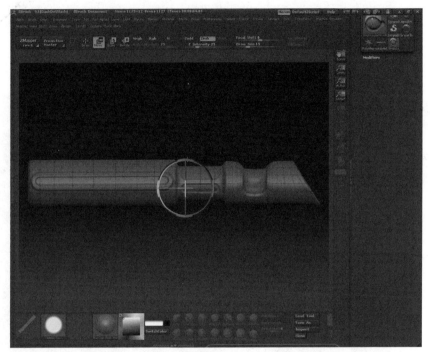

FIGURE 14-6

Now for cool trick number two! In Projection Master you can copy and paste strokes to replicate them. So if you now press **Shift+S** it will duplicate your previous stroke, and by using the Move transform tool you can move this identical stroke into another position on your model. This is a very powerful option for times when you need a lot of identical strokes, such as repeated details on a model in a regular pattern like stripes or a grid of dots. While we are on the subject of "cool Projection Master hard surface tricks," I'll give you one last one. Once you have made a stroke, you can use the [and] hotkeys for stepping up and down the brush size by increments of 10. This allows you to resize a stroke you have made on the fly.

Set your brush to **Zadd** and its size to **9** and make another stroke in the center of each line you have just made. Make use of the Shift+S duplicate trick along with the Move transform here, and remember to

step back into Draw mode again. Now zoom in on your model near the
front portion of the part where it is "scooped." Make a vertical stroke
here at a Draw Size of **10** and move it into position, then duplicate it and
position the second stroke. You should be noticing by now how the
duplicate trick speeds things up considerably. The Move, Rotate, and
Scale transforms can be used to move the strokes that we drew while in
Projection Master. As these last two strokes are drawn from the outside
edge of the model, the part where they reach the very edge of the
model where the opposite side starts will now be faded out according to
the options we set before coming into Projection Master.

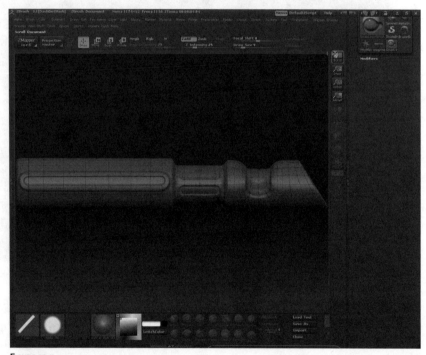

Figure 14-7

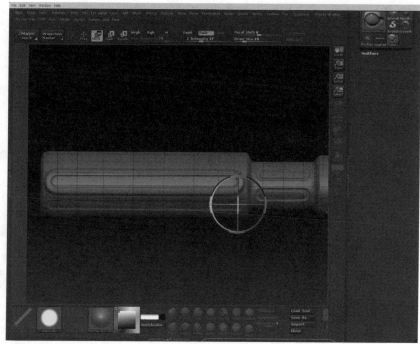

FIGURE 14-8

Using Zsub, set ZIntensity to **37** and draw some horizontal lines on the last part as shown in Figure 14-9. Then scroll back across to the largest section of the subtool again and add a couple of strokes horizontally here as well using the duplicate trick. Now press the Projection Master button again to open the settings and press the **Pickup Now** button to return once again to 3D space.

I changed the MatCap at this point to my favorite, BW film skin, which is provided on the companion DVD. I use this one and a couple of others I keep for sculpting as they help me to read the forms a little better than the default Red Wax MatCap.

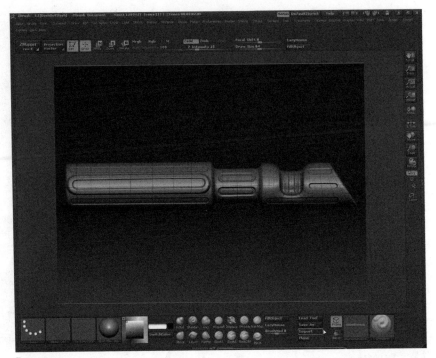

FIGURE 14-9

Now rotate your model so that you can see the top-down view and lock this into place by holding down the **Shift** key when you are nearly at the top. This helps to make sure that once things are mirrored to the opposite side in Projection Master they don't get off center. There's nothing worse than a hard surface sculpt that looks like it was made by a drunken engineer.

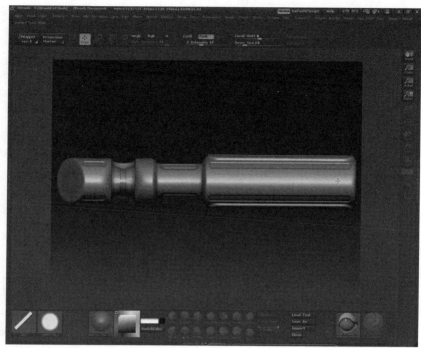

FIGURE 14-10

Enter Projection Master again to add detail to the top and bottom part of this subtool. Draw a line with a Draw Size of **21** and the brush set to **Zsub**, then reset the size to **12** and the brush to **Zadd** and add another stroke in the center. Make use of your Move transform tool as needed from now on in this project.

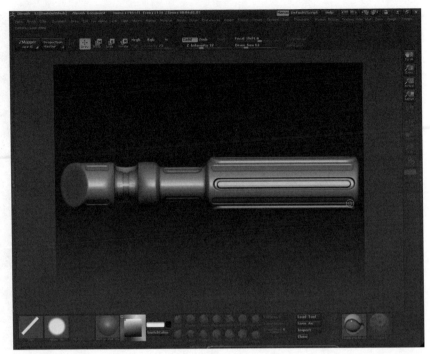

FIGURE 14-11

Now set your brush size to **7** and **Zsub** and add a line in the center of the middle section, then set it to **Zadd** and a Draw Size of **12** and add a stroke in the center of this. Add a line to continue the ones already there on the front section using **Zsub** and a Draw Size of **12**, and then another in the center vertically toward the other side of the notched section. (Use a ZIntensity of **37** for this stroke.) Once you've done this, exit Projection Master and return to 3D space once more. The first part is now finished.

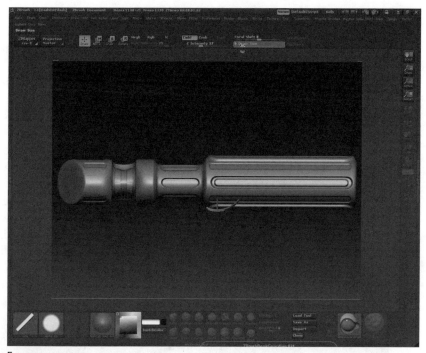

FIGURE 14-12

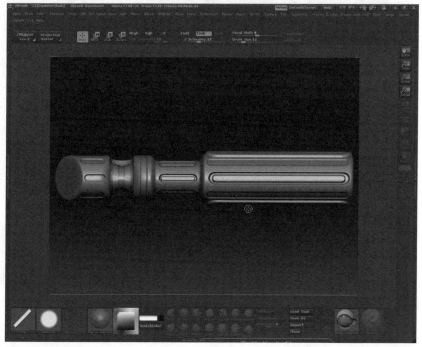

FIGURE 14-13

Since this workflow is basically repeated for the majority of the rest of the parts, I'll just provide you with a series of images for each part so it doesn't become too repetitive to read. I will give information for any parts of the workflow that may be confusing, though.

Now let's move to the next part of the barrel of the gun. (We'll leave the two blades until near the end.) On this particular part we have a polygon count of just a shade less than half a million to work with. Since this isn't a very large part, it should be enough for what we need.

Draw out four wide vertical lines using **Zsub** to start to give the part a bit more interest. Now we are going to change our stroke type to another that's very useful for hard surface sculpting, the **DragDot** stroke. Using this, add a raised dot to each of the "stripes," then use **Zadd** with the Line stroke to draw a short line both above and below each of the round dots that you've just drawn. When you've finished, exit Projection Master. Now switch to a top-down view and go back into Projection Master to add the series of inset dots and the line shown in Figures 14-18 and 14-19. When you're done, once again exit Projection Master. That's our second part sculpted.

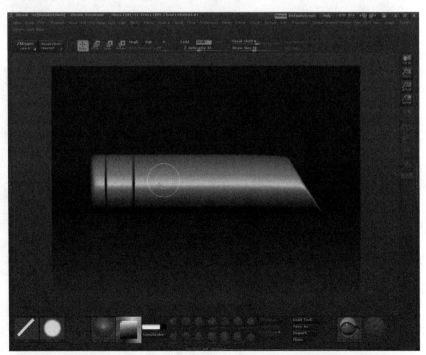

FIGURE 14-14

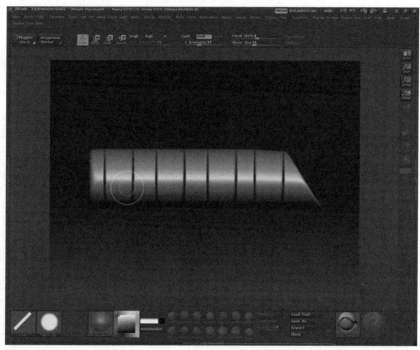

FIGURE 14-15

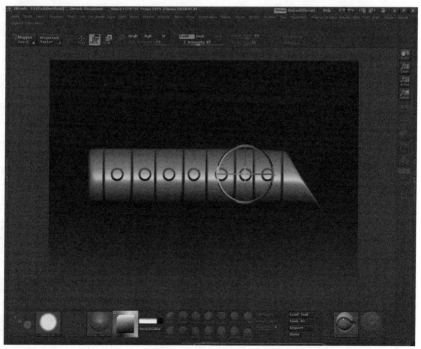

FIGURE 14-16

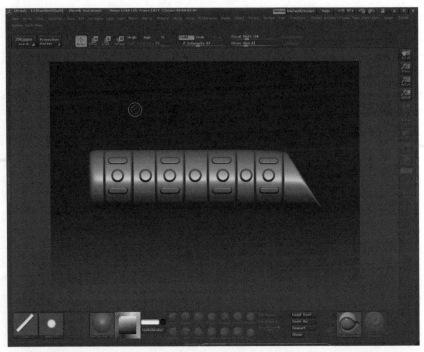

FIGURE 14-17

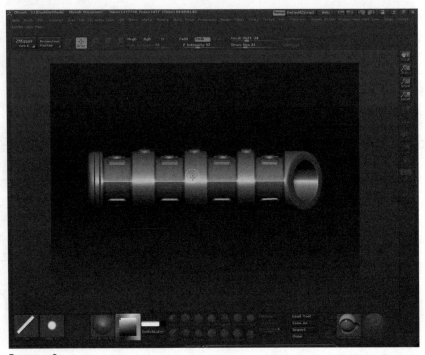

FIGURE 14-18

FIGURE 14-19

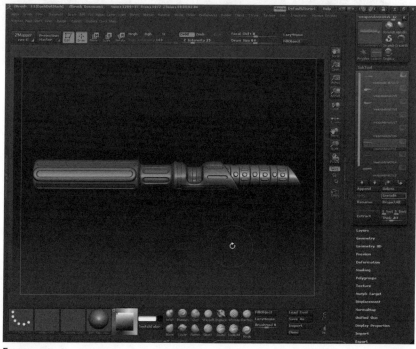

FIGURE 14-20

Now let's move on to the very short cylindrical part. Bring it into Projection Master as usual and add the three indented lines shown in Figure 14-22. Then add some thinner Zsub lines in the raised areas between the lines you have just sculpted as shown in Figure 14-23. That's the easiest part so far.

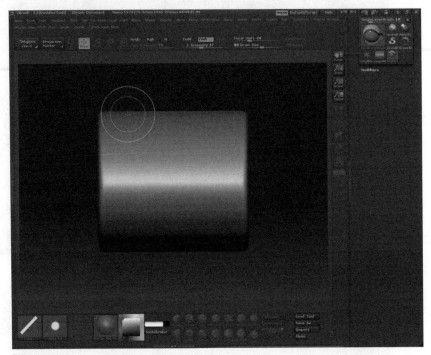

FIGURE 14-21

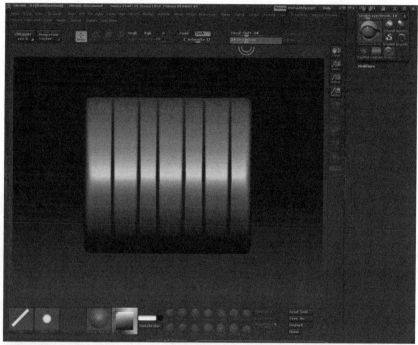

FIGURE 14-22

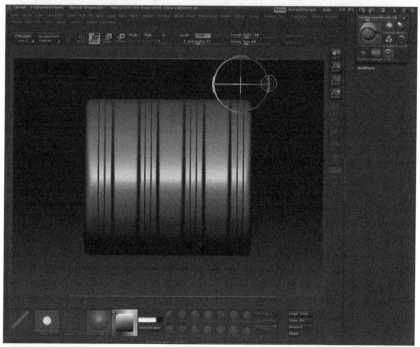

FIGURE 14-23

Now we can work on the shorter of the two blades. Again, take it to its highest subdivision level, and then open it in Projection Master for detailing. The one difference this time is to make sure that you have the central main gun part visible as well. This is because we want to check that we do not screw up the intersecting geometry with detail that won't look right. Draw in the lines shown in Figures 14-25 and 14-26, then add the two Zadd dots with two smaller Zsub dots inside as shown in Figure 14-27. Finally, draw a **Zsub** stroke using the **Grid** stroke type between the two dots.

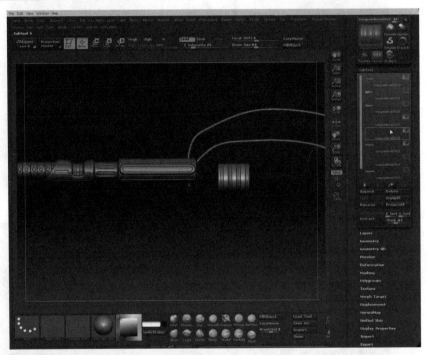

FIGURE 14-24

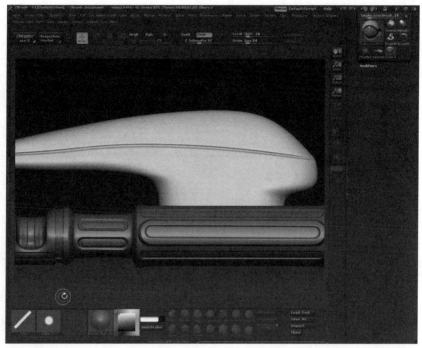

FIGURE 14-25

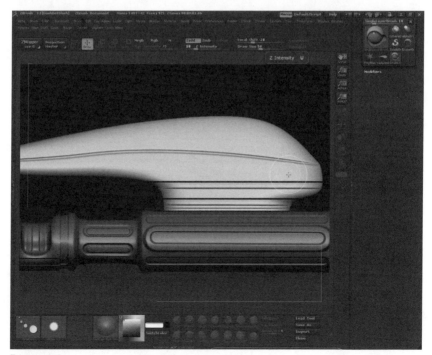

FIGURE 14-26

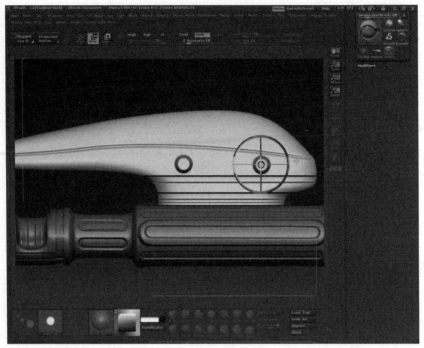

FIGURE 14-27

After exiting Projection Master, move to your second blade and repeat what you have just done, adjusting the stroke sizes accordingly. After finishing both blades, the whole gun/blade combo weapon is finished and we just have the staff itself to tackle.

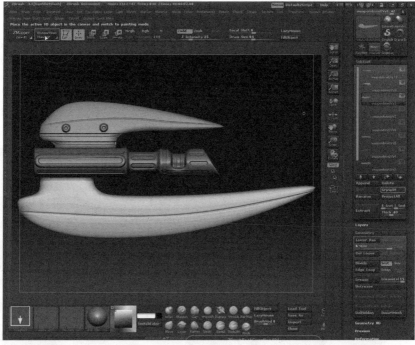

FIGURE 14-28

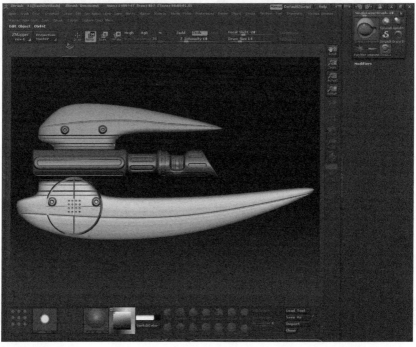

FIGURE 14-29

For the staff I made use of a specular texture created from my color texture in Photoshop. The texture was created for the low-polygon model before it got anywhere near ZBrush. This texture for the wooden handle helps to do 90 percent of the detailing. So import the specular map texture and mask it by its intensity as detailed earlier. Then change the Deformation section's Inflate setting to **5**. You can then use the **Slash1** brush set to a low ZIntensity and small Draw Size to add other detail to the woodgrain to make it look less "regular."

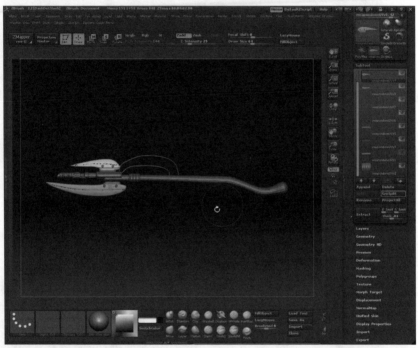

FIGURE 14-30

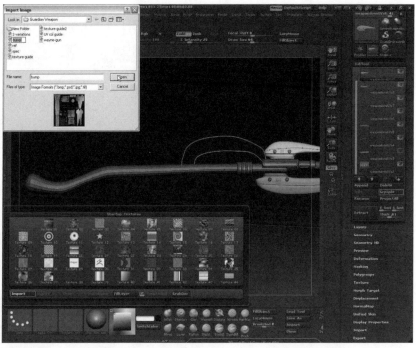

FIGURE 14-31

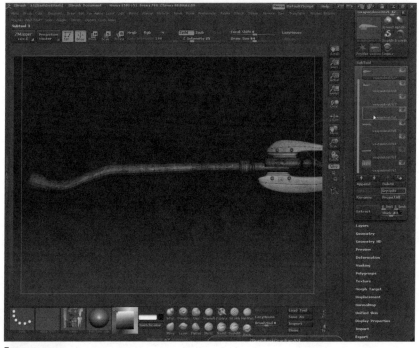

FIGURE 14-32

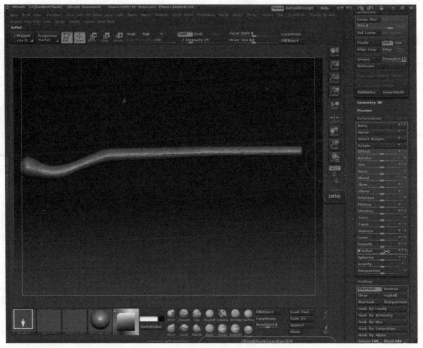

Figure 14-33

We start off by adding a few small vertical lines in Projection Master. After you've added them and are back in 3D space once more, change to your Clay brush and the FreeHand stroke type. For the part of the handle that the Guardian uses to both hold and control his weapon, we'll be using a different non-hard surface technique. Use the brush to round out and make the area look a bit more organic. Then make the grooves to make the handle look like it is wound with leather. Once you've done this to your satisfaction, you are just about done.

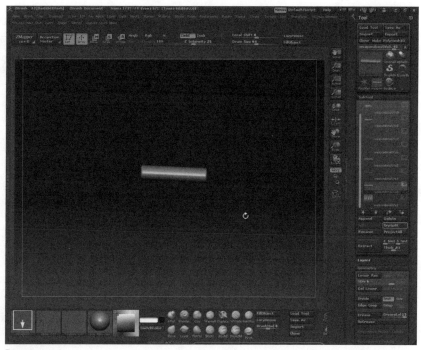

FIGURE 14-34

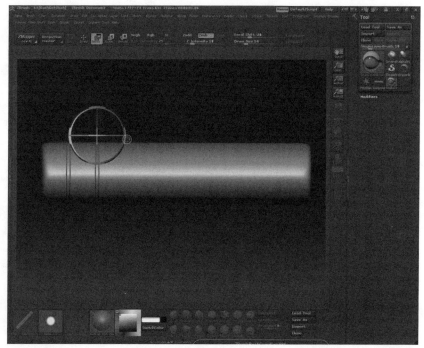

FIGURE 14-35

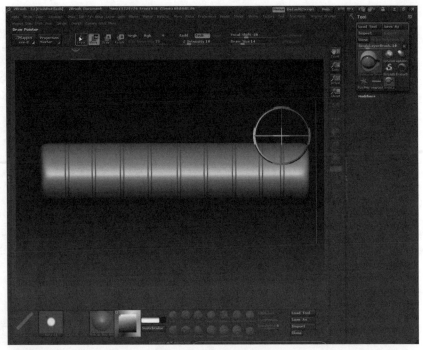

FIGURE 14-36

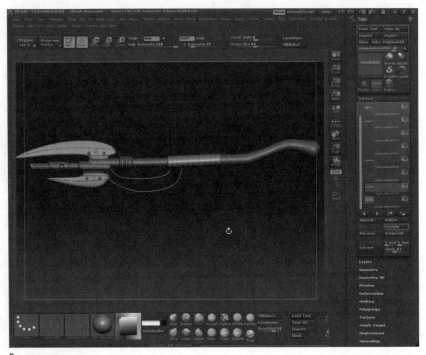

FIGURE 14-37

Now it's just a matter of merging all the subtools together. To do this, we'll use the ZBrush plug-in called SubTool Master. I would advise that you first save your non-merged subtools because once they are merged, the merge operation cannot be undone.

Set all your subtools so that they are visible and then open SubTool Master from the ZPlugin palette. Press the **SubTool Master** button, then choose the **Merge** option from the box on the left-hand side of your interface, and sit back until it's finished. After this, save the tool and you are done.

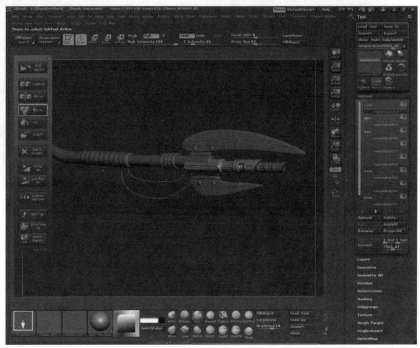

FIGURE 14-38

So that you can generate your normal and cavity maps, import your newly merged weapon into a brand-new tool. Then import your original base mesh as a subtool and subdivide it, and then project the details from one version to another. Yet another way is to use arbitrary mesh baking in ZMapper. Or you could even bake each single subtool (if you do not merge them) and then recomposite them together in Photoshop.

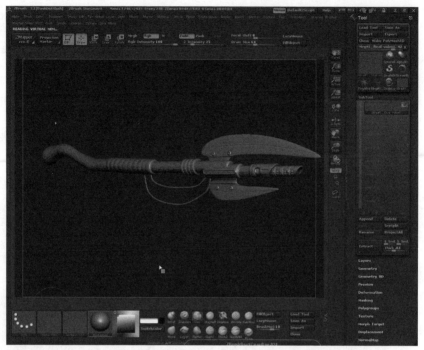

FIGURE 14-39

15 Environment Modeling: The Stone Surround for the Door of Secrets

About the Workflow

In Chapter 13 we sculpted a door for the main scene using a variety of hard surface sculpting techniques that demonstrated how easy this can be. In this chapter I want to do the same with an example of environment modeling for the stone surround of the door. For this we are going to use a very basic base mesh that again I made in about five minutes in Silo. It's not going to challenge anyone but the newest of polygon modelers, but if you like you can get the base mesh from the book's companion DVD.

Environment modeling is a much broader subject than hard surface sculpting, so I will only cover the basics. Once you have used ZBrush for a while and understand how to digitally sculpt, you will find many other methods on your own.

For the texture we will use a simple repeating pattern placed onto a render of the UV layout, making sure that the stonework doesn't stretch too badly anywhere. The mesh we provide on the DVD already has its UVs in place and was done in a traditional polygon application. We will be changing the color texture later though, and I will walk you through that process. We will also be covering normal map and cavity map generation as well as making a specular level map. (As stone doesn't have a highly reflective nature, we don't need a specular color map in this case.) We start by outlining our main forms before moving on to the details. I also use only the default alphas that ship with ZBrush because I want to show you a workflow that depends heavily on a large number of custom alphas that you may not have access to. Once you have the workflow down you can use as many custom alphas as you feel you need when sculpting an environment for your own scenes.

The final render is game friendly with a very low polygon count and maps that are only 2K (although these could be reduced to 1K with little problem). I only use the larger maps so that I could render out the cover image with plenty of detail. Okay, let's get down to sculpting an environmental piece.

Sculpting the Door Surround

First of all, import the base mesh provided and then apply the basic stonework texture. The texturing could also be done in ZBrush if you wished, but as mentioned before I prefer to do it in Photoshop. I have kept the sculpt itself as basic as I dared so that new and experienced users alike won't get into a complex and scary looking workflow. All the projects in this book are intended not only to give you skills, training, and knowledge, but also to build your confidence as a sculptor.

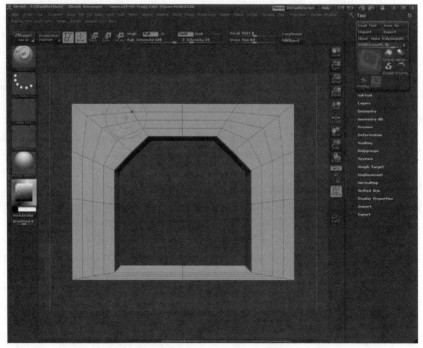

FIGURE 15-1

I would now like to take you through subdividing the model because if you simply subdivide the usual way, the mesh will round off and end up being totally the wrong shape. We used this same trick for the hard surface door. The first two times that you subdivide, turn off the **SMT** button under the **Geometry** section of the **Tool** palette. This will simply tessellate your model (not change its shape, just add more polygons to it) without smoothing it at all. Then continue to subdivide up to level 8. This then gives us 2.5 million polygons to sculpt with, which is plenty for something of this size.

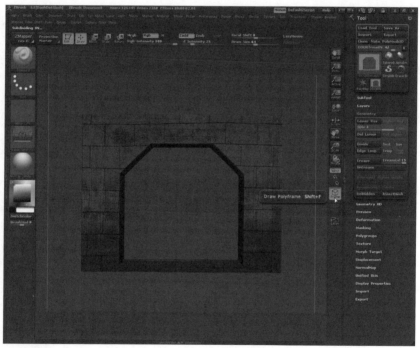

FIGURE 15-2

With your basic color texture applied I would like you to scroll down to the **Masking** section of the **Tool** palette, and then press the **Mask By Intensity** button. This will make a mask based on the intensity of the colors in the map, although it will be the inverse to what we actually need. So then press the **Inverse** button to invert your mask. Now we are ready to start blocking in the main forms on our digital sculpture. Since this is a sculpture of a doorway, its main forms are not muscles and bones but stones and mortar, so we need to sculpt in the mortar between the stones as our main form in this particular case.

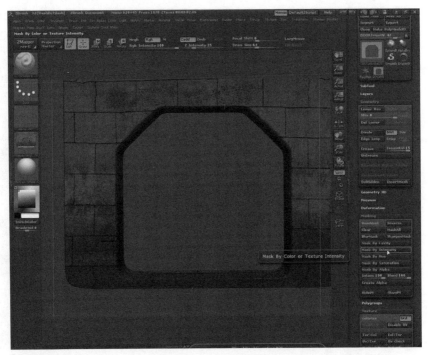

FIGURE 15-3

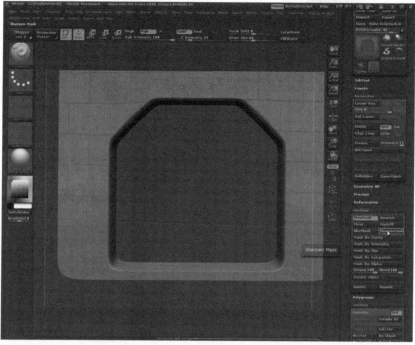

FIGURE 15-4

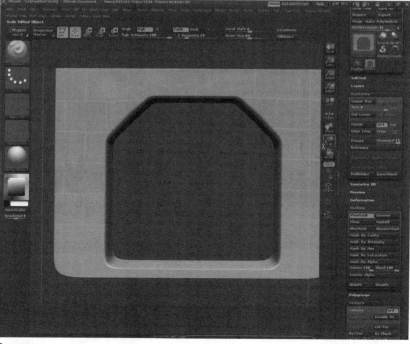

FIGURE 15-5

So to start adding the gaps between the stones for our mortar, we first need a visual clue to help us since the texture itself is too dark to be able to see a whole lot. Go to the **Deformation** section of the **Tool** palette and set **Inflate** to **–10**. Why use such a low setting when you could "crank it up" and add the gaps for the mortar in one fell swoop? The answer is that the texture we are using would become very jagged and not very stone like. The light indented lines we make will be a visual guide so we can sculpt them properly ourselves.

Take your **Standard** brush and set it to the **FreeHand** stroke type and select **Alpha 13**. Set your brush also to **Zsub** with a ZIntensity of **27** and activate **Lazy Mouse** by pressing the **L** key or by choosing it from your Stroke palette. What I want you to do next may seem like a very long, tedious job, but trust me — it only takes a few minutes to do. Using these brush settings, I want you to trace along every indented line that was produced by masking and using the inflate deformation. You could try to do this without the Lazy Mouse switched on, but unless you have the steadiest of hands it'll take a while and not look as good. Also remember to cover not just the front, but the inside where the door itself goes and the top and sides as well. (Just in case we need to change angles at any point in our renders.) Once you've done this you are ready to sculpt some stone.

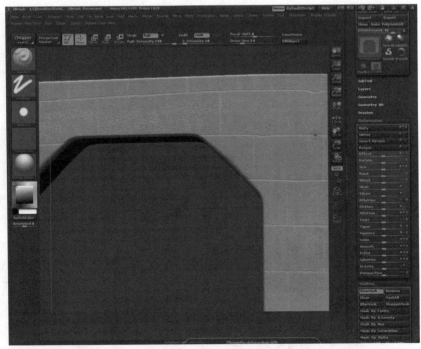

FIGURE 15-6

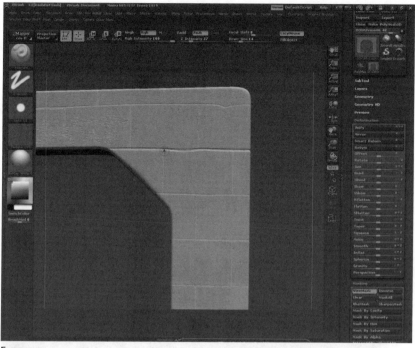

FIGURE 15-7

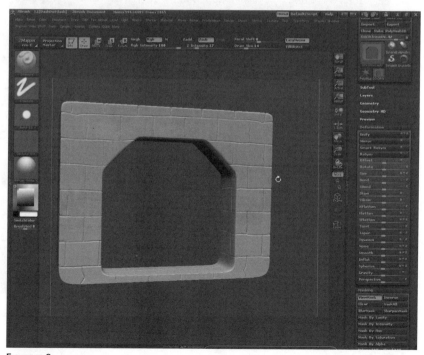

FIGURE 15-8

Sculpting stonework is a task that is usually dreaded because most people imagine having to sculpt every single nuance of each stone. In this example, however, we use a texture for the details to help the viewers believe that it is stone. Producing an untextured environment piece for a traditional looking sculpture would require all that detail, but since a production environment restricts our time, we have to get the job done quickly. So the rule is to make it look good...but work fast. You won't have a week to sculpt a single wall and you may have hundreds of such pieces to do, so you need a robust and simple workflow.

Set your **Standard** brush to the **Spray** stroke type and choose **Alpha 04** with a **Zadd** ZIntensity of **21** and a brush size about half the height of one of the stones. Now start to run this brush over every stone on the front, where the door goes, the top, and the sides. Do not try to be too precise! Work with X symmetry enabled if you wish at this stage, although you will need to turn this off later to avoid it looking too "regular" on both sides of the door. Now use a smaller brush size and zoom out of your mesh a little and go over the whole model again to add both small and large protruding detail.

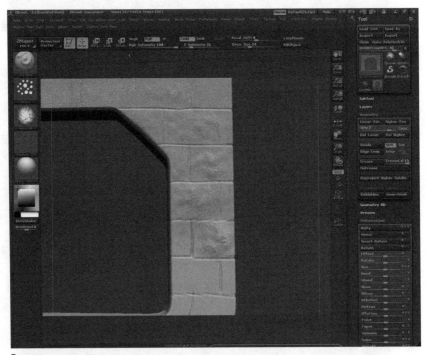

FIGURE 15-9

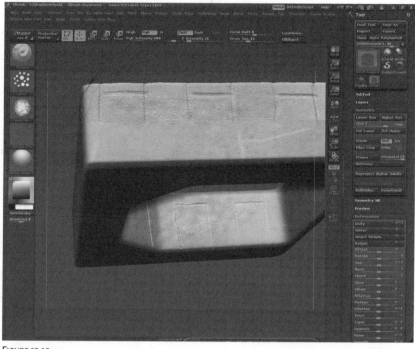

FIGURE 15-10

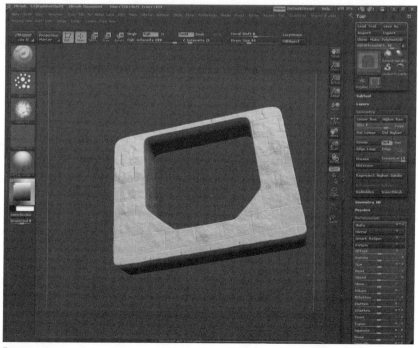

FIGURE 15-11

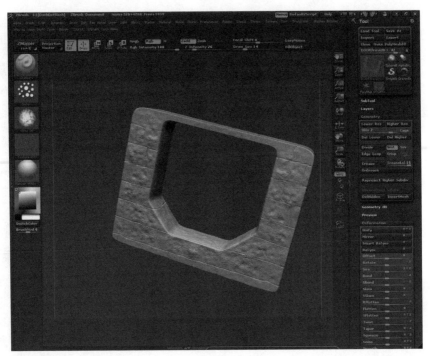

Take your brush size down now, change to **Zsub**, and cover the model again to add the inset detail. Turn your ZIntensity up to **26** or higher and with Zsub still active, start to add some deeper details, although be sure that Symmetry is turned off. This is the "creative part," as you can (and should) treat each stone as a separate thing. Once you've sculpted each stone, go back with Zadd active this time and add some slightly more aggressive protruding details.

To make this doorway look even more real, we need to simulate the battered areas that appear on the edges, where the stonework loses chunks and bits here and there. So you can now use exactly the same alpha to take some chunks out of the corners of the stonework around the door and at the tops and sides of the surround. As a final pass at detailing (*you have been noticing how we've approached it in "layers" of detail, haven't you?*), change to **Alpha 16** and with a large brush size and a ZIntensity of **6**, go over your entire model again. This will add some finer stone-like detailing. So after about 10 minutes of work you have your sculpted environment piece that will look great once the textures are applied and some nice lighting and shading are added.

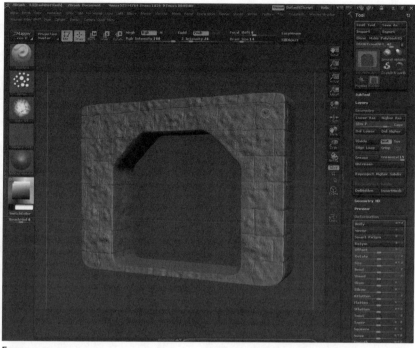

Figure 15-13

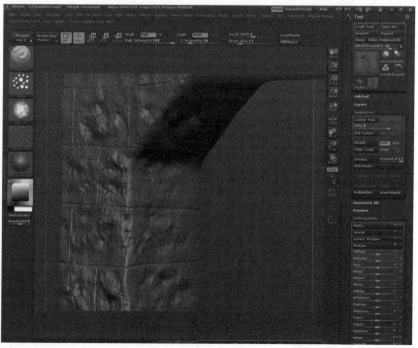

Figure 15-14

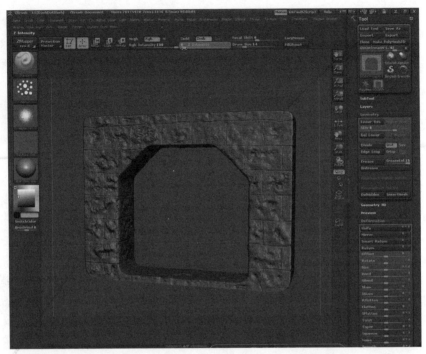

FIGURE 15-15

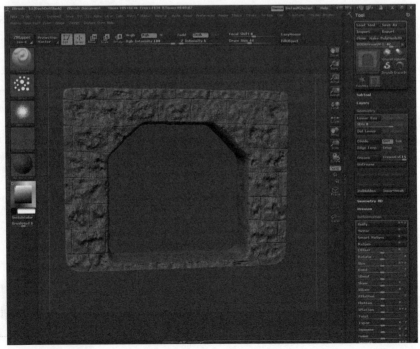

FIGURE 15-16

Making the Maps

The Normal Map

Now we want to make our normal map. However, if you step down to level 1 of our UV'ed mesh you will notice its changed shape. If we generate our maps from this shape, it will end up having some very nasty stretching issues at render time. So reimport your base mesh again to correct its shape before continuing. Press the **ZMapper** button to enter ZMapper and open the preset for your particular render engine or application. Then press the **Create NormalMap** button. For a detailed explanation of ZMapper and its interface and settings, see Chapter 8. Once you have done this, press the **Escape** key to exit back to ZBrush and export your map.

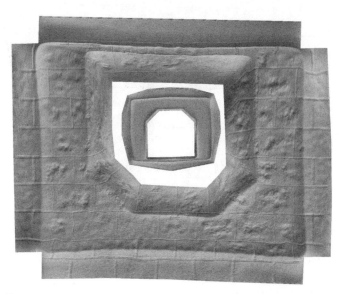

FIGURE 15-17

The Cavity Map

Now from the Texture palette, create a new white 2048 x 2048 texture and enter ZMapper again, this time to create our cavity map. This time select the **!Default TangentSpace_BestQuality.zmp** preset and turn the Cavity Blur slider up to at least a quarter of the way across and the Cavity Intensity slider three-quarters of the way up. Now press the **Create CavityMap** button to generate the cavity map. After this has completed, press the **Escape** key to exit back to ZBrush and once more export your map.

FIGURE 15-18

Making the Other Maps in Photoshop

Making a Better Diffuse Map

We are now going to use the cavity map we have generated along with our basic color map to create a more exciting diffuse map and a specular level map. It is assumed for this that you have at least a basic understanding of Photoshop, as it is beyond the scope of this book to cover it in great detail.

Open up both the basic color texture and the cavity map in Photoshop and copy the cavity map onto a layer above the basic stone wall texture. Set the layer blend mode of the cavity map to **Multiply**, which will only let the dark colors through. The nearer to black a color is the more it will be visible, while white will be invisible. Right now the cavity map will be far too dark to produce a believable texture, so turn the Opacity setting down to **30%** and it should start to look a lot better. The whole point of this is to darken the gaps where the mortar is and to add some darker areas for those areas we removed around the door. (They won't be too visible right now, but don't worry.)

Go to **Layer > Duplicate** to duplicate the basic stone texture to a new layer, and then go to **Image > Adjustments > Auto Levels** to lighten it up a bit. Change the layer blend mode to **Multiply** again and turn its opacity down to **53%** to fade it back a bit. We need to change the color of the stonework a little now as it's very boring in its current mucky brown color. (And since we are going to use a soft yellowish light it would end up too colorful if we don't change it.) Go to **Image > Adjustments > Hue/Saturation** and set it as follows:

Hue: 56
Saturation: 24
Lightness: 0

Now fade this Hue/Saturation layer's opacity back to **49%**, then go to **Layer > Merge Visible** to merge all the current layers into one. *(You may want to make a copy of your original stonework texture for comparison later.)* Now save out your finished color/diffuse map.

Making the Specular Levels Map

With the diffuse map that you just created open in Photoshop, duplicate the layer by going to **Layer > Duplicate**. We now need to remove all the color information on this layer. One way to do this if you are on the PC is to simply press **Shift+Ctrl+U**. The resulting grayscale map will be far too light for use as a specular level map for stonework because dry stone doesn't usually have a lot of specularity. So change the **Brightness** and **Contrast** settings from the **Image > Adjustments** menu to:

Brightness: –39
Contrast: +17

If you feel at this stage that the bottom of the wall is not going to have the right specularity, feel free to add another brightness/contrast and mask off all but the bottom of the wall. With this done, save out your map. The whole surround asset is now ready for render.

FIGURE 15-19

FIGURE 15-20

16 The Guardian Project: Sculpting the Head

Introduction

So far in this book we have tackled a few simple projects to help you to gain not only an understanding of the program itself but also some confidence in digital sculpting. So with that in mind, and assuming that you have practiced what's been outlined so far, we are going to tackle a much larger and more complex project. It will continue to build on what we already have learned as well as show you some new skills.

We'll be tackling the figure in stages, starting with the head. While trying to come up with a concept for this piece I first roughed out a number of head designs. I personally find that the head of a character to a large degree dictates what sort of body and even pose the final character will have. So I sat down for a couple of nights and made a number of possible creature heads, and then picked the one that I felt was the best overall design and worked best with the concept I had in mind.

We'll be building the Guardian from a number of pieces of geometry that I've purposely kept as simple as I can at this stage. My reason for not using a traditional polygon model for my base was so that users at all stages can learn from this project and not just those of you with good poly modeling skills. Everything you see in these chapters can be done equally as well with a polygon mesh. Another reason for starting from very low-resolution and simple geometry for some of the model is that it makes for a better learning process. I'm a firm advocate that if you can sculpt something starting only from a sphere or low-resolution model, then you can sculpt just about anything. When you do get to use a polygon model it will feel like a walk in the park and be much less limiting.

Character Back Story

I always feel that if you are to make a believable character you must
know the character well. The more you know about the person or thing
you're sculpting and how it would live its life, the better job you can do
in interpreting that information while you sculpt. So who, what, why, and
when are the important questions that we first need to answer to get
some feel for this character we will be sculpting.

Who is he? Well, the Guardian is a non-human bipedal creature from
a futuristic society. He is guarding a locked door from entry by any living entity. Why is he doing this? First, it is his job, and one for which he
was chosen at an early age and trained. A Guardian must be highly
trained and able to defend or attack others, whether a single person or
an army. He must be agile and of great intelligence and can be of great
age by the time his services are finally called upon. Primarily he is not a
warrior, but more of a keeper of secrets behind the door, and in the time
of the scene his society has begun to see his role as primarily a cseremo-
nial one. But he must stand and look after the Door of Secrets until such
time as he has to call upon another to take his place.

What is he? His race started out eons ago as a water dwelling race
descended from amphibians, although over time they have evolved into
a land dwelling species. When does this scene take place? It takes place
— in the tradition of all space operas — in a futuristic civilization
(although whether this is the far future or the far distant past is
unclear). The scene itself will reflect the futuristic nature of the place as
well as a sense of tradition and age with both sci-fi type elements and an
ancient look to the surroundings.

So with this basic outline in place we can start to flesh out the character of this creature a little to give us a guideline as to how he would
look. We know that he may be a little old and almost religious looking as
his current role as a ceremonial figurehead would dictate. As this is a
traditional role he may well be carrying a weapon of some age or
renown. His skin would have features such as fine wrinkles denoting a
creature not only of great age but also as a side effect of this ancestry
from his race's water dwelling past. He will have some fish- or amphib-
ian-like features, but will bear a resemblance to both man, because of
his bipedal anatomy, and animal.

We can surmise that since he has spent most of his life guarding a
door of secrets that he is a man of great wisdom. There's a fine chance
he will know what is behind the door and have to check on the things
behind it at least occasionally. He will give off some sense of serenity
when at rest because he's become very used to waiting alone over the

many years he has spent in his role. He obviously treats his role with great seriousness and reverence. But once called upon, he can spring into action at a moment's notice.

So there we have our basic story outline that gives us enough information to continue with the character. While it may seem to be a pointless exercise to create a detailed back story such as this, it really helps with our design and modeling of the character. I've found that when you have no back story for a character as you sculpt it, it often ends up cold and emotionless. Imagining details for a character makes it more interesting and easier for the artist to bring it to life. The back story should only take a few minutes to develop and is certainly worth spending the time on.

Behind the Door

So what is behind the Door of Secrets? While it's part of the fun that each person will have to work out for themselves what they think is behind the locked door, I can give you a few hints. First, there are things of great power and hence great danger locked away that could spell very bad things for either the Guardian's race or the current system of government. It is a group of things that would shed "new light" onto their civilization and as such must be kept locked away from all but the Guardian to keep safe the current order.

Part of the artistry of the scene is that each viewer will have his or her own interpretation based on personal experiences, ideas, and even bigotry. So now that we've got our back story and interpretation of the scene out of the way, let's get on with some digital sculpting in ZBrush!

Sculpting the Head

To start off we are going to sculpt the head of the creature from our ever-popular polysphere. The reason for this, as I outlined earlier, is that once you can sculpt the design in your mind starting from basic geometry, sculpting from a "proper" base mesh is far easier. This technique also helps improve the "concept design" part of your skill set, which is important these days for a digital sculptor.

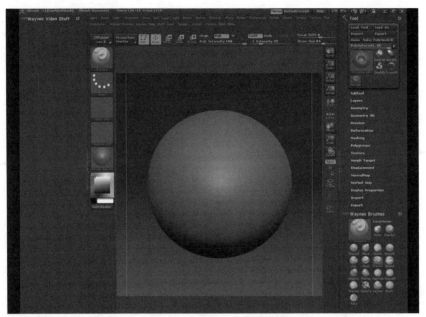

Figure 16-1

Once we have sculpted and refined our head a bit, it will eventually be retopologized. It also means that we can interchange the head and other body parts for later reuse, which is especially useful in a production environment.

Starting Work

With ZBrush open, choose the **PolySphere** tool from the startup splash screen or from the ZTools folder in ZBrush 3. Press the **X** key to make sure that you're in Symmetry mode along the X axis, which means that everything we do on one side of the model will be mirrored to the other.

We will be approaching the sculpting of this "spherehead" in a somewhat different way from our first polysphere head sculpture back in Chapter 5. This time we'll start with the mouth area. By starting from the mouth you won't feel locked into a somewhat "human" head design and you will have plenty of polygons in the mouth area to adequately give the detail that we need. We will add the other features in as we progress.

We won't change the shape of the head at this stage, as that would only make sculpting the mouth, tongue, and teeth areas more difficult. By sculpting them on the front of the sphere, we will be able to reshape the whole head afterward and keep the mouth we have, while just adding the shapes that we need.

Select your **Standard** brush with no alpha selected and **Dots** as your stroke type. Set the Draw Size setting to **124** and the ZIntensity to **25**. Make sure that you still have Symmetry in the X axis switched on, then make a round indentation in your polysphere as shown in Figure 16-2. This is the very start of what will eventually become the inside of the mouth. Take the Draw Size down to **74** and make two upward lines on either side of the center of the model to form what will be the tonsils. Even though this is an alien creature, it helps to make the mouth area look more "mouth like." Take your Draw Size back up to about **114** and further hollow out the inside of the mouth a bit. At this point you should have been sculpting on subdivision level 3; every now and again I step back down to level 1 and press the **Reconstruct Subdiv** button to help even out the polygon flow a bit, so do this now.

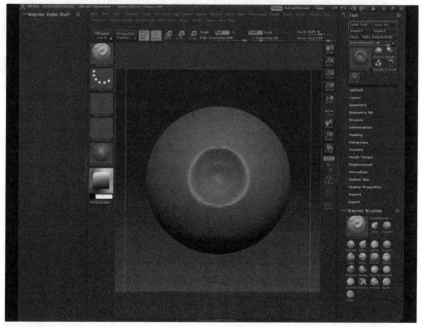

FIGURE 16-2

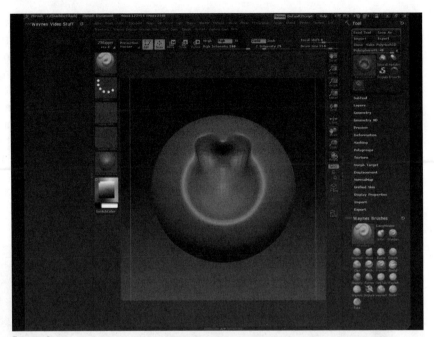

FIGURE 16-3

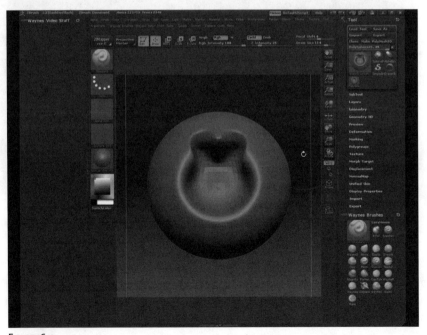

FIGURE 16-4

Take your model back up to its highest level and subdivide it to level 5, as we are going to need a little more detail. We are going to be sculpting in a fair amount of detail in the mouth before we even touch any other part of the head, so we are going to need these polygons. They also make the sphere look a fair bit smoother. Holding down the **Shift** key, draw a mask in the shape of a tongue as shown in Figure 16-5, then invert it so that the tongue shape is the only part of the sphere unmasked. Now bulk up and start to fill in a very basic tongue shape with your Standard brush. We will be refining it as we go along. Invert the mask again and hollow out the area behind the tonsils some more and also at either side of our rudimentary tongue.

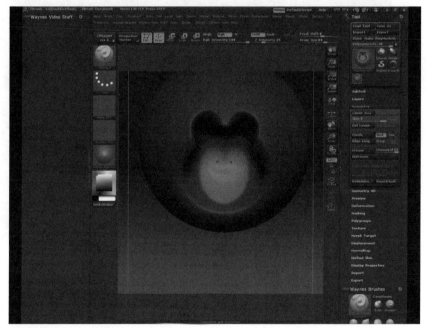

FIGURE 16-5

Zoom out a little from your sphere and use the **Standard** brush again with a Draw Size of **74** and add a curved line above the tonsil area. (Don't worry; this will all make sense in a moment.) Take your Draw Size down to **34** and carve in a line under this quite close to the tonsils themselves. Then bulk up the area at the bottom of the mouth for what will eventually become our lower lip. You may need to run your brush a few times over this at larger sizes to bulk up the area sufficiently.

Switch to your **Move** brush with a Draw Size of **114**, rotate your model to just past the three-quarter view, and pull the tonsils downward and back a little. Pull the corners of the mouth backward as well. Remember, the mouth is not flat but rather curved, so we want to add that curved shape pretty early on since most other things in the face are affected by it.

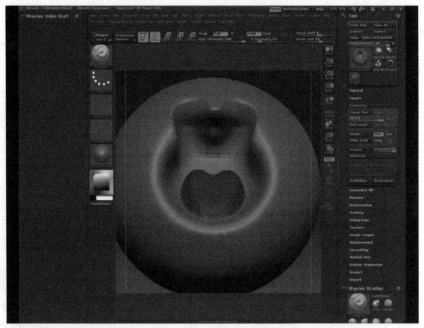

FIGURE 16-6

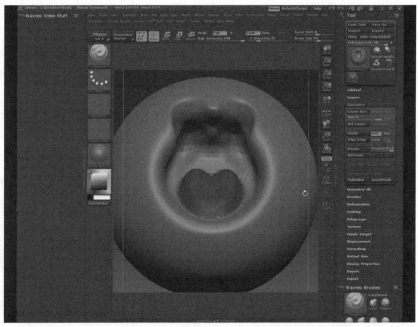

FIGURE 16-7

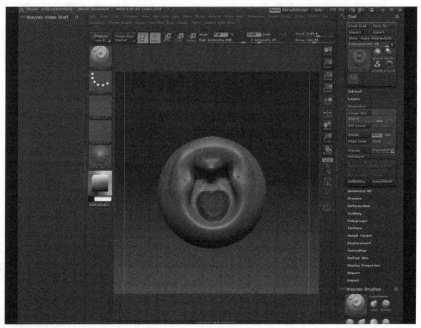

FIGURE 16-8

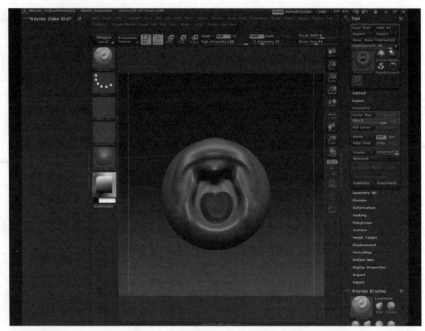

FIGURE 16-9

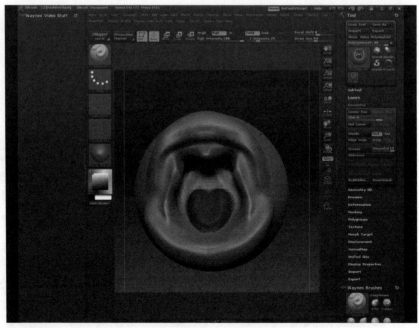

FIGURE 16-10

Zoom out again and pull the center of the upper lip area out using a larger brush size (~**114**) for your Move brush, and then do the same thing for the bottom lip. Zoom in slightly to the mouth in a three-quarter view, then with a Draw Size of **74** move the parts of the mouth just inside the ends of the top lip inward a bit. Those parts were sticking out too far, and it is important that you correct any mistakes you make early on as they can have a massive effect later in the sculpting process. You can now remove the mask that has been on the tongue all this time, then step back down to level 1 and press **Reconstruct Subdiv** again to even out the polygons a bit more.

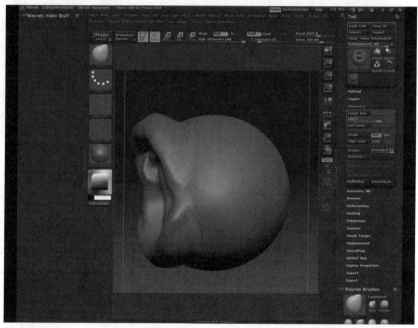

FIGURE 16-11

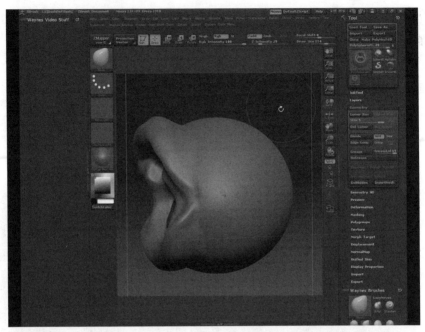

FIGURE 16-12

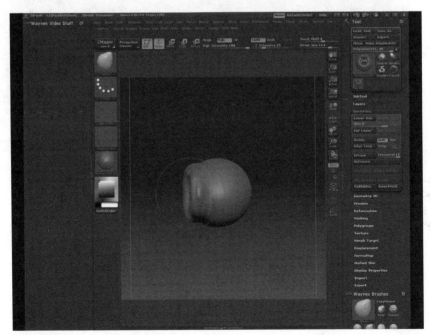

FIGURE 16-13

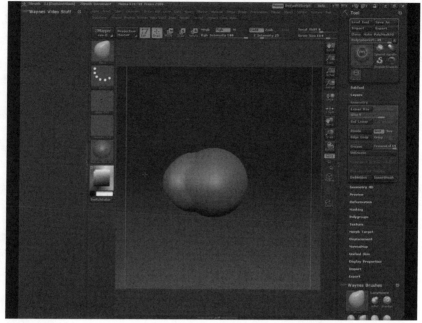

FIGURE 16-14

Step your model back upward to divide to level 6. It's time for us to add some teeth in the mouth so we can visualize things a bit better, so rotate your model and make sure that it is front on.

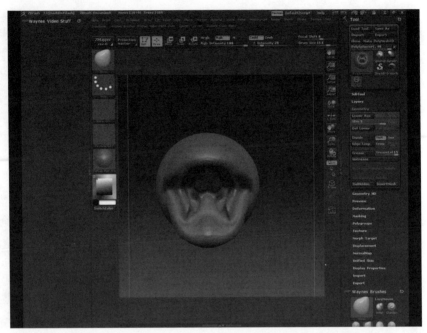

FIGURE 16-15

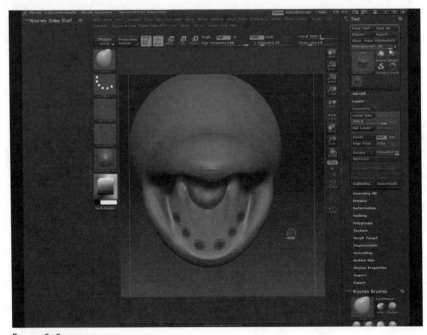

FIGURE 16-16

With your **Move** brush still selected, draw three dot-like masks on each side of the lower lip to give us six in total as shown in Figure 16-16. Now invert the masks. Using your Move brush, pull them upward to form the teeth. At first they will appear too low polygon to use, so smooth them by holding down the **Shift** key and very slightly pull them out again. As we add more subdivision levels to our sculpt, they will look better, but for the moment they will act as placeholders. We now repeat this process on the inside of the upper lip, only this time with one large masked dot on each side. Before doing so it is best to subdivide to level 7 because we will most definitely need more polygons for the upper teeth. At this stage you should be able to recognize a rudimentary mouth starting to take shape.

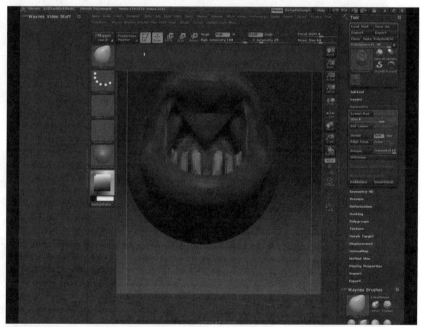

FIGURE 16-17

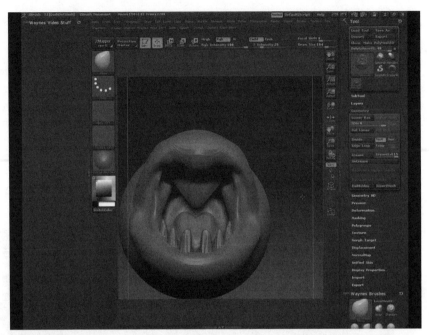

FIGURE 16-18

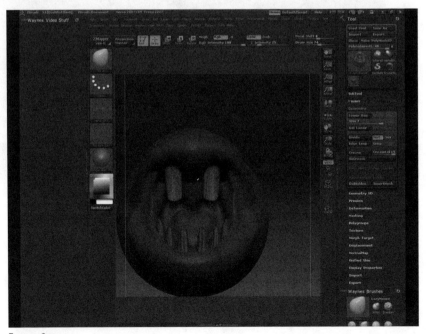

FIGURE 16-19

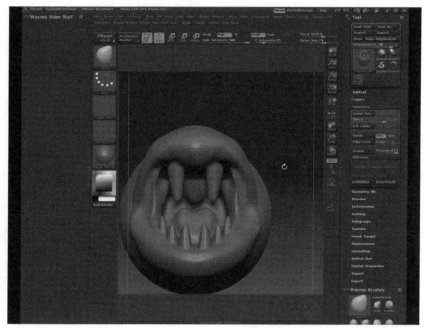

FIGURE 16-20

Switch to your **Standard** brush with **Alpha 35** selected, a ZIntensity of **13**, and a Draw Size of **44**. Now zoom in on the bottom teeth so we can add the gums. Draw around the bottom of the teeth, taking particular care to fill in between the teeth a bit as well. At this point we are simply adding a bit of bulk to the area for the gums. Now do the same thing for the upper two teeth as well. Try to get as far behind the back of the teeth as you can, but don't worry if you can't reach all the way around. We will be coming back to this area later on.

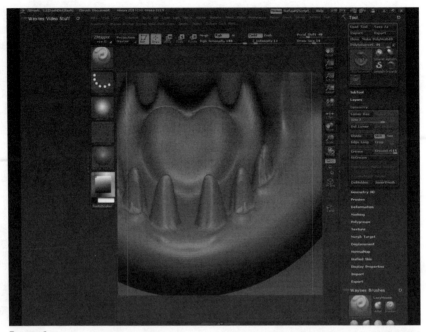

FIGURE 16-21

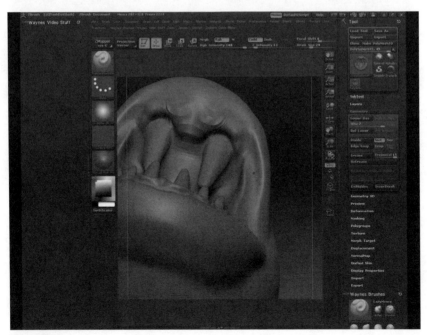

FIGURE 16-22

We now switch to the **Displace** brush and select **Alpha 36** and a Draw Size of **24**. Start using this brush to first carve a rough line between the gums and the lip. Carve in some more lines on the inside of the sides of the mouth that we can add some more detail to later. I always add a couple of fine lines to the front of each tooth so they don't look too smooth. With a small brush size, carve in the line between the lower lip and the gums.

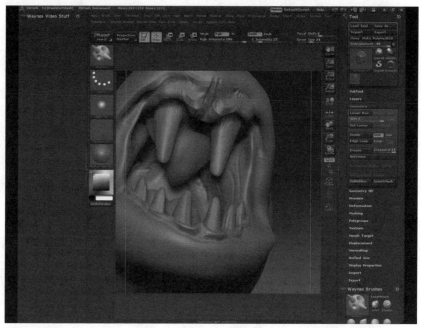

FIGURE 16-23

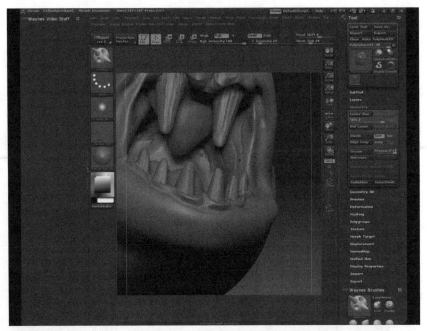

FIGURE 16-24

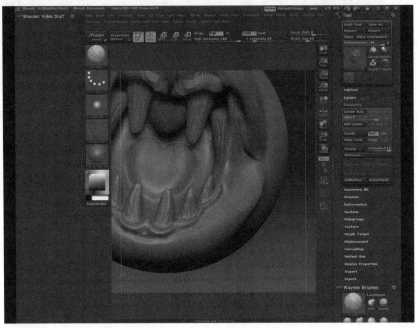

FIGURE 16-25

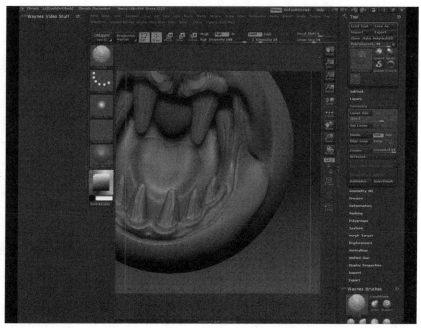

FIGURE 16-26

We need some sort of delineation for the mouth that we can also use later to add more bulk and weight to the lips. Carve another line from the outer edge of the upper lip to the outside of the mouth and another one around the edge of the tongue. The lines on the outside of the mouth will be used to add some detail later, while the lines carved around the tongue will help separate the lower mouth from the tongue. If you switch back to the **Standard** brush you should also be able to add the gums for the inside of the bottom teeth at this point. Rotate the model as needed.

We will now add a few lines and wrinkles, or at least the beginning of them, by again taking our **Displace** brush and carving in some lines at the edge of the mouth. Some of the lines will be running under the bottom lip and over the outer edges of the top lip as shown. Take your **Standard** brush again with a ZIntensity of **13** and **Alpha 01** selected, and then start to fill in the areas between these lines. Think of these lines we've carved as a sort of railway track that we use to guide the brush. We don't want to go mad just yet, so be gentle and make sure you can still see the lines themselves.

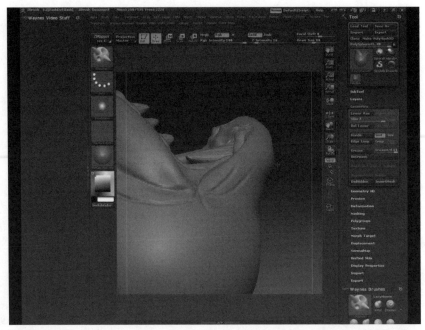

FIGURE 16-27

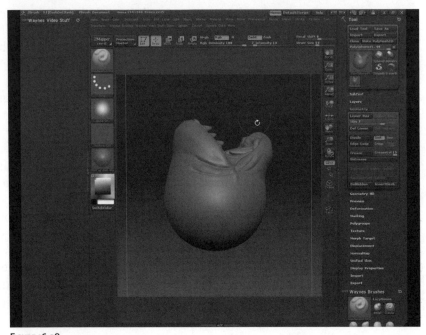

FIGURE 16-28

Now go back to the **Displace** brush with **Alpha 36** selected and a small brush size and carve in some lines at the edge of the mouth as shown. Next, with **Zadd** active, make some strokes between these to bulk that area up just a little. Feel free to add other wrinkles horizontally from the outer edge of the mouth and make sure all wrinkles meet properly at the end of the mouth. Lightly smooth the edges of each wrinkle to help them blend in a bit.

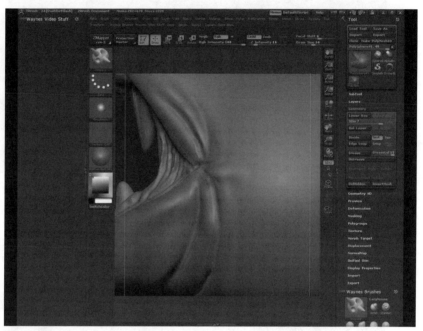

FIGURE 16-29

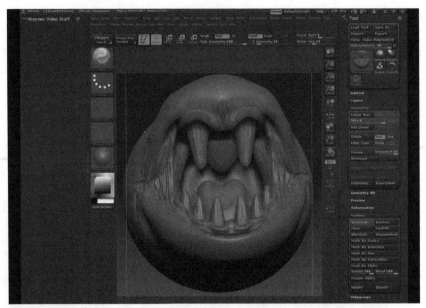

FIGURE 16-30

Subdivide your model to level 8 at this point as again we are going to need more polygons. This may appear to be a backward way of working to some of you, but for a creature such as this one it is important to "nail" the mouth and teeth area as it's one of the biggest features on the head.

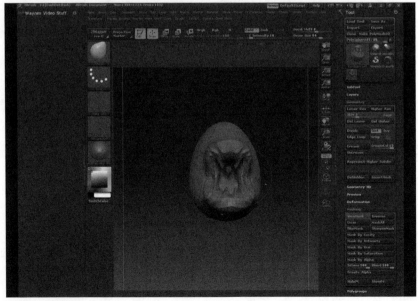

FIGURE 16-31

Take your **Pinch** brush and start to nip together the line between the upper gums and upper lip a bit, then do the same around the base of each tooth as well. Don't worry about any large gaps between the gums and teeth because we will sort those out later. Also use the Pinch brush around the edges where the tongue meets the bottom of the inside of the mouth to help it "sit" better. Move toward the wrinkles at the corners of the mouth and start to gently pinch those together a bit as well to give them a more "wrinkled" appearance.

Take your **Inflate** brush with no alpha selected and a fairly large brush size and add some bulk to the lower lip area. As we carved in a line between the lips and gums earlier, this should be a fairly easy job. Take your time and use gentle strokes until you feel it looks right and matches the images well, then move to the top lip and do the same thing.

We've now got the mouth fairly well blocked in and looking decent enough for the moment, although we will come back to it several times. Digital sculpting, like traditional sculpting, is a "layered" process. Think of the forms and detail you are adding as passes, with each pass adding more detail to the sculpture until we consider it done.

It's now time to shape the head so that we can add some other features. So switch to your **Move** brush and step down to subdivision level **3**. Make sure you have zoomed out quite a way from your model as shown and have a fairly large brush size as well. Start to pull the head shape into place until it looks like the one in Figures 16-32 and 16-33.

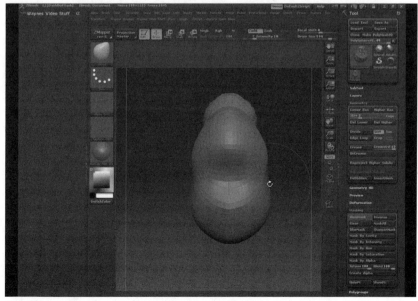

Figure 16-32

If you rotate to the front of the model you will notice that the head appears somewhat flat. We'll tackle this in a moment, but first let's use our **Move** brush to move the outer edges of the mouth inward as shown. Pull under the chin outward a little and then rotate to a side view so you can pull the top of the head up a bit and make the base of the cranium a little higher. Rotate to a top view of the head so you are looking downward on it and add some breadth to the head to make it look less flat. Go under the jaw and check that it is "horseshoe"-shaped. If not, pull it into the correct shape. Also pull the base of the cranium so that it is a bit broader while you are there. If we now step back up to level 8, we should have a nice head shape to continue with.

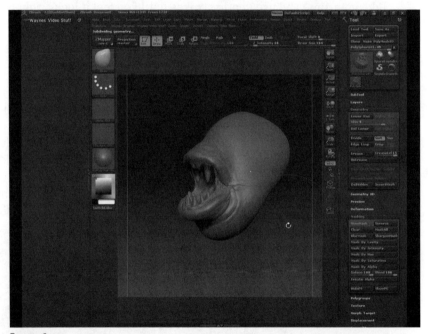

FIGURE 16-33

Let's start to add a little bit of detail in the head itself to give us some points of reference for the eyes we'll add soon. So switch over to the **Slash1** brush with a ZIntensity of **47** and the **FreeHand** stroke selected (which it should be by default). Drag a few lines above the upper lip that we'll think of as the "nose area" even though he won't have a nose. Then smooth it over very slightly, especially over the edges of them to help them blend in. Do the same to add some lines for wrinkles outside the corners of the mouth. Next we need to draw out a line that will act as an eyebrow placeholder so that we get a better idea of where to place the eye itself. So start from the edges of one of the "nose" wrinkles and make an arc over where the eye will end up as shown in Figure 16-35, and also add a line to denote where the jaw will join with the upper skull. When sculpting you should always keep in mind the underlying muscle structure and bone structure. This not only helps you avoid anatomy mistakes but also makes digital sculpture more believable in the end.

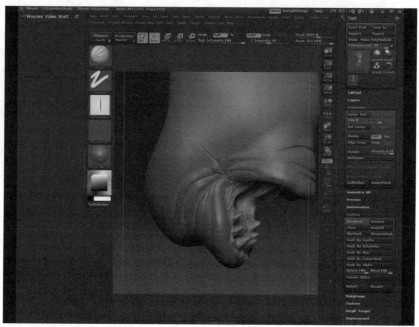

FIGURE 16-34

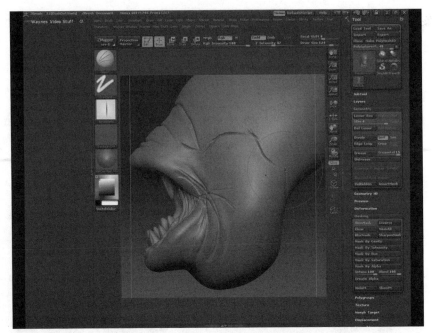

FIGURE 16-35

Change to your **Standard** brush with **Alpha 01** selected and draw a mask in the shape of a circle for the eye as shown in Figure 16-36. This is the area we will eventually hollow out and make into an eye shape before adding the spheres for the eyes. So invert this mask, hold down the **Alt** key, and sculpt out the circular area. We can now take our **Move** brush and move and stretch the eyehole into the right shape. Paint a mask around this whole eye shape right up to the brow line we carved in earlier and invert this. Using the **Move** transform tool, pull this out a little. If the transition is a bit too harsh between the masked and unmasked area, undo this and blur your mask either by **Ctrl**+clicking on the mask itself or by choosing **BlurMask** from the Masking section of the Tool palette.

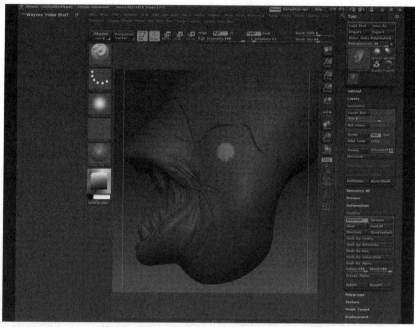

FIGURE 16-36

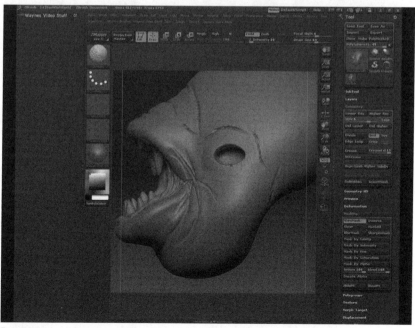

FIGURE 16-37

We now need to isolate this area, so we can later curve this area outward for the eyelids. So hold down **Shift** and **Ctrl** and drag an area over the eyes to isolate them. Make sure that you have held down the Shift key and "clicked" the model into a side view first to save on any misalignment problems later. With the eyes isolated, go down to the **Display Properties** section of the Tool palette and click on the **Double** button to make the model double-sided. This means that we will be able to see both the inside and outside of the mesh, making the job of moving the eyelids into position a fair bit easier.

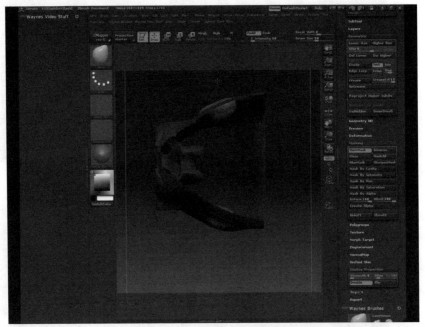

FIGURE 16-38

So switch now to your **Move** brush, and from the top "inside" of the head move the lid outward, making sure that you have a nice curvature to it as shown, then do exactly the same thing to the bottom lid. On a human, the bottom eyelid extends farther than the top one, so make sure that you add the same features here. As we want our creature to look a bit humanoid, it is important to add small details like this. With the eye sockets now ready for the eye, I felt that the head shape needed to change a bit so I pulled the top of the head up and back out a bit with the **Move** brush. I then had to move the eye holes up a little in the head again with the Move brush. It's important that you maintain the balance of your design as you go along.

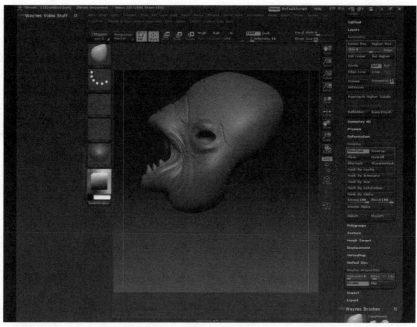

FIGURE 16-39

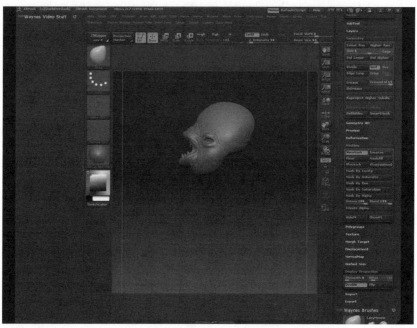

FIGURE 16-40

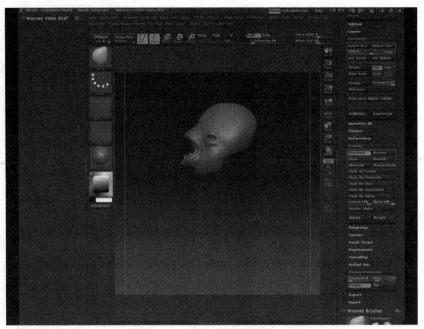

FIGURE 16-41

Using the **Inflate** brush, inflate the wrinkles in the nose area and add an inflated area over each eyebrow above where the brow lines were carved in earlier. At this point I also added some gravity for my Inflate brush with the Gravity setting at **67** to help pull these folds downward a little and add a little bit of weight to them as well. Obviously you will need to change the size of your brush as required.

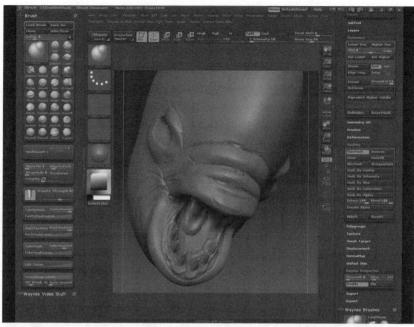

FIGURE 16-42

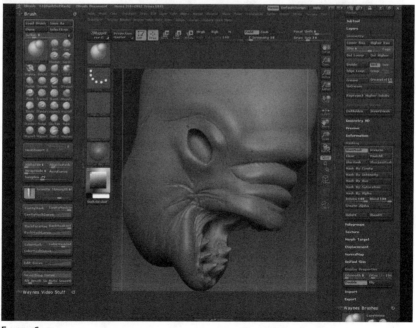

FIGURE 16-43

Draw a masked line over the corners of each eye (inner and outer corners) and slightly inflate the upper eyelid right up to these masked lines. This helps to give the eyelids a bit of weight, although we won't notice this much until later on in the process.

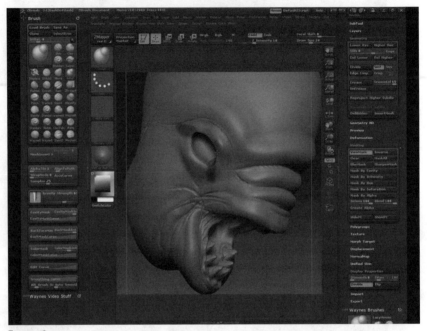

FIGURE 16-44

Where the upper eyelid meets the brow, use your **Inflate** brush to push this inward a bit and then smooth it out a little so that you don't end up with ragged looking polygons in that area. Draw in a mask for the cheekbones and invert this so that we can now run our Inflate brush with a large size over this to create some cheekbones. Remove the mask and smooth the edges of the cheekbone transitions a little until they fit in well with the rest of the face.

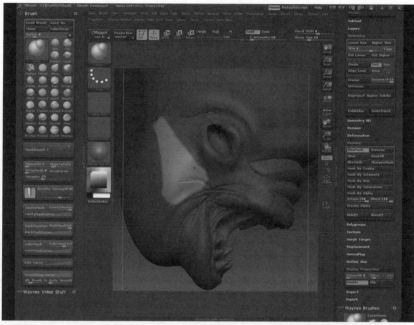

FIGURE 16-45

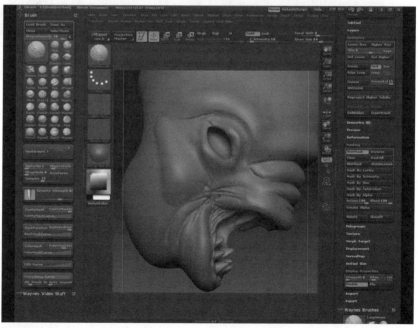

FIGURE 16-46

Using your **Standard** brush again, carve out the area on the under-side of the jaw to create a hollow part where the jaw bone curves around to meet the sides of the head. Be sure to smooth out any nasty transitional areas before continuing.

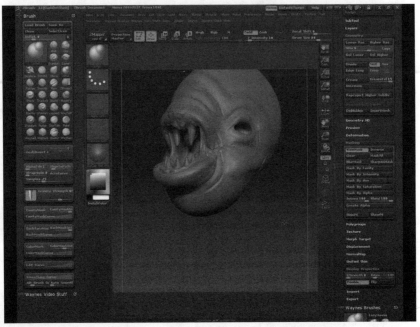

FIGURE 16-47

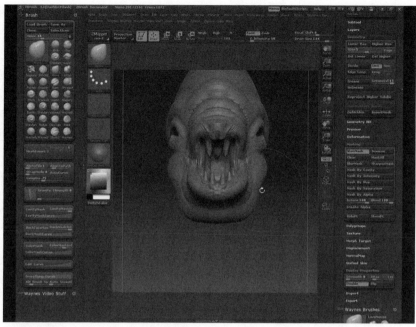

FIGURE 16-48

Move again to a side view by rotating your model with the **Shift** key held down. Slightly flatten the sides of the head and add a curved line running from the brow toward the back of the head as shown in Figure 16-49. Feel free to bulk up the eyebrows or any other areas that you feel may have been knocked slightly off by these changes before moving onward again.

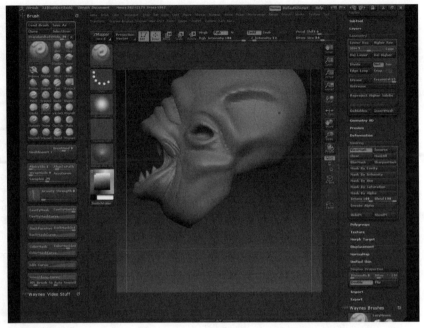

FIGURE 16-49

At this point I want to change from the default Red Wax material to a black and white one of my own making. I mainly do this to get a fresh view of things. The worst thing for any digital sculptor is when you lose your objectivity when sculpting a model. If changing materials or lighting doesn't work, save your model out and take some time away from it. When you come back, you'll likely have a fresh perspective.

The basic shape of our creature's head is now looking roughly the way it does when we get it to the final stage. All that is missing is a few of the details that we are going to do in passes. Currently the polygon count of this head is 1.5 million, which is pretty good bearing in mind the amount of detail we need in some of the low-resolution areas such as the mouth. Obviously if we retopologized the head at this stage we would save a lot of polygons, but as ZBrush can handle very high polygon counts with ease, why not make life easier first?

Using the **Slash1** brush, carve a couple of lines from each corner of the eye and smooth the ends of them out a little. Carve a few more coming from the nose area down in front of the eyes and smooth them until they are barely visible.

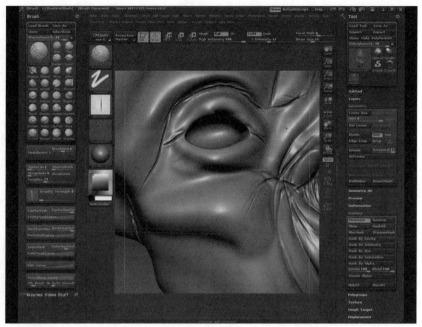

We are now going to add some eyeballs to our creature's head so that we can get a better idea of the sculpting that we need to do on the eyelids. So left-click on the model's thumbnail at the top of the **Tool** palette and pick the **Sphere** tool. Remember that this is not yet a polygon mesh but a ZBrush primitive, so we need to press the **Make PolyMesh3D** button to create a copy that is in fact polygons. With this done, switch back to your main creature model and open the **SubTool** section of the **Tool** palette. Press the **Append** button and choose the polymesh sphere that we just made.

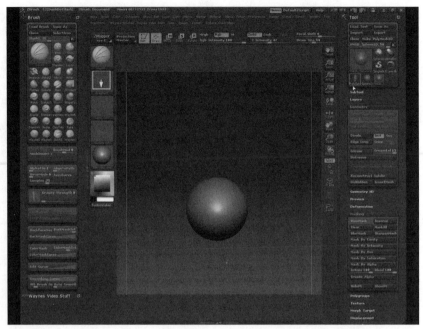

Figure 16-51

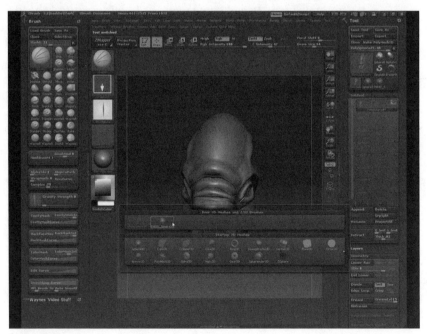

Figure 16-52

The sphere will probably be too big and in the wrong position, so we will need to use our transform tools (Move, Scale, and Rotate) to both move it into position and make sure it is the correct size. First of all, let's scale it to roughly the correct size with the **Scale** transform tool. So click on the **Scale** button on the toolbar and draw an action line over your sphere. Holding down the Shift key will constrain it from flying back into the distance if one of the ends of the action lines goes beyond the model. Grab inside the circle at the end of the action line (making sure that the other end is in the center of the sphere) and scale your eyeball down to roughly the correct size. We can make any further adjustments later if needed.

Change to your **Move** transform tool now and grab the sphere by the center of the middle circle on the action line to move it into place. If you are still quite new to using action lines, the more you practice using them the better you'll get. If your eyeball still needs some scaling or relocating, make it the correct size and placement. One tip I would add is that if you turn on **Transp** you can help to line up your eyeball with the help of the transparency. Once you have your eyeball lined up and the correct size, go back to the top of the Tool palette and hit the **Clone** button, which creates an exact duplicate. If you go back down to the SubTool section again and hit the **Append** button, you can then pick this as your second eyeball. It currently shares the exact position as the first one, but we can change that by opening up the **Deformation** section and hitting the **Mirror** button (making sure that it is set to X). You should now have two eyes in your creature's head and be ready to continue. I find that once I put the eyeballs into a character it starts to look more "real" and suddenly gets a lot more interesting. Switch back to your main subtool of your creature head before continuing. This is usually a good point to save your model; I always try to save multiple times in multiple locations so that I have incremental backups of any model.

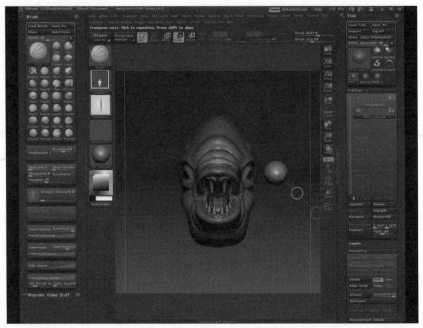

FIGURE 16-53

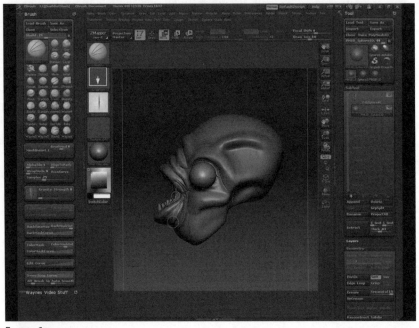

FIGURE 16-54

FIGURE 16-55

First do any corrections that are needed on the eyelids of your model. On my version it was a simple matter of cleaning up the area where the upper eyelid meets the eyeball and correcting the shape a bit. Change to your **Clay** brush and start to block in some areas of transition between the eyelids and the rest of the face. I added a stroke on the edges of the upper and lower lids to add a bit of weight and to help them "gel" with the rest of the model. At the moment the eye area seems to stick out a little too far and I feel it weakens the design, so run the Clay brush over this indentation below the lower lid to help to fill it out a little. Remember that one feature of the Clay family of brushes is their ability to melt together two pieces of intersecting or nearby geometrical surfaces, so they are great for filling in areas such as these. Plus their slight flattening effect helps us to shape the planes of the face easily.

FIGURE 16-56

Run a very small size **Standard** brush over the outermost edge of the upper eyelid where it meets the eyeball to help give it some thickness. Remember that eyelids are not paper thin and do have some thickness to them. Plus, the very inside part of the eyelid (for want of a better description) is pretty flat for most of its journey and only rounds out near the edges of the eyelid. So take your **Flatten** brush with a ZIntensity of **29** to **32** and a very small size and flatten this inside area to help give the user a better idea of its thickness. If we leave it more rounded, the light will not catch this as well, and it appears to be thinner than it actually is. Continue to do the same thing with the lower eyelid, and if you feel it is currently too thin, then use the **Inflate** brush very lightly to add some bulk to this area. Once this is done, take a look at the overall shape of the eyelids and make any corrections. The eyes require special attention to make any character believable.

Using a very small **Standard** brush size, start to carve out the area at the corner of the eye nearest the nasal area. This is often overlooked by beginners, but if missed can make the eyes look more like holes in a mask. Switch again to your **Displace** brush with our small sized alpha and press the **L** key to activate the **Lazy Mouse** feature. We are now going to add some wrinkles and lines to help catch some of the shadows on the eye area. So run a line just above the edge of the upper eyelid.

You can make it fairly deep because we want it to be in shadow most of the time. Do exactly the same things to the lower eyelid area.

These lines are important because in reality we are sculpting not with polygons or digital clay but with light and shadows. These along with any specular highlights are what tell the human eye what shape something is. Add some further wrinkles below the eye and fill between these a bit using the **Inflate** brush. Take care to smooth the ends of each wrinkle a little to keep the ends from looking too sharp. Vary the brush size as you need to. You'll notice that by this point I'm not giving brush sizes as often because you've probably already found the sizes that work best for you. So the images should give you enough clues that you can follow along with no problem.

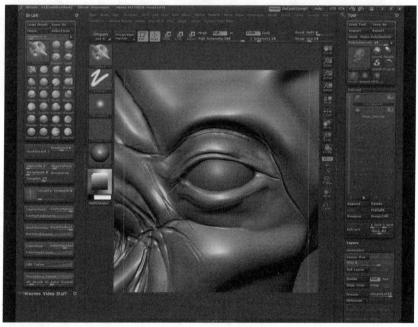

FIGURE 16-57

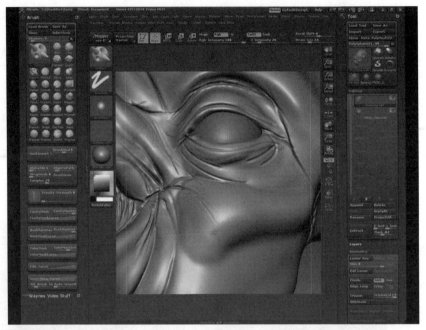

FIGURE 16-58

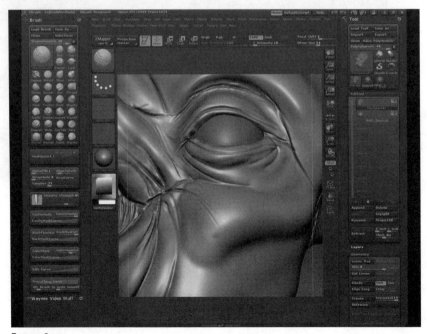

FIGURE 16-59

We are now going to go back and work on the area under the mouth, so change over to your **Slash1** brush before going any further. I want you to run a number of overlapping lines from the current ones on the sides of the mouth to under the bottom lip as shown and then slightly smooth them. Run some more down from the bottom edge of the nasal area to the side of the mouth as shown. I'm treating these a little like the nasal labial folds on the human face.

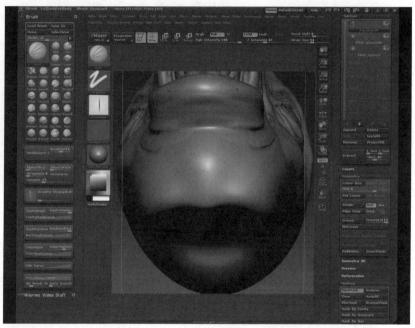

FIGURE 16-60

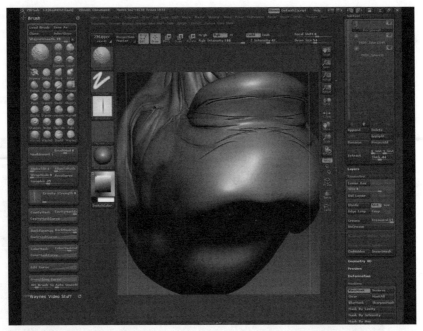

FIGURE 16-61

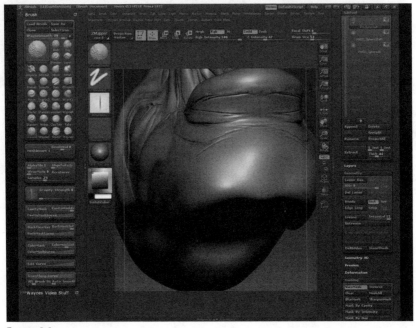

FIGURE 16-62

I felt that some sort of indication of a nose was needed even though this creature does not in fact have one. Again, smooth those out a little once you're done. While we have the **Slash1** brush active, let's also run some overlapping lines over the top of the brow area as you can see in the images. This is an area that is very active when we make facial expressions and so would have some wrinkles. Watch for areas that would have wrinkles or folds because they help give your character both believability and "life." Add more lines over the brow area and as usual smooth them out a bit. The farther back toward the back of the head they go, the smoother they should be. Add some finer lines and then smooth in between the folds in the nose area and down toward the eyes. The eyes and the wrinkles are important to facial expressions, so we must add some sense of movement there. Also, since the character is older he will have more wrinkles in these active areas. I also added a few more lines to the edges of the mouth for the same reason. This is a good example of how our initial character back story helps us in the modeling process.

FIGURE 16-63

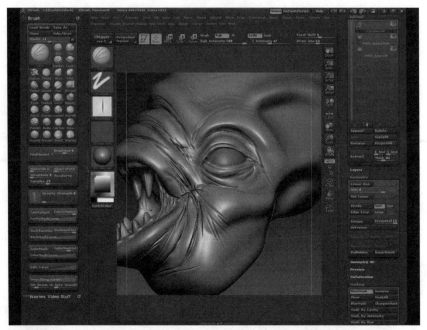

FIGURE 16-64

Add lots of fine lines below the eyes and a few above them as shown and blend them in a little. Wrinkles around the eyes are also good indicators of age. I added a few rough slashes on the sides of the head as placeholders for gill-like structure development later on in the sculpting process. These were a last-minute addition to the design that I felt might be needed as our character does have amphibian ancestry.

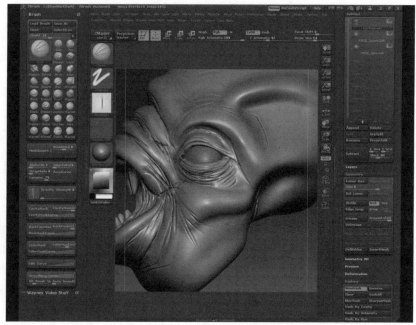

Figure 16-65

Change to your **Inflate** brush with the **FreeHand** stroke type selected and **Alpha 01** active. What I would like you to do now is go back to all the areas where we have just added wrinkles and lines with our Slash1 brush and add some mass between them. Remember to treat the lines like they are railway tracks for our Inflate brush. Work your way over the model, changing brush size and pressure often to keep things from looking too "regular."

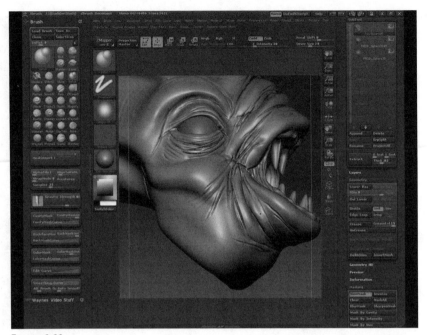

FIGURE 16-66

Remember that organic items usually have a somewhat irregular and unpredictable surface, so to imitate that we must try to add some irregularity where we can. That is one of the keys to organic digital sculpting and an area in which ZBrush excels. If some of the smaller areas of lines and wrinkles are difficult to push with the Inflate brush, you can use the **Displace** brush with a smaller alpha (such as **Alpha 36**) and a low ZIntensity. You want to keep your strokes slow and flowing and avoid jittering or jagged strokes that can produce a lumpy look that used to be known as the "ZBrush look." Now that digital sculpting techniques in ZBrush have evolved, that look is easily avoided.

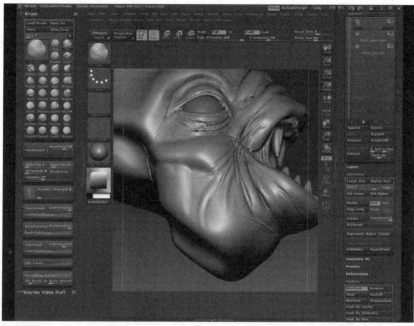

FIGURE 16-67

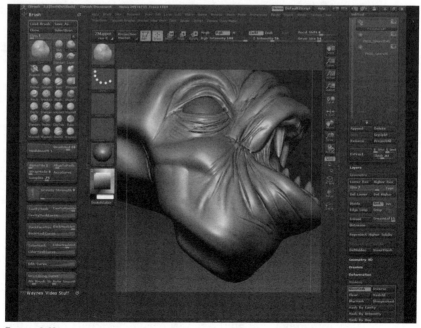

FIGURE 16-68

After doing all this, change to your **Clay** brush again, step down to subdivision level **7**, and add some mass to indicate the jaw area. The slight flattening effect of the Clay brush works wonders here and is much quicker than a rounded brush such as the Inflate or Standard brushes. Remember to smooth out the transitional areas as you go before moving on to add some mass under the mouth and on the chin area. Again, if you feel any part of the design needs modifying after making these changes, do that now. In my case I felt that the cheekbone area needed some modification, so I ran the Clay brush over that area, then flattened the whole cheek area down a little with the **Flatten** brush set to a ZIntensity of **29**. I also ran the Flatten brush over the outer part of the brow curve to help it fit in better with the rest of the creature's head design. Step back up to subdivision level 8 again for the next part of the sculpting process.

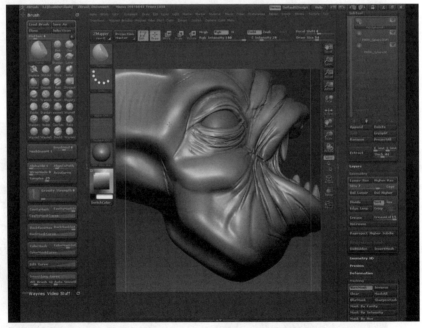

FIGURE 16-69

Using the **Clay** brush, start to add a little more detail to some of the wrinkles and folds under the eyes. I felt the intersecting area of the upper lid meeting the eyebrows needed to show more weight, so first I ran over it with the Clay brush and then again with the Inflate brush.

Now remember that all the time we have been using the **Inflate** brush we have had Gravity set to **64**, which has helped to add a little more of a fold each time we used it. Use this Inflate brush over any areas of the face you feel could use some fill between wrinkles or some softer additional wrinkles. This part of the process is up to each individual artist's style and preference. Remember, in art there is no right and wrong... only "different."

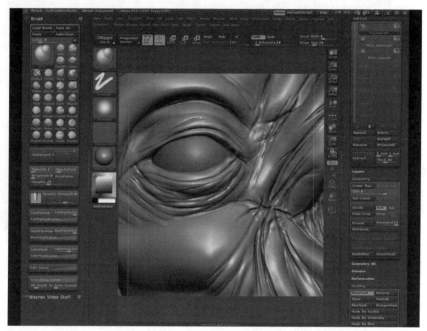

FIGURE 16-70

I also want to fill between the wrinkles we made earlier inside the mouth a bit to give it more of an organic feel. At this subdivision level we are still a little short of polygons in this area at the moment, but we will be coming back to it again later. As we are in the area of the inside of the mouth, it is high time we sorted out the tongue and got it sized and positioned correctly.

So hold down **Shift + Ctrl** and drag a green box over the area you wish to be left with (in this case the bottom part of the inside of the mouth where the tongue is). Now step right back down to subdivision level 5 this time. Doing this is going to make it much faster and easier to make what amounts to large changes in our sculpt without affecting any of the upper level detail. It also makes it a whole world easier for ZBrush as it has fewer polygons to worry about.

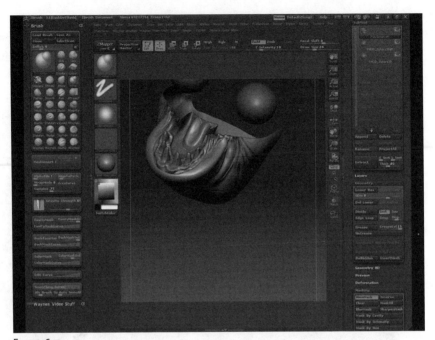

FIGURE 16-71

Using your **Move** brush, pull the edges of the tongue to make it both wider and longer, and in the front make sure that the area behind the gums and teeth is deep enough as shown. Once you have the tongue the right size and position, step all the way back up to level 8 and use the **Clay** brush on the tongue area to refine its shape. If you feel at this point there is anything to adjust in the gum/teeth intersection area, do so using the **Standard** brush.

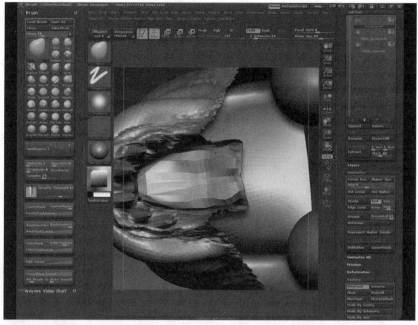

FIGURE 16-72

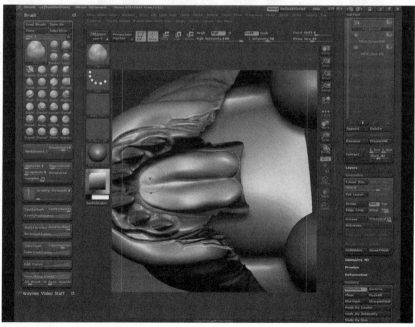

FIGURE 16-73

It's now time to get those gums looking like they actually fit the teeth a bit more, so switch to your **Pinch** brush and carefully pinch together these intersecting areas with a smallish size brush. Work your way with care around each tooth on the bottom set. (You should still have some of the model hidden from before.) Unhide the rest of the head before continuing onward.

Step back down to subdivision level 3 as we need to broaden the back of the skull a bit. The back of the head still looks a bit narrow in Perspective mode (activated and deactivated by pressing the **P** key). So rotate your model to a top-down view and switch to the **Move** brush with a large size, then pull the sides and back of the head outward to broaden it a bit. Now rotate your model until you get to an underneath view looking up from under the jaw and again broaden the back of the cranium a bit. If you do not do this from underneath you will end up with a fairly odd-shaped cranium.

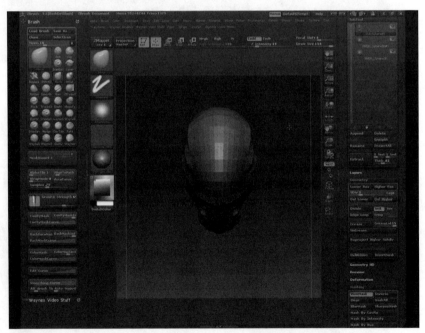

FIGURE 16-74

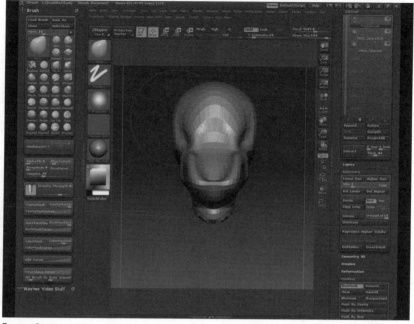

FIGURE 16-75

We want the head to be roughly human-like. From a side view, make sure that the dome of the top of the skull is correct as shown to complete our editing of the skull shape. We are now finished with correcting the skull shape so we can step back up to subdivision level 8 again.

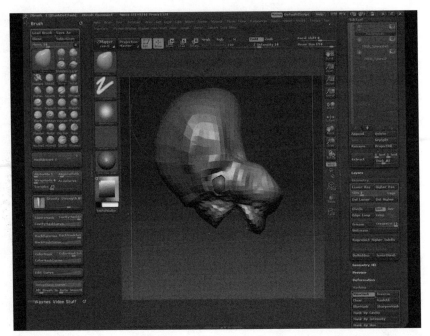

FIGURE 16-76

Switch to your **Inflate** brush and inflate some of the folds and wrinkles around the upper brow area, adding folds where there would be some due to pulling of the skin and muscle movement. Look back to the finer wrinkles in the nasal area, and if needed use your Inflate brush between them as well to again help add that sense of weight. Work your way around in similar fashion to the wrinkles at the edges of the eyes and the corners of the mouth, being careful to smooth the edges out to make them fit in with the rest of the sculpture.

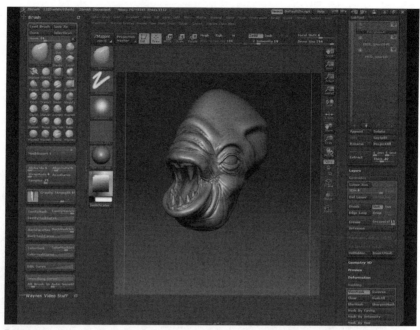

FIGURE 16-77

FIGURE 16-78

I want you to change the alpha for your Inflate brush now to **Alpha 58** (this is the one that has five vertical wavy lines). We are going to use this with a **FreeHand** stroke type to carve in some finer details; you will find that when it comes to detailing, this alpha is a perfect "one size fits all" that can give many different looks depending on the brush you use it with. When using it with your Inflate brush, make sure that you are using the **Alt** key to reverse from Zadd to Zsub. Test it out by lightly dragging it over the area where the lower eye meets the bottom of the brow ridge. Wrinkles in this area will help make the character look old.

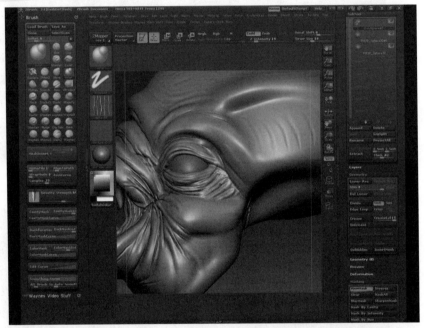

FIGURE 16-79

It's time to add some detail to the lips, so with your **Inflate** brush with **Alpha 58** still active, use short light strokes to carve out some fine lines along first the bottom lip and then the upper lip. You can now increase your brush size a fair bit and use the same sort of stroke on the upper brow area, the eyelids, and even the cheekbones. As you'll notice, this immediately adds some sense of life and extra fine detail to the digital sculpture that we'll be expanding on before we finish off the head. Working your way around the jaw and under the mouth area, make sure that each stroke is made in the direction that the surface is traveling and not against the grain. Also, rather than just one stroke, make two at a slight angle. This gives a far more pleasing result than just simple straight lines.

FIGURE 16-80

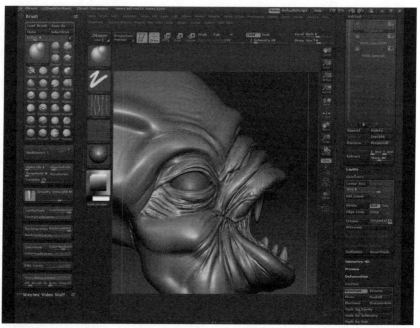

FIGURE 16-81

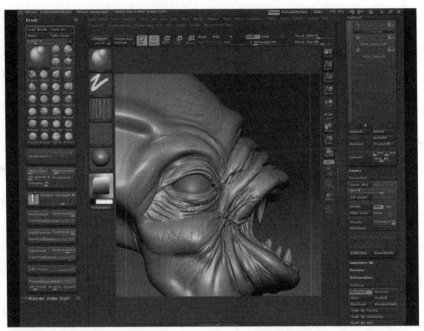

FIGURE 16-82

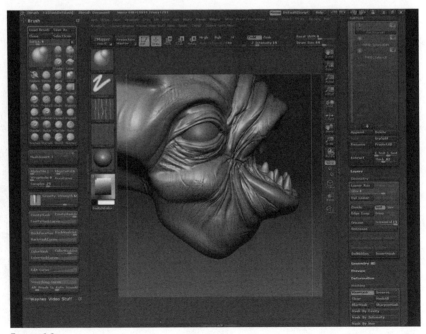

FIGURE 16-83

Continuing up to the brow area and then behind the brows, cover the rest of the head in the same way using a variety of brush sizes. Make sure that you do not use exactly the same pressure each time, as varying it will help to add some unpredictability to the surface. It is very important that each set of "lines" flow with the surface because that movement is what makes the skin look believable. This is a key part to making any character look photo real. Remember, though, that it is no use whatsoever in adding details such as these until you have totally nailed your main forms. Adding details too early can make a digital sculpture look amateurish and unconvincing. A good guideline for when your model is ready for the fine detail is this: Could it stand on its own as is with no detail? If the answer to that question is "yes," then it's time to add any fine detail that is required.

Figure 16-84

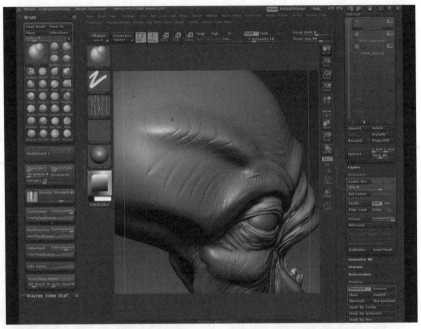

FIGURE 16-85

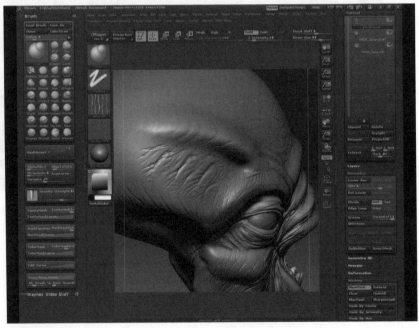

FIGURE 16-86

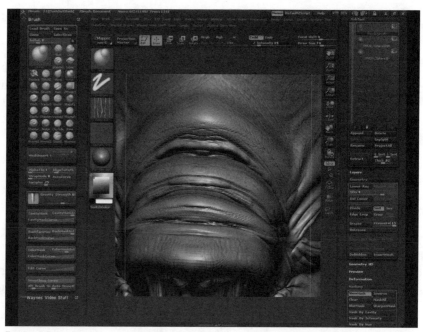

FIGURE 16-87

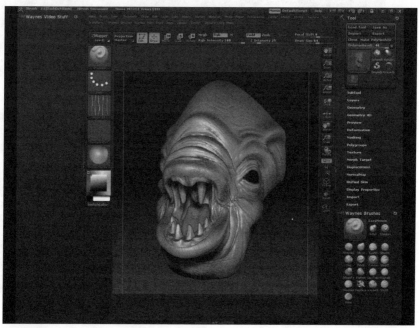

FIGURE 16-88

At this point I recommend that you take a short break from modeling before getting to the really fine detailing. Without a fresh perspective, you get too used to a model and can miss vital things.

At the moment our Guardian's head stands at a perfectly respectable 1.5 million polygons, but we'll be subdividing it to level 9 to finish it off so we'll need those extra polygons for the fine details. This will take our polygon count to about 6 million polygons, so if your computer cannot comfortably handle that polygon count, feel free to use HD geometry so that you can follow along.

Note: Nowadays just about everyone's computer is capable of a polygon count of 6 million, and ZBrush itself can handle many more polygons than that. My personal record is 1.2 billion in a test run. As you can see, ZBrush is extremely stable at such extreme poly counts.

This is the stage where we get to add all those lovely über details that really start to make this sculpt look like a real living, breathing thing and not just a cool design. So subdivide your model again from the **Geometry** section of the **Tool** palette and get ready to roll.

FIGURE 16-89

Switch again to your **Standard** brush with the **Alpha 58** selected and a **Dotted** stroke type, and set **Zadd** to **18** and your Draw Size to **84**. We are going to use it very lightly indeed to add some further lines and wrinkles to our model. This is the part in the process where you need to use your own artistic judgment, but I'll outline how I approach it so that you can get an idea of how to approach your own models. I'm aiming for a light cross-hatched effect with the lines I'm gently carving into my model. As before, I'm making one stroke and then another at a very slight angle to the first to help create a bit of irregularity. Make sure you take your time and only put the fine details in the direction the skin would travel and also where you think they would be needed. Don't just add them everywhere or randomly, or it will end up killing the design and making your digital sculpture look very bland indeed.

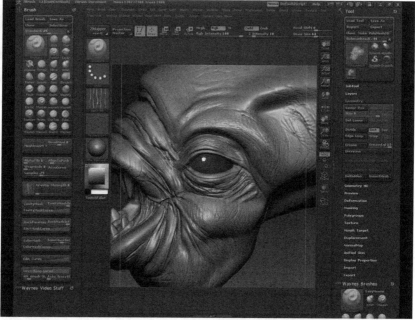

FIGURE 16-90

FIGURE 16-91

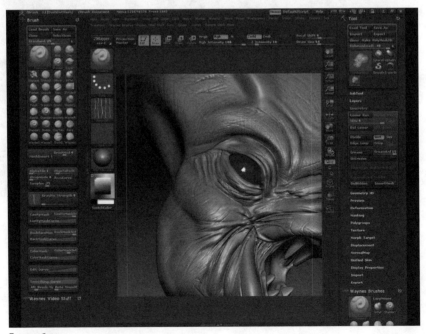

FIGURE 16-92

I started by adding some fine wrinkles to the cheek areas, then the upper and lower eye. Once I was happy with the effect there, I moved onward to the nasal area and worked especially on the existing wrinkles there. I made sure to add plenty of these fine wrinkles over the existing heavier ones to make the surface look like old skin. If you look carefully at the skin of a very old person, you will notice that wrinkles appear to have "layers," with the heavy wrinkles surrounded by increasingly finer and finer ones. This pattern is individual to each person and usually becomes more pronounced with age.

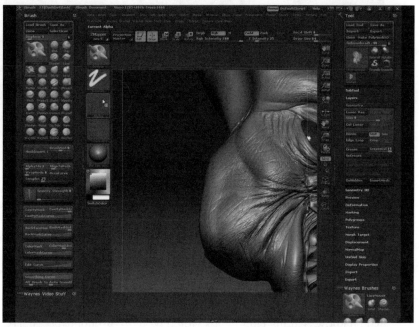

FIGURE 16-93

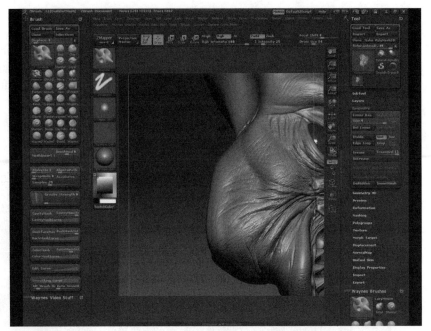

FIGURE 16-94

One area to make sure you take some time getting right is where the nasal area meets the edges of the eyes. This area will likely have the most and largest variety of wrinkles than any other. Keep the back story of our character in mind as well, because this is going to help tell us how he would live his life and give us valuable information in the sculpting process.

For example, if we knew he was a happy and jovial type of guy, we would know that his laugh lines would be more pronounced. Since we know this guy takes his role very seriously, chances are that he will probably worry and frown a lot, so that information will tell us where to put these finer details. Now you can see why the exercise of writing a back story is actually vital if something is to be made believable. And the deeper you get with the back story, the more detailed and believable your model will become as a result.

So with the information given to us by the back story as well as some artistic license of our own, work your way around the model adding fine wrinkles. Work on areas such as the brow and below the mouth until you are happy with it. While you're working on these details I strongly urge you to switch off your X symmetry so your digital sculpture doesn't end up looking "too CG." This will double the amount of work you will have to do, but you will reap the rewards once you are done.

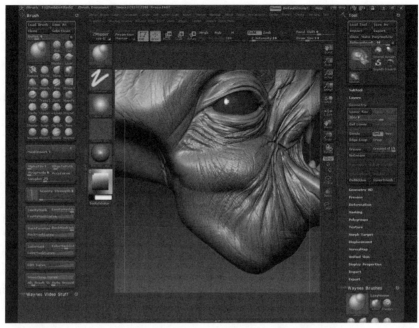

FIGURE 16-95

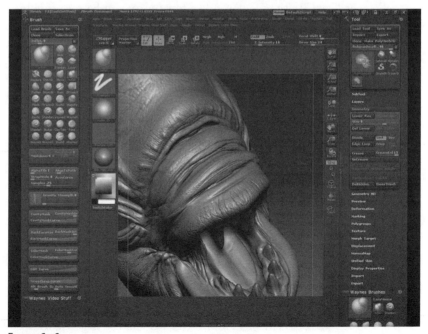

FIGURE 16-96

Also make sure that while you work your way around the model adding these fine wrinkles you vary the brush size as well as the pressure that you use. You may even want to turn the Zsub up and down a small amount. If all your wrinkles and folds are the same size and depth, the sculpture will not look as "real" or be as good as it could be. The only time I break this "rule" is if I am speed sculpting to get something done in a given time limit. But on all other occasions I try to add as much asymmetry as I can in the later stages. You could even sculpt your entire model asymmetrically from the start, although it is going to at least double the time that it will take to do it.

Once you have gone over your model and added the fine wrinkles, I want you to return to places such as the eye/eyebrow intersection area and add wrinkles going in the opposite direction. You can't do this with the whole model as it would soon make it look very muddy and messy, but in specific areas it can help to again pull off that sense that the skin moves over bone and muscle in certain places. Also at this stage I up my brush size a fair amount and add some larger wrinkles using the same brush but very, very lightly over the cheeks, sides of the mouth, and under the chin area. These have to be very light indeed — so light that you can hardly make out that they are there. Digital sculpting at this stage is all about subtlety. Those faint details really help to sell a piece as "real" to the viewer. Add a few more faint larger wrinkles carefully to the upper and lower lips, again using that slight cross-hatching stroke we've been doing of late. Follow this up with some deeper large ones, but use them very sparingly.

This kind of lip detail is something you just have to practice. Sometimes reference photos can be helpful, but there will be times when you will simply have to use your imagination and artistic ability.

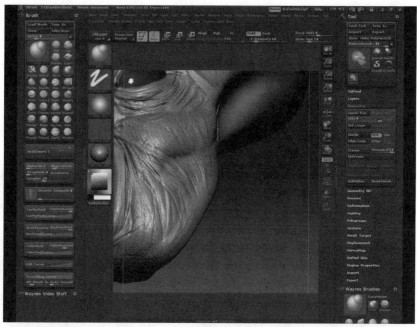

FIGURE 16-97

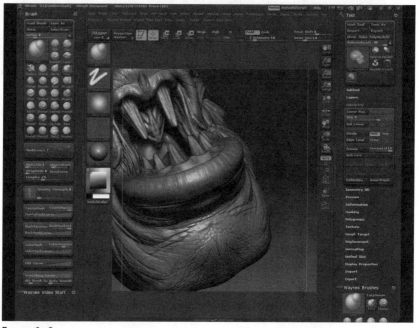

FIGURE 16-98

Change to your **Displace** brush with a **FreeHand** stroke type selected, **Alpha 36** active, and a ZIntensity of **25**. With this brush we are now going to carve out some wrinkles and folds — some that are older ones we've done that may have gotten slightly lost in the detail and others that are new. So start creating lines of wrinkles/folds radiating from the corner of the mouth area using this brush with the **Alt** key pressed. (Imagine that you are drawing an asterisk with each of the arms a line radiating from the center point. In our case, the corner of the mouth is the center point.)

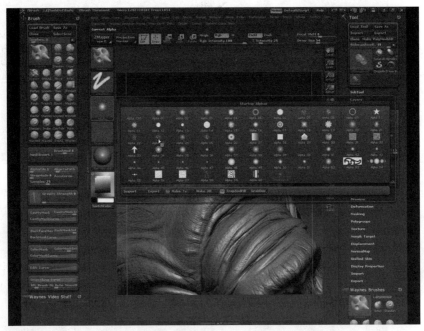

FIGURE 16-99

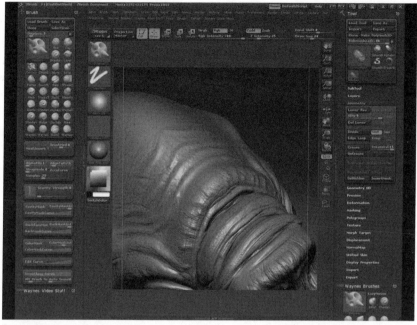

FIGURE 16-100

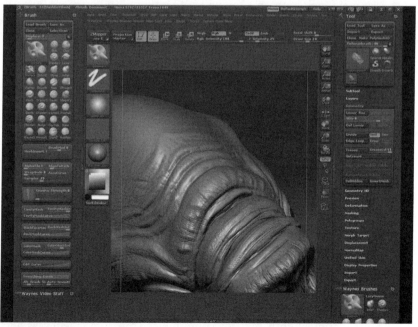

FIGURE 16-101

The back of the jaw currently is a tad boring and we need to add some medium-resolution detail for a few folds running from under the cheekbone and fading out just before the jaw turns back underneath. Be sure to make these only slightly visible and not too deep, as we don't want to have to smooth this area and redo our previous detailing if we can help it. Check the folds that run from the corners of the mouth down under the mouth to make sure they haven't gotten "washed out" in our detailing process. One thing that many newer digital sculptors forget is that when you add fine detail your medium-resolution forms can get a bit lost, so it's important to go back over areas that need it.

This would be a good time to take a brief break. When sculpting in ZBrush for long periods of time you need to give your brain time to get used to being creative on demand. When working to create high-resolution models, you will not always have the luxury of being able to be creative only when you feel like it. While it's never good to force your art, you do have to actually eat and survive to be able to make these wonderful digital sculpts, and as such the ability to sculpt on demand is one that you need to develop.

Change to your **Inflate** brush with **Alpha 35**, the **FreeHand** stroke type selected, and a ZIntensity of **10**. What I would like you to do now is take a really good look at the fine wrinkles on your model. (I do mean a *very* good look at them.) You will notice that at the moment 90 percent of them are merely cut in lines and have no sense of mass or weight pulling on the skin and no bulging at all. Although the model may look fine at a cursory glance, those who study the detail (especially other artists) will notice the lack of weight and realism. So start very slowly and lightly at first to build up the areas between some of these fine and medium wrinkles in areas that you think are believable. This is up to personal artistic interpretation to a large degree, so rather than giving you details stroke by stroke, I'll just outline general areas for this part of the sculpting. That way you will hopefully gain the benefit of the reason why I'm doing it and not rely on exact instruction.

I find good areas to start with are the cheeks and sides of the face area. This is a personal choice, but I feel it's easier to work out the sense of weight and movement for this area than the others. Plus it often helps to give me the information that I need to add to the other areas. I work with a very small brush size and carefully inflate only those areas that I feel need it and contribute to the actual detail, not between every wrinkle. Digital sculpting is to a large degree all about creating an illusion of detail, so as such I pick and choose areas that I feel inflating slightly will add something to the digital sculpt as a whole. I would urge you to pay extra attention to your medium-resolution folds at the sides of the mouth and make sure that these do in fact convey a sense of mass and gravity pulling down on them.

One trick I would like to share with you as a way to save time and to make sure that things remain "organic" is what I call "widdling." Remember that organic things rarely have straight lines or an overly organized look. By their very nature they are irregular and controlled not by logic but by nature and chaos. So to simulate this without having to spend immense amounts of time, I created a shortcut that was inspired by latex makeup artists who work on films. When painting a texture for something such as a monster, they will often use a light continuous wiggling stroke to add that extra sense of organic chaotic randomness. I use a similar technique with the Inflate brush to give that randomness to the inflating between small wrinkles. I use a continuous winding wriggling stroke over a small area at a time using a brush size that is slightly larger than the areas between the smallest wrinkles. I keep randomly working over an area at a pretty fast speed until I've covered about 50 percent to 70 percent of the total area between the wrinkles I wish to inflate before moving to a new area. Using this method you can detail vast areas extremely quickly.

Once the areas between the wrinkles are inflated, I up the brush size and add some lines radiating from the sides of the eyes outward toward the top of the eyebrow, gently fading them out as I go. Even though I have fine detail in this area, I felt that it still needed some more medium-resolution details to help keep things looking interesting. Digital sculpting is all about refining things as you go, changing your mind about an area, and improving it. It is rare that you will do a sculpture that turns out great without some sort of modification at some point in the sculpting process. That is what helps an artist to put his heart and soul into a work and not just go through the motions.

Do the same between the wrinkles in the nasal area to again add some medium-resolution "interest," then work on the areas between the wrinkles on the top lip. Finding the balance between the medium-resolution detail, the major forms, and the fine detailing is not an easy one to be honest. Getting this balance correct is really a matter of personal preference. You will also want to inflate between some wrinkles in areas on the lower lip in a similar way.

While we are in the mouth area, add a few soft carved in lines to show that the tongue is more than a lump of flesh. If we were to retopologize the head model at this stage, we could even add detail to the tongue such as the taste buds, but in this case the distance the model will be seen from and the final render size mean that we don't need that amount of detail. Go in and sharpen up some of the lines we made to the teeth and make sure they haven't been washed out while we worked on the rest of the model. Feel free to add further detail to this area, but remember that the mouth area of this model isn't going to be seen close up. Work your way around the inside of the mouth in a similar way, adding detail where it's missing and sharpening up what is already there. Although we don't need to go mad with detail in these areas, it is important to have enough to stand up to scrutiny in the final shot.

Add a few lines to the bottom part of the top lip where it meets the gums that up until now have been pretty hard to get to. Switch to your **Displace** brush with **Alpha 35** and the **FreeHand** stroke type selected and add a few outward folds to the brow area as shown. You need to think carefully about how the skin would look in this area if you are to make it believable. If you're not sure, look for reference photos of old men. Using the same brush but at a smaller size, carve in lines between these folds that will be deep enough to catch some shadow when the model is lit. Another area that needs work is the lines coming from the corner of the brows. So using the same brush, add some folds to give more weight and "life" to this area. A couple of strokes with the brush will do wonders.

Figure 16-102

Another area that is conspicuous by its lack of detailing is the bottom part of the side of the head. So I ran the same brush in an upward direction, starting near the underside of the head, between the lines we carved in much earlier on. I made sure to check that I faded them out as I drew each stroke to avoid smoothing the area too much. Do the same thing for the top part of the side of the head where the two ridges run down the length. Again, make sure as best you can that these folds are running between the lines already there and that they fade out nicely.

You may have noticed that in early stages we were often smoothing a stroke after creating it, but now we don't. The reason for doing so early on was to make sure that every line we carved faded out and sat as perfectly as possible. Now that we have some fine detail, though, we want to preserve it as much as possible. With practice, you will learn to better control your strokes in ZBrush. Something I learned from an old tattooist is that "line quality" is of major importance. So for a digital artist, this means that we must strive to have total control of our brush and the forms it creates.

There is an area on the side of the head that hints of gills that may be relics of evolution, so run over each of these to give them a bit of depth so that they don't just appear as random marks on our mesh.

Step down to subdivision level 7 again as we need to sort out the area where the top teeth meet the gums, or to be more accurate where they fail to meet the gums. Switch to your White Pearl MatCap material as it will give us a better view of the mask I need you to paint over each tooth. Paint these masks in carefully, then once you've got them masked, invert the mask by either going to the **Masking** section of the **Tool** palette or by holding down the **Ctrl** key and clicking on an empty part of the viewport. Then switch to your **Move** transform tool and draw out an action line on one of the teeth. We are going to use this to help us move the teeth back against the gums a bit more. Move them back until they meet the gums at the point nearest the front of the mouth. If you now go to a side view of the area, you can draw another action line from the gum to the end of the tooth, then use your **Rotate** tool until it looks correct. Adjust the location against the gums with care.

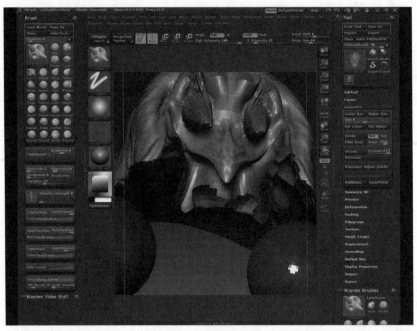

FIGURE 16-103

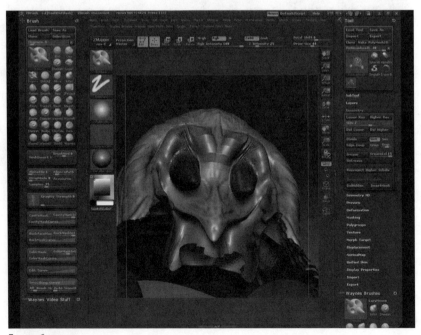

FIGURE 16-104

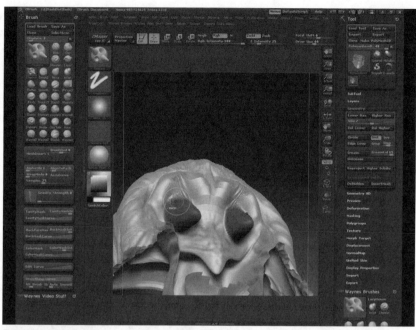

FIGURE 16-105

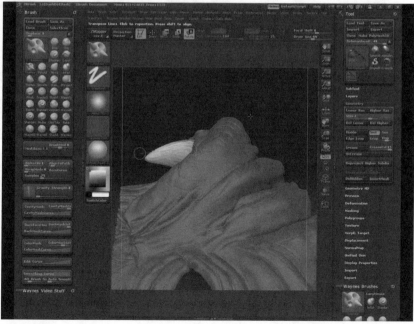

FIGURE 16-106

Step down now to subdivision level 4, switch to your **Inflate** brush with the **FreeHand** stroke and **Alpha 01** selected, and make the size big enough, and stroke up over the cheeks and up over the brows. This is best done from a side view. Also do another stroke down the sides of the jaw toward the front before slightly inflating the chin area, since at the moment the Guardian is basically chinless. Look at the underside of the chin; if there has been some movement in the jaw line from inside, switch to the **Move** brush and move this area to its proper "horseshoe" shape.

Now mask off everything on the head apart from the jaw area. You want to move the back of the jaw where it meets the head back and down a little to better help the design of the creature's head. Each form and curve will later be reflected in the shapes of the body and give us design ideas. Once you've done this, we can step back up to subdivision level 9 again to continue onward. I also switched from the White Pearl MatCap back to my original black and white material that I use often. Feel free to use your own favorite MatCap for the main sculpting stages or make one for yourself.

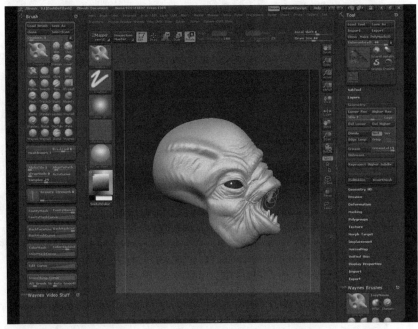

FIGURE 16-107

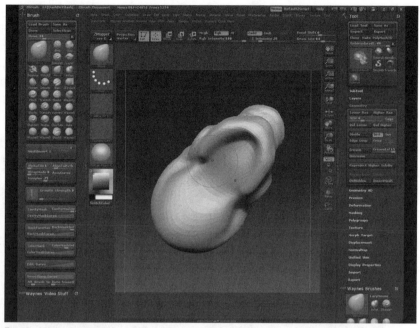

FIGURE 16-108

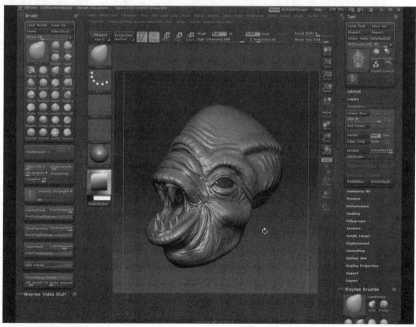

FIGURE 16-109

It's time for us to start detailing the rest of the head such as the scalp and the back of the cranium. We won't try to detail every last bit at this stage; we'll do that once we combine it with the body. So change to your **Clay** brush, choose **Alpha 57** and the **FreeHand** stroke type, and start to "scribble" over the scalp to add some texture to it. This scribbling is another shortcut (along with "widdling") to add detail to large areas quickly.

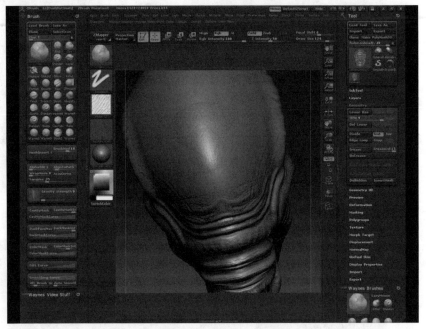

FIGURE 16-110

I made scribbling motions in overlapping continuous arcs down the scalp. Then go to your **Alpha** palette and increase the radial fade on the alpha by setting the **RD** slider to **6**. This will give the alpha a softer edge for the rest of the work we will do with it. Increase the Draw Size of your brush to about double the size it has been and fill in the back of the cranium, then run under the cranium to right behind the jaw. This ensures that there aren't too many "blank areas" on our sculpture, although much of the area underneath the head will not be seen once we add the neck and the rest of the body to the digital sculpt.

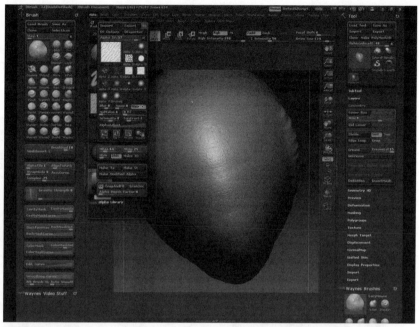

Figure 16-111

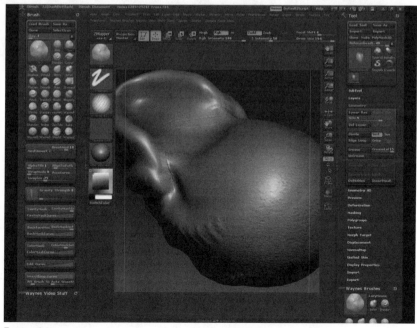

Figure 16-112

Switch to the **Slash2** brush and scratch out some lines between those folds we added on the bottom part of the side of the head as shown. Then carefully scratch in some of the gills as well. The gills shouldn't be too obvious because our back story dictates that this species was water based long ago, but those features have faded with evolution.

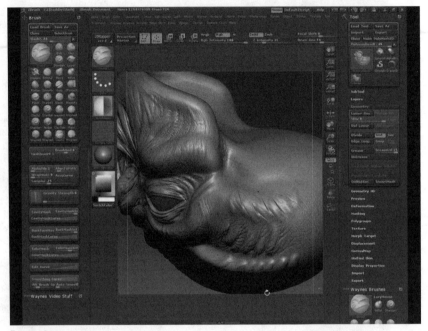

FIGURE 16-113

Using the Slash1 brush, we carve some more lines over the areas at the sides of the head to further sharpen them up a bit. The balance between soft and harsh detail is important to my style of sculpting and can be a difficult balance. Too much soft detail can make a sculpture look washed out, but too much hard detail can make it end up looking cold and artificial. So finding this balance is one that I continually work on. I also added some "slash work" for the "gill" area and the lines running from under the skull and the top ridge running along the skull. Lightly now, add some scratched lines that come from the corner wrinkles of the eye. Remember to try to keep these as "organic" looking as you can.

This is the point where our usage of the Slash1 brush is going to change a bit. Either by using a very light pressure or by turning the ZIntensity down a fair bit, add some very lightly carved in lines on some areas of the face to add some extra visual interest. Start by running a few over the cheekbones, making sure that they are not all perfectly aligned in the same direction. You want a variety of stroke direction while still maintaining a common direction.

Add others to further deepen the folds in the skin that are near the edges of the mouth (under the cheekbones). We need to reinforce some detail that looks too soft at this time. Remember not to simply carve a single line, but rather a series of two or three overlapping slightly criss-cross strokes to help maintain that organic skin look. Using this same overlapping stroke technique, we need to now look at adding some sense of depth between the forehead wrinkles. These can be made deeper than the ones we carved into the cheek area because they need to catch shadows well. So start to do this between the forehead wrinkles, remembering to not make the strokes identical in size, direction, or depth.

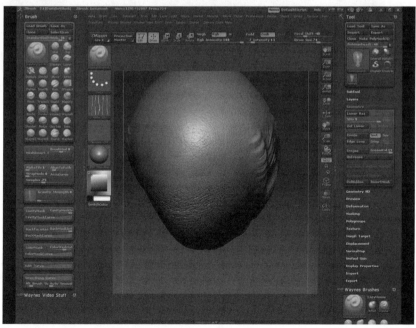

FIGURE 16-114

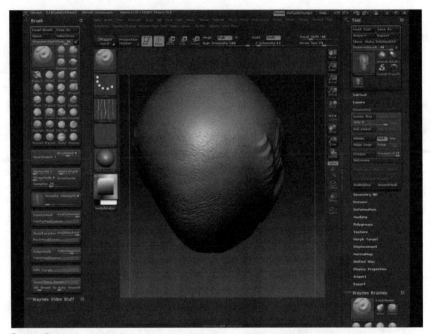

FIGURE 16-115

Change now to your **Standard** brush with **Alpha 58** and the **Dots** stroke type selected, and set the brush to **Zsub** with a ZIntensity of **13**. We are going to use this brush over most of the head to add to our existing surface skin detail. A while back we added a simple skin surface to a large area using a single alpha. Although this may look okay, it does not yet look like a believable skin texture.

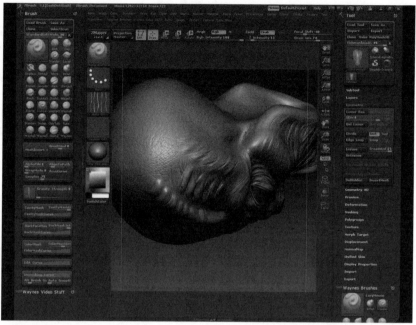

So we need to add a second layer of detail. A believable skin texture is one of the hardest things for a beginner to achieve and one that invariably takes more time than necessary. Skin texturing should never be added until the digital sculpture can stand up on its own perfectly well without it. It should just be the "icing on the cake" and not the cake itself. Up your brush size so that it is pretty large and make the scalp of the head nearly fill the viewport. Now use a series of overlapping circular motions over the scalp, moving toward the back of the cranium a bit. This will add a really nice texture to the head that we will continue down the back of the cranium. Carry this underneath the head to just behind the jaw. A little overlap onto the jaw is allowed and may even help to tie these areas together.

Start to do the same with the sides of the head, only this time use strokes that follow the direction of the surface. This helps to add very fine stress wrinkles in the skin that give the impression that it is stretching over bone. Again, make sure you vary the depth of your stroke by using more and less pressure. If you don't have a graphics tablet, these steps will take considerably longer.

Creating believable skin texture detail is usually a matter of approaching it in a series of layers, just like we did with the head. On the head we started with our main forms before moving onward to the medium-resolution forms and then the finer details (getting increasingly finer with each pass). With skin texture we first added an overall texture using a simple off-the-shelf ZBrush alpha, then used another layer and a different ZBrush alpha to add some complexity and believability. So now we need to add some lumps and bumps to keep the main forms from looking too "spherical," which is a dead giveaway of a CG model. To do this we are going to use a brush that we haven't used before and one that is often overlooked — the **Blob** brush. This brush does one job exceedingly well: It adds lumps and bumps to a digital sculpt in a variety of ways depending on stroke type, ZIntensity, brush size, and the alpha used (if any).

So switch to your **Blob** brush with no active alpha and the **Spray** stroke type set to a ZIntensity of **25** and a Draw Size of **124**. As we are not using an alpha, we will get softer lumps and bumps. Of course you can keep on adding layers of detail as long as you wish and get some highly complex skin textures. What I'm showing you here is a shorter version that covers the main concepts. So make some movements over the back of the cranium and the top of the scalp with your Blob brush. The Spray stroke type creates a random pattern of the alpha selected, whereas the DragDot stroke type gives us one instance of a selected alpha.

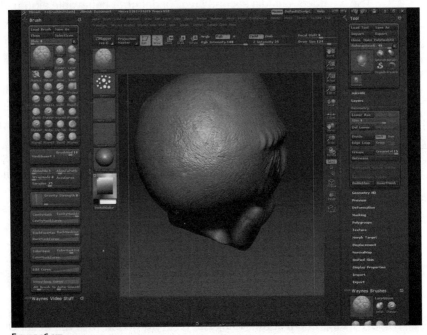

FIGURE 16-117

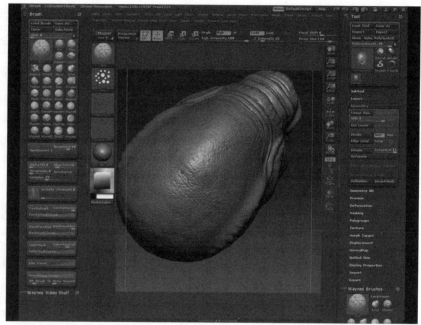

FIGURE 16-118

Now switch to **Alpha 23** and set ZIntensity to **8**, and do the same thing over the same areas. This will add many smaller and somewhat sharper looking lumps and spots on the skin surface.

Now take your brush size down a fair bit so you can make much smaller lumps over the eyebrow area. Add more of the same type of detail over the nasal and brow folds before gently fading your pressure as you move back toward the scalp once more. Do a pass over the chin area and lightly over the cheeks as well. This helps to blend everything together so it doesn't look like separate details in separate areas.

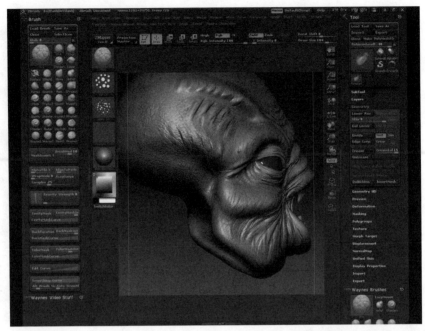

FIGURE 16-119

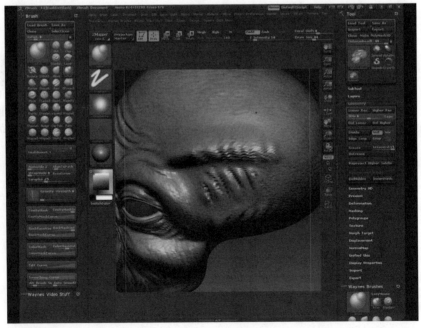

FIGURE 16-120

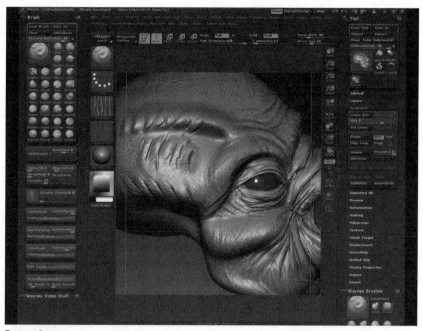

FIGURE 16-121

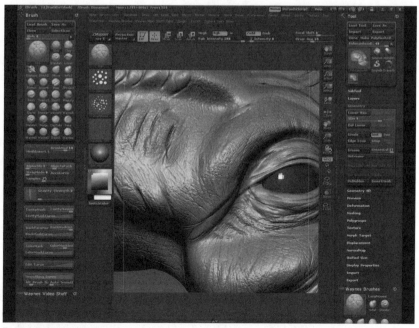

FIGURE 16-122

Change to your **Displace** brush with **Alpha 36** and the **FreeHand** stroke type selected. We are going to use this to carve a couple more areas inward and sharpen a few details so they aren't lost in the overall details. So go back over the lines we carved earlier on the top ridge and bottom part of the side of the head and then move toward the gill area and add some sharper lines there as well. This should help them to stand out a bit more. Step down now to level 6 as we are going to use our Inflate brush to inflate between the lines we just recarved. If we try to use the Inflate brush on subdivision level 9, we will end up with a nasty and muddy-looking surface that we would have to smooth out. So if we step to a lower subdivision level, only the polygons in this level will be inflated and they will be reflected in the higher ones without losing the detail we need to keep. So using your **Inflate** brush on level 6, inflate the areas between the lines carved into the top ridge and the bottom of the side of the head, then step back up to level 9 again.

Now take your **Pinch** brush and nip together all the lines that we carved in on the side of the head to help create the look that we are after. Also nip together the forehead wrinkles and those under the mouth if you feel that they need it. Things should be starting to look pretty fine at this stage, and we are not far from the end of the process for the head of the Guardian. While you have the Pinch brush active, check for any other wrinkles that need nipping together before we change from this brush to another.

We are now at the finishing off stage where a lot depends on the look of your own sculpture. This is the time to start to pull everything together toward the final look for the head. So I again switched to the **Blob** brush with the same settings we used before and added some very small bumps and lumps with it using a small brush size and low ZIntensity in places such as the side of the head near the gills that I felt could do with it. I also added some very tiny ones over the bags of the eyes in the corners where they intersect with the rest of the face. Go over the tongue with the Blob brush as well to add the look of taste buds and some extra interest. I used the **Pinch** brush on the lips/gums intersection on the top lip as it was still bugging me a little. The bottom set of gums I felt were also a little too flat at this stage so I used the **Inflate** brush to round the tops of them off a bit until I was happy with their look. We want to get to the point where we only have to make minor changes once we integrate it with the body.

Carve a few soft lines on the tongue running from the center outward, making sure that they follow the surface direction. Finally, add some lines and folds using the Inflate brush at the very back of the inside of the mouth to make sure that should anyone be nosy enough to look (or should it actually show in our final render) that there is indeed some detail there.

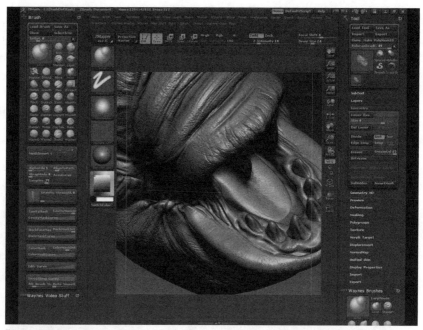

FIGURE 16-123

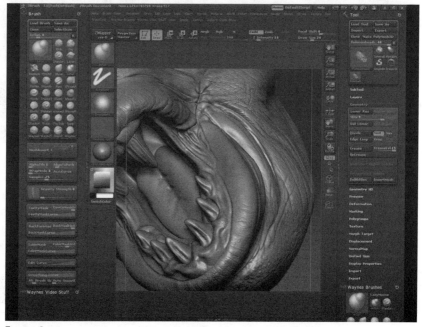

FIGURE 16-124

Before finally calling this head "done," take a short break, then take a last fresh look. Check every feature of your digital sculpture before you move on the next stage. You don't want to have any worries about the quality of the head before moving to the body. There's an old saying that "art is not released, but rather it escapes." So once you know that it is good enough, save it out (a couple of times in multiple locations for file security), and go take a rest and pat yourself on the back. The sculpt that you have just completed has taught you not only the concept of how back story can be used to help develop a character, but also how to deal with a complex design in layers of form and detail. The things that you have learned in this section will be things you can use for a long time to come in your own digital sculptures.

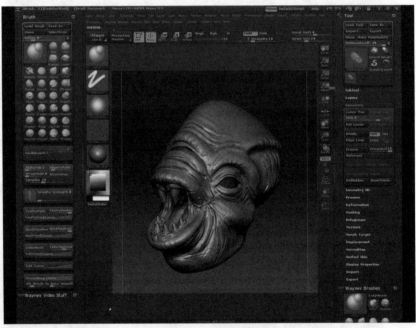

FIGURE 16-125

You could think of this part of the model as the "easy bit" as we started with a simple sphere. In the next sections about the creature and the scene we will be dealing with more complex geometry for our base meshes. By the time you complete the entire scene, you should be thoroughly at home in ZBrush and be a competent digital sculptor, but remember that practice (and lots of it) is a must if you are to progress as an artist. You will only get out of digital sculpting what you are prepared to put into it. By completing this complex head sculpture, you have put in both time and practice that as a result will stand you in excellent stead for the next parts.

17 Retopologizing the Guardian's Head

What Is Retopologizing?

Topology is the layout of edges and edge loops that create the polygon flow of your model. So if you use one mesh to sculpt on to a high level, you sometimes may have to retopologize it near the end to create the correct polygon flow. This was the case with the head sculpture of the Guardian. We started sculpting from a basic sphere, which is good from a sculpting standpoint but has bad topology if we plan to extract maps from it or if it were to be animated at all.

Topology is especially important for models intended for computer games, as these models must make the best use of every single polygon. They also have to deform well once they are rigged and animated.

Topology also affects how well we can extract color, normal, cavity, or displacement maps for our model. For example, if we have too many polygons in one place and not enough in another we can end up having to use a much larger map than is really needed. So while a base mesh for sculpting would ideally have a fairly even distribution of similar sized polygons with more polygons concentrated in areas that are going to get a lot of detail, this mesh wouldn't be of much use elsewhere in a pipeline.

Why Do I Need to Retopologize a Model That Isn't Animated?

Good topology is not just needed for models that are going to be animated, although that is a common requirement. It can also help with the actual sculpting of your modeling process; by retopologizing a model once the main forms are established we then get polygons in the areas that we need them. This can enable us to use far fewer polygons than we otherwise would.

By retopologizing the Guardian's head, approximately 2 million polygons allow us to have the same amount of detail as our 6 million polygon version. This savings gives us the option (should we actually need it) to take our model to a still higher level of subdivision. In the case of the Guardian's head, 8 million polygons would certainly be over-kill, but if you needed an extreme close-up of the head, then you may need to increase the polygon count.

So topology is just as important to a digital sculptor as it is to a rigger or animator, plus if there is even the slightest chance that at some point your model will be animated, then retopologizing is a good idea anyway. So as a general rule, it's best to take the time to create a good layout of edge loops for a much tidier model that as a result is easier to use and transfer from computer to computer.

Retopologizing in ZBrush

To retopologize in ZBrush we make use of that most important tool in the ZBrush toolkit: the ZSphere. Up to this point we've used it primarily as a way of generating a quick and usable base mesh, but ZSpheres are capable of so much more. In fact, you could nearly fill a book just about the uses of ZSpheres and little tricks with them.

In this section I'll outline the basic workflow for retopologizing. Later on I'll give you an actual example that shows how to retopologize the Guardian's head.

Basic Workflow Guide

To start with, you need to have your high-resolution model ready and at its highest level of subdivision. If you keep it at a lower level, then you will only retopologize your model to that level and not its highest one. Now go to the ZSphere and select it to make it the active tool.

Draw your **ZSphere** in the viewport and make sure that you press **T** for Edit mode. Scroll down the **Tool** palette to the **Rigging** section and press **Select** button. Select your high-resolution sculpt from the pop-up box. This tells ZBrush what we are actually going to retopologize.

Now go to the **Topology** section and press the **Edit Topology** button so we can start to draw the new topology for our model. Make sure that you have X symmetry turned on (by pressing the **X** key), and start to create your geometry. (We'll cover this in detail in the example section, but it is basically a matter of clicking where you want a vertex to be.)

One thing you must remember is that ZBrush will only create a polygon if the face is closed on all sides. So if you have four vertices for a face and only three of them are connected, the face will not be created. It is possible to create topology with triangles in ZBrush, although in my opinion it is best to avoid triangles at all times where you can.

Once your model is retopologized, you can preview it (or at any time during the creation process) by hitting the **A** key or the **Preview** button in the **Adaptive Skin** section of the **Tool** palette. This will preview your model based on both the number of subdivisions set in the Adaptive Skin section and whether or not you have Projection turned on. If it is turned off, it will not project the details from your high-resolution model onto your retopologized one.

Once you are happy with the results, simply press the **Make Adaptive Skin** button and it will then appear under your main selection of tools. I would suggest turning off the preview on the working copy you have been using in order to save on system resources. Once you've done that, make sure that you save your retopologized mesh out (which will have all its subdivision levels up to the one that you generated the mesh from).

Other Uses for Retopologizing

Retopology does not just have to be about correcting topology; it can also be used to make items and accessories that are in physical contact with your digital sculpt, such as clothes and armor. So if you wanted to retopologize the shoulder area to create a piece of armor, you would turn up the **Skin Thickness** slider to give it some actual thickness before previewing or exporting. You can then export it to another application for some further polygon work if you need to.

So basically if you are making something that will come into physical contact with your sculpt, this is a great way to do it.

Editing Existing Topology

You can also edit your existing topology or project from a retopologized version of your sculpt that was created with software such as Topogun. (At the time of writing, Topogun was still in the late stages of beta testing.) So you can just as easily import your topology to the correct size by making a clone of your high-resolution sculpt and then deleting all but the lowest subdivision level. Then when you import your new topology over the top it will be of the correct size.

Then instead of just hitting the **Edit Topology** button when you are at the ZSphere part of the workflow, you can select your retopologized mesh and project the details onto that.

Should you think that your existing topology is "nearly right" but just needs a few minor tweaks, then you can use a similar workflow. Simply clone as mentioned and delete your existing upper subdivision levels. Once you have the lowest subdivision level, select it as the active topology mesh after selecting your high-resolution copy as the mesh you wish to take the details from. Then just delete vertices that are unneeded and add some edge loops where you would like more. Then follow the above workflow as before.

So as you can see, the topology features of ZBrush are very versatile and do not limit you to using the retopology features of ZBrush on its own. They can be used in conjunction with other tools to give you the fastest and most robust workflow.

Guide to Retopologizing the Guardian's Head

Painting the Reference Lines

To those new to ZBrush it may seem strange to start a section about how to retopologize a model by painting a texture on it. As you'll see,

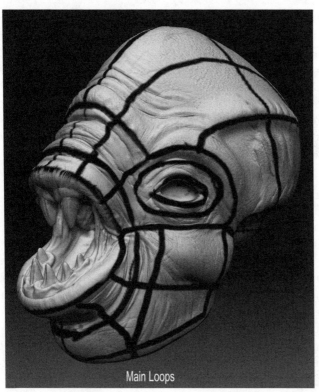

FIGURE 17-1

Main Loops

though, polypainting a reference set of lines that indicate where each polygon goes is a good standard practice because the lines give you the guidance you need while you are retopologizing.

So take your high-resolution model up to its highest subdivision level and fill it with a white color and the white MatCap. This will allow you to see things much better once we get around to the actual retopologizing stage in a moment. Take a smallish brush size with one of the sharper round alphas and make your active color black. Turn off both Zadd and Zsub and set your RGB Color Intensity to **100.**

Knowing where to place the lines for the topology comes from experience and research. For example, if you search Google for "*topology + edge loops*," you'll get thousands of images and information about it. As a general rule though, when starting to paint your edge loops it's best to bear in mind that each major form will need some supporting edge loops. So for a raised area you would need a loop running over the highest point and loops running along the low sides. This allows you to capture it using far fewer polygons.

Start with just adding lines around the main features and forms as shown in the figures before even thinking about the rest of the topology. This allows you to make sure that you will have the most important edge loops in place before you start to refine and add the other edges. Add edge loops only where you need them and do not be tempted to go edge loop crazy. Remember that each time your model is subdivided your polygon count increases by a multiple of four.

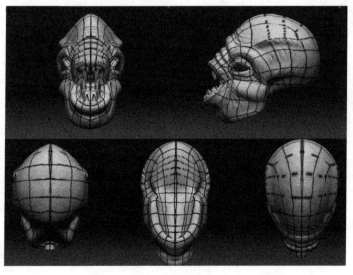

Figure 17-2

Slowly work your way over your model, painting lines for the topology and making sure that you are careful to use only four-sided polygons (known as quads). While ZBrush can retopologize a mesh with triangles in the topology, it's not a good idea as a rule. Keep to an all-quads "watertight mesh" where possible.

By "watertight" I mean imagine that your retopologized mesh is actually a water filled balloon; if there are any holes, the water would stream out. So make it watertight because edges around holes can prove troublesome when it comes time to extract normal or displacement maps from them.

Retopologizing

Let's start by making sure that the model we wish to retopologize and take the detail from is active in our viewport and at its highest subdivision level. As mentioned earlier, if we are at a lower level we will only capture detail to that particular level of our high-resolution mesh. Make sure that the set of topology reference lines that we painted a moment ago are active, then make the ZSphere your active tool and draw it in the viewport.

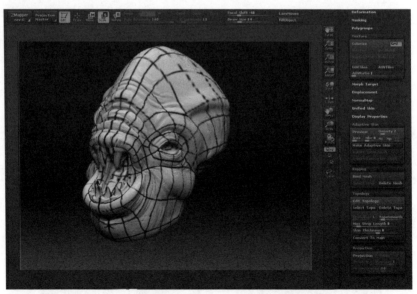

FIGURE 17-3

At this point open up the palettes listed below. We will be making use of all of them before we are finished:

Adaptive Skin
Rigging
Topology
Projection

Scale your ZSphere down to a fairly small size using the **Scale** transform tool. As ZSpheres do not use action lines, it should be easy for you to control. Also place it in the center of the model.

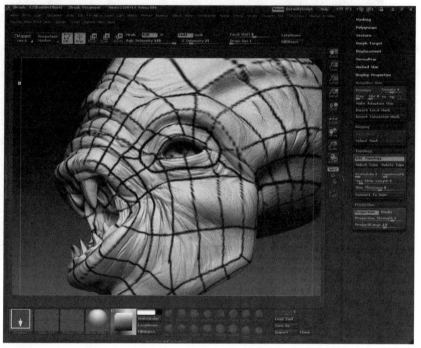

FIGURE 17-4

Press the **Edit Topology** button and start to left-click on each intersection point on your topology reference texture. Since we filled our model with the white MatCap everything should be easy to see. Work your way around your model until the whole thing is done.

There are a few techniques that you will need to know to achieve this. If you are creating a long line with a series of clicks, things will work as you probably expect them to, but if you move to another area you will find that ZBrush expects it to be attached to the previously made area. To start on a different area or a different section of your line, just **Ctrl+click** on the starting vertex/ZSphere, and then continue. For example, to add a set of polygons around the eyes, you would need to make it a separate area.

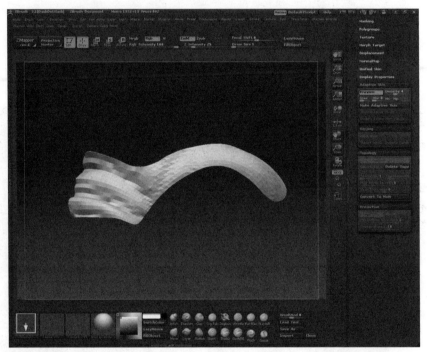

FIGURE 17-5

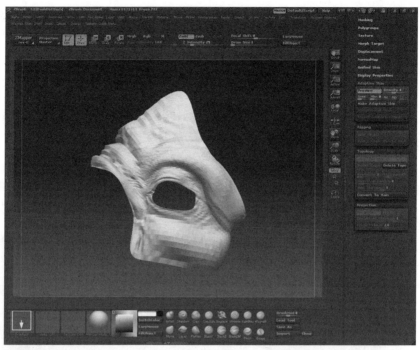

FIGURE 17-6

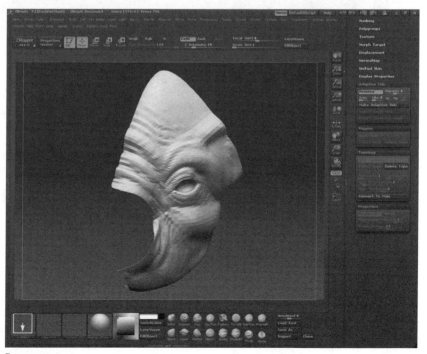

FIGURE 17-7

Create the line for the innermost section of the eye around the inner eyelids. Then **Ctrl+click** to start on the corner of the eye and draw from there outward to the edge of the eye and continue to make the outer loop of the eye. You can then connect these together by **Ctrl+clicking** on a vertex on the inner eye and then clicking on a corresponding one on the outer eye.

Working in this way you can cover the entire model. So what happens if you add something that you later wish to remove? To remove any point that you have added all you need to do is **Alt+click** on it. You may have noticed that every time you hover over an existing point it is highlighted with a small red circle. So by working in this way and regularly previewing our retopologized model, we can work our way around our model fairly quickly.

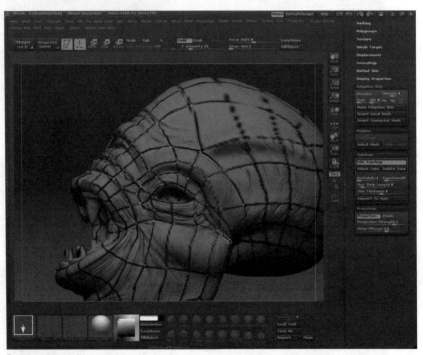

FIGURE 17-8

It will take you a little time to get used to the way that you need to work with the ZSpheres, but the more you practice, the quicker you'll get. To start to capture the details from your model with preview turned off, press the **Projection** button in the **Projection** palette. Then preview again. If you turn your levels up for the preview (using the Density slider), you will notice more and more details being captured. This also allows you to see any vertexes you have added that are not working so you can correct them.

Note: I recommend a density of 2 or 3 while working because higher levels will slow your preview considerably.

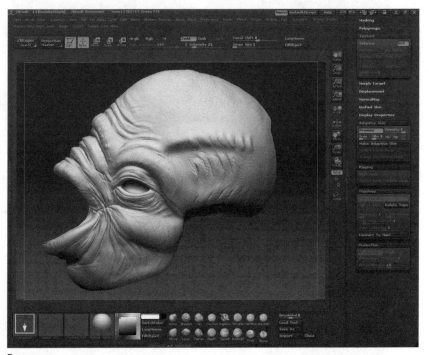

FIGURE 17-9

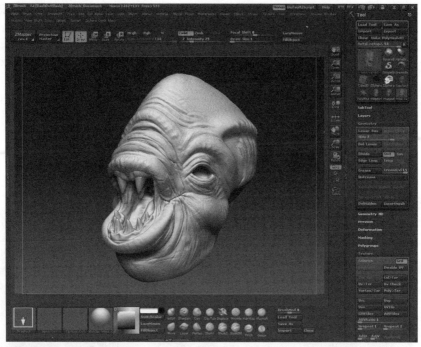

FIGURE 17-10

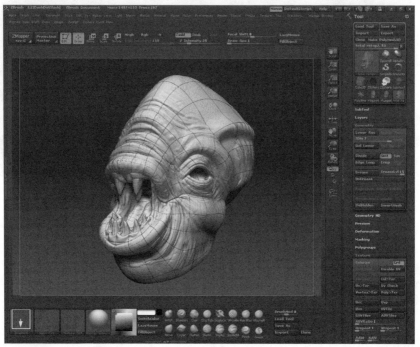

FIGURE 17-11

Note: Remember that when your model is subdivided, polygons will be added by a power of 4, which can also help to add loops in places that you need. So you can start by retopologizing at a pretty low level and use a level version of your model as your base should you need to.

Exporting the Final for UV Mapping

With the head now totally retopologized, we are ready to convert it to an adaptive skin. To do so, just press the **Adaptive Skin** button, making sure that your preview has been set to the level that best captures every detail of your model. You can then choose it from your tools list and save it out.

If you need to export it for UV'ing in an external program, I recommend taking it down to its lowest subdivision level and then exporting this lowest level. Just about very traditional polygon application can do UV'ing these days, and I've used quite a few of them over the years. My current tool of choice is UVLayout Pro by headus, but it doesn't matter which application you use to lay out your UV map as long as you are comfortable with it.

You can then import it back into ZBrush to transfer the UVs over. To do this just clone your retopologized mesh from before and delete all but the lowest level, then import the UV'ed mesh over the top. (We do this to make sure that the UV application hasn't changed the scale of the model as some do.) You can then export it again since it is the correct size.

Now switch back to the retopologized version of your digital sculpt, open the Morph Target section of the **Tool** palette, and choose **StoreMT**. Import the new UV'ed mesh and once it is back inside ZBrush, go back to the Morph Target section and press the **Switch** button, followed by the **DelMT** button. This will delete the morph target so that it doesn't cause any problems in ZMapper when creating normal maps, but also keeps the UV information now transferred onto your retopologized sculpt.

Then you are ready to extract any normal, cavity, or displacement maps that you need from your model.

18 Sculpting the Guardian's Body

Body Blocking Stage 1

For the main character in our scene we are going to use the Guardian head we have already sculpted to a high resolution from a sphere and the Guardian body base mesh made in Chapter 6, "ZSpheres." So with the head already sculpted, it is now time to move on to the body itself. First let me outline a few concepts about how we are going to approach this part. When you made the base mesh from ZSpheres in Chapter 6, it produced a base mesh with two subdivision levels. The lowest level of these (level 1) has a polygon count of 280.

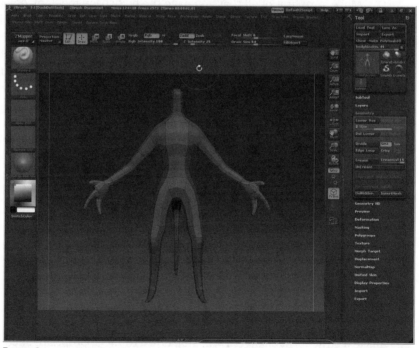

FIGURE 18-1

We are going to start right back on this lowest level to get our initial forms correct before moving up the levels, subdividing as we go and refining the forms and anatomy each time. We'll be using the back story from Chapter 16 as a guideline for the body, along with some basic knowledge of anatomy. I would strongly urge any digital sculptor specializing in organic bipeds to have a few anatomy books and other references handy and to make a concerted effort to understand how the organic machine that is the human body works. Only then can we be sure that we are producing a believable character. Even though this character is not human it must have a basis in proper anatomical structure. Yes we can tweak the anatomy a little to fit our character's story, but its overall basis must be that of a human.

For this character I'll be outlining some of the more important features of the human body as we go along and describing where this character is a little different. This is not intended to take the place of a proper study of human anatomy but rather as a very brief introductory guide as we sculpt the character. Those of you with a knowledge of anatomy will obviously find this project a little easier than those without. So let's get right down to doing the first blocking of the Guardian's body.

Make sure first of all that you have the body base mesh made earlier in the book active in your viewport and that it is the Adaptive Skin version and *not* the ZSphere one. We are going to use our Move brush with a very small Draw Size (between 1 and 5) to move some of the points around to very roughly block in some of the most important bits of anatomy of the skeleton. I prefer to treat sculpting any biped as working from the inside out. So I start with getting the bone structure correct before moving into the main muscle groups, then the minor muscles and fat distribution, before getting down to the skin, hair, and other details.

Note: If you need to, you can use the bodyblockin.ZTL file that is available on the companion DVD.

Subdivision Level 1

So with your base mesh at level 1 it will look very "boxy" at the moment and not at all like the finished character. This is because it is far easier to manipulate a small amount of polygons than a larger group of them when making large changes to form. Whenever I am about to make a large form change, I will step down to the appropriate subdivision level. Currently the rib area of our base mesh is just a large cuboid, and the human ribcage has a definite shape that we need to reflect in this base mesh. The main feature I want to try to capture first is the shape of the front of the ribcage where it curves around to the back that is somewhat flatter. Since we do not yet have enough polygons to reflect this curve we will treat it instead as a flat plane.

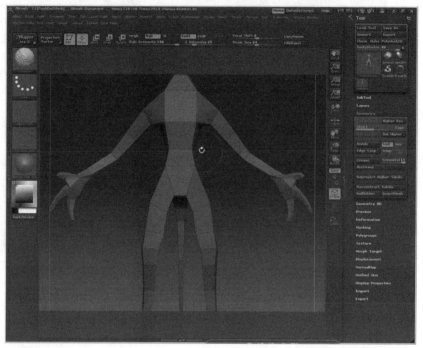

FIGURE 18-2

Notice in Figure 18-3 how I have pulled the points in at the front of the ribcage and chest using the **Move** brush to rough in that form. We will continue to tweak this form as we progress through the subdivision levels. In fact, all that we do now is a basis for our later sculpting. So make sure that you broaden the pectoral area of the chest and from a side view, pull it outward just a little.

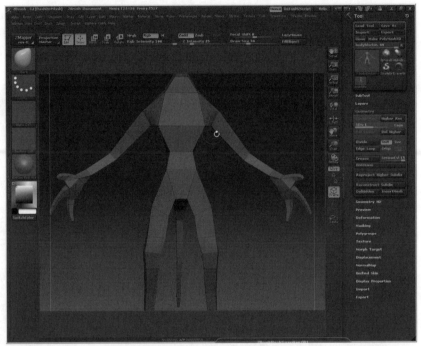

Figure 18-3

Move down to the crotch area and move the points at the very base of it so that both the back and front set are closer together. This will help to maintain the important form of the area between the legs, and keep the creature from looking bowlegged.

Let's now move to the neck and shoulders area. The neck is a little too wide, so pull the points in this area inward some. I'd also like you to check that the line in the area where the belly button would be is not flat and in line with the front of the ribcage when looking from a side view. (Remember that you can snap to any view by holding down the **Shift** key while you move the model.)

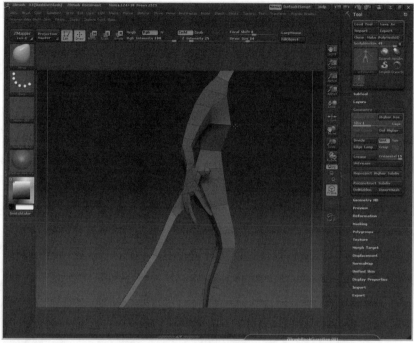

FIGURE 18-4

Now let's move to what is probably the hardest part of this blocking in stage…the hands. The hands are an area that give many modelers the most trouble, so let's grab the bull by the horns early on. Concentrate on the hands only and zoom in tight by holding down the **Alt** key and then left-clicking and dragging downward.

I purposely made sure our creature's hands only had a thumb and two fingers to make them as simple as possible. So start by moving the area next to the base of the thumb outward some, and check that both the back and the front of the hands match in this respect. Also pull the length of the thumb out a little as it seems a bit stubby in relation to the rest of the hand.

The last area that I'd like you to look at while at this particular subdivision level is the feet, so zoom in on them now. Pull the bottom of the back of the heel so that it looks less rounded, and check that the foot/leg intersection area is in the correct place and width. Remember that we are starting out with human body shapes and adapting them to our needs for this creature. Before you set up to subdivision level 2, have another good visual check against some skeleton references and what "looks right." One area I would suggest paying special attention to is the hips and buttocks area, as these can easily end up the wrong shape.

Subdivision Level 2

Now is a good time to introduce one of my main methods of nailing down the form of the body. While researching this book and studying traditional sculpting methods and workflows I noticed that the way traditional sculptors work with a series of flat planes joined together is particularly useful to digital sculptors because it allows us to correct the initial forms before rounding them off and adding the finer details. So if you turn your Wireframe view off for a moment and just look at your model with the default Red Wax MatCap you will see a number of areas that while "flat" are vaguely representative of the human body. To help fix these areas, as well as add some edge loops where we will need them as we continue to subdivide our model, we'll start moving some of them. So first we need an edge loop that follows largely the line of the bottom of the ribcage. This is especially important at the front of the body as it will help us later to define the stomach area.

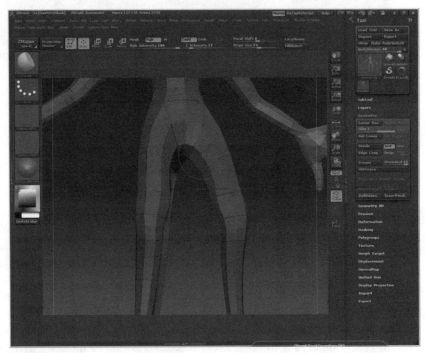

FIGURE 18-5

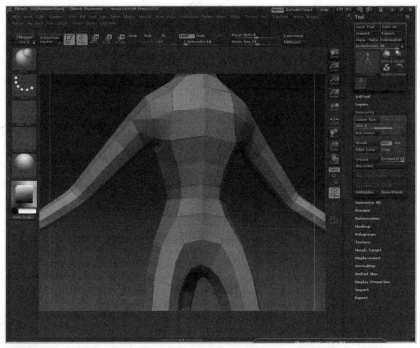

FIGURE 18-6

We also need to go over some of the areas we worked on in subdivision level 1, such as the neck/torso intersection area, and continue to pull these points into the correct places. If you pop back into Wireframe mode, you will notice a five-pointed star formation of edges that are roughly where the nipples would be on the pectoral muscles of the chest. Follow the line down the sides of the stomach to check that it pulls inward once we get to the main stomach area. If it doesn't, then gently move these into position. Go back to the hands and pull any points needed to keep the shape looking right and following the forms of good anatomy before moving downward to the legs.

The tops of the thighs can be a big problem area for a digital sculptor and can take a while to get right, so I'll try to point out some anatomy facts that may be helpful as we progress. Notice that the area on the thighs between the legs has a flat plane that runs from near the center where the pelvis is to about halfway down and toward the back of the leg. This area is not a "tube" as many beginners sculpt it, but rather a series of complex planes and curves that need to be nailed to look correct.

You will see me going back to this area quite a few times before I am totally happy with the area. So switch to your **Flatten** brush with a ZIntensity of **25** and very slightly flatten this area on the interior area of the front of the thighs. Use **Ctrl+Shift+click** to isolate the polygroup for just the legs and then flatten the interior of the back of the thighs in the same way. The continual refining and correcting of the form is an essential part of the development process. **Ctrl+Shift+click** outside the model to show us the polygroups for your model once again. We isolated the legs when flattening the back of the thighs because it would have been too easy to end up affecting the buttocks area. It is easy to isolate an area either by its polygroup or by masking areas off. Make sure that the center of the rib area at the bottom where the left and right side meet has a more pointed look at this stage than you'll need. Remember that things will smooth out as we subdivide the model, so at lower subdivision levels we need to exaggerate the forms sometimes.

Looking at your model from the back now, use your **Move** brush and broaden the shoulder blades and back area as shown in Figure 18-7. On most men the back is always broader than the front of the body. Also pull the vertices at the center of the front of the crotch outward a little. Remember that this area is not flat and on an athletic person appears to protrude outward more than the stomach area.

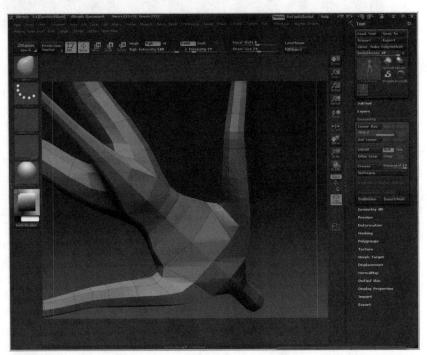

FIGURE 18-7

At the moment the area where the legs join the body in the hip area of the pelvis does not look correct. We need to pull the vertices at the top of the legs at each side of the body to create the curve of the iliac crest. If you need to, take a look at some skeleton references to help you shape this area correctly. Once done, start pulling the curves of the leg into place. It's best to do as much at this stage as we can to avoid a lot of work later. So using a larger brush size for your **Move** brush, pull the curve for the front of the thighs into shape from the side view. Hide the main torso polygroup by first isolating it and then **Ctrl+Shift+ click** on it again. Then pull the base of the spine inward a little to give it a more natural curved shape. We'll continue to smooth things out as we go, and will come back to a number of these areas later.

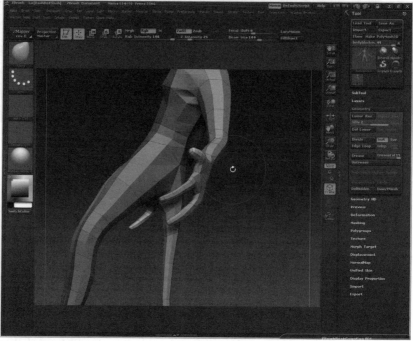

FIGURE 18-8

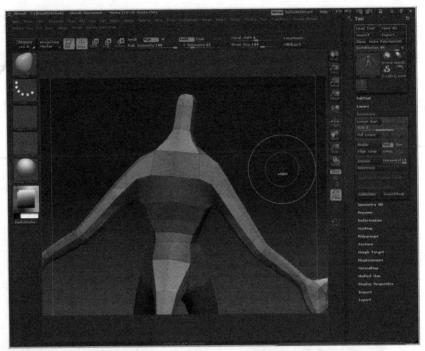

FIGURE 18-9

Subdivision Level 3

We now need to further subdivide our model so we can add some additional forms. Go to your **Tool** palette and press the **Divide** button to go to subdivision level 3. Remember that not only will the polygon count increase by a multiple of four each time we subdivide our model, but also some of the forms we added in the previous level will be washed out a bit. (This is why we often exaggerate them during the sculpting process.)

With your **Move** brush active, gently shape the line of the chest area if needed. Also gently pull the shoulders back a little while looking from slightly below them as we eventually want the pectorals to run under the deltoid muscles. The insertion points of the muscles are very important and so it is imperative that we get them right. Sculpting is all about shaping and correcting a form as many times as needed.

Another very important job that we have to do at this stage in blocking out the form is the stomach area itself. Let me explain a few landmarks that we will use to check that our proportions are correct.

The nipples will almost always line up with the sides of the stomach area on a fit, athletic person. The stomach area should also be a flat plane at this stage in our blocking out process. So remembering that the two five-pointed stars on the chest are our rough guides as nipple locations, pull the stomach area out until it lines up with these. We can correct them later in the sculpting process, but at this stage we simply need our planes in the right ballpark.

Moving back to the thigh area, we need to start to get the curves of them looking right from a front view. So using a largish size Move brush, gently pull them into shape, starting with the inside of the thigh. The upper legs are fairly complex forms, so it might take a little while to get the legs looking right. You may even need to revisit your anatomy books and get an in-depth understanding of how they work as organic machines. Doing a number of in-depth studies of any area that gives you trouble is a great way not only to be able to sculpt it but also to show you "what" to sculpt and "why" it is that shape.

Move down to the bottom half of the legs and in the side view slightly pull out where the kneecaps will be and then use your Move brush to block in the rough shapes for the calf muscles. We are only going for rough forms at this stage and not the final sculpt. Move next to the feet area and pull the heels into the correct shape and start blocking out the feet themselves. In the final sculpt, our Guardian will have webbed feet, but at this stage I would recommend making them look fairly human first. When blocking in the feet it is important to check your forms from each side so that you can see their general volume.

The important shapes of the feet of a human are the arch of the foot, the shape of the bottom of the foot, and the wedge-like shape of the outer side. You will get an understanding of this by looking at your own feet.

The next form we are going to change is not anatomically correct but does help to add a sense of life and movement to a character and is commonly used. What am I referring to? Taking a large brush size and adding a very slight curve to the lower leg bones. I always exaggerate this as it really does seem to add that extra something to the lower leg. Knowing when to bend or even break the rules is an important part of being an artist because that is what makes our art unique. It is really important not to lose sight of the fact that we are artists and not merely technicians.

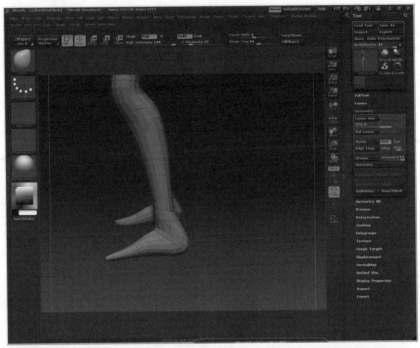

FIGURE 18-10

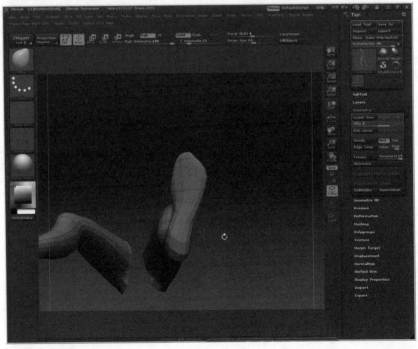

FIGURE 18-11

The tail is obviously not a human shape but is something that we need to address as well. For this I used a number of animal references and previous sculpting experience to come up with a tail I felt looked like a cross between a mammal and an amphibian. I added a bit of a curve to it to help give it some basic movement. I was thinking of it in terms of a kangaroo tail that is used for balance and also has a lot of muscle and weight to it.

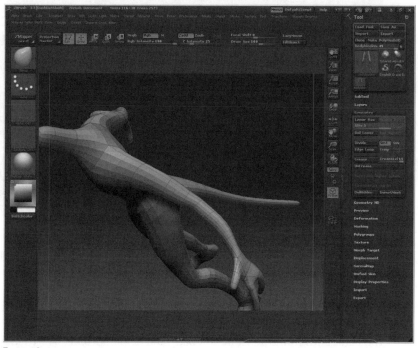

FIGURE 18-12

I felt at this point that the joints in the arms were a bit low and the proportions didn't "read" correctly. So I took the Move brush and pulled them a little bit further up the arm. I then added a similar bow in the lower arm to the one I did in the lower leg, and for the very same reasons. Remember though that the lower arm is made of two distinct bones that can create some complex forms and vastly affect the shape of the arm. This is why understanding anatomy is so important.

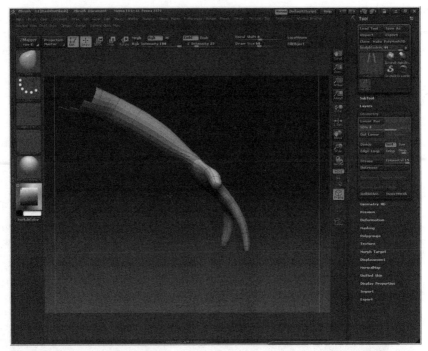

Figure 18-13

Shift+Ctrl and **left-drag** a green selection box over both hands (you can deselect the center section of the torso). We do this because we need to go back to the hands so we can continue to block in the forms now that we have a few more polygons to work with. I would recommend using your own hand as a reference and checking the shape of the palm both from the front and back and also in profile. Try to match it as best you can with the polygons currently available.

Notice that the area between the fingers appears "taller" when viewed from the palm. It's these small things that are very important to get right and can help with the believability of a model. If you imagine the arm as a line and the hand as another line, when seen from the side the hand is offset slightly inward in the palm direction. There is a very noticeable curve to the back of the hand and the way that the fingers emerge. There is also a distinct curve at the base of each finger. The middle finger forms the apex of this arc and the little finger is the lowest point. This is actually much easier to see than it is to explain, so take a look at your own hand now and you will see exactly what I mean.

I pulled very slightly upward the area where each knuckle would be. This is mainly as a placeholder and reminder for later on and not the final shaping. Now unhide the rest of the model before continuing onward.

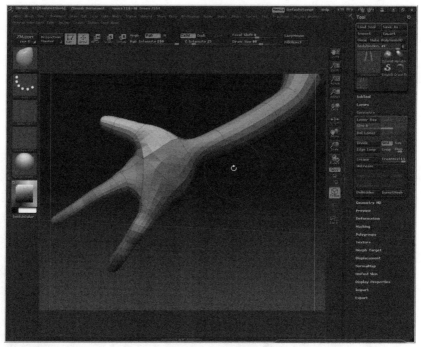

FIGURE 18-14

Taking your Move brush again, pull in the base of the neck area toward the center to continue the work we did at the beginning. The area where the neck and clavicle intersect is an area in which we will do a lot of work because it is a very defining part of this character's anatomy.

Body Blocking Stage 2

Subdivision Level 4

Subdivide your model to bring it up to level 4. Remember not to have any parts of your model masked or hidden when subdividing.

We are going to start blocking in some of the most important features of the model from this point, so we need to have enough geometry to do this. Subdivision level 4, however, is a bit too "blocky" for what we are about to do.

Subdivision Level 5

Subdivide your model once again. Now we have plenty of geometry. We are going to start off in the neck/shoulder/clavicle area first of all, so mask off those areas now. After inverting the mask, use the **Move** brush to pull this area first inward and then back a bit before lightly smoothing over the area. (Be careful not to totally wash out the work we have just done.) Now remove the mask before we move on.

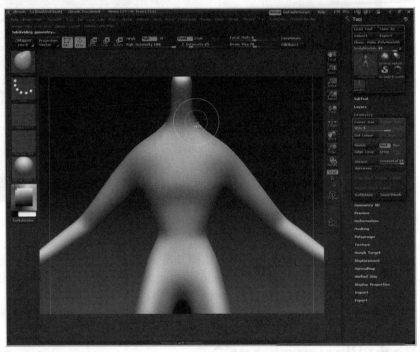

FIGURE 18-15

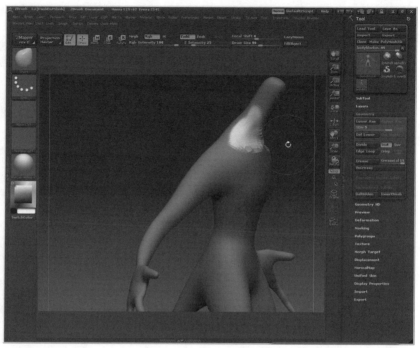

FIGURE 18-16

Switch now to your **Clay** brush, which we will be using a lot for the blocking in stage at this point. We will be using it to both add and carve out areas that we need to define the form. (Instead of just adding to a model, it is often better to take geometry away so that your model doesn't end up far broader than you envisioned.) Let's start with the base of the ribs. Most people would inflate or bulk up this area when in actuality they should be removing some mass from beneath the ribs. If you only add bulk to your model it will obviously get bigger and can end up looking nothing like you wanted it to. So as a result we will take away mass where we can and only add bulk where it has to go.

Note: Technically you are only sculpting a model when you are removing from a mass. When you are adding to it, this is more properly termed modeling in the world of traditional art media.

FIGURE 18-17

Now let's look at the torso and chest. As I mentioned earlier, the ribcage has a definite shape that you must capture early on, so we made sure it was broader at the back than at the front and that it was as near the correct shape as we could get. I also talked about the use of flat planes to help visualize and interpret the shapes and forms. So what we will now do is a two-fold operation that sounds more complex than it is. We need to remove some mass from under the sides of the pectoral/deltoid intersection while starting to block in a flat plane for the side of the ribcage. The idea is to get the main forms correct early so you don't have a massive load of work to do later.

So using the **Clay** brush, remove the mass from under the edge of the pectoral intersection area and smooth the rest of the side of the ribs to make your flat plane. Don't worry if your model looks very blocky and rough now — we're concentrating on the main forms.

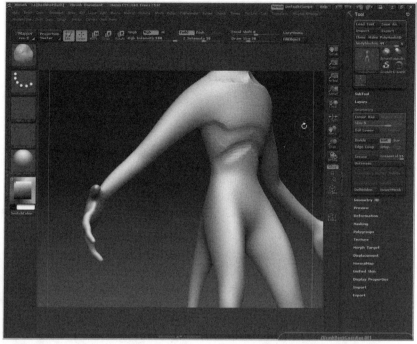

FIGURE 18-18

Again using your **Clay** brush, start to block in the shape of the clavicles, and remember that they are not just straight lines but shaped more like a set of handlebars on a bike. If the shape and location of important areas such as the clavicles are off slightly, it can throw the entire sculpture off visually as a result. But do remember that we are going to refine and correct areas as we go.

Now I want to show you the masking technique I use for the main part of my workflow when blocking in the muscle forms. This technique is certainly not something unique to myself, but isn't as widespread as I think it should be. I often use masks when I sculpt as a way of controlling areas and forms, and I've came up with a variety of ways to use masks. One way is to paint masks for each muscle and invert them. This allows me to bulk in the mass of muscle, and because I am painting the mask it helps me get the correct shape of the muscle as quickly as possible. So for the next few pages I will outline the muscles I am sculpting and use a mask for each one.

I'll outline in detail how I approach the deltoid and then you can apply this technique to other muscles. For these muscles it is very important to have references handy so that you can get the shapes as correct as possible the first time.

So now paint in the front part of the shape of the deltoid. I paint the deltoid in two sections because it has insertion points both on the shoulder blades and the clavicle. Since it effectively goes around to the back of the model, it is best to treat it as two separate entities that work as one. So paint the shape in and then invert the mask (remember the shortcut of **Ctrl+clicking** on an empty part of the viewport to invert your mask).

When blocking the mass of the front part of the deltoid, I would like you to run your Clay brush in the direction of the muscle's flow and not against it. You should do this with every muscle on the body because it helps us to maintain a rhythm and flow to our sculpt and it helps to make sure we have less to correct later. We will be working like this on each muscle until I tell you otherwise, so I won't be repeating the same instructions.

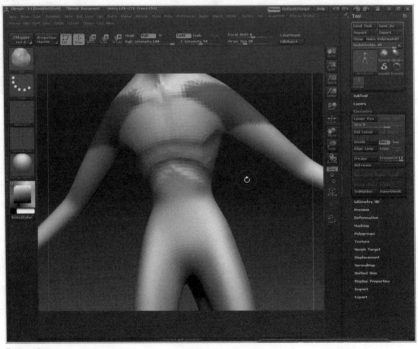

FIGURE 18-19

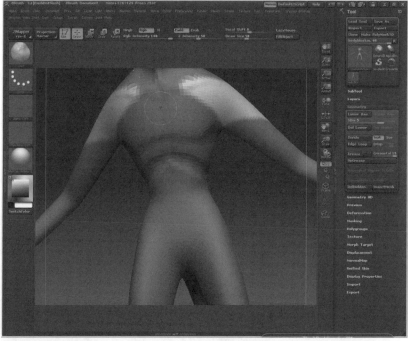

FIGURE 18-20

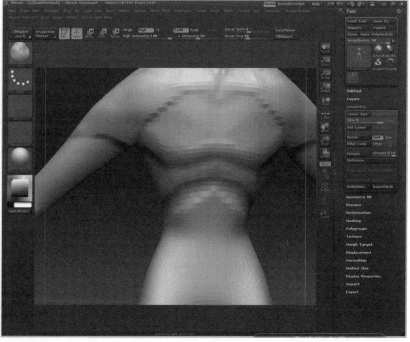

FIGURE 18-21

Once we are done blocking in the front of the deltoid we can simply invert this mask and use it to help us block in the pectoral muscles. Start by using your Clay brush to run along the bottom of the pectorals to start bulking this area up a little. When blocking out the back part of the deltoid I also make it a habit to block in the shoulder blades as well (the scapula) because they share similar planes and directions. Remember to go with the flow of the muscles to block them out and that they carry a fair amount of mass along with the scapula, so don't skimp on the bulk. Now we want to go over the back part of the deltoid again, this time isolating just that part of the deltoid and not the scapula as well, so paint in your mask (maybe downsizing your Clay brush if needed) and block in this area.

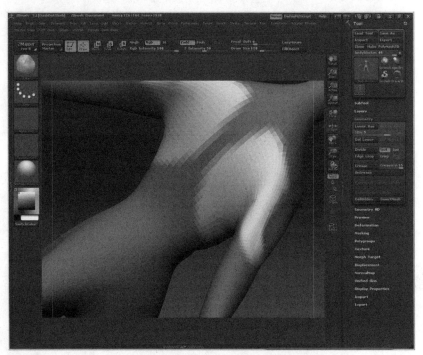

FIGURE 18-22

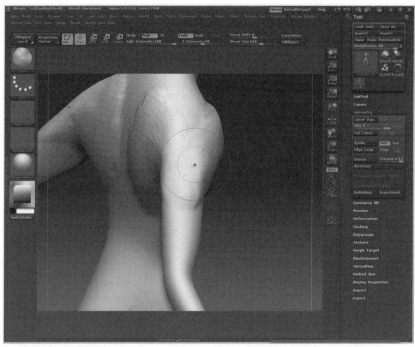

FIGURE 18-23

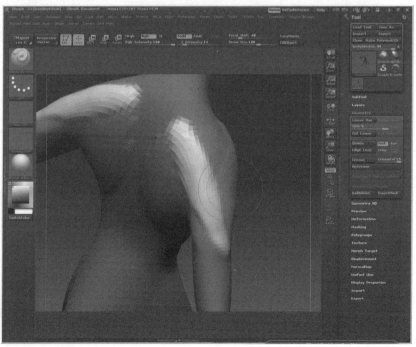

FIGURE 18-24

Subdivision Level 6

At this point, subdivide your model to level 6. The torso area has less geometry than other areas of our model, so to compensate we need more polys. Once we have the model to a final stage we have a couple of options for getting a higher poly count, ranging from local subdivision or retopologizing our mesh to splitting our model into parts.

We will now block in the main parts of the chest area by splitting it into a number of intersecting planes. Each plane will be created by painting a mask (which is inverted) on the area we wish to be flat and then smoothing over the area to flatten it. Should the smooth not flatten enough, feel free to use the **Flatten** brush with a ZIntensity of about **20** instead. So let's start by painting in the first plane, which is a triangle shape running along the deltoid and side of the chest area, and flatten that out first of all. To complement this, take your **Standard** brush and run it softly along the deltoid part and the bottom part of the pectorals again. I also beefed up the clavicle again since I use this as a point of reference that I like to keep oversized until near the end as I find it personally helps me to judge the forms correctly. Softly smooth over these areas again to help them to fit (but do not smooth over the area we have just flattened).

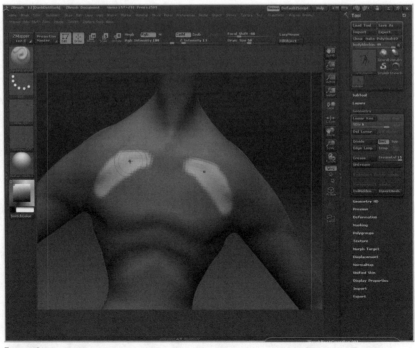

FIGURE 18-25

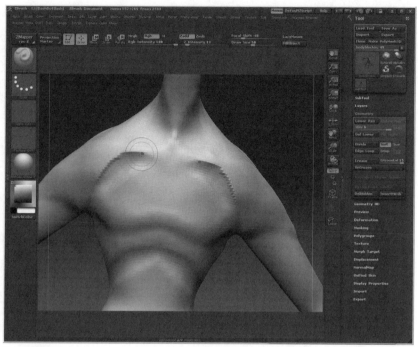

FIGURE 18-26

Paint a mask for the sternocleidomastoid muscle running from the clavicle up the neck (and eventually to behind the ears; although the head of our model is separate I include this information for the sake of completeness). Use your **Standard** brush (or the Clay brush would do just as well) to bulk this area up before smoothing the transitions out a little. There is a hollow form I add in as well that helps to define the trapezius muscle that I also hollow out at this stage while I am in the area. Carve a line again under the pectorals where they join the front of the ribs. This area had lost some of its definition due to the smoothing effect we get each time we subdivide, so as a result we sometimes have to go over the same area several times to maintain the shape. In a similar way I also added a very small amount of mass to the very bottom of the pectoral muscles to compensate.

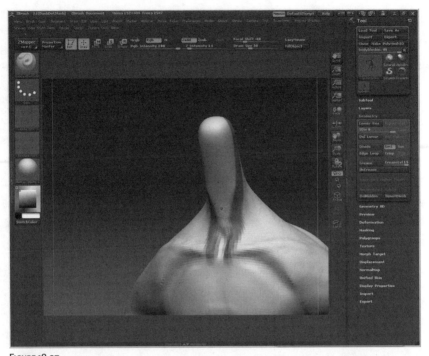

FIGURE 18-27

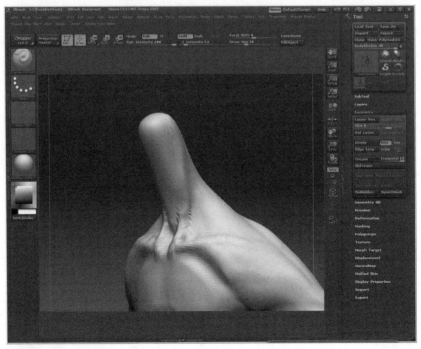

FIGURE 18-28

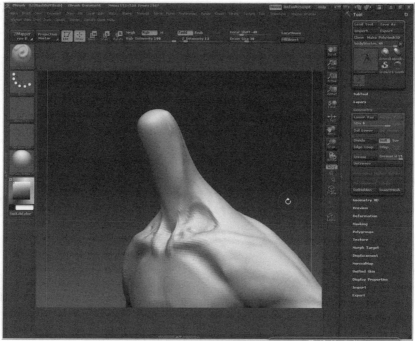

FIGURE 18-29

For the stomach muscles I like to start by drawing a mask in the shape of a figure eight. Although the male and female body differ in many areas, including the stomach area, the male's stomach does have a similar shape if somewhat overdeveloped in comparison to the female's. So I start with the more female figure eight shape, which I then overdevelop into a male one. I will be keeping the muscles on this character overdeveloped until nearer the end to make it easier to visualize the forms.

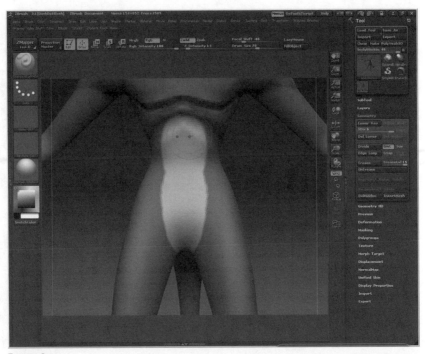

FIGURE 18-30

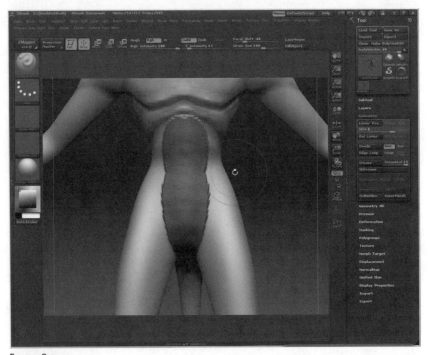

FIGURE 18-31

Once your figure eight-shaped mask is done and inverted, smooth it over to make it flat. The stomach is a plane all its own and as such we don't want it to curve toward the sides of the torso at this stage. Once you have it nice and flat, run a large Standard brush over it to increase the mass and give us something to work with later. Invert the mask again and smooth the transitional areas a little. (By keeping the area masked we will not be totally smoothing the edges out as we do need some definition.) Then lightly use your **Standard** brush to push these areas nearest to the stomach inward a bit. Remove the mask and again smooth the transitions a little.

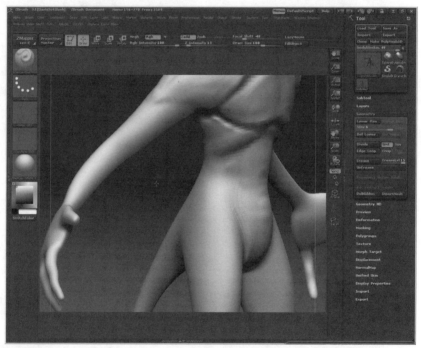

FIGURE 18-32

Paint a mask for the love handles and increase the mass like we did for the stomach. We will be tweaking this area several more times. Remember to smooth over the transitions as normal. Switch back to the **Clay** brush again for the next series of blocking in moves.

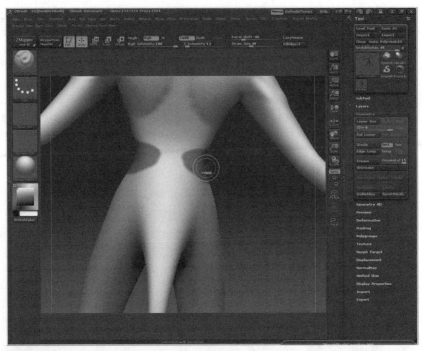

FIGURE 18-33

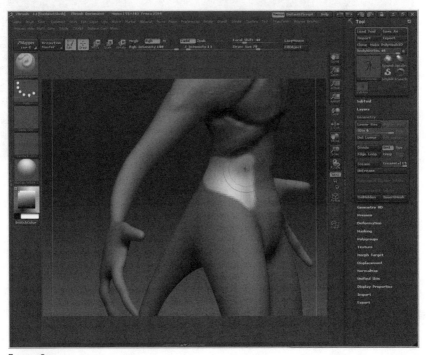

FIGURE 18-34

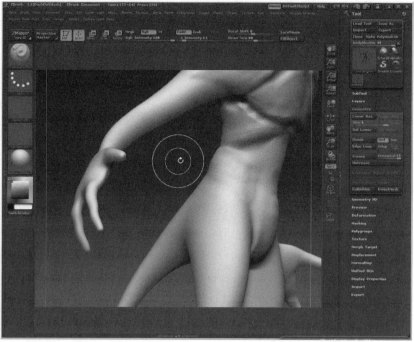

FIGURE 18-35

First, make three or four strokes running from the sides of the ribs toward the stomach area to help blend these muscle groups into one another. Then add more mass onto the stomach as shown to what will eventually become his "six-pack." Also add some mass to help define the iliac crest of the pelvis at the edge of where the torso meets the legs. The transitions between both the muscle groups as well as the bones and limbs are crucial. If done wrong, they can make a good model look bad; if done well, they can make an okay model look great. This takes time and practice and is something you will always need to keep on top of while sculpting.

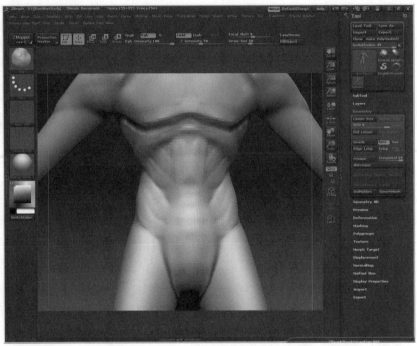

FIGURE 18-36

It's now time for us to move to areas such as the arms and block in the main muscles there. So let's start with the bicep by painting a mask and using the **Standard** brush to add the mass to these areas. One thing to watch out for is that the bicep is not in the center of the arm but toward the outer edge of it, so make sure you get the insertion point right. Another point to remember is that the shape of the bicep depends on whether or not it is being contracted. You may need to check some references to get an idea of what is actually happening to it if you do not already have a good idea. At the moment I am sculpting the default pose, but we will go back and change the shape of some muscles such as the biceps later once he is posed. For muscles in places such as the arms you will need to check the forms from all angles to get a good overall view.

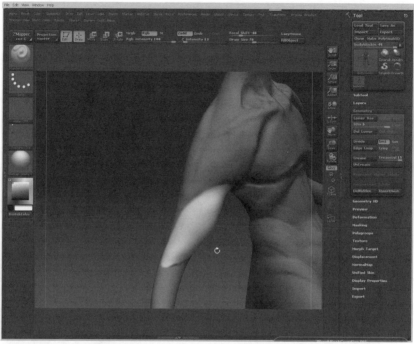

Figure 18-37

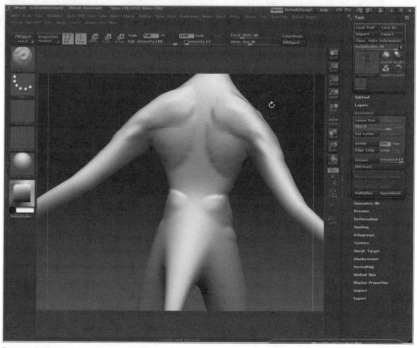

Figure 18-38

Paint a mask in the correct shape as shown for the latissimus dorsi muscles and fill these out a bit. As with the triceps, the lats are also visible from the front of a person to some degree. Remember that they are fairly bulky muscles, so give yourself enough room to sculpt them in properly as we get further into the sculpting.

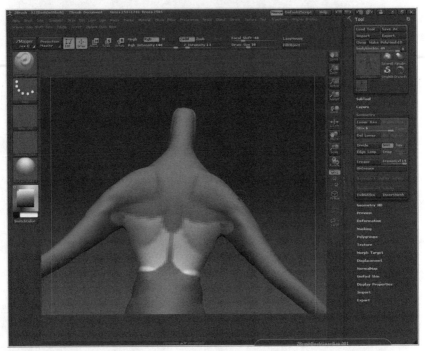

FIGURE 18-39

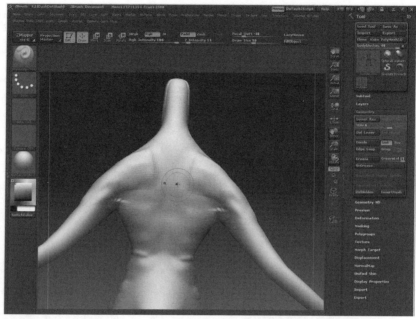

FIGURE 18-40

Next up it's time to rough in the trapezius muscle, which is diamond shaped and runs from between the lats right up the neck. It also wraps around and inserts into the clavicle area, so think of it a bit like a cloak. As such it can be a little harder to keep running your brushstrokes in the direction of the muscle and you may have to do a little more smoothing as you progress. Note also that it does not insert into the back but rather into the upper arm. Don't forget that there is a gap in the center for the spine as well, which is our most important landmark for the back area. Take your brush size down and carve a line down the back to denote where the spine is.

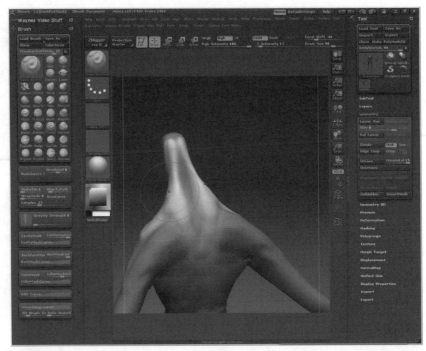

FIGURE 18-41

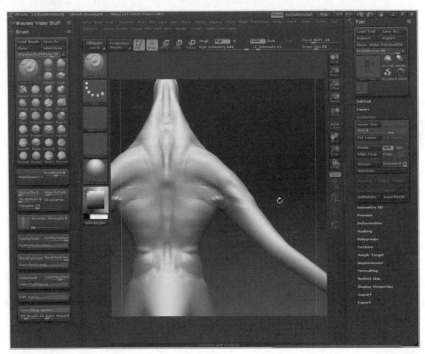

FIGURE 18-42

To sculpt in a basic form of the triceps, we need to approach it in three individual masked sections. We start with the center section by masking that off and adding mass to it, before doing each side. The two side parts of the triceps have a lot in common with the deltoids in that they actually run around the arm (whereas the deltoids run from back to front, clavicle to scapula).

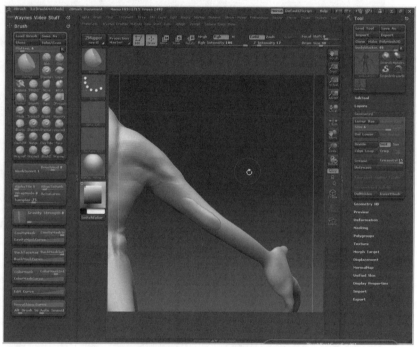

FIGURE 18-43

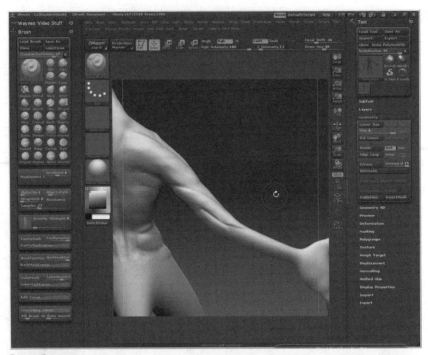

FIGURE 18-44

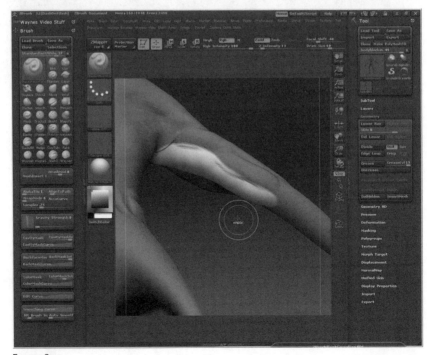

FIGURE 18-45

Keep working until you have the form blocked in correctly. For some areas I use the **Standard** brush because the Clay brush has a flattening effect that we don't really want.

It's time again to move back to the chest area and work on the pectoral muscles that we blocked in earlier. So split it into the planes as I previously mentioned, starting with a triangular-shaped mask running from the deltoid/pectoral intersection to a point that is near the interior edge (near the center of the chest). Select your **Flatten** brush with a ZIntensity of about **17** and invert this mask, then flatten it out to create your first plane. Now paint a second triangle that runs from near the center line at the ends of the clavicle to the bottom of the pectoral area and again flatten this out the same way to make a second plane.

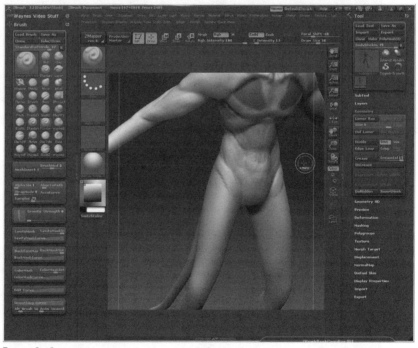

FIGURE 18-46

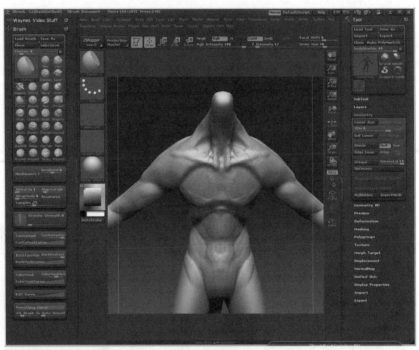

FIGURE 18-47

FIGURE 18-48

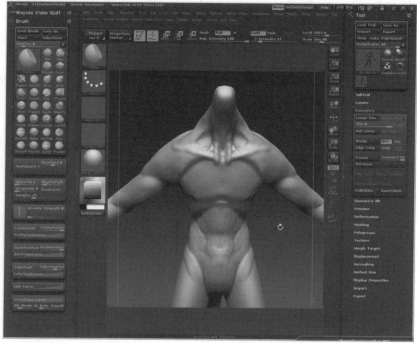

FIGURE 18-49

Smooth the pectoral area out a bit. Then using the **Flatten** brush, convert the front of the deltoid into flat planes with one at the front and one or two at the sides. This is a way to check that the existing forms are correct, and if they are not, it will help you to correct them. Flatten the stomach area in a similar way, treating each muscle in the "six-pack" as a separate plane.

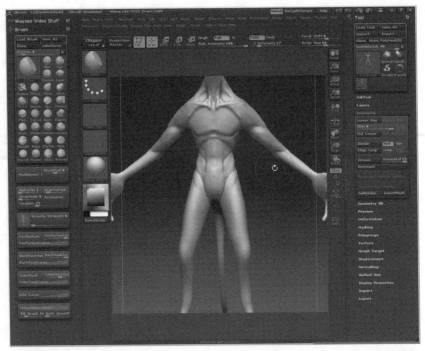

FIGURE 18-50

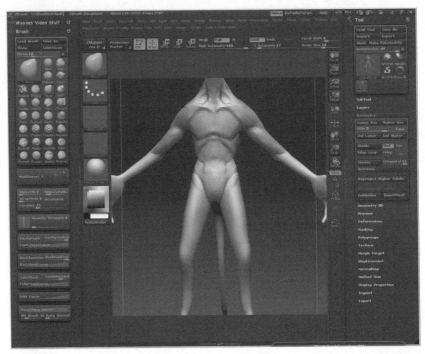

FIGURE 18-51

The time has come to correct any proportional problems we see at this point. On my model the shape of the bottom arch of the ribcage needed to be a bit sharper, so I used the **Move** brush with a largish size and pulled this into place. I also pulled the stomach muscles so that they were broader and more in line with where the nipples will be, and corrected the shapes of the hips. You'll find that once you start to get some of the muscles blocked you will start to see other areas that need correcting because you have better visual references. I also felt that the armpits were slightly too low in relation to the pectorals, so with a small brush I moved them upward a little. I also beefed up the triceps a bit more to make them more visible from the front view. Stepping down to subdivision level 5 for a moment, I also pulled the lats out a bit, so that they were more visible from a front view and help to make him look a little more balanced.

The next correction I made is a fiddly one that meant I had to **Shift+Ctrl+click** the torso polygroup to isolate it first. The planes at the sides of the torso had become misaligned when I broadened the lats, so I had to go back in and correct these angles as shown in Figure 18-52. I also corrected the arch of the ribcage again and pulled the sides of the stomach area back very slightly to help the stomach forms read better. The stomach itself I felt looked a bit "weedy" so I painted a mask on two-thirds of it and blurred this mask before pulling the top part of the stomach area inward to accentuate the rib intersection. (This was a design decision as opposed to an anatomical one.) I then unhid the rest of the model by **Shift+Ctrl+clicking** in an empty part of the viewport and stepped back up to subdivision level 6.

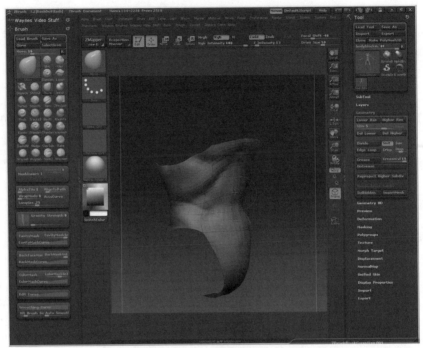

Figure 18-52

When doing some of the work on this digital sculpture I regularly step in and out of Perspective mode for some jobs. The reason I do this is because in Perspective mode I can sometimes only see part of an area, but in Orthographic mode I can often see more. As a general rule, though, I sculpt in Perspective mode.

As the curve of the ribcage and lats were a bit too extreme I masked off the biceps area and moved the lats and ribcage inward a bit to help straighten them out. As a result I had to go back to the side of the torso area with the Flatten brush to re-establish the planes again. As no doubt you will have noticed by now, at this stage onward when you tweak one thing you often end up affecting other parts that then need correcting as a result. I removed the mask and continued. So now that I've outlined the problem areas I corrected in my model, go back over your own and correct any areas that need it before moving onward.

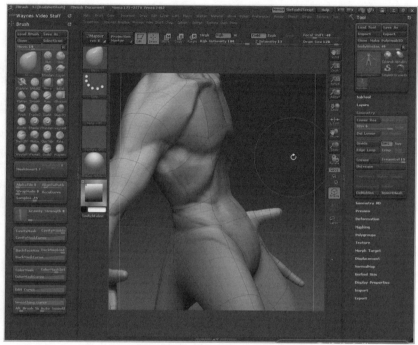

Figure 18-53

Okay, let's go back to the chest area again to start to add a bit more roundness to it and help it start to look a bit more like a chest and less like a series of flat planes. So take the **Clay** brush and start to add some mass to the bottom of the pectoral area and then round it out a little before changing to your **Standard** brush to add more volume to this area and again smoothing it off. **Shift+Ctrl+drag** over the torso area to paint a mask over the edge of the neck as shown. The mask will protect it from the work we will do using the Move brush in a second.

Move the front section of the clavicle backward a bit to help the shape of the chest, then gently correct the "hang" of the chest and deltoids. Move to a front view and pull the corners at the bottom of the chest outward toward the arms a bit more to add some more defined shape. As you will see, the chest area is something I keep refining as I progress with the model because it is such a defining feature that affects the overall look and muscle balance of the character. (I also pulled the crotch outward a bit along with the entire lower stomach to get a better overall shape.) Unhide your entire model and zoom out.

FIGURE 18-54

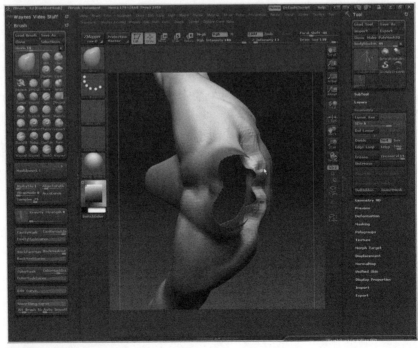

FIGURE 18-55

Subdivision Level 7

Subdivide up to level 7 now, and start smoothing over the chest area a little. I have found that smoothing at a lower level means you have a lot of corrections to do to get the overall forms back, while smoothing at a higher level helps the forms fade into one another with a more pleasing result. It's a small trick but a useful one to know.

Your aim at this point is to take the existing shapes and make them work together with some smoothing and some very light use of the Standard brush where needed. So start working over everything you have done up to this point. Make sure no forms have gotten lost or mis-shapen due to the smoothing effect of subdividing, and correct them if needed. What you are aiming for is simply a smoother version of the last subdivision levels, with any corrections that you feel are needed.

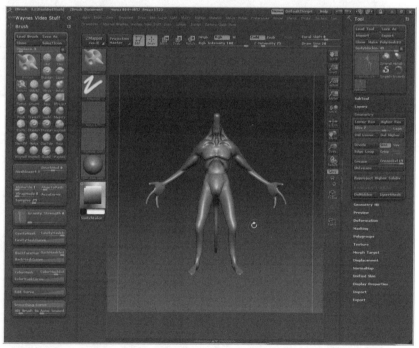

FIGURE 18-56

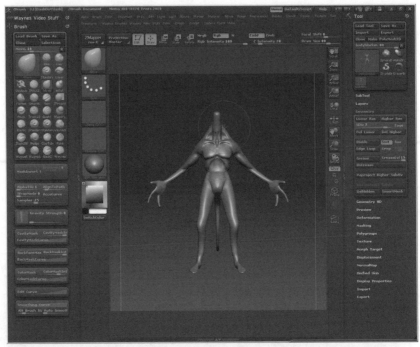

FIGURE 18-57

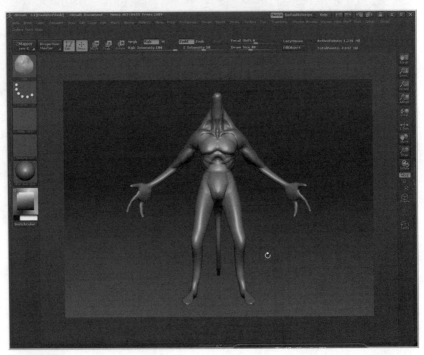

FIGURE 18-58

Body Blocking Stage 3

As we are currently working mainly on the torso, it's time to add a few medium-resolution details to it to help it "work" as a design. So select the **Displace** brush with no alpha selected and the default ZIntensity of **25**. Use it to reinforce the existing lines of the forms and outline areas for further work.

Taking your **Move** brush at a large size, pull out and broaden the neck and shoulders around the trapezius area. This will help him to look a bit more muscular and more in proportion. One of the biggest problems for digital sculptors is that we can sometimes get so caught up in anatomical correctness that we forget things have to work together to look right as well as be anatomically perfect. Sharpen the existing lines, edges, and carved in areas using the **Pinch** brush, as we need to use these as points of reference as we continue onward. In the final version we will wash out details such as these once their job is done. But for now we need them to help us place medium-resolution and finer forms.

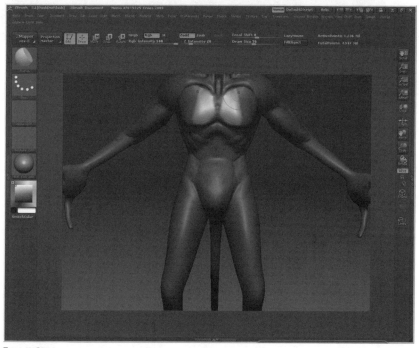

Figure 18-59

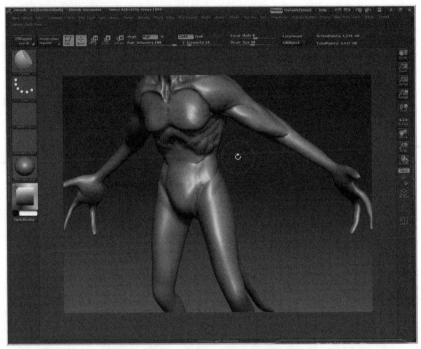

FIGURE 18-60

Use the **Flatten** brush again to re-establish the planes of the chest before smoothing them out, as shown in Figures 18-59 and 18-60. We'll be doing this quite a lot in the chest area to keep it in tune with the rest of the model as it changes. Everything on the model must work not only in isolation but also as part of the whole. Move the clavicle downward a bit so that it has a very slight "V" shape that is typical in many males.

Starting to Bring the Torso Together

Well, we've finally gotten to the stage where our torso is blocked out pretty well and it's time to start pulling it together as a design. You may wonder way I'm doing the body in sections up to this level of detail and not as a whole. The reason is purely for teaching purposes. I find students get a lot less confused working in one area at a time (especially with "favorite areas" such as the torso) than jumping around to different areas.

So now we have the main shapes ready to have some features added to them. By "features" I mean of course points of interest and anatomical detail. Bear in mind we will be overexaggerating the anatomy on this sculpt compared to a human's anatomy.

Before continuing onward I'd like you to switch to the **Clay** brush with no alpha selected. Now that it's time to start bringing things together for the torso, we'll start by beefing up a few edges and adding some mass. The Clay brush is great for this as it's fast and allows you to quickly create organic shapes before you even start to add detail. Let's start with the curve on the lower part of the ribs and add some more mass to this area all the way around the curved section at the bottom. Make sure that once done you smooth out any transitions for this and the other parts we are going to work on. (This will save me having to repeat basically the same phrase over and over again.)

Then gouge out the area just under the center of the ribs to create a bit of a cavity. We need this in order to create a nice shadowed area that will help define the form. Remember that in many ways we are not sculpting with polygons but rather with light and shadows. Slightly build up the love handles and smooth the transitions out again; this area will receive a lot of work as we go through the modeling process.

Also start to work the areas such as where the deltoid meets the bicep and the insertion point for the bicep itself that runs under the deltoid and pectoral area. Getting the order of the insertions is really important to making the chest and upper arms look correct. The deltoid sits on top of the pectoral muscles that insert under it, and the bicep sits under the pectoral muscles and inserts underneath that. At this point we need to work on the edges of the muscles where one transitions into the next and add mass where needed. This is to a large degree a judgment call on your part as your artistic style may be vastly different from mine. So make your creature look the way you prefer or try to copy the way mine looks at this point.

The serratus muscles, which start under the lats and run to the separate ribs, are probably familiar to anyone who has drawn comic book characters. They can look quite different depending on the build type of the person and the position of the body, so this is where anatomy knowledge comes into play again I'm afraid. So using your **Clay** brush, block these in using a single stroke for each, making sure that each would feed into a separate rib.

Go back to the love handles and make sure they look correct from a side view, as their shape is rather complex. Then build up the crotch area and the base of the abdomen a little, as we need some weight here to help balance out the character.

Making sure your character has a sense of balance and doesn't look as if it is about to fall over is something we have to make sure of. As a general rule, the head must be over the feet of your model, but you must also bear in mind where the center of gravity is. A good way to get a feeling for balance in poses is to look at some videos and stills of dancers. After a while, you will develop an innate sense of whether the character is balanced or not, although some poses are more difficult than others.

We are now going to go back and re-establish the planes of the pectoral muscles again, as after all this time they are starting to look a little off. So let's start with the triangular shape that runs down the center of the chest. Mask it off, invert it, and then use your **Flatten** brush on it. After the plane is established, smooth it slightly in the transitional area before making the one that runs nearest to the deltoid. Smooth things over a little until they are looking correct once again.

Let's do some work on the hands now as they have been rather neglected. Isolate each hand by pressing **Shift+Ctrl+drag** over the hands and torso (see Figure 18-61), then removing the torso section in the center until you have the hands on their own with just a little bit of arm attached to each one.

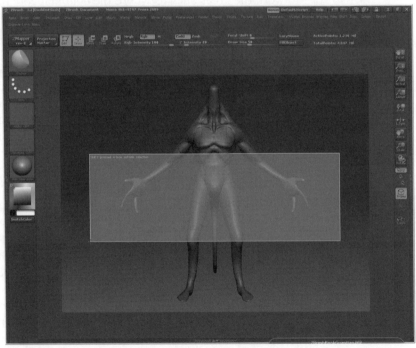

FIGURE 18-61

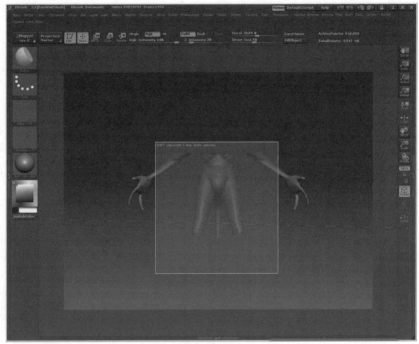

FIGURE 18-62

Our first job is to add the knuckles at the base of each finger and the thumb, so use the **Inflate** brush for this. Then from the back of the hand, since you are in the area, remove some mass from between the fingers and from between the thumb and index finger. Draw a line to represent the tendons running over the back of the hand from each finger and the thumb. At this stage these are simply placeholders (although we won't be adding a whole lot of detail in the hands since they are not seen close up). Add the joints to the fingers and thumb as well so that it starts to look a little more like a hand. One of my favorite ways to quickly block in the knuckles is to paint a mask for each and then simply invert and run the Standard brush over these areas.

Smooth things out until you are happy with the way the hand looks. Since this is not a human, you can overexaggerate the knuckles to give a bonier and aged look. I'd also like you at this point to start to improve the transitions between the fingers and between the index finger and the thumb using the **Clay** brush. Block in the way that the skin would lie, checking against your own hand should you need to.

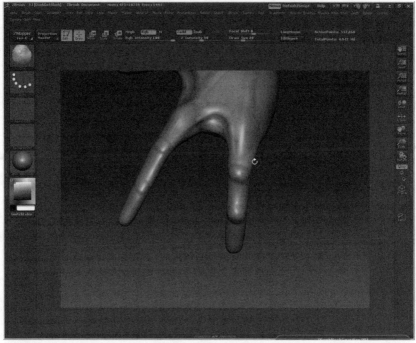

FIGURE 18-63

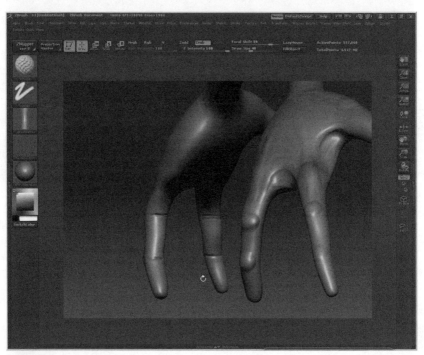

FIGURE 18-64

Move now to the palm of the hand and start by drawing some masks as fold lines where each finger bends at the joint. This will allow us to add the wrinkles in these areas with no danger of affecting the other parts of the hand (this is a pretty cramped area to work in). Add the wrinkles using the **Slash1** brush, the **Displace** brush, or any other favorite harsh brush that you prefer. I use a variation on the Slash brush posted at ZBrushCentral a while back.

These harsher "carving" brushes all do basically the same job, so use the one that feels right to you. Using the same brush, then start to carve in some of the major lines in the palm of the hand. Don't try to add all of them, only the major ones. We'll be using these to guide our brush when inflating between them. So take your **Inflate** brush with a size that is just larger than the space between these lines and carefully inflate between them to add the look of folding skin. Inflate also the pads of the fingers between the lines we put in a moment ago. The tips of the fingers are usually larger than the rest of the finger when seen from both the top and side views.

Figure 18-65

Now it's time to start adding the fingernails. (Although amphibians don't have them, we added them here to show you how for your future sculpts.) We are going to use a nifty trick to add them quickly and accurately. Paint a mask for each nail on the fingers and thumb and inflate around this, then invert and inflate the nail itself just a little. You've just created a fingernail!

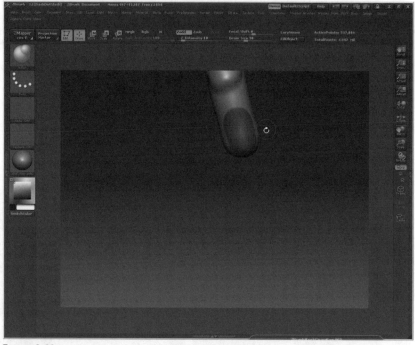

FIGURE 18-66

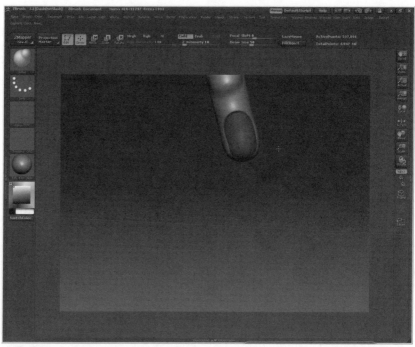

FIGURE 18-67

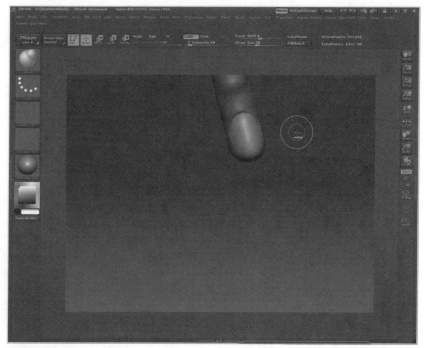

FIGURE 18-68

When you are painting your mask, remember that the base of the fingernail is curved and the top is usually flatter. If you wanted long fingernails, you could use the Move brush to drag the nail outward a little. You can then run your **Inflate** brush very lightly on the edges of each finger between the knuckles as the finger does have a certain roundness in that area. Repeat this for the other fingers and the thumb.

Subdivision Level 8

Subdivide to level 8 as you are going to need a little more geometry to add the wrinkles and folds on each knuckle. To carve in the lines that we will be using as guides for our Inflate brush, use the **Displace** brush with a smallish alpha. Now make a series of opposing and slightly flattened semicircular lines on each knuckle and then inflate between them. How deeply you want to go into this area is entirely up to you and how closely they are to be seen. (While you have the Displace brush active, feel free to add some wrinkles between the fingers and between the index finger and thumb.) Once all of this is done, the hand should look pretty good from a distance, although close up it will still look somewhat sketchy. As our Guardian will have a weapon in one hand, I didn't go overly mad with the palm since it wouldn't be seen. My theory is to sculpt only what is seen to any level of serious detail.

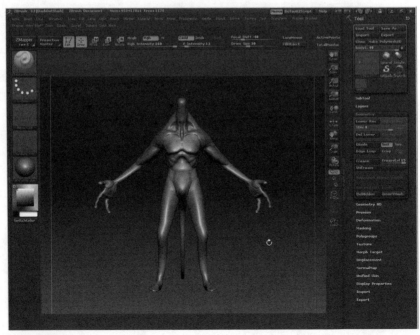

FIGURE 18-69

Take your **Standard** brush with **Alpha 58** selected and the **FreeHand** stroke type and start to carve in some lines in the direction of the skin flow for the palm of the hand, fingers, and thumb. Smooth these out a little as they are there only to keep these areas from reflecting too much light, which incidentally is a dead giveaway of lack of detail. If any of the lines you carved into the hand need redoing after this, feel free to do that now. One thing often left out by beginners is the bone on the back of the wrist that is on the opposite side of the thumb. While this isn't always visible on all people, on more athletic or bony types it is. Finally, add the tendons running from the back of the carpal tunnel area at the base of the hand to the lower arm to add a bit of tension to the area. Unhide the rest of your digital sculpt to prepare to move onward.

Step back down to subdivision level 6. We are going to start adding in the muscles for the lower arms and this is much easier at a lower subdivision level. As a general rule, I would block in all the muscles in the body at the same time, but I have broken them up into sections to make them easier to describe.

We'll use the same technique of painting a mask for each muscle and then invert it before adding the actual mass. The lower arm has some fairly confusing anatomy, and the forms change dramatically depending on the position and pose of the arm and what it is actually doing. It is worth learning the insertion points of the muscles of the lower arm in detail so that you can make this area look realistic. So mask off and invert the first muscle before using the **Standard** brush to add the mass, then be sure to smooth out the edges of the muscle before you remove the mask. Smooth over the area again lightly. We will return to this area later on in the sculpting process to adjust the muscles to fit the pose.

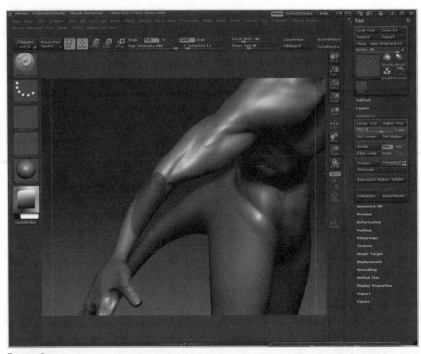

FIGURE 18-70

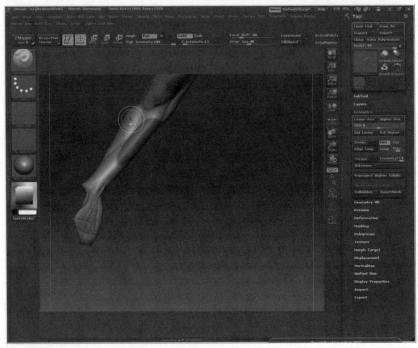

FIGURE 18-71

Switch to your **Clay** brush and block in the rest of the muscles in the arm. For the larger ones you will need to apply and invert a mask, while smaller ones you can sculpt in freehand if you like. For some of these larger muscles, use the **Standard** brush as before, since the Clay brush has a flattening effect we want to avoid for these larger muscles. We will then need to revisit the triceps area once the lower arm has been smoothed a little bit to make sure it fits correctly with both anatomy and the overall look of the character. So we need to beef up some of the forms on the lower part of the triceps as well as add the indentation on the elbow. Remember that the lower part of the triceps down to the wrist is only blocked in at this stage and will need to be refined as we continue onward. When dealing with these areas I find it useful to isolate them first.

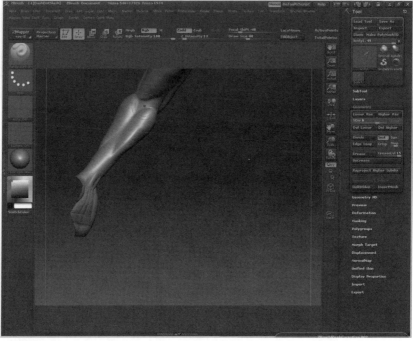

FIGURE 18-72

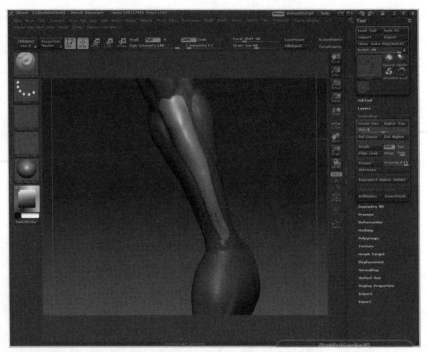

Once those areas have been blocked in to your satisfaction, unhide the rest of your model. Now go back to the back part of your model and continue to correct and refine the muscles there such as the deltoids, the trapezius, and the lats.

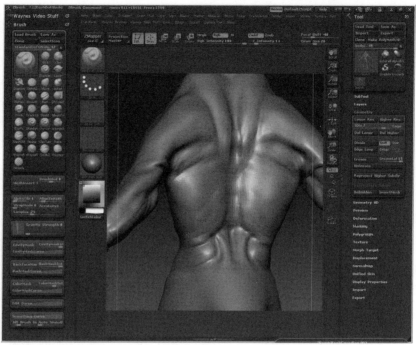

FIGURE 18-74

Work this area until you are happy with it, referring to references if you feel the need to. After doing this work (the majority of which can be done with the **Standard** brush), go back to the front and lightly add in some placeholders for the nipples. The nipples are very important landmarks when checking your proportions. Up to this point I've been estimating where they would be. If you draw a line through the nipple to the belly button, it should line up with the shoulder at the very end of the clavicle. Once you've added the nipples, use this method of reference to line up where to put the belly button on your model before adding that in as well as the line to represent the horizontal skin fold in this area.

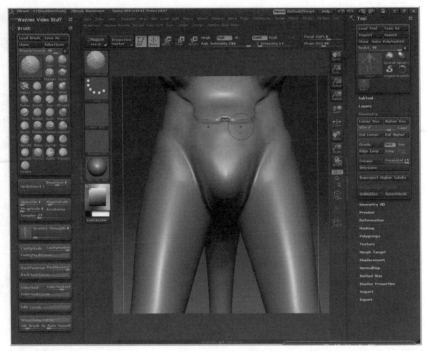

FIGURE 18-75

I've purposely waited to add in the stomach muscles so you could visualize the underlying forms. Add them now using exactly the same workflow as the majority of the other muscles by painting in the masks, inverting them, and then using the **Clay** brush to block them in one set at a time. At this time we are looking only to block in the shapes as flattish planes for later refining. When blocking in the mass of these muscles I start each stroke with my Clay brush from the center line outward as we want them to gel nicely with the rest of the torso muscles and not stick out like they have been added on as an afterthought. I should also point out that not every male character you sculpt will have a standard "six-pack." Only add features that will fit the design and body type of the character you are creating.

Let's look once more at the serratus muscles and how they feed into the stomach muscles as this is key to getting the stomach of a male character believable in my opinion. Notice how each set feeds into one of the abs, with each insertion the next down. So using your **Clay** brush, make sure that they align correctly with the stomach.

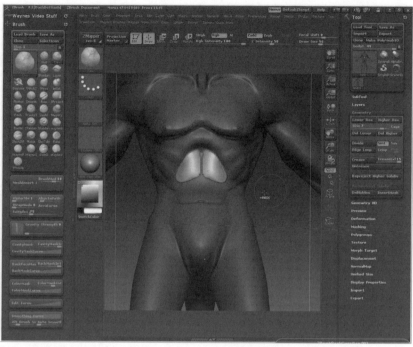

FIGURE 18-76

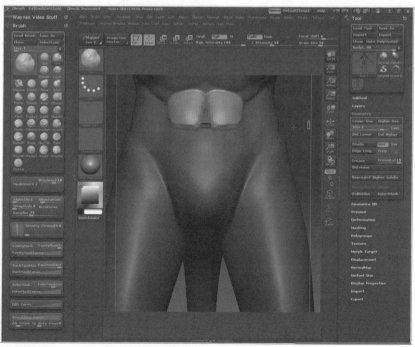

FIGURE 18-77

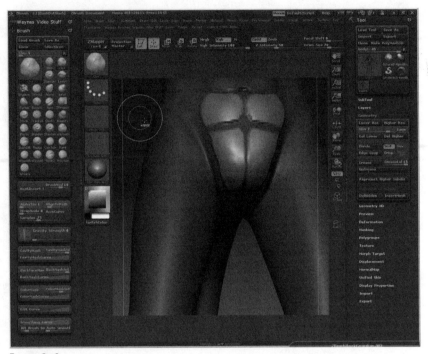

Figure 18-78

With things blocked in on the stomach area now, you should start to see the upper body take shape. There is still plenty of work left to do though. Rotate the model around in the viewport and look at it from every angle to check for problem areas to later fix.

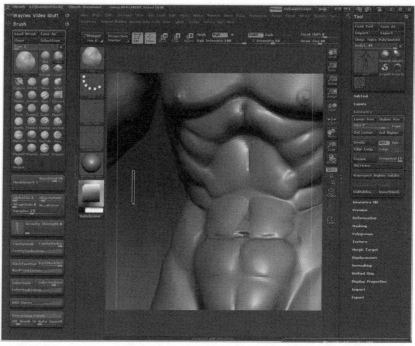

FIGURE 18-79

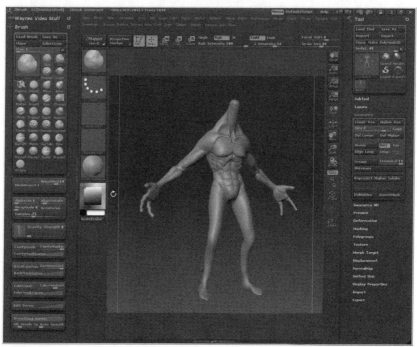

FIGURE 18-80

I'd also recommend changing the material you are using as well because the cavity shading effect can make the geometry look a little deeper that it actually is. If you preview the model with only a simple shader, you'll be able to see some things you might not notice otherwise. Indeed, some digital sculptors I know never sculpt with MatCap or use only a simple one such as the MatCap White. The way you choose to work is a personal choice, but it is good to be aware of how the optical effects of some materials can fool the eye during the sculpting process.

The Lower Half of the Body

Now that we've got the upper part of the body blocked in it's time to start on the lower part of the body. Legs used to give me a major headache when I was learning anatomy, especially the thigh because it has a relatively small number of muscles that go in a number of different directions. If you have problems like I did, I would advise practicing the part you have trouble with in isolation. Get as much information as you can about the part you are having problems with and keep practicing until things fall into place.

I find it best to start with the kneecap when blocking in the upper leg. It doesn't have to be perfect since we are using it only as a point of reference at this stage, but it gives us something to measure against when we are placing the muscles. We will be blocking in the muscles for the upper leg in the same way as all the others by using masks. So start with the kneecap first and check that you have it in the correct place. Remember that its placement and orientation depend on what the leg is doing and how it is posed. For now just concentrate on getting the placement right; the rest we'll worry about later once the character has been posed.

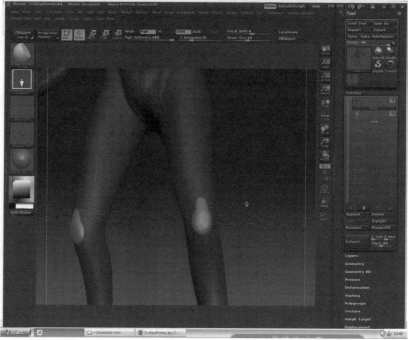

FIGURE 18-81

After blocking in the knee, start to block in the other muscles of the front of the upper leg until you have the basic structure correct. These will need to be tweaked as we progress of course, but for now we have a basic outline. For the main muscle mass I use the **Standard** brush and start adding the outside muscle, working my way inward. I normally block in the shins as well, but I leave the actual main forms of the leg for later because they depend on how the leg and foot are posed. I would advise keeping an anatomy book open while you sculpt to refer to if any area is giving you issues. Save the muscle in the center of the thigh for the later stages because it is one of the most visible and it is also on top of some of the other muscles. Be sure to check the thigh in profile from the side view as well as from the front and three-quarter views. Getting the lines and forms correct help to maintain balance in your sculpt.

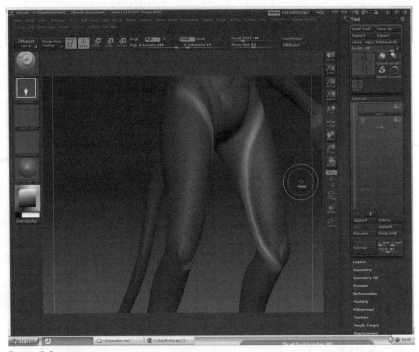

FIGURE 18-82

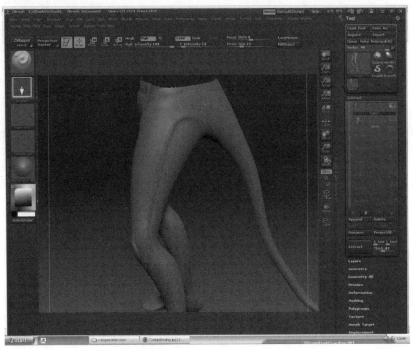

FIGURE 18-83

The single most important muscle of the upper leg is probably the one nearest the crotch on the inside of the leg. Many people forget it is even there because it is usually a bit underdeveloped and difficult to see. Remember that like the arms, the legs have many complex interactions of forms. Block in all the muscles in the front part of the thigh, but don't smooth them too much at this stage. You'll need some of those harsher lines later on in the process. One tip I would add is that if you sculpt your leg muscles on a layer in ZBrush, you can then use this to fade things in and out as needed. Layers can be a real aid to your sculpting process.

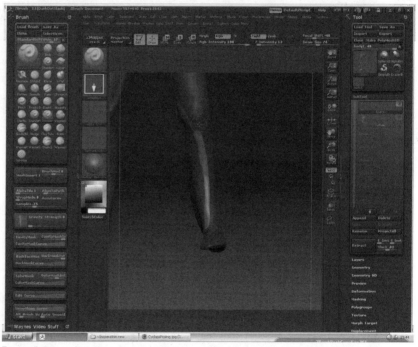

FIGURE 18-84

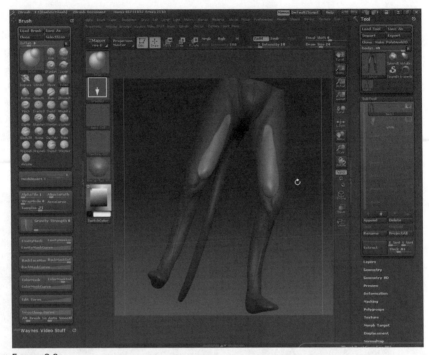

FIGURE 18-85

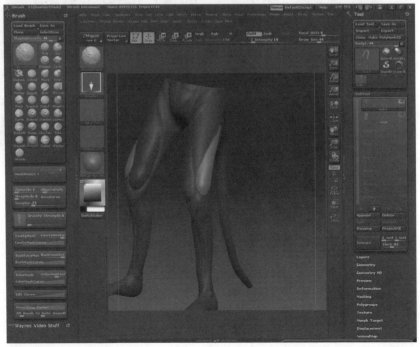

FIGURE 18-86

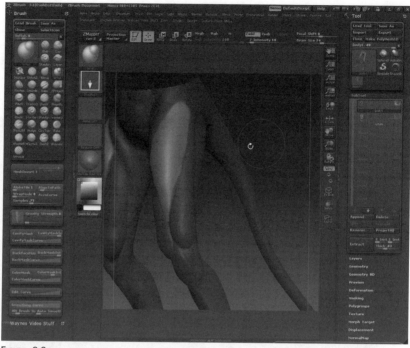

FIGURE 18-87

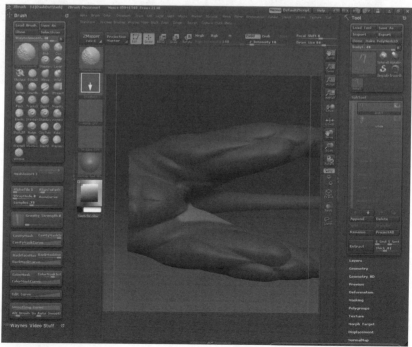

FIGURE 18-88

Using the **Clay** brush, add some weight back to the iliac arch of the pelvis and start to add some shape and mass where needed on the muscles we've just added on the upper legs. Try to use strokes that fade either into the mass or out of it to get a smoother transition where you can, and feel free to smooth out any other transitions in this area that don't work.

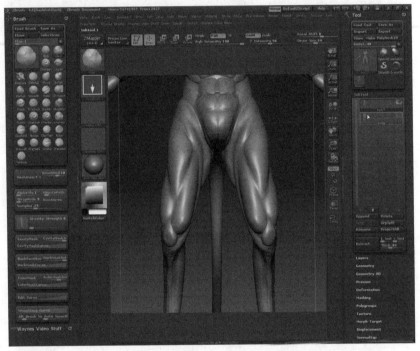

FIGURE 18-89

Let's start to block in some detail for the tail. I free styled this part because I wanted something unique but not overly distracting. I tried to use pleasing interlocking lines and forms that would be interesting but not draw the viewer's eye too much. The trick is to make the tail look like it is growing out of the area rather than being a separate item tacked on as an afterthought.

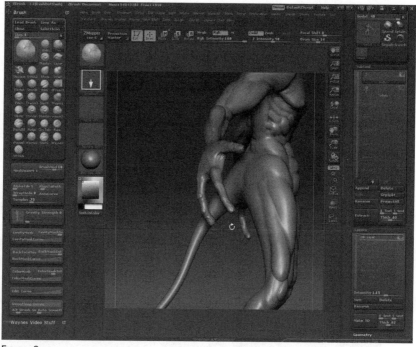

FIGURE 18-90

I then used **Alpha 55** along with the **Displace** brush to carve in some interesting lines that would complement the muscle structure in the legs and back and help the tail look like it "belongs." Try to maintain strong lines and not get lost in a sea of alpha induced detail. Often you will notice that the strongest sculpts are those that look good at a pretty low level and do not have to be detailed to high heaven. So when detail is added to such a piece, it's just the icing on the cake. It's easy to go a little "alpha crazy" until you realize that more is not necessarily better.

Just take a few minutes to check the existing forms of the entire sculpture and add or remove weight in areas that need it before we continue on.

Next up I decided that the lower stomach and abdomen were not technically correct and spoiled the lines of the entire sculpt. So I stepped down to subdivision level 5 and masked off the area from the belly button down the stomach to the lower abdomen and the front of the crotch. I then blurred this mask using the **Blur** button in the **Masking** section of the **Tool** palette. I then activated my Rotate transform tool and drew an action line (with X symmetry still enabled) from the belly button downward to about level with the lower crotch area. I rotated the entire lower abdomen backward a fair bit, removed the mask, and pulled the center of the stomach in a little to refine the shape.

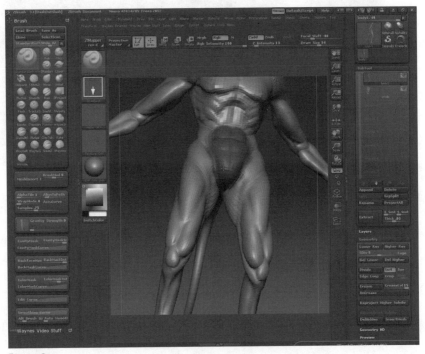

FIGURE 18-91

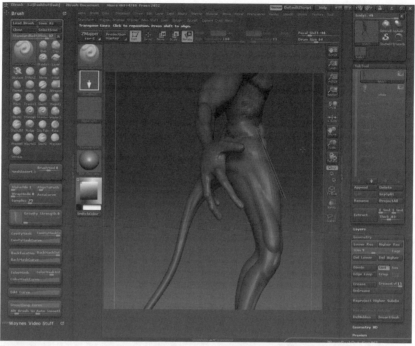

FIGURE 18-92

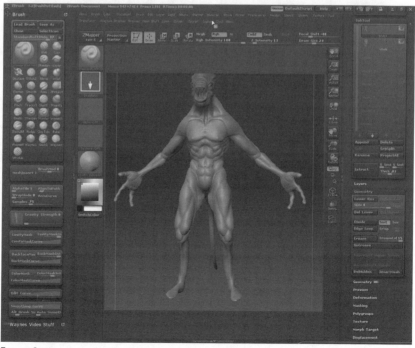

FIGURE 18-93

I then added quite a bit of weight to the sides of the stomach using the Standard brush to fix the overall silhouette of the model. I also realized when looking at my model from a full body shot that the thighs were too bulky. So I used the Move brush to pull these areas back into the original silhouette while still keeping the muscle structure we've added.

I corrected the thigh shape both from the front and three-quarter views to check the lines of the forms until I was happy with them. The thighs from a front view should fade into the top of the pelvis. The trick at this point is leaving yourself enough room for the detailing you will have to do later. At this stage I am ready to correct and improve areas and noticed that the top pair of muscles of the stomach had become a bit flat in the sculpting process, so take a **Standard** brush and add the weight back if you have the same problem with your sculpture. Make sure you are then back at your highest subdivision level.

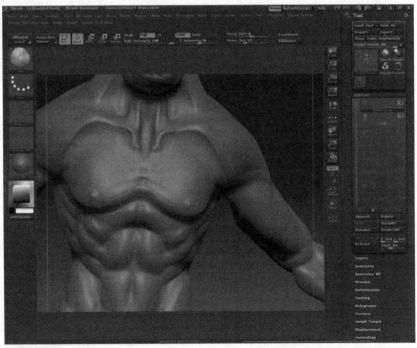

FIGURE 18-94

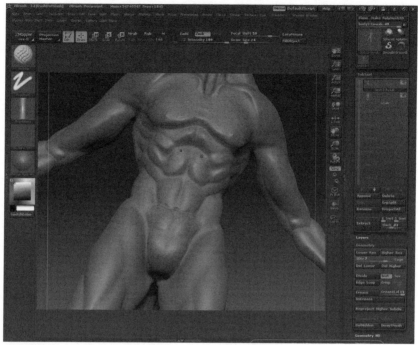

FIGURE 18-95

Both the serratus and the deltoid intersection with the biceps have became washed out in the process of detailing as well, so I went back and corrected these by adding some weight with the Standard brush again. When making corrections, try using a few different materials and check the forms with different MatCaps. Some MatCaps can have cavity effects, plus changing the look of your sculpt helps you get a new perspective on things.

Using the **Clay**, **Standard**, and **Flatten** brushes, we now need to start changing a few minor things in the stomach. What we are really looking at is the way the muscles interact and work together, so knock the muscles leading into the stomach back a little with the Flatten and Clay brushes so they don't stand out too "proud." Take the Clay brush and make these muscles fade into the main six-pack so that the transition is hardly noticeable, and then do the same with the love handles. Our aim is to make things look a little more organic at this stage. We now need to do a bit of work on the biceps starting with the insertion point into the lower arm. The shape got lost when we added the muscles of the lower arm a while back. Again, check the shape of the biceps from all angles.

Now let's revisit the thigh area by first stepping down to subdivision level 7. These are large forms and it's better to sculpt them at lower subdivision levels. A good guideline is to sculpt finer details at high subdivision levels and large ones at lower levels. This helps to prevent any "blobbiness" on the surface of the mesh caused by insufficient smoothing. Also, smoothing, correcting, and adding forms is easier when the polygon count is lower. So switch to your **Inflate** brush and starting on the outer muscles, try to improve the transitional areas a bit more without spending too long on it. Make sure that each muscle is believable both on its own and in conjunction with the others. Make sure that they fade out as they head toward insertion points and that any areas of mass are not just "lumps" but appear to be the muscle contracting. Don't go too far into the kneecap area as this is going to be changed by the pose we put him in later on.

Step back up to your highest subdivision level (level 8 at this time) and switch to your **Displace** brush with a fairly small alpha. We are going to start cutting in a few finer lines starting directly under the pectoral muscles to the skin folds. So work down the stomach and add some nice lines that will become folds later between the individual muscles. As we will have lost detail in the serratus area, sharpen that up again using the brush as well. I'm guessing that by now you have started to see a pattern. We sculpt at a subdivision level, and then add forms until we need to step up to the next level. We then correct any forms washed out too much or knocked off by adding further details. Add to this we correct any areas as we sculpt, and you see the pattern of a basic digital sculpting workflow.

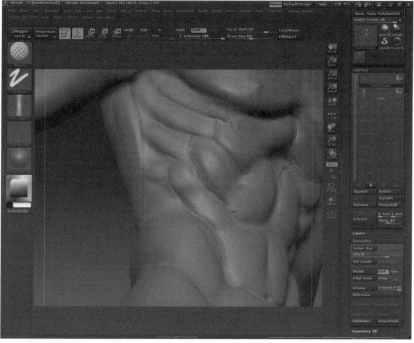

FIGURE 18-96

Use these lines you are carving in as a way of strengthening the forms and keeping them from looking too "wishy-washy." (I hate sculpts that look either all harsh or all washed out and have no sense of "light and shade.")

Now carve in the backs of the thighs an inverted elongated "Y" shape that we will once again use as a guide line for us to inflate and add mass to this area. So far we haven't touched the backs of the thighs at all, but even though they won't be directly seen in our final render it is still a good idea to add details to a fairly fine level. Also carve in lines for the calf muscles in the lower leg running right down to the Achilles tendon. I like to think of these carved guidelines as light pencil drawings that are later used as a guide for a painting. Remember that the calves wrap around toward the front of the shin a fair bit, so be sure to capture this when cutting those guidelines in. You should end up with a diamond shape on the back of the knee, so if you don't have this shape, then recheck your lines. Now take your **Standard** or **Inflate** brush (either will do just as well) and use these guidelines to add the forms between them. The lines will act as a sort of boundary that prevents the brush from affecting the muscle next, which makes the job a little bit easier.

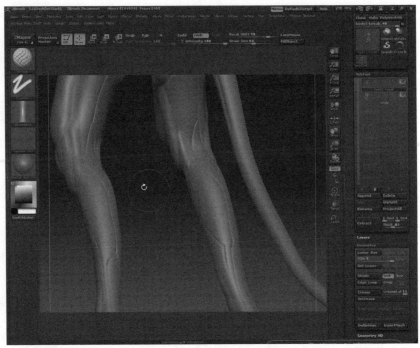

FIGURE 18-97

When dealing with the diamond-shaped form on the back of the knees, I would advise masking this off, inverting, and then adding the form using only the Standard brush, as the Inflate brush can be overkill for this area. Once added, remove the mask and smooth the transitions a bit until things look more acceptable. Make sure that as well as bulging out it also bulges slightly sideways as well for realism. Then remove the mask and isolate the leg polygroups by **Shift+Ctrl+clicking** on them.

Moving onto the calf muscles, I'd like you to paint a mask over the outermost one first and invert that mask. Make sure that your mask runs all the way down the side of the Achilles tendon and then use your **Inflate** brush with a large size (~94) and add some mass to the area. Try to keep your strokes long and even and be sure to fade the pressure out toward the end of the strokes. While inflating this area you will need to check the muscle from all angles to check that the overall shape is correct. With your mask still active, smooth around the edges of the muscle to help it transition into the rest of the forms we are going to add in a moment.

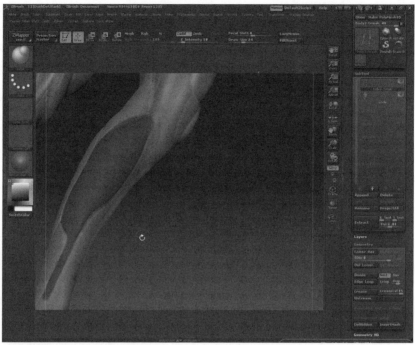

FIGURE 18-98

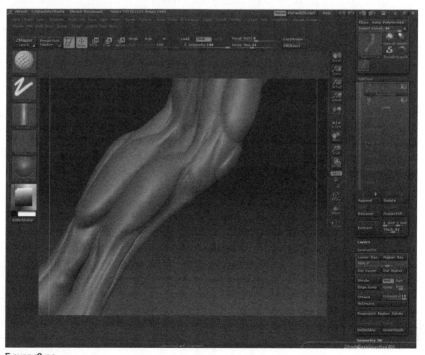

FIGURE 18-99

Invert your mask again and this time hold down your **Ctrl** key and add the areas around (but not including) the other calf muscle. We want to make sure that we have a large area around it masked as we again will be using a large brush size. In this case it was easier to invert and then add to the existing mask than to unmask and create it fresh. If your mask is a bit too large, hold down the **Alt** key along with the **Ctrl** key and paint the area you wish to remove. Again use your **Inflate** brush to bulk up the area, remembering that each calf muscle is a different shape. We just want them in approximately the right ball park for later refining. Again smooth out the edges before removing the mask to fix those transitions along with any imperfections in the calf muscle.

Now take your **Move** brush and pull the calf muscles into shape, remembering that the apex of each muscle is not the same. The outer one protrudes more than the inner one. Many muscles of the human body should be studied from a variety of angles as well as in silhouette. Once you've done this they become easy to remember. If you find you can't get the shapes right with just the use of the **Move** brush, bring the **Inflate** brush back into play to enable you to correct the forms a bit more.

Now I want you to paint a mask, invert it for the Achilles tendon, and then use the **Inflate** brush with a medium size to make this area protrude a bit. Now take your **Displace** brush with a smallish alpha and start to carve some lines into this area, first at the top of the Achilles tendon where it exits from beneath the calf muscles to help it look like it is "emerging" and not just sitting on top of them. Also carve some lines to help the calf muscles in this area look more defined. You can then add some lines to represent the other muscles in the lower leg, and carve in some lines to make the tendons running down the inside of the knee stand out a bit more and look a bit tighter. Your aim is to try to make each muscle in this area look like it is emerging from under the muscles it is supposed to. Adding this gives a sense of layer and depth to your sculpt and is something we will be repeating as we work on other areas of the model. Correct any areas that look off as a result of this "layering" work on the lower leg muscles. Although the lower leg is still far from done, it will do for now.

Using your **Standard** brush, start to add some shape and bulk to the heel of the foot, which has been neglected. I want a more sphere-shaped heel than a human's to exaggerate it and to help with the feet's balance and proportion with the rest of the design. We started with a fairly human foot and now we want to change the shape to more of a duck-like shape. So start by removing the geometry where the arches of the feet would be.

While on the subject of feet, let's point out a few main things about human feet. Like all forms on the human body, the feet are made up of some rather simple shapes that when combined become more complex. The arch that runs from the lower leg down to where the toes begin is higher on the inside of the foot than the outside by quite a margin, and the shape of the heel is fairly rounded.

A common method of learning to draw the human body is to see the forms as a series of simple shapes such as spheres, cubes, cones, and cylinders. If a form looks too complex to you, then chances are you haven't broken the form down into simple enough parts yet.

You can study your own feet to help you block out a very basic foot shape. But don't add toes; just pretend that all the toes are glued together as this creature will have a webbed, duck-style foot. Blocking in human form first gives us enough information to later change the shapes to fit the character. One trick I learned long ago is to think of the shape of the sole of the foot first. Most people can remember the shape of a footprint, so this information is helpful when modeling the upper foot.

Using your **Clay** brush, start to block in the interplay between some of the major tendons and the front of the foot. We are exaggerating this anatomy for the Guardian.

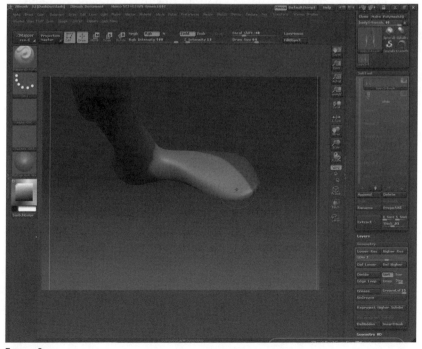

FIGURE 18-100

Now go back over and check and correct all the transitional areas between the different muscles on the entire lower leg, making sure that muscles emerge where they need to and interplay correctly. Then work around the upper leg in the same way, correcting those transitions and helping it to look a little more "real." Feel free to step down a subdivision level when dealing with larger forms such as the quads as this will make working on them far easier and yield smoother results on the surface of your digital sculpture. If you isolated the legs while working on them, make sure that you have your entire model visible again. Some of our work will have a direct impact on how the upper body looks, so as a result we may want to tweak a few things.

Let's work again on the transition between the obliques (love handles) and the ribs and pelvis area. Like before, make sure that it appears to emerge from under the lats and inserts into the stomach area. The layer of fat in this area affects how this area lays, so more fat means it will bulge out or even downward. Try to capture the complexity of the shape as it wraps around the sides of the torso and over the iliac crest. Melt it nicely into the lower set of stomach muscles to help the whole pelvis and stomach area appear less like a sum of complex shapes and more like a living thing. When trying to "nail down" the shape of the oblique muscles, remember that a muscle (which you can't see) runs under and connects from the bottom ribs to the arch of the pelvis. Once you understand how the muscles you can't see affect the ones you can, things will make a lot more sense. Once all of this is done, step back up to subdivision level 8 again.

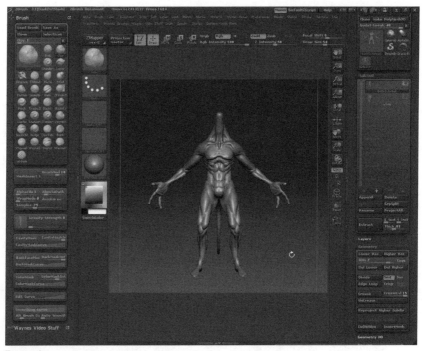

FIGURE 18-101

Sorting Out the Polygroups

Up to now we have been living with the polygroups that ZBrush handed to us when we first generated our base mesh from ZSpheres, and they have done the job very well. However, as we are going to be dealing with the hands now we need to put them in their own polygroups. At the moment, each finger, thumb, and palm of the hand are in their own polygroups, which makes it difficult to hide and show just the hands themselves when working on them. So I would like you to step all the way back down to level 1. Use a combination of **Shift+Crtl+dragging** to isolate polygons and **Shift+Ctrl+dragging** and then lifting the **Ctrl** key to remove an area to isolate the hands. When making polygroups at the lowest subdivision level, we are affecting how all the polygons that are subdivided from these are grouped.

Once you have just the right and left hands showing, go to the **Tool** palette, open the **Polygroups** section, and press the **Group Visible** button. If you have trouble getting exactly the right selection, try turning on Double Sided mode in the Display Properties section using the Double button. Once this is done you can unhide the rest of your model, then when you have **Frame** switched on you should now see the hands in their own polygroups and you can step back up to the higher subdivision levels again.

Take your model to subdivision level 6 and again isolate just the hands polygroups so that nothing else is visible.

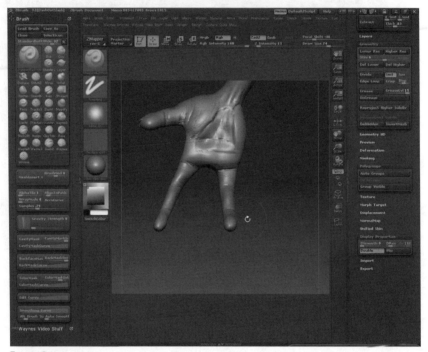

Mask off the center portion of the palm of the hand and using your **Standard** brush with a slightly larger size than the area, push it inward a little to give the palm more shape. The reason we stepped down to subdivision level 6 to do this is because if we tried it at the higher levels we would be washing away some of the detail and forms we added earlier. At lower levels we keep the details and only affect the larger forms that we need to. On my model the bulged areas between the finger joints on the front of the hand have been washed out a little due to both subdividing and work on the area, so re-establish them again to where they were previously. In a similar way, if the pad at the base of the thumb is getting a little lost and looks too flat, bulk it up a little.

Activate your **Move** transform tool and drag a topological mask over the hand to isolate the first finger. Then without removing the mask go back into Draw mode and edit the mask until it looks like the one shown in Figure 18-103. Now go back to your Move transform tool and drag an action line the length of the first finger. From the side view, move the whole finger upward a little to increase the curve of the area where the fingers connect to the hand. This is the easiest way of making this major form change to the hand without making a huge mess of it. Once you have checked that the resulting transition is not too harsh, remove the mask. Redisplay the rest of your mesh again by pressing **Ctrl+Shift** and clicking on an empty part of the viewport.

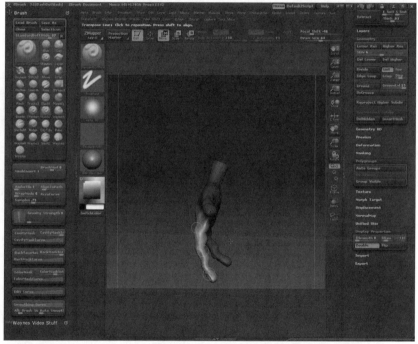

Figure 18-103

At the moment the wrists are far too thin for the size of the hands and muscle structure, so we need to bulk these up a bit. The easiest way to do this is to use the **Move** brush to gently drag out the sides of the wrist area just below the hand.

Move now to a back view of your character and mask off a large area over each shoulder blade, but make it much larger as we are now going to bulk this area up quite a lot and want a fair bit of space to do it in. Once you have the area masked off and inverted, we need to do a little editing of the mask to get proper deformation. So paint in a mask by holding down **Ctrl** and using your left mouse button. Then change to your **Rotate** transform tool, and draw an action line from the edge of the deltoid/shoulder blade area to a little short of the midway point. (Make sure that not the whole center of the back is unmasked, as you will need to leave a line down where the spine is still masked for this to work.) Now move to a top-down view and gently adjust your action line to rotate the shoulder blade area outward using the deltoid side as your pivot point. Then remove your mask totally. This is a relatively painless way of adding this basic form to the shoulder blade area for many humanoid bipeds, as it allows you to sculpt in the detail early on and keep the main mass for nearer the end when things are coming together, meaning that you can check that the forms are working together well as a design. If the base of the area you've rotated near the bottom of the back is too far out, simply smooth it back in gently.

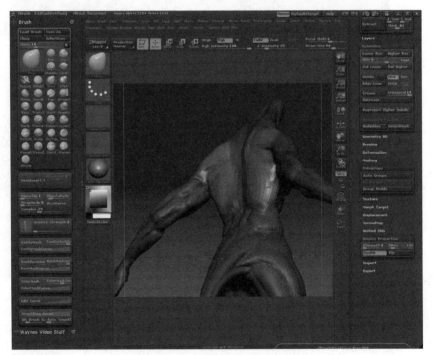

FIGURE 18-104

Moving back to the neck again, switch to your **Clay** brush and refine the forms as we did before, making sure that there are no unintentional lumps or bumps. We are adjusting the shape of the neck so it works with the head of the model (although at the end we will have to tweak this once it is in position and textured). So just eyeball this for now. But again make sure that the muscles of the neck do not just appear to be stuck on with Super Glue, and do originate from somewhere. Where your muscles come from, where they are going, and where they emerge and insert is really the key to organic digital sculpting.

At this point I stepped up to level 7 (where my layers were) and created a new layer before stepping back down to level 5. I wanted to thin out the waist on the Guardian a bit as I felt he was starting to look a little too stocky. So mask off the whole torso area and then invert it. This should leave you with the limbs masked off and the waist and chest area exposed to work on. Now using the **Move** brush gently pull the waist of the character inward. The best part of using layers is you can actually move it in further than you need to and then use the layer controls to fade in or out the effect to control the waist size when you are back at level 7. When changing the waist size, use a large brush and zoom in so that the torso fills most of the screen. Once you're done, remove your mask. I then rotated my model until I was looking up at the torso from the feet area and gently pulled the center line between the pectoral muscles inward just a fraction.

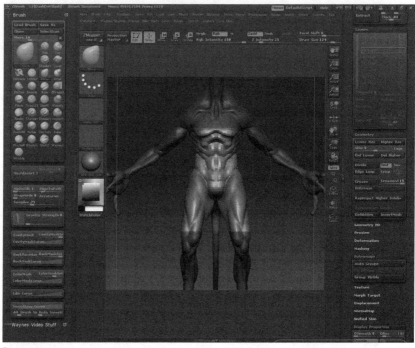

FIGURE 18-105

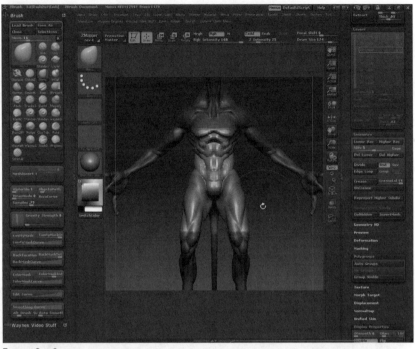

FIGURE 18-106

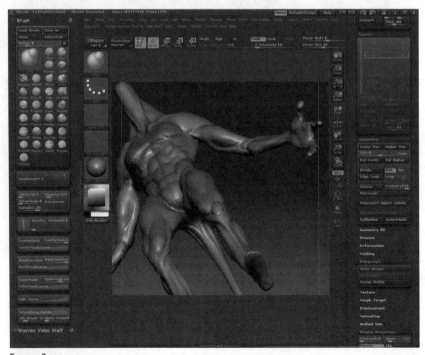

FIGURE 18-107

Most of this work on the stomach and chest was done with Perspective mode turned off. This can be toggled with the **P** key or from inside the Draw palette. Work again over the deltoid and then down the arm, correcting any forms you don't like and that don't seem correct at this stage. By now you will have noticed that one change can act like a domino effect to knock other things slightly off design wise. We then need to keep going back over these areas to pull them back so that the design continues to work. Don't be tempted to ignore these issues and decide to sort them out all at once, as this only means you increase the risk of getting in such a mess that you forget what the original design problem was anyway. So although it can be annoying to keep going back over areas, it makes more sense to do it while you see the problem. Once you've done this clean-up job, step back up to your highest subdivision level and switch Perspective mode back on.

Bringing It All Together

We are just about ready to bring the whole character together to its initial level before we start posing and correcting the forms for the character. We will add some finer details that help to "sell" the character. Notice that we haven't gone too wild with the polygon count for the body on this model. This is because although we are going to subdivide once more, the final scene will be rendered externally so we need to keep the polygon counts to a manageable level. Once the character is done we will also need to add the base mesh for the weapon, pose it with him, and detail it, so we don't want to end up with a polygon count greater than our machine can handle.

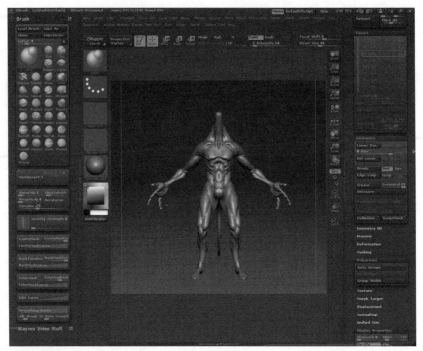

FIGURE 18-108

There is nothing more heartbreaking than finding that you cannot finish a scene because your machine cannot handle the poly counts needed. It has happened to all of us at once time or another, but as you get used to what your particular setup can and cannot do before going into HD geometry, you will be able to find the balance needed. I also wanted to keep things at a manageable level for most ZBrush users. So let's get on with bringing things together.

Let's start in the stomach area by first masking it off from the end of the ribs down to the crotch excluding the legs. We are dealing with the front only, so do not mask around the sides of the torso. Invert the mask and switch to your **Move** brush before we start to tweak the look of the center muscle strip on the stomach. Remember very early on in the chapter when I mentioned using a female stomach shape to generate the male shape? Well, that shape is going to be useful now to help us define the look of the stomach. From the front view, a female stomach shape is often described as a "figure eight" shape. Although this shape is not as pronounced in a male, there is a difference in the width of the bottom, middle, and abdominal areas. It is not a straight line as we can currently see on our model. So use the **Move** brush to pull the top and bottom of the stomach muscle strip outward a bit. We also have a lot more leeway with regard to the look of the stomach area than we would on a human anatomy study, so we can make this area of the character more unique.

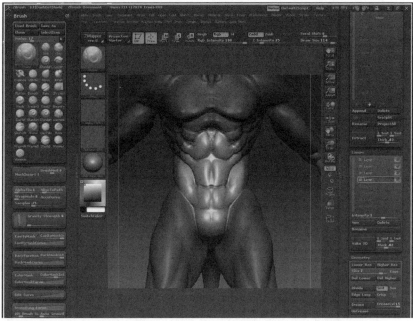

FIGURE 18-109

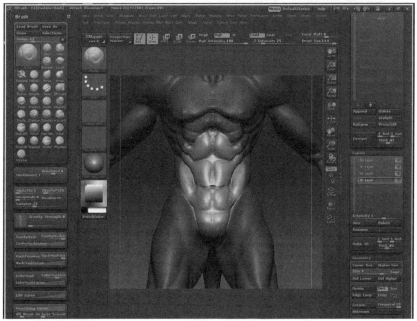

FIGURE 18-110

After doing all the changes to that area, check that the surrounding forms and their transitions are still correct and...well, you know what to do by now, don't you?

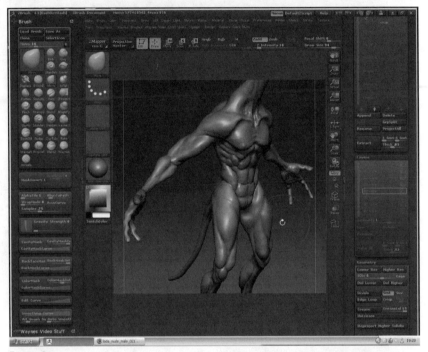

FIGURE 18-111

If the shape of the thighs is not correct when viewed from the front or they appear unbalanced due to changes, then step down to subdivision level 6 and use your **Move** brush to pull everything back into place.

Now move to the back view and use a smaller brush size to pull each side of the back of the knees inward just a little to help with the overall shape of the area. Move back to the calf area and start to improve the silhouette, taking your time and making sure that the forms are checked from all angles and not just the one that you are working in. As I mentioned earlier, we are going for a bit more of a bow to the lower leg than you would find in a human in order to make it look more balanced. Your artistic interpretation of the anatomy is an important part of creating a unique character.

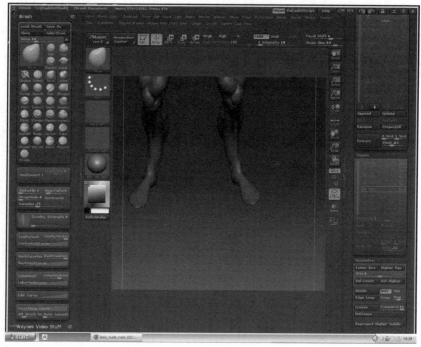

FIGURE 18-112

Now it's time to make the feet look a bit more like duck feet. Isolate the leg polygroups and move down to the feet area, then using your **Move** brush start to pull the shapes into what looks like three toes with webs between them. I would recommend starting with a largish sized Move brush and pull the outside of the foot first before the inside. I switched PolyFrame on for this to give me information regarding how many polygons are in the area I'm working on and how they are distributed, as I knew the polygon count in the feet area is not very high. We can then amend any creative decisions if we find that our design is simply too complex for the polygon distribution of that particular area.

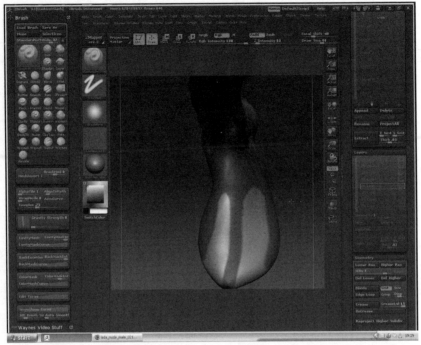

Figure 18-113

Look at the foot now from the bottom up, and again pull the shapes into place. As I mentioned earlier, the information that we get from the sole of the foot is very helpful. Pull the front of the foot forward a bit to make it larger than a human foot. At some point in the evolutionary past the creature's race would have used these shapes to help them swim and they would as a direct result be a little oversized.

I found at this point that the feet when viewed from the front were slanting slightly to the outside, so go in with your **Move** brush and carefully adjust them so that they are more flat. Also increase the size of the arch on the inside of the top of the foot leading from the lower leg down to the toe area.

Step up to subdivision level 7 this time and switch to your **Standard** brush so we can add some shapes to the feet. Paint some masks for where each of the "webs" are going to be and invert them. Then use the **Flatten** brush to push in this area a little before moving to the **Layer** brush with a low ZIntensity and continuing to remove a little of the geometry. Make sure that you work right up to and slightly over the edges of the foot to keep the illusion solid when we pose the character later. Remember that the Layer brush allows you to cross over a continuous stroke without building up the point of overlap, so try to keep the work in one stroke if at all possible. Then remove the mask and use the Layer brush again, this time to add some mass to the "toes" as shown. Then switch to the **Standard** brush and add even more mass to those areas so that we will catch some nice shadows as a result of the geometrical changes between the toes and the webbed part of the feet.

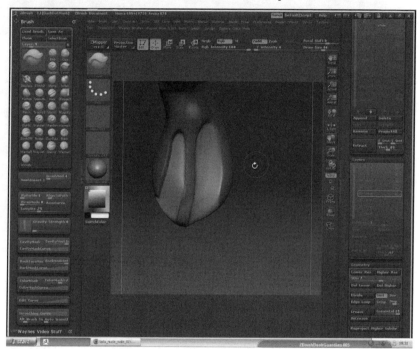

FIGURE 18-114

Smooth out the areas some without smoothing out the actual transition areas too much. To make the webbed areas look like they are slightly stretched between the toes, use a smallish sized **Move** brush and pull these areas inward. Once you have done this, smooth the area a bit.

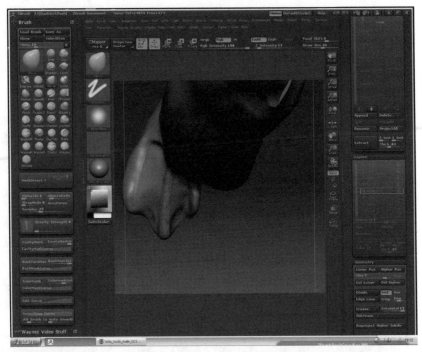

At this point I would like you to solve a common problem I've intentionally created in this workflow. If you look at the soles of the feet, you will see all sorts of nastiness created by the **Layer** brush affecting not just the side we were working on but also the back-facing polys as well. So how do we prevent this from happening in areas where two geometrical surfaces are so close together? We use the often neglected brush option in the Brush palette that allows us to turn on "backface masking." I'll give a quick reminder of what it does, but for a full explanation see the section about the Brush palette in Chapter 4. With Backface Masking on, only the areas that face the viewer will be affected. So when two opposing faces are close together, the Backface Masking option prevents the back-facing polys from being affected.

This also gives you some practice at cleaning up problem areas manually with your brushes. So smooth the area until it looks better. If you need to, step down a subdivision level first before stepping back up and smoothing it again.

Now step back up to your highest subdivision level to give us some more geometry to work with in the area. We still don't have a lot of polygons to work with, but we can start to tighten the forms up a little. Take out your **Displace** brush and a smallish alpha and start to reinforce the lines and transitional areas between the webbed parts and the toes.

Also carve in a few lines for where the tendons would go leading up to the lower leg. You'll have to imagine the anatomy for this area. The feet are not really that noticeable in the final scene, so once we work out the size of our final render we can then decide how many pixels will be taken up with the feet. (This isn't going to be a lot, so the feet will be a bit rougher than the rest of the creature.)

Using the **Standard** brush, add some knuckles and joints to the toes of the feet and beef up those tendons a bit from the lines we carved in a moment ago. You'll have to use your personal and artistic judgment about this. Push the areas between the tendons inward a little and smooth out any lumpiness that you may get as a result of working in such a small area.

As we will now have a slight downward bow to the foot we need to rotate the front of the foot back into position. So take your **Rotate** transform tool and drag a topological mask about halfway down the foot, then drag an action line from a side view from there to the end of the foot. (Remember that you can snap to views by rotating and holding down the Shift key.) Then still in this side view, rotate the front of the toes upward a little until the foot is level. You may need to use a few different topological masks and rotate in a few directions until the foot is flat and looks level with our imaginary floor.

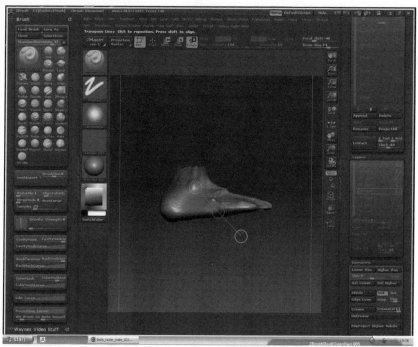

FIGURE 18-116

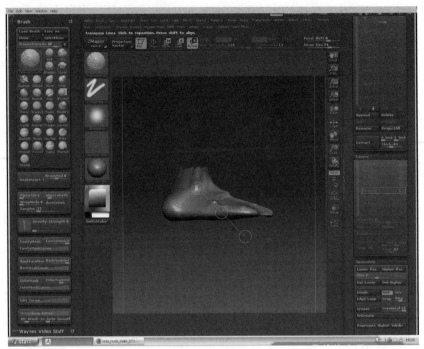

FIGURE 18-117

Exit Perspective mode by pressing the **P** key to toggle it; for the moment we'll be able to better judge what we are doing in Orthographic mode. Taking your **Move** brush, pull the kneecaps forward a little. Now step back down to subdivision level 5 as we are going to make some changes to larger areas that will be far easier at a lower subdivision level. At this lower level, as it is less smooth looking and a little more "blocky," sometimes you can better judge your forms and muscles. So start to correct and round off some of the flatter areas of muscles on the leg and again try to strive for believability.

Step back up to your highest subdivision level (level 8 at this time) and make the **Layer** brush your active brush. Set its ZIntensity to 4 with no alpha selected. We are going to use this to give a little more character to the nipple area, so first we want to block in the outside part of the nipple by drawing a circular shape in one smooth movement. Then zoom in a little and make a smaller circle inside the previous circle to represent the nipple. It's now looking a lot more nipple like, but we'll come back to add a few finishing touches later on.

With your **Layer** brush still active, we are going to use its unique functions to help add some detail to our digital sculpture. The Layer brush is often overlooked as an organic sculpting brush and used more often in hard surface sculpting in ZBrush. But its highly predictable way of working and the results it gives can be a real boon by allowing us to either carve in or add mass and smooth one side (or both of the edges) to quickly get the look we are after. So first let's use it in **Zsub** mode (which as you know by now you can get to from Zadd mode by simply pressing and holding down the **Alt** key) to carve some lines into the center of the chest. These are basically echoing the lines we made in this area that have now become lost. Draw each line as a continuous stroke and then smooth over it to help its transition into the forms of the chest. Repeating this way of working, also carve a line directly under the center of the pectoral muscles, but don't smooth it right now.

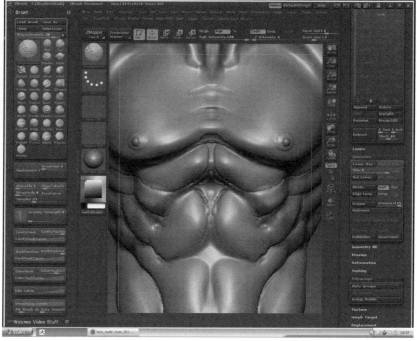

FIGURE 18-118

Now we can refine the areas we just carved into the chest by using the Layer brush in **Zadd** mode, running it above each carved in area, and then smoothing. This helps to add a sense that the skin wrinkles and folds here regularly. Also do the same above the line you carved in directly below the pectorals, so this line we add will be at the very bottom of the center chest line on the pectorals themselves.

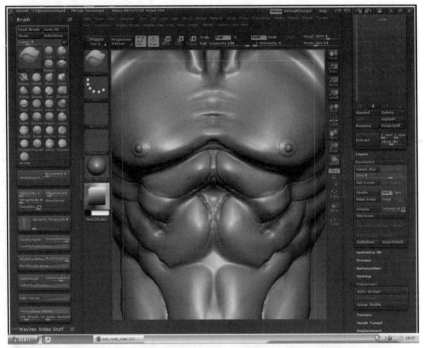

Figure 18-119

Now zoom out from your model, scale it to fit within the viewport, and activate the head. For this design process I copied the head and deleted the last two subdivision levels, leaving me with a lower polygon version that makes ZBrush highly responsive. Later on when the body has been textured I will use the fully textured and retopologized head. The head is crucial for getting the design and balance of the character correct, so by using a lower polygon version of it we save our system resources for the polygons that matter in the body while we work on it. There is no point in wasting system resources to show the high-poly version of the head when we aren't working on it.

As we now have both parts of the body visible, let's make the modeling experience as enjoyable as possible. I personally don't like seeing the different colors on the subtools caused when a material is active but not applied. I know this is a personal issue, but if you find that having the head and body slightly different shades of the same material is distracting, then apply the same color and material to both parts of the model. A small thing like this can really help with the experience of sculpting because it eliminates the distraction or slight annoyance.

After a quick look over your entire model (mentally logging anything you would like to change later on), make sure that the body subtool is active and that you still have the **Layer** brush selected. I would like you to now zoom in on the belly button area so that only the bottom part of the torso is visible. Take the Layer brush down to a very small (but still big enough to be usable) size and remove some mass from the belly button. Then carve out the line that runs from the belly button sideways across the stomach where it folds. Next, use your brush to add a thin amount of mass directly above this line to give the sense of some weight above the fold line and then smooth one side of this (the upper part of it) out a little.

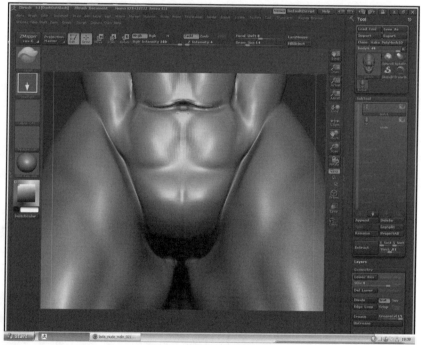

FIGURE 18-120

If you zoom back out you will notice that this one small addition has brought more life to the character. Although styles and artistic philosophies vary greatly from artist to artist, my personal belief is that you are far better off with a few very fine details on a model than smothering it in an alpha induced haze of details. Art is about contrast. Contrast between light and shade, high detailed areas and low detailed areas, and getting this balance right is part of the attraction to me personally. But ask any five digital artists their personal artistic philosophy and you will no doubt get five different answers, as there is no right or wrong, only *different*. I just want you to see where we will be going style wise with this and why. Although we will add some skin surface detail at the end, it will hopefully still retain a balance of light and shade and detailed and less detailed areas.

I'd like you to make your **Displace** brush the active brush now and pick one of the smaller alphas and the **FreeHand** stroke type. We are going to use this to add a few finer details and the start of some folds on the back area of the model. So taking it at a small size, carve in a few lines to denote the fold areas on the lats and lightly smooth them out until they are just visible. Start the longer ones from the armpit area (where the lats insert into the origin point in the upper arm) and run along the surface flow of the muscle toward the center. Then add some more in a similar way from the base of the center of the muscles up and outward again, following the surface flow direction. Carve a line or two to again make the trapezius muscle a bit more visible (remember, we are purposely going for an exaggerated anatomy). When carving these lines, try to give them a little variety to make the model look more realistic. Skin folds are rarely a continuous line of the same depth, but rather a combination of a few overlapping or staggered lines. So make sure that you don't use a single line, but rather a few of different depths and sizes, then smooth the transitions out a little. Also I'd like you to block in a few lines to later develop into stress lines from the spine outward across the muscles and then smooth them out until they are barely noticeable.

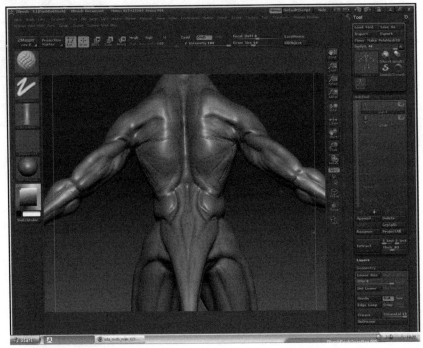

FIGURE 18-121

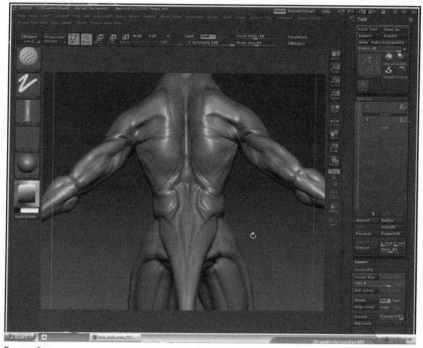

Figure 18-122

Start to tighten up the other muscles on the upper and lower back by sharpening the transitions a bit using the **Displace** brush over those areas that look washed out. Move on to the triceps area and, using a set of staggered carved in lines, start to outline the way the tricep muscle stretches and moves. Add some wrinkles to the elbow area as well. Although the back will not be seen in the final render, it is still best to develop it to at least some degree for the practice and to help judge the way the other muscles should look.

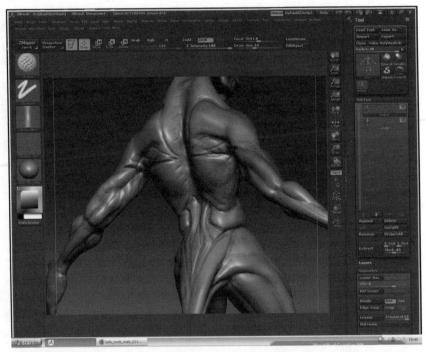

FIGURE 18-123

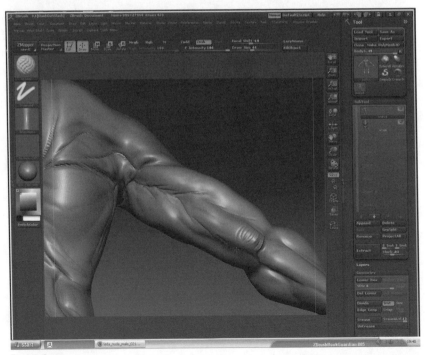

FIGURE 18-124

Using your **Standard** or **Inflate** brush (either will do equally well), add some mass between the folds we added coming from the spine. This is where the workflow for the sculpting of this character risks getting a bit boring as basically we are doing much the same thing over many areas of the model. We just want to use the same methods to tighten up the overall look of the way the muscles intersect, overlap, and insert under each other to help bring the model a bit nearer to completion. So for each set of lines you've carved for folds, add mass between the lines to give it a sense of weight. To avoid repetition, I will just concentrate on a few areas that are unique and only briefly mention the areas I am tightening up. (The footage of the entire modeling and texturing process of this character is available on the DVD.)

Before starting though, I want you to step back down to subdivision level 5 and use your **Move** brush to gently pull and push some of the muscle shapes to correct anything that is now out of whack as a result of our work. Take particular care with the muscles of the arms, legs, and chest, checking them from a number of views and angles. I found that on my model the area between the upper bicep and the deltoid had become a bit lost in a sea of washed-out detail, so I used the **Displace** brush to bring that back a fair bit. I also made the area at the bottom part of the biceps a bit harsher to help maintain the design balance. Now using the techniques I mentioned above, work your way around the entire front to the torso and tighten it all up. If you find any of these carved in lines a little too harsh, don't be afraid to wash them out a bit or totally redo them. Once you have tightened the front of the torso to your satisfaction we can move on.

FIGURE 18-125

Take your **Inflate** brush and correct any shapes on the legs that
may need to be bulked up or rounded off a bit more. The muscle structure should be fairly well sculpted now, so it's time to get things looking
as good as possible. If you have been keeping a set of layers going with
different parts of the detailing process, you may be able to use them as a
backup plan for major corrections. I always use layers once I get beyond
the basic blocking in stage for this very reason.

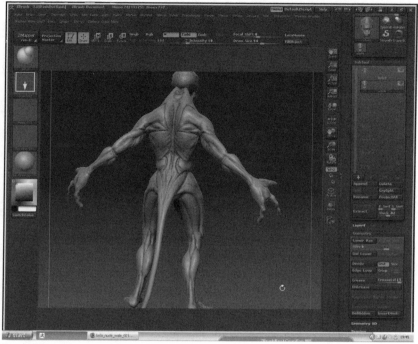

FIGURE 18-126

After all this work it is again time to try a few different MatCaps to change the way the preview looks over in the Render palette. This helps to give us a fresh perspective that will let us see any areas that are wrong. It's very easy to get so used to a model that you actually can't see its problem areas anymore. Keep this in mind, especially if you do extended modeling sessions, because without breaks you can end up making things worse instead of better.

One thing the new MatCap did was show me that some of the carved in lines still need to be tighter. So I took the **Pinch** brush to nip the lines together a bit more.

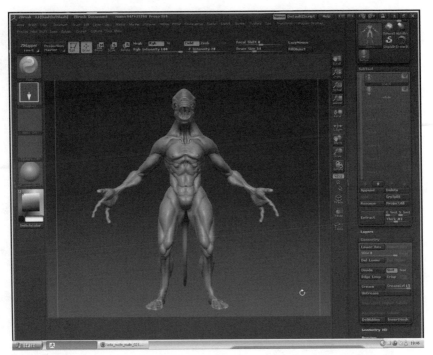

FIGURE 18-127

Posing the Guardian

We have done about as much as we can before we pose the Guardian, as the pose will change the way a lot of the muscles look. For the pose we will be switching off X symmetry and starting to sculpt each side independently since the pose is asymmetrical. To determine how he was going to be posed, I first had to plan the final composition of the scene in my head. So my final idea for the pose was that he would be blocking the way toward the Door of Secrets as if the viewer were coming a little too close.

Although **Transpose Master** had just came out when I posed this model, I wasn't able to use it because of a (now fixed) bug that meant using a polysphere in your model would delete the upper subdivisions as a result. So since the head was sculpted from a polysphere, I had to do this the "old-fashioned" way. This issue is fixed now, so you will be able to take full advantage of the plug-in to make the posing process a bit easier. So with that said, this section shows how I posed the model by hand as body and then head.

Take your body model down to subdivision level 4, which gives us the right polygon count and flow for posing a model of this type in my experience. Activate your **Move** transform tool and drag a topological mask (with X symmetry still enabled at this stage) up to the waist of the character, then drag an action line from the edge of this mask up above the head while holding down the **Shift** key. (Holding down the Shift key will prevent the action line from zooming off into space in the viewport when you drag an action line beyond the edges of a model.) Once this is done, move to a side view and move the action line by the edge of the center circle to the point where the spine is in the body. Now switch off X symmetry and check that the action line is in the very center of the body from a back view before continuing. We are now ready to make our first move in posing the body part.

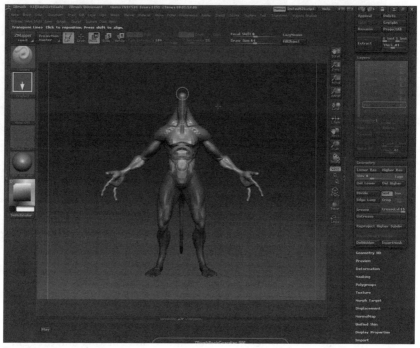

FIGURE 18-128

Switch from Move Transform mode to **Rotate Transform** mode and rotate the body to the side using the upper circle handle. Then rotate the upper body forward a little so he appears to be leaning over a bit. Draw another topological mask up to the neck area and draw an action line down the center of the back of the neck. Rotate it first when looking from a back view to the right, and then from a side view rotate it backward a little so that the head will appear to be looking upward and toward the viewer once we add it.

Let's move on to the legs now, which are rather important to the entire balance of the character. Remember that the head and at least one foot must be in line. So drag a topological mask up to the edge of the left leg where it meets the pelvis and then drag an action line that is aligned with the bones underneath the skin from both front and side views. To correctly pose limbs we have to consider the actual skeleton of the character as well as the body type (the arms in particular).

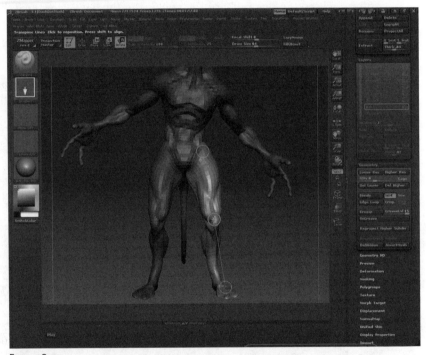

FIGURE 18-129

Rotate the leg sideways so that it faces outward more by using the center transform circle on the action line and clicking and dragging within the center of that circle. Now go to a side view and rotate the entire leg forward. Right now he looks like he's about to kick someone, so we need to pose the lower leg. Drag a mask over just the kneecap and then drag out the action line to align with where the bone would be within the leg. We can now rotate this leg back a bit to maintain some sort of balance.

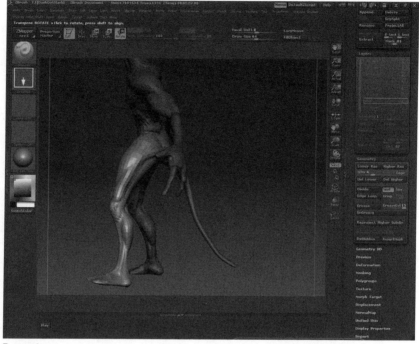

FIGURE 18-130

I find when posing the feet of a character that it is best to exit Perspective mode for a bit because it allows me to rotate the foot forward without fear of misalignment. So draw a mask to about ankle level and rotate the foot until it's positioned as shown. You can also adjust the foot's rotation from a front view if needed.

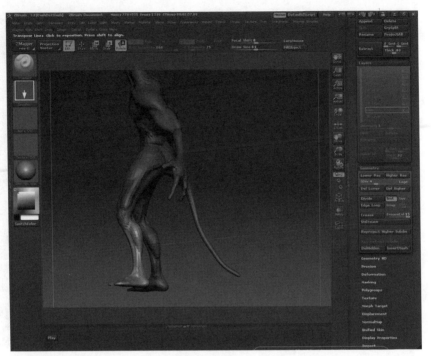

FIGURE 18-131

For the rest of the pose I'll just outline what you need to do and you can simply repeat the same steps to get there. Mask off up to the pelvis point so that the other leg is the only thing unmasked and rotate this leg backward a bit, then mask just below the knee and rotate this into a slightly bent position as well. Next move to the foot and align it with the way the leg is bent.

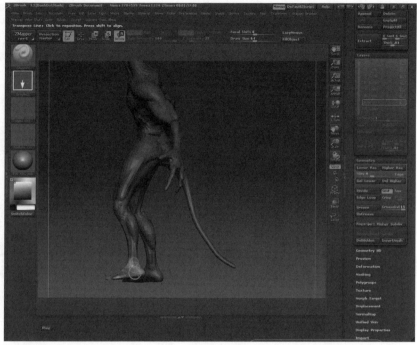

FIGURE 18-132

Chances are that this will make the toes align below the base of the opposite foot, so we will need to correct that. Again mask to just beyond the knee and move the bent leg more until the toe is level with the sole of the foot on the other leg. As he is going to be standing on a floor, we need to resolve these issues at this stage and not find out later on. The leg now needs to be moved sideways a little to give a better sense of balance, so mask it off leaving just the right leg, and then rotate it outward as shown in Figure 18-134. We've now got our initial pose for the legs and torso.

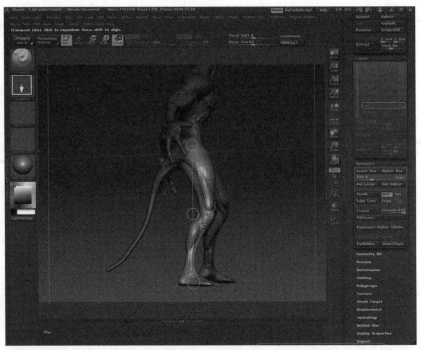

FIGURE 18-133

FIGURE 18-133

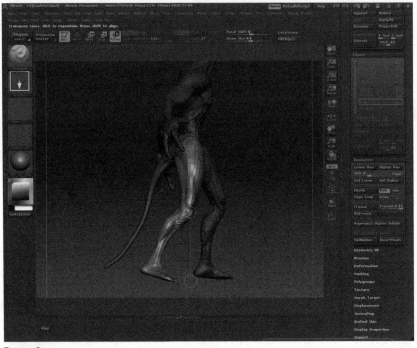

FIGURE 18-134

Masking the arms so that they rotate correctly can be difficult if the topology doesn't have the poly flow we need, so I'll show you my solution. The left arm won't give us any issues because you simply align the action line with the shoulder joint both from the front and above after using topological masking to mask it off. Then rotate this arm inward toward the body more. To add the twist that we need to pose the hand correctly so that the palm is facing the body, simply mask until halfway down the lower arm and draw an action line to this point. Then using the center of the middle circle, rotate the arm so that the palm faces inward. We can then leave only the left hand unmasked, draw an action line down the back of the hand, and rotate this a little more toward the body. Now the pose is looking a little less stiff.

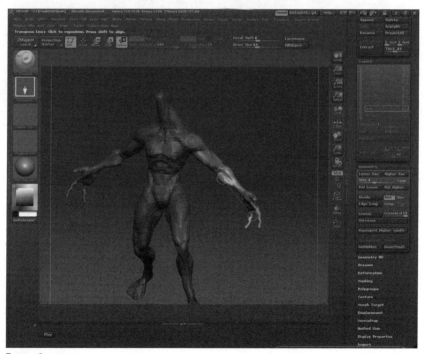

FIGURE 18-135

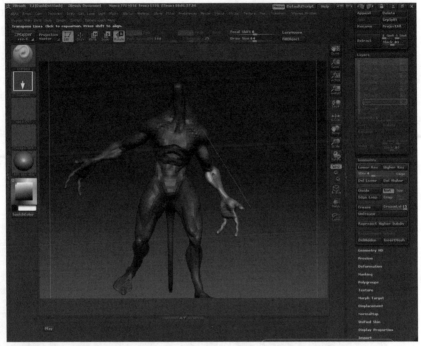

FIGURE 18-136

For the other arm, you initially mask it off using the topological mask like we did the first arm, but now you need to go back into the standard Draw mode to edit this mask to get the correct deformation. So in Draw mode holding down **Ctrl+Alt**, remove the mask on the shoulder blade as we need this to rotate with our arm to maintain a good pose. Blur this mask and then draw an action line from the shoulder joint like we did for the other arm. Rotate this arm backward and up a bit.

We can now correct anything that needs to be; in my case I needed to realign the sole of the foot with where the floor will eventually be and add a bigger bend to the left arm.

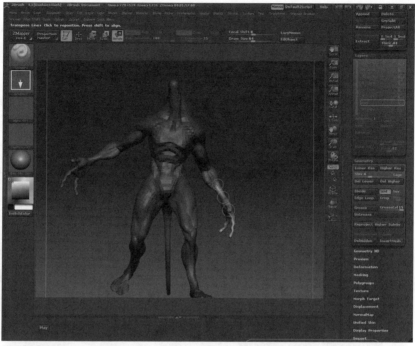

FIGURE 18-137

FIGURE 18-138

One area in our body pose that looks very stiff at the moment is his tail, so we are going to go in and try to add a little life to it to help both the character's balance and the rhythm of the pose itself. Keep in mind that one of my inspirations for the tail was a kangaroo's tail, although unlike a kangaroo's tail I want it to be a bit less straight.

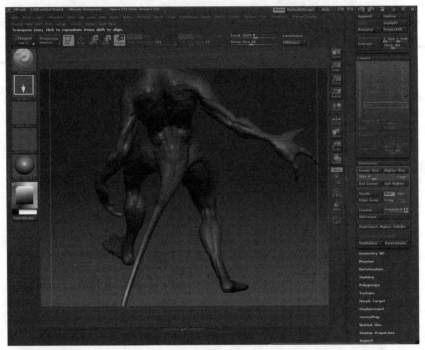

FIGURE 18-139

So draw a topological mask that masks the entire body apart from the tail and then pull out an action line from the base of the tail. Rotate the tail to the left, then drag the mask a bit lower down and redraw your action line. Now rotate it to the right until it is almost at the same angle as it was to start with before moving the mask down a bit more and then rotating to the left again. Without removing the mask, go to a side view with Perspective mode temporarily turned off and rotate this end part of the tail upward a small amount. Now drag a topological mask from just beyond the base of the tail covering part of the tail itself and rotate the tail downward a little. Again do not remove the mask but turn Perspective mode back on by using the **P** hotkey. Go to a front view and rotate the tail to the left, then mask off from the base of the tail, leaving the whole tail unmasked. Rotate it again to the left from a front view to finish off the posing of the tail.

Take your body subtool back up to subdivision level 7 and select the **Inflate** brush now so we can start to correct some areas that are now incorrect due to the pose. In this pose some of the muscles will need adjusting. For example, the muscles in the right arm (on our left looking at the model from the front) are extended and stretched out (and so need to be thinner), and the ones in the left arm have been compressed so they need to be fatter. So we need to go in and do some initial inflating of the left arm biceps, deltoid, and muscles of the lower arm. Correct these areas first before continuing on.

Also since he is leaning slightly to one side his stomach muscles will no longer be as symmetrical as they were. So using your **Inflate** brush add a little more mass to the muscles on the left side that are being slightly compressed as a result of the pose. Also, because of the way he leans, the love handle on the left side needs to be a fair bit fatter than the one on the right side, so bulk that up also. (But don't go too crazy yet.) Looking further at the pose you will notice that while the majority of the muscles on the left side are now compressed, those on the right should either be stretched or in a standard pose. For this pose I wanted to show you how the muscles react to their positions and illustrate how to make an asymmetrical pose look lifelike. Since the leg is bent forward on the left side, the muscles in the quads are compressed and hence larger, so we need to bulk these up a little, but try to be subtle with it at the same time. Using the **Clay** brush, start to tone down the cavity areas on the knees a bit by gently running the brush over those areas.

Moving now to the calf muscles, you will notice that it is the right calf that is going to be fatter as the lower leg is bent into a more extreme position than the left leg. So use the **Standard** brush to bulk up the right calf muscles more than those on the left.

The neck is an area that often gets overlooked in a pose, so let's look at that now. Due to the fact that the neck is bent to one side, the muscles on the right (left as we look at the model from the front) are going to be fatter. Remember that those on the other side will need to be thinned out a fair bit too. So use the **Inflate** brush on the right side of the neck, and then flatten the curve of the muscles as we see them from the front with the **Move** brush so that the muscles appear to be more correct. Note that much of the way the muscles behave may seem to be very subtle, but if you compare the "corrected" muscle structure with the one from just after the pose, you will see that it makes a world of difference.

Now moving to the back area, the first thing we need to do is to correct the angle of the shoulder blade in relation to the right arm. So using your **Move** brush, push that inward toward the body a little more since his arm is extended out and backward, and pull the tip of it downward a little to better reflect the angle of the arm and hence the change to the position of it. These minor changes will do for the moment, although once we pose the head we'll have more corrections. So step back up to subdivision level 8 and switch to your head subtool.

Why bother to pose the stand-in head that is only a low-poly version and not our final head? The reason is to nail the angle and position of the head so we can use it as a reference when we later bring in the real head sculpt. As the "real" head is higher in polygons, it's best to minimize how much work ZBrush has to do to move every single vertex each time you move the sculpt when posing. So I prefer to use stand-in geometry where I can until later in the process and avoid undue stress on my system resources.

So let's start getting the head into position by selecting the head subtool, activating the **Move** transform tool, and dragging out an action line down the center of the head. Make sure you have X symmetry turned off before you move anything, or the head will try to go in two directions at the same time, which isn't pretty! Start by moving the head from a front view to the center of the neck, then switch to a side view and align it with the neck from this angle as well. We want it to appear that the neck is growing from just beyond the chin toward the front of the face a little; this allows us more options when posing without having to retopologize the entire model as a single piece for the final render. (Obviously if this were an animated model we would have to retopologize the entire model anyway.) Draw your action line this time from the corner of the jaw and rotate the head slightly forward. Now move to a front view and draw an action line from the top lip upward and rotate the head into a pleasing position as shown. Remember that he is challenging someone and blocking their path, so try to reflect this in the pose and position of his head.

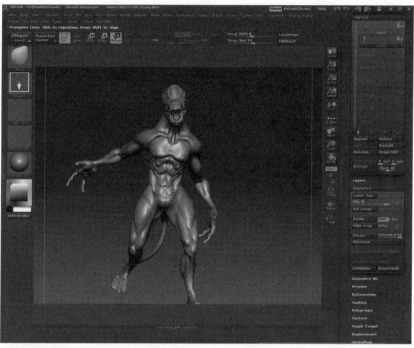

FIGURE 18-140

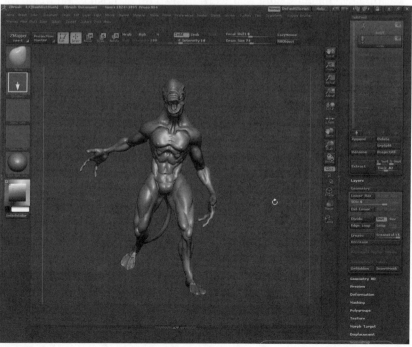

FIGURE 18-141

Go now to a top-down view and draw an action line from the center of the head backward and rotate the head so that he is looking straight forward. Since his body is not facing forward, this gives us a rather nice pose that should give the look we are after. Check again from a front view to make sure that the rotation angle is still correct. I want the slight head tilt to one side to show that he is quite curious about the person who intrudes. Now go back to Perspective mode again and now take a good look at your pose. Look at your model from every angle and try a few MatCaps to try to find any problem areas on the body that you may have missed. If you have made a new layer before posing your model, you can now switch the pose on and off if you need to (meaning of course that should you need a more standard pose at some point for this character, then you will already have one).

Now that our character is posed, we have some pretty serious corrections to do before we are ready to texture the entire character.

Final Tweak and Tidy Up

We've finally got to the stage where it's a matter of just tidying up and tweaking the model to get it completed in regard to the sculpting stage. There are still a few jobs that we need to do though, including putting the love handles right that were thrown off by posing and fixing the clavicle area that we've left overexaggerated as a landmark. So let's step back down to subdivision level 7, select the **Clay** brush, and start to refine these forms first of all.

Zoom in on the waist area. Notice that now that the legs are posed and the waist is bent slightly to one side, the area where the legs and the torso intersect is now off kilter. So we need to work on each of the love handles independently to make sure they are in the correct shape for the pose. You can see that there is a bit of a sharp pinching to the posed areas, so take your **Clay** brush and start to add some mass to the right side to compensate for the pose. After working on that side, move to the other side and correct that. Be sure to treat each side as an independent form and not simply mirror what works for one side onto the other. Remember that extended muscles will be thinner than compressed muscles for joints and bent areas. You are going to need to reflect this where you can in your model. Once the love handles on the waist are blended in well to the other muscles and cradle the stomach muscles on each side, increase their mass some by using the **Inflate** brush.

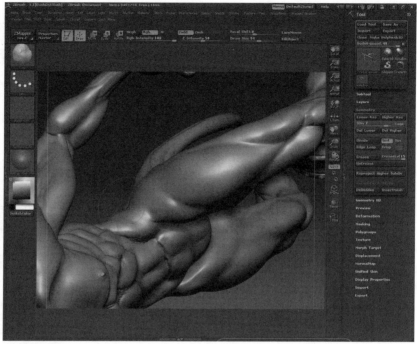

FIGURE 18-142

Before we start work on the clavicle area, let's isolate it by hiding our stand-in head geometry and then select the upper chest area by holding down **Shift + Ctrl** and dragging over it. You should now have the area isolated and ready to work on without the distractions of the other parts of the model.

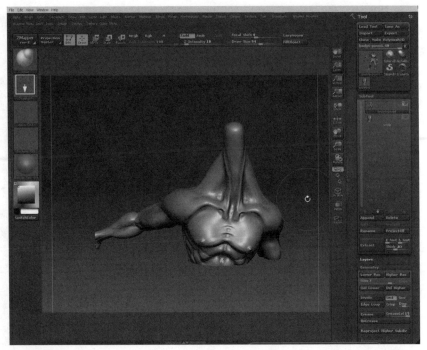

FIGURE 18-143

Remember how I said that we would be leaving the clavicle exaggerated until near the end to help us with placement and proportions? Well, the time has now come to blend it back into the model a bit more. Smooth over the lower section of the clavicle that is closest to the chest so it doesn't stand out so far. Use your **Clay** brush to refine the overall shape of it. If you find that the neck needs to change slightly as a result, be sure to do that at the same time. Take particular care with the deltoid/clavicle intersection where the deltoid inserts onto the clavicle. It's crucial to nail this area correctly, so be sure to take your time to make it look right. We now need to move the clavicle into the correct position because with all the sculpting we have done it will have pulled too far forward. So taking your **Move** brush, start to pull each side back some until you get the familiar "handlebar" shape of the clavicle when viewed from above. As we are sculpting asymmetrically, remember to do each side independently to ensure it is in the right place for the pose of each arm. (The clavicle pivots when the arm is lifted or lowered.) After moving the clavicle, the shapes on the intersecting area with the chest will need to be corrected again.

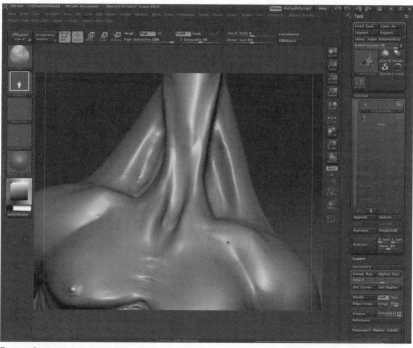

FIGURE 18-144

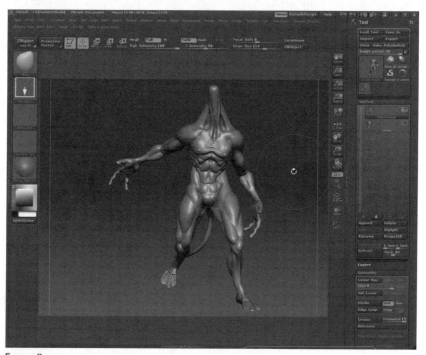

FIGURE 18-145

Some of the forms on the back of the shoulders may have collapsed slightly due to posing, so go back and add the mass needed with your **Standard** brush set to a fairly large size. Using a large size brush will help to avoid any surface unevenness. A smaller brush size may help to get the forms right, but the surface would not look as smooth as we need it to be. The serratus muscles on the sides of the chest that insert into each rib will have also flattened out a fair bit, so go back in with your **Standard** brush and re-establish the shapes as you did earlier. Take a good look at the areas you have just done and smooth over any surfaces that are looking rough or uneven. At this stage in a digital sculpt, many of the tasks are somewhat repetitive, but if not done they can end up ruining a perfectly good model. So it is worth taking the time and care to pull everything together.

One major adjustment I made at this stage was to change the straight horizontal look of the clavicle into more of a V shape. I took the **Move** brush set to a very large size and pulled this down from the center (while in a front view) to help the model "read" better. Although this was one simple brushstroke with the **Move** brush, it made a world of difference to the overall design and attitude of the character. Once you've done this, step back up to subdivision level 8 again.

The pectoral muscles are also still in their original positions and since one of the arms is now stretched out to the side, this muscle needs to be reshaped again. So pull it upward from about the nipple area so that it reads better and is more believable. The other pectoral muscle needs to be pulled downward at about the nipple point. For both of these procedures, use the **Move** brush with a pretty large brush size and zoom in fairly close to the chest area for a better view.

We also haven't done much with the lower leg and as such it is not up to the standard of development of the rest of the digital sculpture. So I stepped down to subdivision level 7 and smoothed out 80 percent of the forms on the entire lower part of the lower leg and redid them. Sometimes rather drastic steps such as these are actually the quickest and easiest way to correct an area. New users often find the idea of smoothing out an area they may have spent a while on a bit frightening, but often it is the best way to approach an area that is a big problem as the lower leg was on this sculpt.

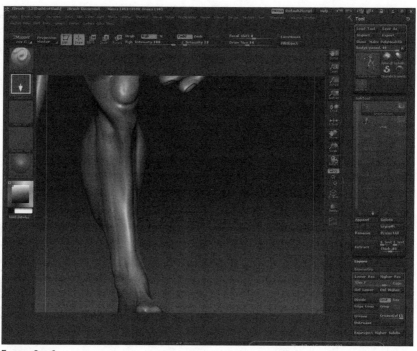

FIGURE 18-146

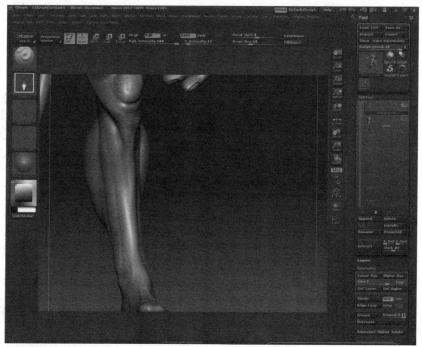

FIGURE 18-147

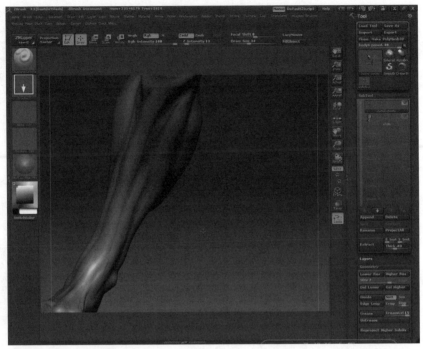

FIGURE 18-148

If you are redoing the lower leg, try to be much more mindful of the insertion points and how the muscles lay on top of one another and create the complex forms of the lower leg. Do this for both legs until you are happy with the result. (Feel free to isolate each lower leg to keep the other parts of the model from distracting you while working on them.)

Making sure that your whole body subtool is visible now, slightly smooth the thigh area with special attention to the quads to get rid of some of the harsher transitions. We are aiming to keep the muscles apparent while making sure they are not too obvious with sharp transitions. Do this also on the back of the legs as well as the lower and upper back to wash out some of the harsh lines there. Then subtly work over the rest of the body so that the muscle structure "gels" as one and no area sticks out like a sore thumb.

What we are about to do now may not make much sense after the smoothing that we have just done, but I'll explain why in a moment. I'd like you to take the **Displace** brush with a small size and one of the smaller round alphas active and start to carve out some fine lines in the transition areas where the muscles are compressed together and add some fine detail there. You don't need to do it all over the digital sculpture, but rather only in a few select areas. So why have we just added more detail back after just spending time washing it out?

The answer goes back to contrast. While before we had many details all over the muscle structure of the body, none of the lines were fine enough (or smoothed out at the ends like the ones we are doing) and they covered basically the whole model so there was very little contrast between areas. As a result it made the design look far blander than using detail in just a few select areas. So find areas that you think would be believable places to put such details. I added them in the back/tail area, the sides of the torso, the front of the torso in some places, and some parts of the legs for starters. What we are trying to do is to simulate the layer of fat above the muscles and how this can form skin folds (that are sometimes quite small) in areas where one large muscle is pressed against another or in areas that bend often. Each time you add one of these sets of fold/wrinkle lines, remember to fade it out as it progresses rather than maintain the same intensity its entire length.

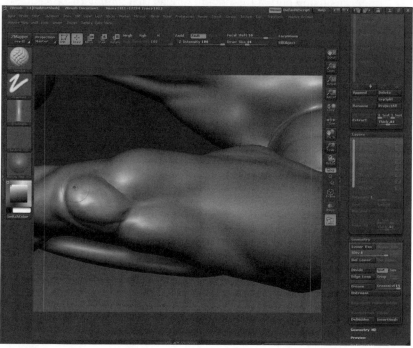

FIGURE 18-149

We mentioned earlier that all wrinkles and folds are not the same size or depth, so please make sure that yours aren't either. While it is far easier to have each fold the same size and depth, it won't help the sculpture to look "real" at all and sometimes will only help to reinforce the CG look of it once done. Note that this can be a rather long and intensive process, so if you find that you are starting to lose patience, take a break and come back to it later. Although it is said that artists must "suffer for their art," no one said you have to be miserable.

The ability to do long, extended sculpting sessions comes with time and experience unless you are lucky enough to have a rock solid attention span. Once you have covered the whole model though, you will notice a massive difference. The addition of a select amount of fine detail suddenly brings it far closer to the final stage. How much detail is enough? That is a call only you can make as it is a personal choice that helps to define you as an artist with your own style. Don't be put off by your first few attempts; this skill takes time and practice to develop.

Let's start to add a little bit of surface texture to areas like the kneecaps using one of the default alphas that ship with ZBrush. So select your **Standard** brush and **Alpha 56** and the **DragRect** stroke type. Before we use this though, we are going to have to invert the alpha. So go to your Alpha palette and scroll down until you see the button labeled **Invert** and press it. Then set the Blur slider to **2**. This will invert your alpha so that now we have a number of lines that we can use to add a surface texture the exact way that we want to. Now set your ZIntensity to **11** and set your brush to **Zsub** so that each time we drag out a rectangular section the white lines of the alpha will take geometry away in that area.

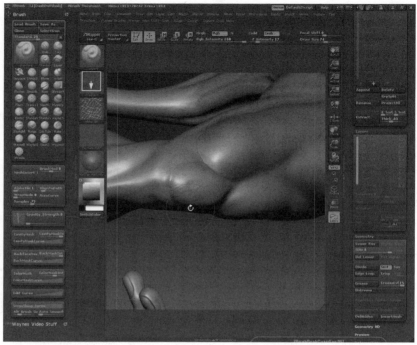

FIGURE 18-150

Drag this out a few times over each kneecap to add some surface texture to them and click with your **Smooth** brush once on each knee-cap very lightly. This will wash away 90 percent of the detail you just added but leave in its place a very subtle amount that keeps the area from looking too smooth.

Go back to the waist area and increase the volume on the sides of the stomach a little. Use a **Standard** brush with a large size to do this. Using the same brush, beef up between the triceps and biceps (the brachialis muscle) to make the arms look like they are capable of lifting some weight and less weedy. Looking back at the upper leg muscles on the front of the leg, make sure that you now round off the muscles themselves and that there are no flat areas where there shouldn't be. Most of this work will now need to be done very lightly to not ruin what we already have done. At the very end after texturing we will again go back to these areas to check all silhouettes and correct any shapes needed. Textures can make areas that are slightly wrong stand out even more, and the colors of the texture can cause an optical illusion that make perfectly good areas suddenly look "wrong." So from experience I've learned to do a set of minor final tweaks at the very end before I call the model done.

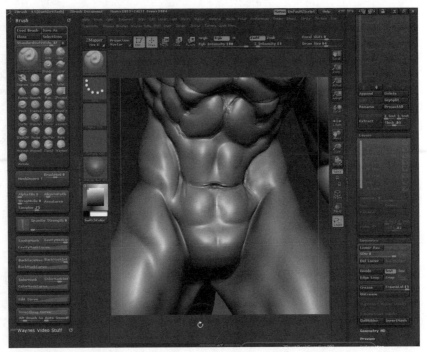

FIGURE 18-151

Using your **Displace** brush with a smallish alpha, start to add some
stress folds caused by stretching between the legs. Once we add some
clothes these won't be seen, but since we don't yet know where the
clothes will fall it's good practice to add them whenever they might be
needed. If you look at your model and see any areas of muscle transition
that need some definition to help "sell" them, then do so now. (Certain
parts of the legs and arms are good candidates for this.) Go back and
refine the muscles of the lower arm, making sure again that the underlying muscle structure is solid and reads well for the pose of the model.

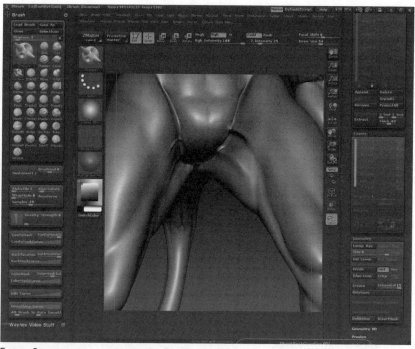

FIGURE 18-152

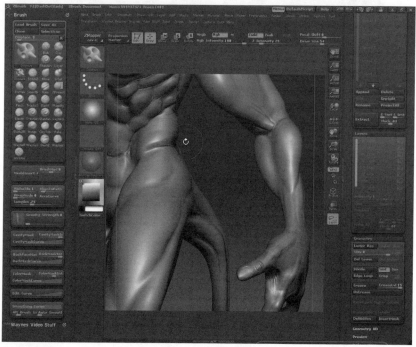

FIGURE 18-153

Add the tendons that feed from the wrist into the hand. These tendons are very important and help us to visualize the structure under the skin.

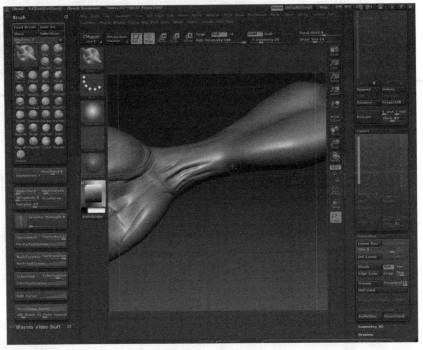

FIGURE 18-154

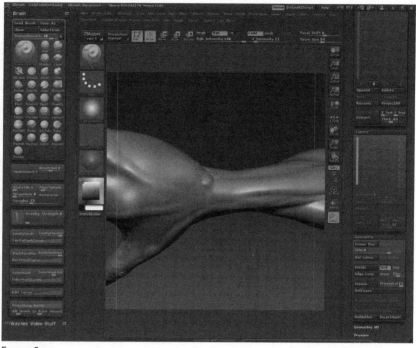

FIGURE 18-155

On the front of the torso use the **Slash1** brush to lightly redefine that area just a small amount, and then smooth over it to help those areas catch the shadows and highlights a bit more. This will be quite important to us when we do our final render. Areas that are either in shadow or that catch a highlight are areas that help us to make our model look more real once it is well lit and materials are added. Check your model with a few different MatCaps as usual to refresh your eye and help you see any problem areas to fix. If you see any, go back and put them right until you are happy with your overall result.

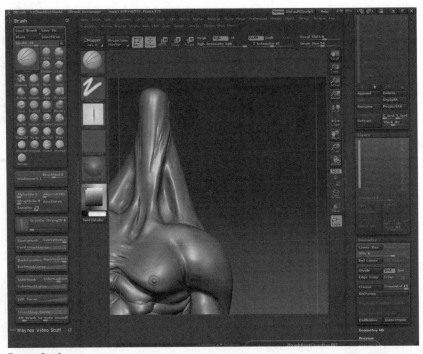

FIGURE 18-156

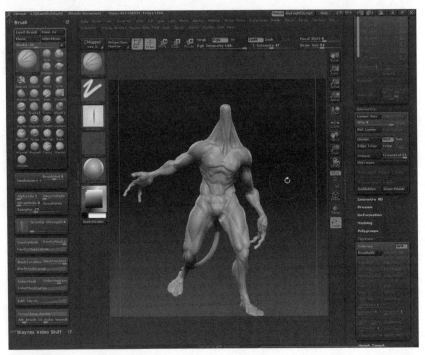

FIGURE 18-157

We have finally came to the end of the main sculpting stages for the head in Chapters 16 and 17 and now the body of the Guardian. It's been a long ride but one in which you hopefully have learned some new things. Next we are going to move on to texturing the body and head before we create the accessories, clothes, and environment for the rest of the scene. In comparison to this sculpting, the rest is fairly easy once we get past the texturing part. So you can rest soundly in the knowledge that the hardest part has been done now.

19 Texturing the Guardian's Body

A Few Words Before We Start

I want to take a few minutes to outline the main points of the texturing workflow that all users will hopefully find interesting. Although this section on texturing both the head and body has many parts that will be of great benefit to both new and advanced ZBrush users, it also contains some theory that may be surprising. One is the way I create the base texture.

So what is a base texture? A *base texture* is what we create or use on our model before doing the "serious painting" that adds the details that we need to the color of the character. A base texture is very important and can actually make or break a character in many ways as color is so important when judging things visually. I've noticed that people sometimes make a very big deal about using the "right texture images" when creating a base texture from photos. These artists expend a lot of time and energy in acquiring the perfect set of textures for use in their projects.

The truth of the matter is that while the actual image is of little importance when using it for a base texture, the colors within that image are important. So for texturing this creature I decided I would illustrate this point by using a few free texture images of random things but with the colors I needed in them from www.imageafter.com. You may be surprised to find that I don't use any skin type patterns at all for my base texture, but rather some images of some very strange and unusual things that when combined make for a very useful base texture.

Here is the list of images I used (keeping in mind I was mostly just interested in the colors that they contained):

green rancid algae
a half-eaten pizza (quatro formaggio as far as I can tell)
rocks
reptile scales

You'll probably be questioning the choice of pizza, but let me explain that I chose it because it had a mixture of reds and yellows and it also illustrates my point that not every texture photo you use has to be of skin or from a very expensive texture set. While the first two images in the list are used as the colors of our main base texture, the other two are simply to add some texture. The rock image will break up some of the larger solid areas later on, and the reptile scales will add some surface detail to our texture. To be honest, we could survive with just the algae and the pizza, though. Any image can be of use as long as the texture fills the image. So a close-up of the pizza gives us a great combination of reds and yellows (and a few oranges thrown in) that when laid over our solid color and combined in some areas with the algae image work very well. It also eliminates the possibility that it will look either too much like someone else's texture or too generic.

Once we have created our base texture we will start the "proper" texturing by hand painting over this base with a couple of colors to bring out the different elevations of the model. The workflow for this texture is very simple really but outlines some concepts that you will use over and over to get some very complex results. In this base texture there are only three stages (solid color, algae, and pizza), but you could increase this number to add even more complexity. I have kept this texture simple yet interesting to save space in this book. Later on we'll use this finished texture on the body to add more detail to the model and to help the two integrate better by making the untextured sculpt fit the texture like a glove.

By the end of the texturing of the Guardian you will have a good understanding of what it takes to texture any model without the use of expensive texture sets by using a bit of creative thinking and some basic painting skills. I should add that this style of texturing doesn't require amazing artistic skills either.

So without further ado, let's get the texturing under way for the body of the Guardian.

Texturing the Guardian's Body

Basic Polypainting

Before we get started it is important that you understand polypainting within ZBrush. Many users don't know how to use an image to texture with when polypainting. All you have to do is make sure that the **Disable UV** button is pressed in the **Texture** section of the **Tool** palette. If you do not disable the UVs, then the image that you want to texture with will instead be applied as a texture to your model and any subtools that contain UV sets.

The simple rule to polypainting, whether it be with images or standard colors, is that the more polygons you have, the more detail you can paint. This is because what you are doing is assigning a color to individual polygons, so if an area is short of polygons, it won't be able to support the detail.

You can paint color and sculpt at the same time should you wish to, and polypainting is also affected by masks and brush settings such as cavity. You can also polypaint on HD geometry, although your texturing will only be visible in that mode.

To polypaint in ZBrush, just pick a brush and a color in your color swatch (or by using the Color palette) and then paint on your model. Your brush will be affected by the alpha and stroke type you use as well as by the RGB Intensity setting. So if you have an RGB Intensity of 100 you will get a solid color, while a setting of 20 would be much lighter. As a rule you will not be using a setting of 100 unless you wish to fill an area with solid color. So in short, polypainting supports all the brush features that you would expect from them if you were sculpting.

You can export your polypainting as a texture, which we'll discuss once we have the Guardian fully textured and ready to roll.

Note: By default ZBrush will give you a texture of 1K, but you can use a texture of any size or dimension that you like, providing you have the UVs and PC memory to support it. Just be sure to create the blank texture before sending the color data to it.

Base Texture Pass 1

Our workflow for texturing the Guardian's body is going to start with a few very simple (but somewhat time-consuming) steps. We start by filling our model with a material that simulates the subsurface shader we'll be using in 3ds Max to render out the final image. The entire body is filled with a base color, so for this particular project I found a few images of amphibians and other animals and saved them from Google and then sampled some of those colors in Photoshop. After selecting the body subtool (and turning the visibility off for the head while we work on the body), I filled it with a medium desaturated green color of RGB 152, 146, 100. Next we load our first texture, so we start with the green algae image. The actual subject matter is of little consequence to us because what we are interested in is the colors, tones, and "patterns." So don't get hung up on the contents of the actual image itself.

I find that for quick access to the textures I plan on using, the **Alpha and Texture library** plug-in available on ZBrushCentral does a good job. It allows you to preview the texture and load it as needed. So I load my **green slimy stuff** image (as I'll refer to it from now on) with my **Standard** brush active. Since we don't want to affect the geometry itself but just add some color to it, make sure that both Zadd and Zsub are off and only RGB is switched on. Select **DragRect** as your stroke type, set your RGB Intensity slider to **31**, and make sure that **Alpha 01** is active. These settings will let you drag out this texture with a nice fade around the edges (to avoid any nasty hard edges) onto our model. We've kept the RGB Intensity pretty low as we want the color and tone and a little of the image's detail without it being obvious that we are using an image of green slimy stuff.

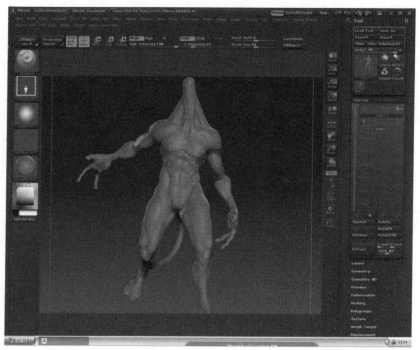

FIGURE 19-1

Before you start to cover your model with what will be the first of a few layers of base texture passes, I wish to cover some basics for the approach. Avoid using the same size of dragged rectangle area each time, and try to make the details on the image the correct size for the part you are texturing at the time. Additionally, make sure the details flow in the direction that the surface is traveling. For example, if you are dealing with a small area such as the eyes, drag a much smaller area than you would for the thighs.

I find that a good place to start is the shoulder and chest area. These areas are usually the largest, so texturing them first lets me know where my boundaries are and means everything else must be smaller. So start to drag out areas along the shoulders and chest, remembering that as you drag you can rotate as well as adjust the brush size. Make sure that there are no areas on your model that do not have any texture on them. A great way to check this is to change your render mode to Flat, which removes all lighting and shading effects and leaves you with a constant (or flat) shading effect that makes it very easy to see any areas left untouched by texturing.

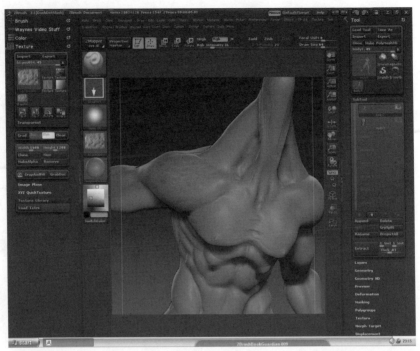

FIGURE 19-2

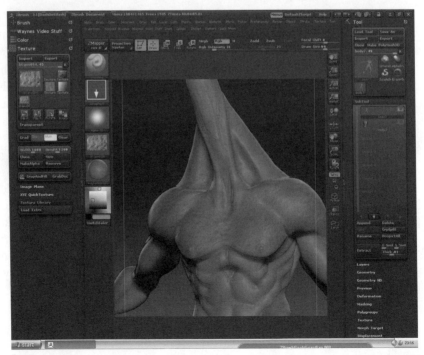

FIGURE 19-3

Work your way down the stomach and along the sides of the torso. Then work your way down the thighs and the rest of the legs, again remembering to keep detail in the flow of the surface and of a proportionate size. Do both the back and the front of the legs. Although we won't be seeing the back of the model in our scene, there may be considerations that would mean we would get some strange effects if we do not fully texture the model. Now work up the back and down the tail before having a good look between the legs to check for any areas you may have missed. (I find that when working primarily in a front and back view that these are areas most likely to get missed.) Work over the feet as well even though the feet will be painted in such a way that the majority of the base texture won't be seen. Work down the arms all the way to the hands.

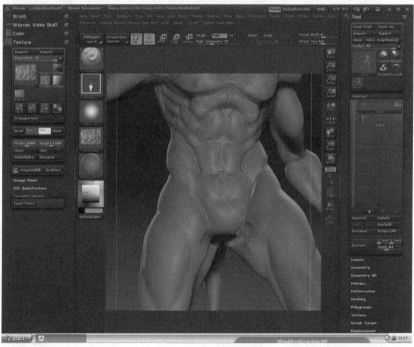

FIGURE 19-4

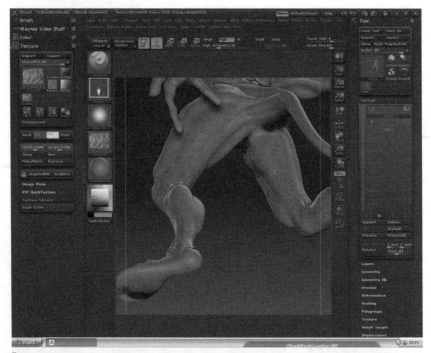

FIGURE 19-5

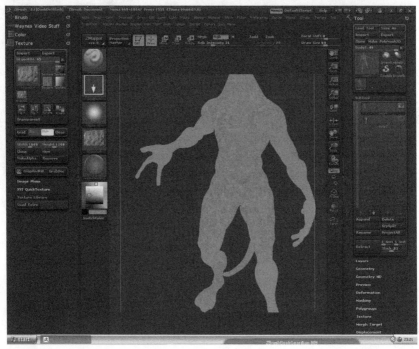

FIGURE 19-6

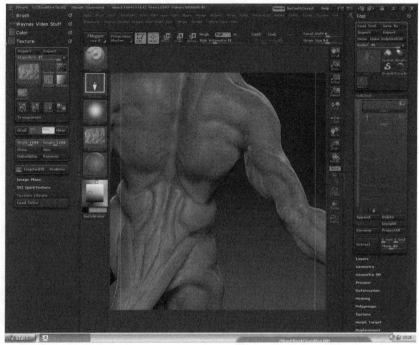

FIGURE 19-7

For the hands, my personal style is to break one of my own rules a bit. Instead of keeping the texture to a size in proportion to the size of the hands in relation to the rest of the model, I often oversize the texture on the back of the hands.

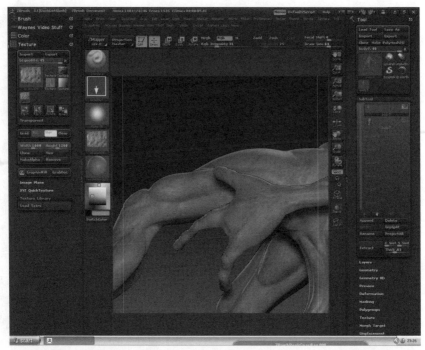

FIGURE 19-8

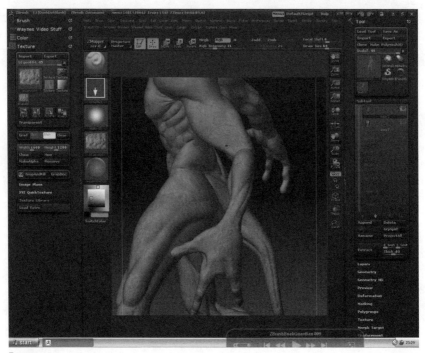

FIGURE 19-9

Once you have all these areas done and the model appears totally covered, go to Flat render mode again and look around your entire model, checking for areas you have missed. It may seem odd to see your model in a flat shaded mode, but you are looking not at your model but at the pure color information. Once you have examined the whole model and are sure that you have covered every single area, we can move on to adding the next texture for our base.

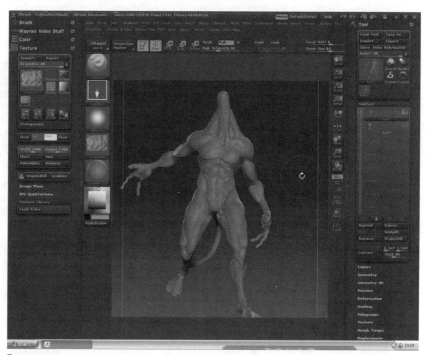

FIGURE 19-10

Base Texture Pass 2

It took me about 15 minutes to do the first pass on the base texture, so as you can see it takes a little longer to describe than to do. We are now going to start adding our second pass of texturing to the base texture. Yes, it's time to use the pizza image. Although this image may seem odd, it has all the requirements we need for this part of the texturing: contrasting colors to our greens and variations in tones and colors.

The brush settings with the exception of the change of texture are the same as last time, except the RGB Intensity slider is set to **18**. When we used the image of the green slimy stuff, we used a low-ish intensity because we didn't want it to be too obvious what the changes in color and tone were from. But with this texture we want it to be a bit more obvious. So why are we using a lower RGB Intensity setting? The answer is to give us more control over how this texture is applied. We can drag out over an area once and get a mild effect, or drag two or three times to get a more aggressive coloring effect, so we can put exactly the amount of the red and yellow colors where we want them.

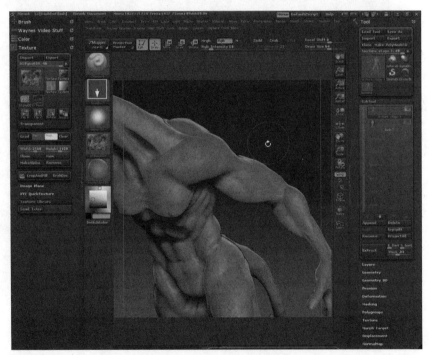

FIGURE 19-11

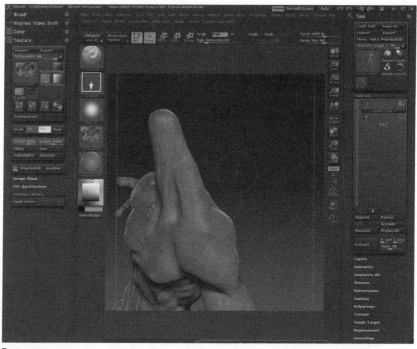

FIGURE 19-12

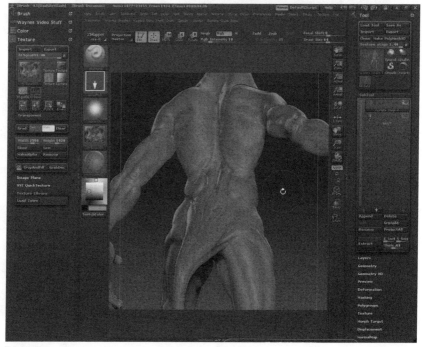

FIGURE 19-13

Rather than randomly add this texture anywhere for the sake of it, we'll apply it on the highest areas of the model. So areas that are raised up a fair amount will get this texture applied to them, and the higher the area is raised, the more coloration we will add for our texture by dragging it out two or three times. Think of your model not as anatomy and forms for the moment but as a series of peaks and valleys. The peaks will be textured with this image depending on how high the peak goes. Later on we'll be using the same method and the reverse to add more finishing touches to our model. This is what I call "old school." It was favored in the early days by guys like Glen Southern (who also designed the weapon for the Guardian), and comes from techniques used by artists who painted latex masks and clay models. In fact you will find that most every texturing technique used today comes from traditional artwork and artists working on latex masks and makeup.

So using this texture, start to drag it out onto the areas that are your model's "peaks." Work as before, starting at the shoulders and front of the torso before working slowly around the rest of your model. This stage took me only about five minutes, so it shouldn't take you very long at all. Once it's done, the colors should be starting to look fairly lifelike.

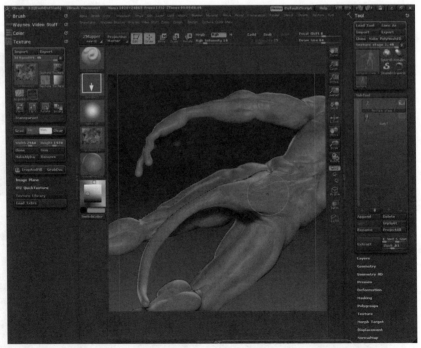

FIGURE 19-14

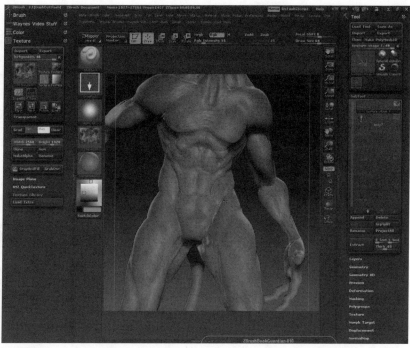

FIGURE 19-15

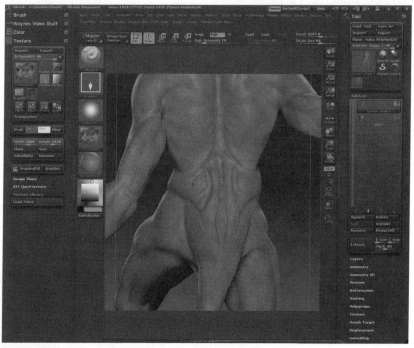

FIGURE 19-16

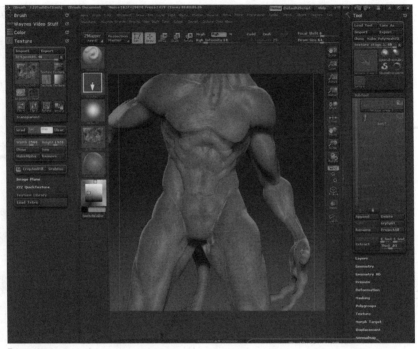

FIGURE 19-17

Base Texture Pass 3

For our third and final pass for the base texture of the Guardian's body we're going to use a simple reptile scale image from www.image-after.com. We'll approach it like we did our first green slimy stuff image. By that I mean that the size of each dragged out rectangular area will be dictated by the size of the area that we are working on. As with the **green slimy stuff** texture, we will be orienting it so that it follows the surface direction of the model. This is *really* important to do for this particular texture as we are dealing with a regular patterned texture of scales. Once we are done with this pass, we'll use this texture that we've completed to bring more details out on our model without actually sculpting anything. So if you get this particular texture stage wrong, it will become very obvious very quickly. Thus, you will want to take time and care with this stage. I realize that applying these textures as bases for later painting and texturing is not the most exciting job in the world, but it is an essential one that helps a great deal with the final look of our model.

Keep the same brush settings as before, only this time I'd like you to change your RGB Intensity slider to **25**. With this texture you will need to be careful when dragging out large areas as these can overlap the edges of your model and produce a stretching or a sudden jump in the texture size as ZBrush will suddenly realize there is no model under your brush. So be ready to undo while you are getting used to the technique.

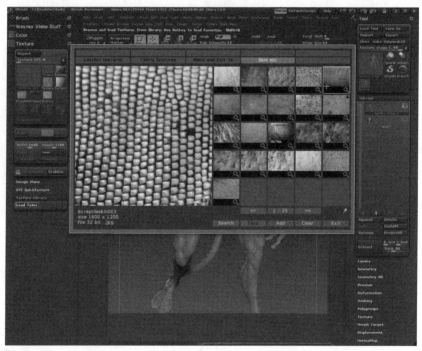

FIGURE 19-18

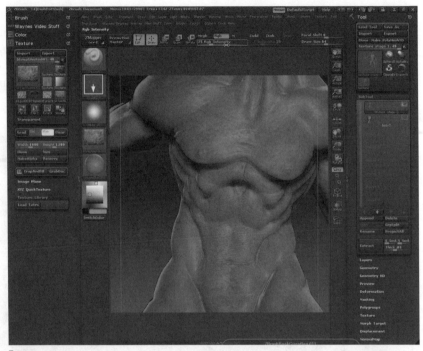

FIGURE 19-19

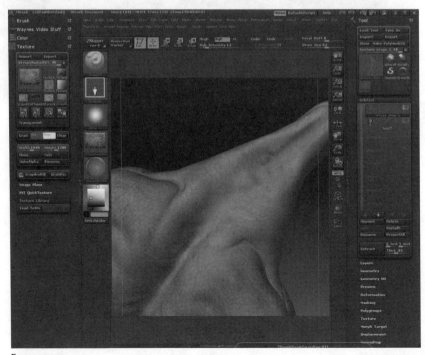

FIGURE 19-20

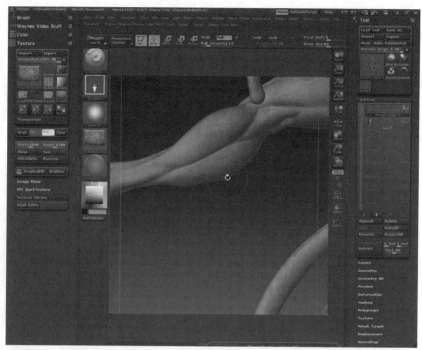

FIGURE 19-21

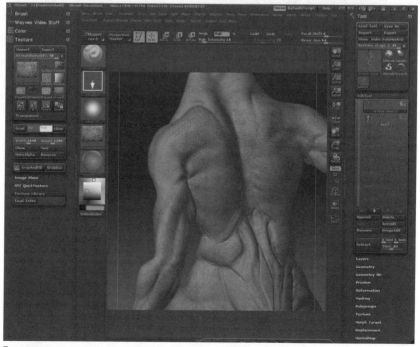

FIGURE 19-22

So now brush over your entire model in the way I've mentioned until you have it covered all over. You can check this by going to a Flat render mode to spot areas you may have missed. Once you are done to your satisfaction, you will definitely want to save out a few copies because we will next be starting the "proper" texturing work on the body. So make a few extra copies you can use to practice your skills. Texturing, like digital sculpting, is something you get better at by practice; as such, there is no real shortcut.

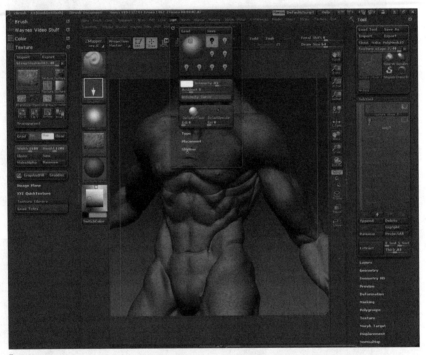

FIGURE 19-23

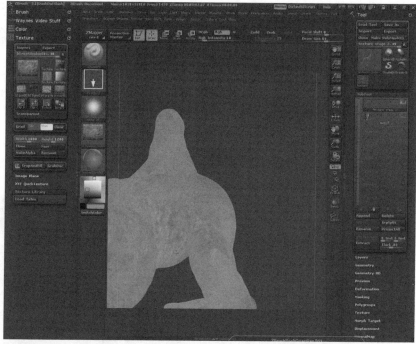

FIGURE 19-24

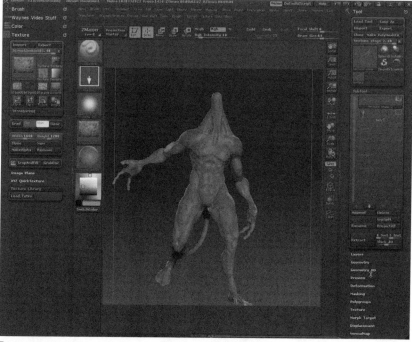

FIGURE 19-25

Painting Over the Base Texture

Now that we have a good base texture to start from that is neither too boring nor too distracting, we can start with the more standard part of texture painting. Think of the texturing process as doing a number of passes, each with its own unique job and reason. So we start now with adding some color to the cavities on the model. We've added the pizza texture to get some nice red colors on the protruding areas, and we are now going to do a similar job but in reverse. Where you were giving the highest areas a red color, we now are going to add some deep brown colors into the cavities.

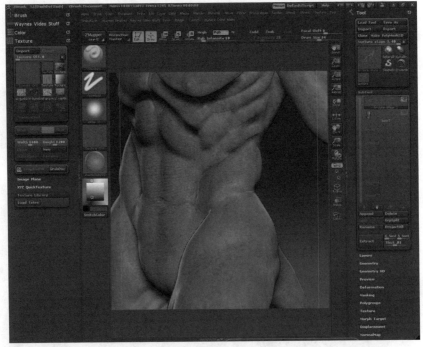

FIGURE 19-26

Texturing is all about helping the eye read the form of the model, so adding a darker color to the cavities makes them look deeper. While ZBrush may have the benefit of cavity shading on its materials, other render engines don't have that luxury, so we need to give the human eye more information to interpret. Start by taking your **Standard** brush as you did earlier, but first change the stroke type to the **FreeHand** stroke. Make sure that you have **Alpha 01** selected and that both Zadd and Zsub are switched off.

We now need to turn our RGB Intensity to a lower level because we are going to be painting a dark color and we do not want it to overwhelm the entire model. So turn your ZIntensity down to about **10** before continuing. For our color we are going to use a dark brown, so pick your color and try not to make it too saturated. (The more saturated the color is, the more it will stand out, and ideally we want this color to be there but not be too noticeable.)

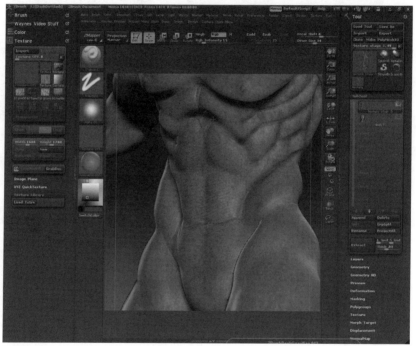

FIGURE 19-27

For this section work your way around the entire model, adding this dark brown color in the areas that are recessed and between the muscles. The deeper the cavity between two muscles, the deeper the color needs to be. What we are doing to a degree is to sort of paint by hand an ambient occlusion map over our base texture. So what is "ambient occlusion"? It is a material effect found in all major render engines in the big applications such as Maya, 3ds Max, XSI, and LightWave. What an ambient occlusion shader will do is shade the entire model white and only add dark areas the nearer two parts of the geometry are together. Basically what we are doing now with the areas closest together, which are the cavities, is darkening them. So instead of exporting to another application and baking out an ambient occlusion map (which does not allow for such a high degree of control anyway), we can paint it by hand, giving us control over the opacity of each stroke we make and what areas we wish to shade a deeper color. Ambient occlusion is often used as a render layer pass along with other render passes for later compositing. Since it helps to bring out the detail in a render, it is especially popular for architectural work.

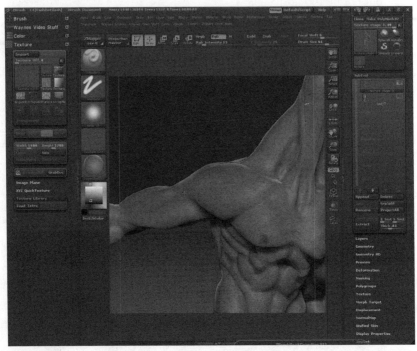

FIGURE 19-28

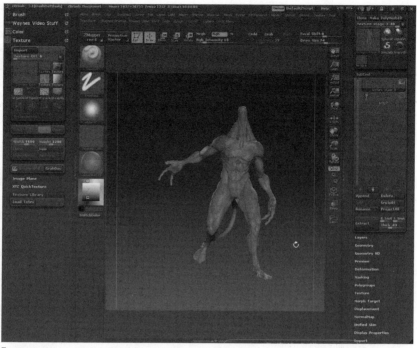

FIGURE 19-29

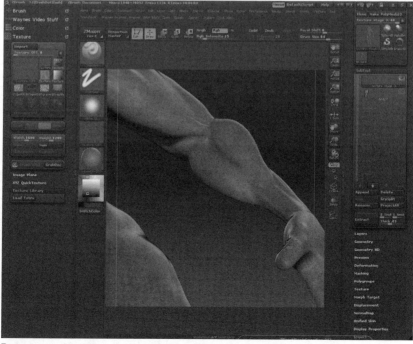

FIGURE 19-30

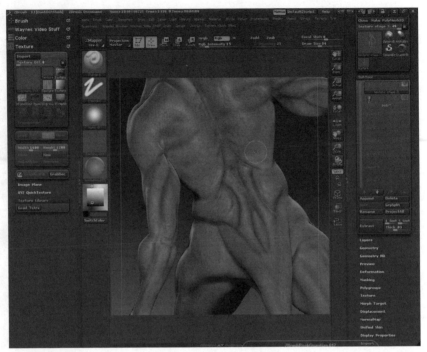

Figure 19-31

Our main objective for the texture for the body once it is finished is to end up with a texture that if previewed in Flat render mode will still be readable to you. If you can still make out the main features of your sculpt while in Flat render mode, then your texture should stand up well in other applications. So let's finish painting the cavities that dark brown color (the ZIntensity of 10 will give it a more washed-out shade and help it fit in a bit better). Go down the sides of the torso and the stomach before working your way up and over the chest and down the back of the model. Remember that any inset area is to be shaded brown depending on how deep and how big the cavity is. (But you will be coloring all recessed areas to some degree.)

Now start to work your way down the arms (back and front), but stop at the hands. Then move to the tail area. Be especially careful with the legs as some of the muscles in the thigh are big but have fairly shallow recessed areas, so you do not want to over-color these areas. Remember that we are simply helping the eye to read the forms and not trying to simulate the lighting at all. Work your way down to the feet, then go back and add some of the brown to the knuckle areas of the feet. Knuckles are areas that often accumulate more dirt and grime, so they need a deeper color. Finish up with the hands by adding color to the knuckles and joints of the fingers, making them a darker color depending on how deep or wide the wrinkles are. You do not need to go too mad in this area though because the Guardian is going to be holding a weapon in one hand and his other will be facing his palm.

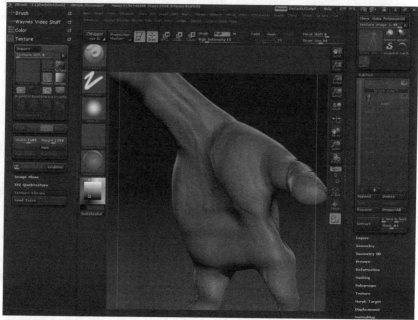

FIGURE 19-32

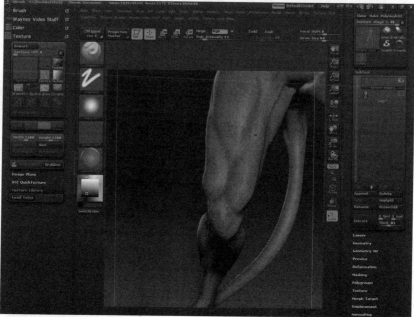

FIGURE 19-33

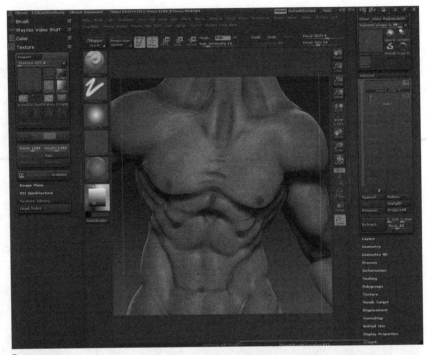

FIGURE 19-34

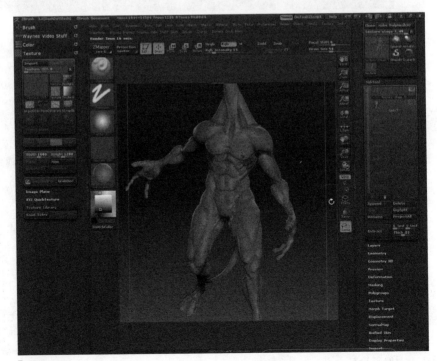

FIGURE 19-35

Once you have worked over your entire model like this, zoom it out and take a good look at it for any areas you feel are not reading as well as they could. You are looking for areas that are either too dark or not dark enough. Hopefully, as you have been using a very low ZIntensity, the only problem you should have is that some areas may be a little too light. Add a bit more of the brown in the cavities until you are happy, then switch for just a moment to Flat render mode and see how well you can read the forms without the benefit of normal lighting and shading information.

This stage took me about 16 minutes, so although it's a fairly easy process, it is a little more time-consuming and there are more areas to deal with. Now it's time to add a little bit more of the red to some parts of our model.

Back in the Red

Our texture is already starting to look more like it should, but we still have some things left to do. First of all, change the color you will be painting from the previous dark brown to a dark reddish wine color. Don't make it too saturated, as we want a subdued and hopefully realistic texture once we are done. Keep your alpha and stroke type identical as last time but change RGB Intensity to **15** because we want to paint very lightly. For those who have painted in watercolors, think of the style as a bit like a color wash done over small areas. We are going to add this wine red color to the protruding areas but in an "artistic" way. The way we choose which protruding areas we will be giving this light red wash is more personal. I decided to add the red first to the ribs and stomach area, as I felt there was way too much "green" there with not a lot of variation for size. Keep in mind that we can only paint details in our texture as fine as our polygon count will allow, although we will be using a few tricks later on to increase some painted detail on the textures for both the body and the head once we exit ZBrush.

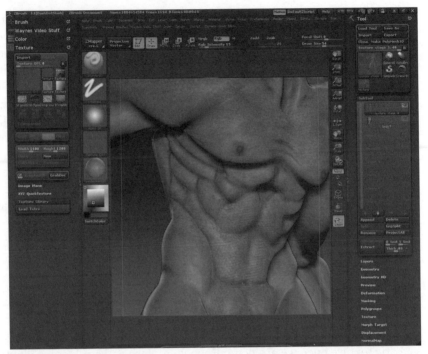

FIGURE 19-36

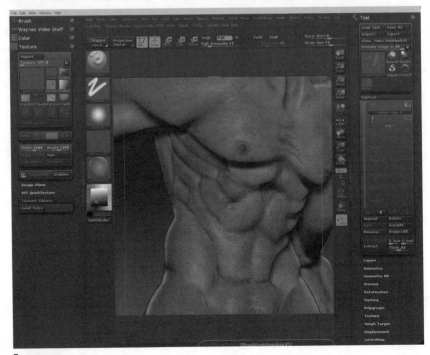

FIGURE 19-37

I also added some more red to both the clavicle and the chest area before moving on to the muscles on the back of the leg and the top of the back in the deltoid region. I also added a small amount of red to the thighs in certain areas and to the shins. As we have to paint on an asymmetrical model, everything will have to be done on each side. I added a touch of red to the knees to keep them from getting lost in a sea of greenness, then moved on to the webs between his toes. I added quite a bit of color to this area to make it dominant for that area.

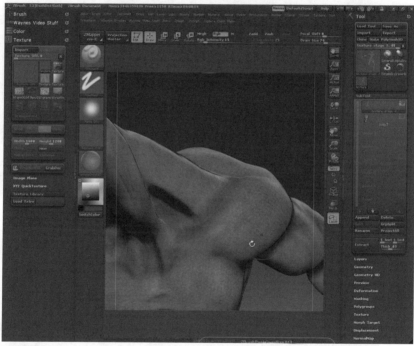

FIGURE 19-38

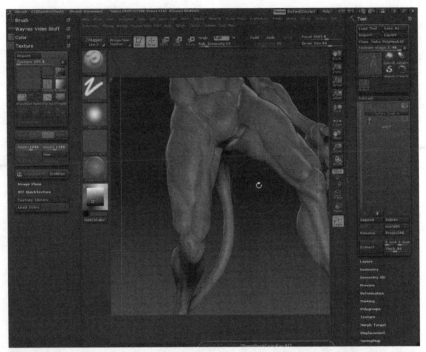

FIGURE 19-39

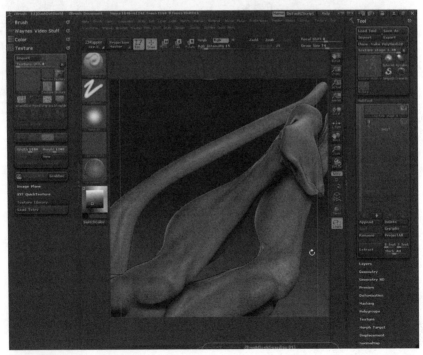

FIGURE 19-40

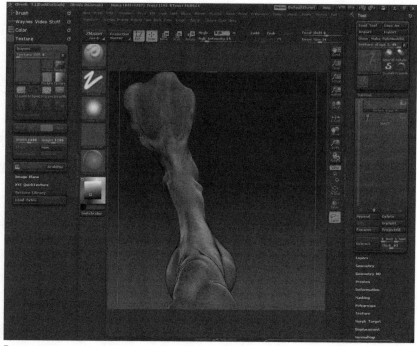

FIGURE 19-41

Next move to the ankles, the calves, and the heels of the feet, followed by some work on the hand area. I added red to the knuckles and a bit less intensely between the fingers and the first finger and thumb. I then added another wash of red to the already red areas on the biceps, triceps, and muscles of the lower arm to help bring these areas out a little more. The stomach muscles still needed more work, so in the center of the stomach each set of muscles in the "six-pack" got the red coloring increased quite a bit more. I wanted this area to contrast with the rest of the torso.

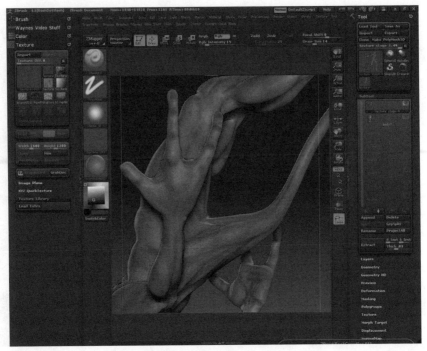

FIGURE 19-42

Once you have added this red wash to areas that you think need it (you may find you have your own ideas where you want to put it), go again into Flat render mode to check the model's texture and see if you can now tell which forms are which. The chances are that you will, although we aren't quite finished yet. Sometimes at this stage I prefer to paint in Flat render mode because once I know I can read the forms, I only have to deal with the color and I don't have to worry about how any lighting and shading information may be giving you a view of your model that is not "balanced." (The way a model is lit and what material you use can vastly affect how you paint your texture, as the way you see the colors changes as you paint.)

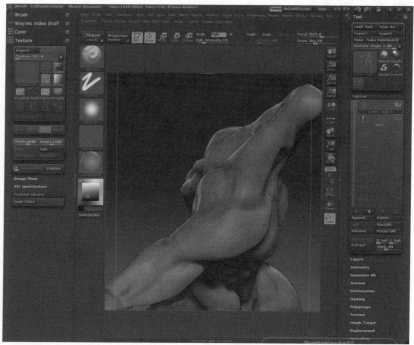

FIGURE 19-43

So while in Flat render mode look for any areas with too much green or that look a tad boring and add a little bit of a red wash to them. I added more red to the trapezius because that area is more exposed and would be more affected by the sun. Go back into your Preview render mode and again check every part of the model for any areas that may need some more red on them, but try not to add it to any recessed areas or you may ruin your texturing effect. Once you have done all this and are happy with the result, you can safely save your model out before we move on to the head texturing stage.

This last stage took me about 10 minutes, but a lot of that time was used for "artistic decisions" and not just painting. But as you can see we have textured the body in a simple way in a fairly short time. There is nothing stopping you from doing further "passes" of texturing and painting to get a very complex texture, but I've purposely kept this texture simple to show that you can get a decent texture quickly and easily.

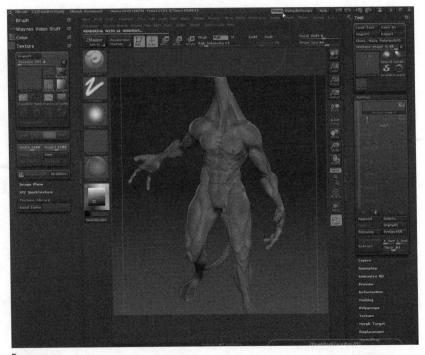

FIGURE 19-44

20 Texturing the Guardian's Head

Much of what we are going to do texture wise with the head of the Guardian is fairly repetitive since we'll be using the same workflow throughout. I'd like you to start off by making sure that you have replaced the medium-resolution version of the head we were using earlier with the higher-resolution version so we don't texture the wrong head by mistake.

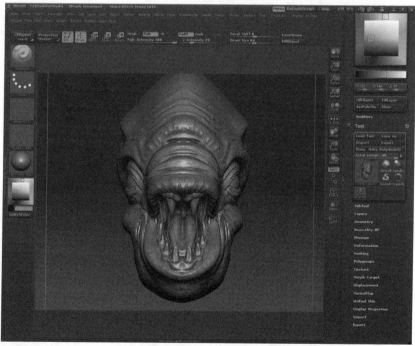

FIGURE 20-1

Start by filling the model with the same base color you used on the body: RGB **152, 146, 100**. Remember that you can fill your model with a color by first making sure that the RGB slider is set to **100** and the RGB button is selected. Then go to the **Color** palette and click the **FillObject** button. This fills your model with the chosen color. (You can also set the material if the M button is selected, or both material and color with the MRGB button.) Once we have our base color selected and our model filled, we are ready to go through the process of adding some base textures to our head model. You can then fill your head model with the material you are going to use for the final. In my case I used the same custom SSS skin shader MatCap I used for the body. Since we'll create the final render with a Mental Ray subsurface scattering skin shader, it makes sense to use a similar MatCap to keep results of the texture work as similar as possible. Lastly, make sure that only the head is visible in the viewport to help speed things up and to prevent unnecessary distractions as you paint.

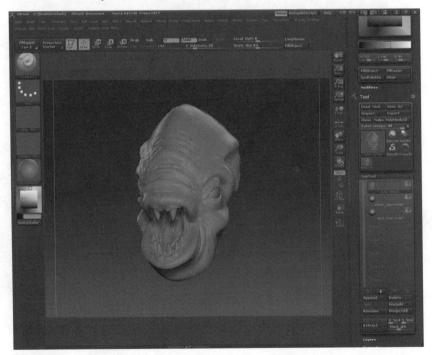

FIGURE 20-2

As we cannot polypaint using textures over a model with a set of UVs, you need to disable them by going to the **Texture** section of the **Tool** palette and pressing the **Disable UV** button. This means we can drag a texture that is currently active in the texture swatch using a

DragRect stroke type to help texture the model. If UVs were enabled, ZBrush would apply this as a texture map to it instead, and as such we wouldn't be able to use it to help with our texturing.

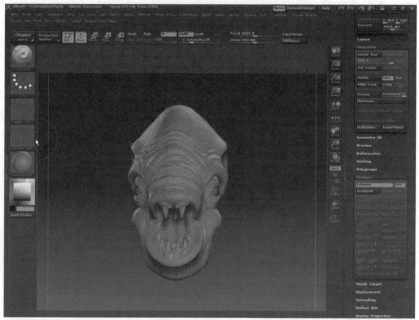

FIGURE 20-3

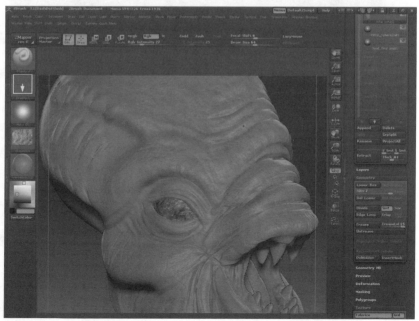

FIGURE 20-4

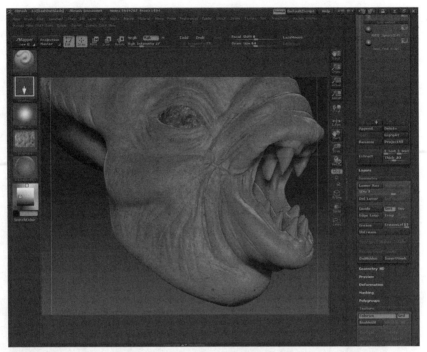

FIGURE 20-5

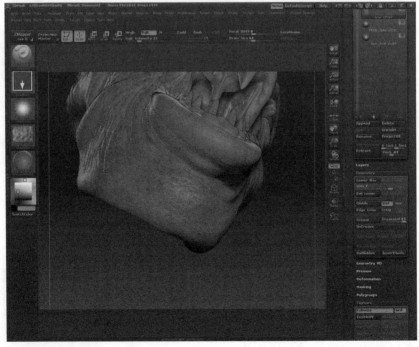

FIGURE 20-6

Since this process is almost identical to the workflow we used for the body texturing stage, I'll just outline the different techniques I'm using to apply the texture. Let's start our base texture with the **green slimy stuff** with an RGB Intensity of **27** and the **Standard** brush selected with **Alpha 01** and the **DragRect** stroke type active. Make sure that neither Zadd nor Zsub is active. Cover the entire head with this texture, dragging out areas that are the correct size in relation to the size of the feature you are working on at the time. So areas that have lots of fine detail such as the eyes will get much smaller dragged areas than the top of the head, which is our largest area.

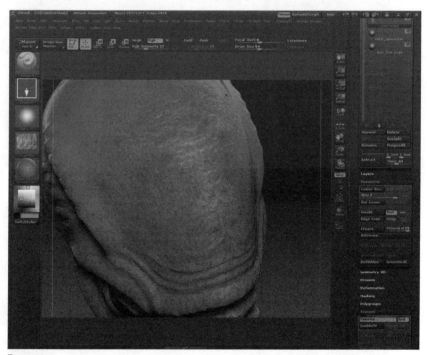

FIGURE 20-7

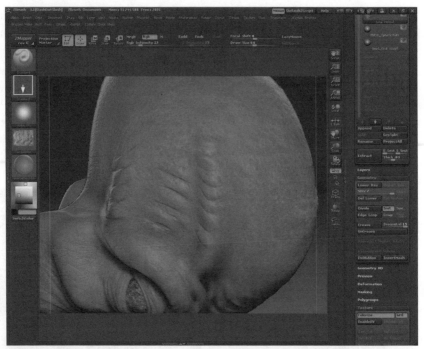

FIGURE 20-8

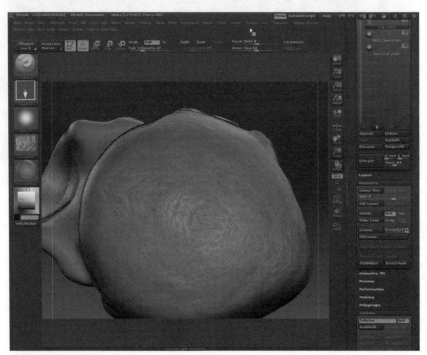

FIGURE 20-9

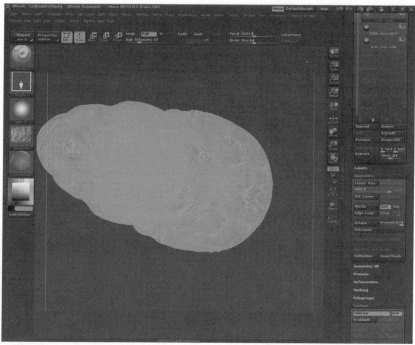

FIGURE 20-10

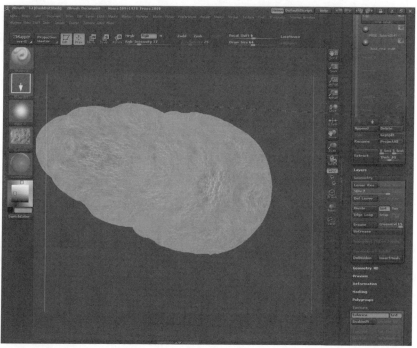

FIGURE 20-11

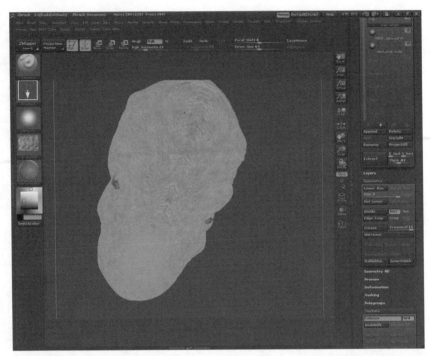

FIGURE 20-12

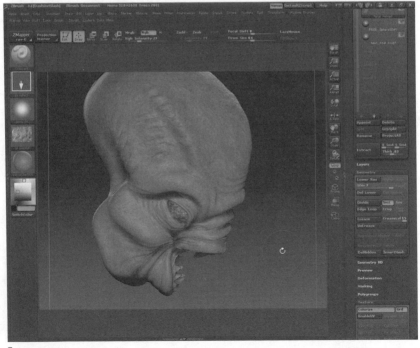

FIGURE 20-13

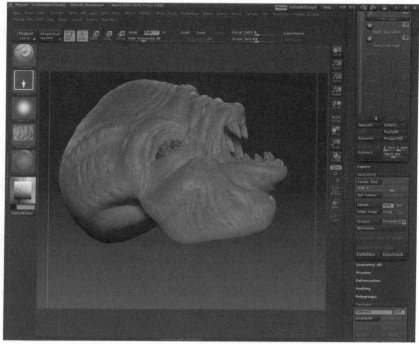

FIGURE 20-14

Be sure to step in and out of Flat render mode to make sure that you don't miss any areas. I even add it to the base of the head in areas that won't be seen once the head is in place again on top of the neck. This ensures that I don't underestimate the intersection areas and leave blank color there. It's better to have more texture than you need than not enough. Once you have covered the entire head with the first texture, you are ready to move onto the second.

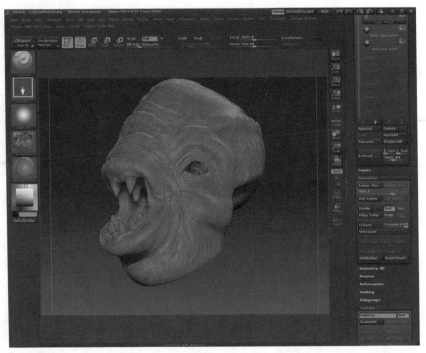

FIGURE 20-15

For the second texture pass we'll once again use the unforgettable half-eaten pizza texture for the raised areas on our model. As there is much more fine detail on the head than on the body, we need to treat it slightly differently to get an effect that will fit in with the coloring of the body. We cannot texture every single raised area red, but must look at the large forms instead and treat the model like a much simpler digital sculpture. So for the moment totally ignore all the fine detail and pretend it does not exist at all.

So with your half-eaten pizza texture active, and the RGB Intensity set to **25**, work on the biggest areas first. So start with the cheeks, eyebrow area, and the bottom of the jaw where the jawbone lies. Then work down the two ridges on the sides of the head and then to the area between the eyes where we can add a fair amount of red. This is a large feature and we don't want it to get lost in a sea of greenness. Add some also to the lips and the sides of the mouth, but much less intense than the other areas. We do not want all the red to be of the same intensity or size, so scale the brush to a size that fits each feature as we did with the previous texture.

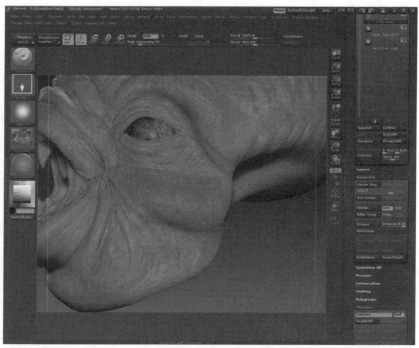

FIGURE 20-16

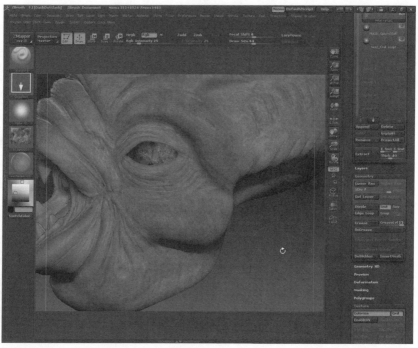

FIGURE 20-17

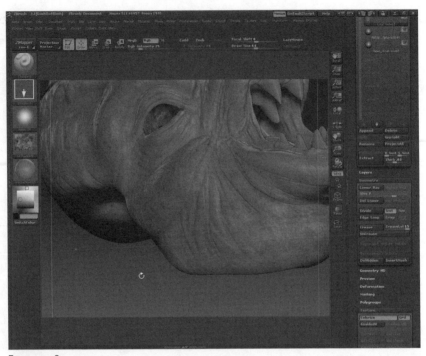

FIGURE 20-18

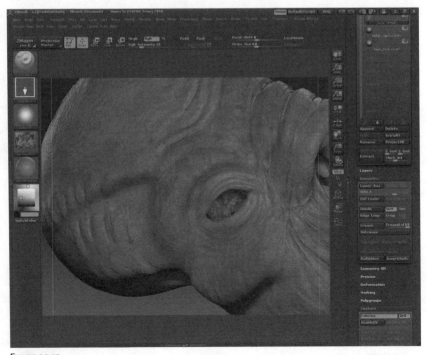

FIGURE 20-19

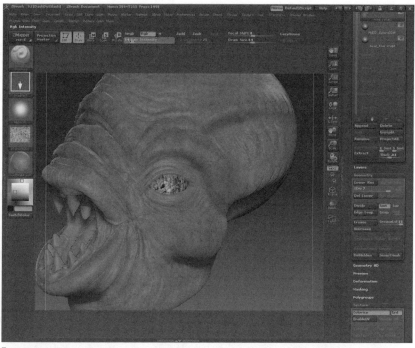

FIGURE 20-20

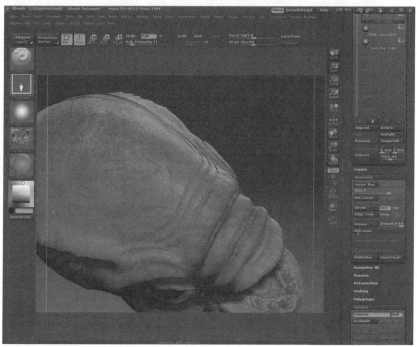

FIGURE 20-21

Now that we've got the base textures in place it's time to start the real texture painting. As our head has a high polygon count and good distribution we don't have to worry about areas not having enough polygons to support the texture. So again pick a nice dark and not too saturated brown color, change your stroke type to the **FreeHand** stroke, and deactivate your texture in the texture swatch. Turn your RGB Intensity down to **11** and get ready to roll.

You are going to do exactly what you did with the body at this stage and paint in every fold, crack, and crevice the brown color to help emphasize these cavities. Remember that we are not working on the very fine details right now, but concentrating on the larger forms. Also check that you have no "dead areas" by switching for a moment to Flat render mode before switching back to preview mode once more. Work your way over the entire head, adding in this darker color.

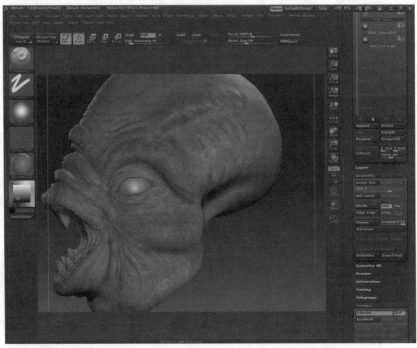

FIGURE 20-22

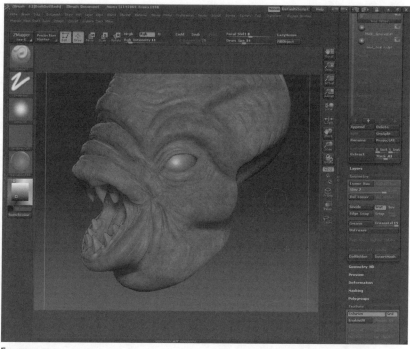

FIGURE 20-23

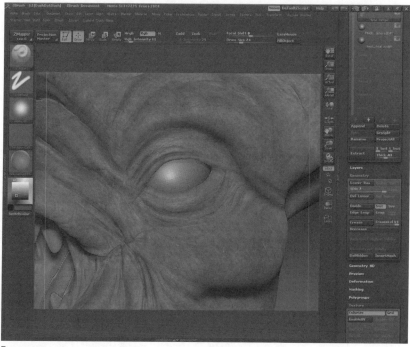

FIGURE 20-24

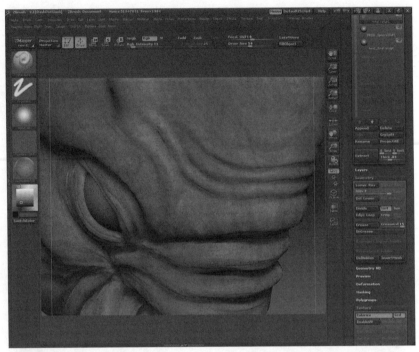

FIGURE 20-25

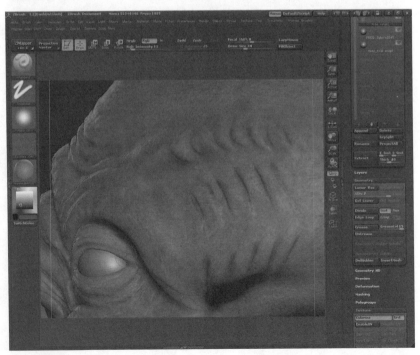

FIGURE 20-26

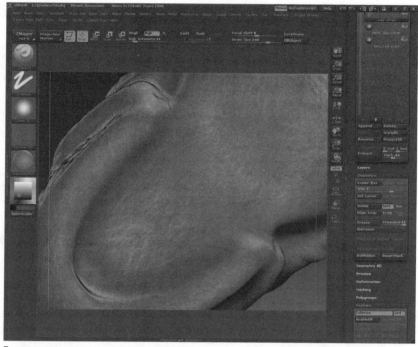

FIGURE 20-27

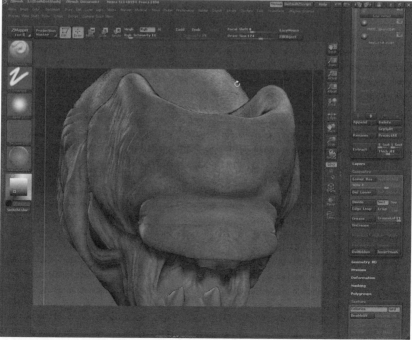

FIGURE 20-28

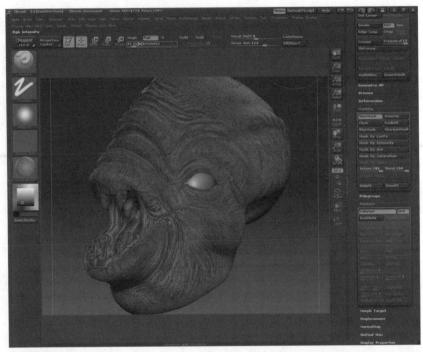

FIGURE 20-29

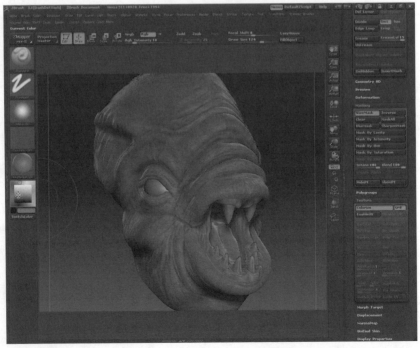

FIGURE 20-30

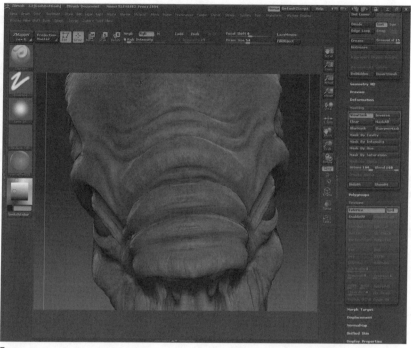

FIGURE 20-31

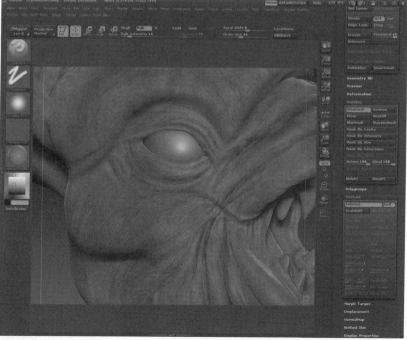

FIGURE 20-32

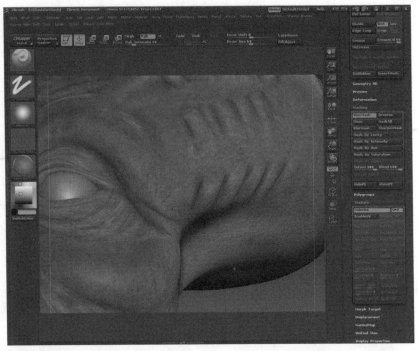

FIGURE 20-33

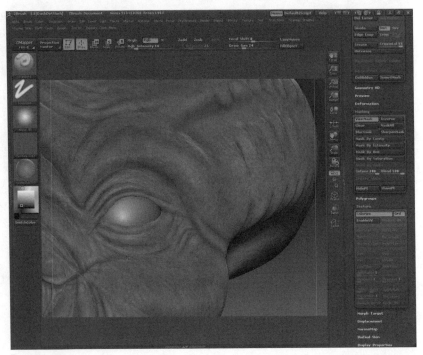

FIGURE 20-34

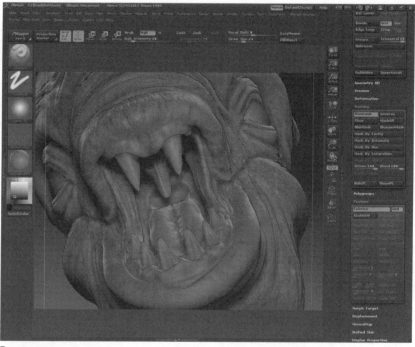

FIGURE 20-35

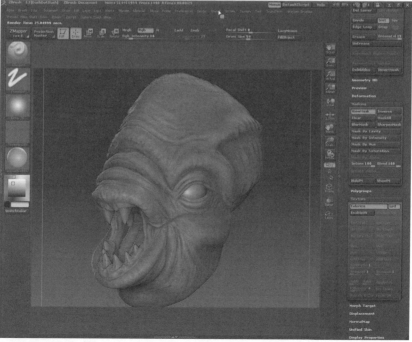

FIGURE 20-36

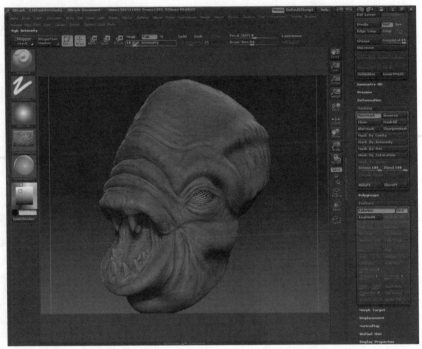

FIGURE 20-37

I'd now like you to switch back to the **DragRect** stroke type, select the reptile scales texture once again, and turn your RGB Intensity to **16**. As you did when working with the base textures for the body, cover the head with this texture and scale each dragged area to the correct size for the feature or area that you are working on. I'd like you to cover about 90 percent of the head. Remember to switch back and forth between Preview render mode and Flat render mode to get a feeling of how the actual texture is turning out without the shading information.

FIGURE 20-38

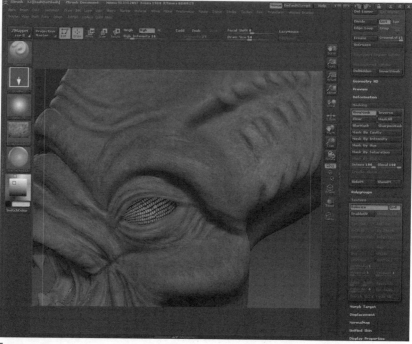

FIGURE 20-39

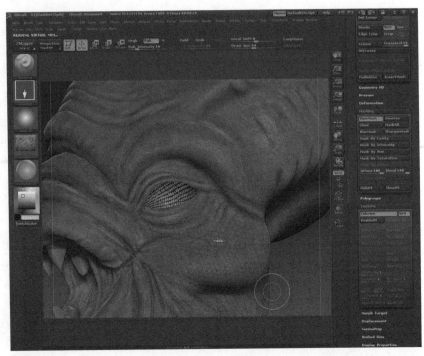

FIGURE 20-40

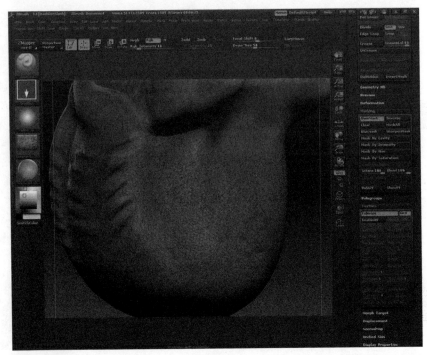

FIGURE 20-41

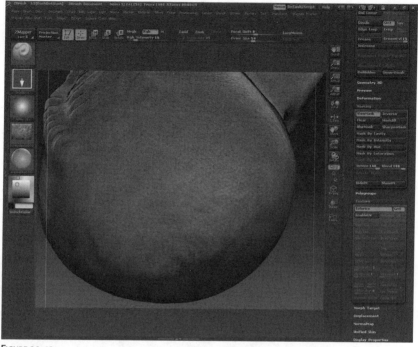

FIGURE 20-42

Fitting the Sculpted Details to Your Texture

This is a little bit of magic that will make the texture details (in this case the reptile skin) create details on the digital sculpture itself. This makes the texture gel better and become an integral part of the model. So first of all go down to the **Masking** section of the **Tool** palette and open it up, then click on the **Mask By Intensity** button. This will mask off your entire head model according to the intensity of the colors on it. We can now use this to detail our model by hand using the Inflate brush or more quickly by using the Deformation section of the Tool palette. I chose the latter simply for speed. So feel free to do it either way, but I'll outline the "easy way" for those of you following along. First of all, temporarily switch off the texture you've painted by deselecting the Texture button in the Texture section of the Tool palette. Then go down to the **Inflate** slider of the **Deformation** section and set the slider to somewhere between **20** and **40**. (How large this number is depends on the overall scale of your model.) You'll suddenly notice if you zoom in that a massive amount of detail has been added just from what you've painted on your texture. Turn your texture back on by reselecting the **Texture** button in the **Texture** section of the palette.

The outside part of the head is now effectively done, leaving only the inside of the mouth to finish.

Texturing Inside the Mouth

I've split the texturing of the inside of the mouth that includes the tongue, gums, the mouth itself, and the teeth into a separate section as it is quite different from what we have been texturing so far. We are going to start with two colors for the flesh inside the mouth and for the gums. I sampled these in Photoshop from a photo I found on Google and wrote down the RGB values of each color. This assured me that I was going to have a color that wasn't going to be too saturated or too bright to be believable. I used RGB 83, 42, 50 (a dark pinkish purple color) and RGB 138, 82, 91 (a light pinkish color).

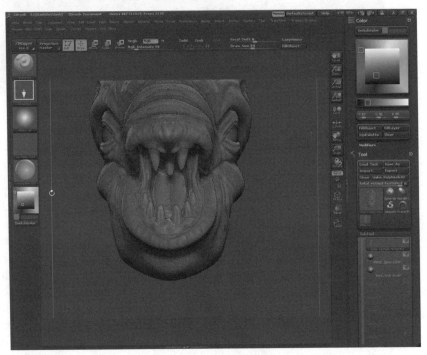

FIGURE 20-43

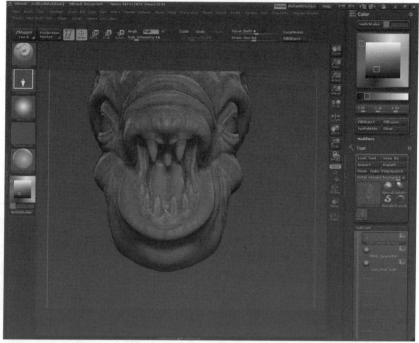

FIGURE 20-44

Let's set up the brush we will be using for texturing the inside of the mouth, so choose the **Standard** brush with **Alpha 35** active and the **FreeHand** stroke type. Set the RGB Intensity to **75** and we are ready to roll. Before we start painting any color whatsoever inside the mouth I'd like you to isolate the area by holding down **Shift + Ctrl** and dragging over the mouth area from a side view. Be careful that you do not hide part of the inside of the mouth. You can turn on transparency by clicking the **Transp** button to help if you need to. Also hide the eyeballs to make sure that you have just the mouth active and ready for us to texture without having to worry about other areas of the digital sculpt.

Turn on Double Sided mode as well from the Display Properties section of your Tool palette as at some point we will need to texture areas of the mouth that are too hard to reach from inside the head. Working deep inside the mouth is not going to be easy, but we can remove the rest of the head and work from inside the head itself for hard to reach areas.

With things all set, we can finally get down to some color!

Set the dark pinkish purple color as your active color using the RGB values from above (83, 42, 50), and start to cover the inside of the mouth with it. So that you do not overpaint onto the lips that you have already done, mask those off by holding down your **Ctrl** key and painting off the area. You want to paint the whole of the inside of the mouth this color with the exception of the teeth. Feel free to work from inside the head (the reverse side of the polygons) if you need to for those hard to reach areas. This is going to be the darkest color that we will later add highlights to. So think of it like an oil painting, where you start with the darkest color.

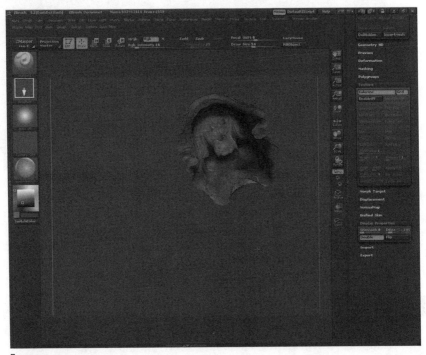

FIGURE 20-45

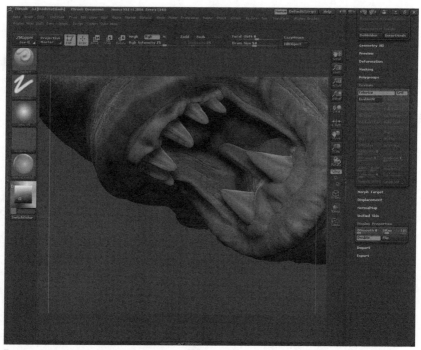

FIGURE 20-46

For texturing most of the mouth area I strongly recommend changing to the white MatCap or a standard material as it will give you a
better view of what is going on inside the mouth. As with texturing the
body and the rest of the head, feel free to pop in and out of Flat render
mode to check for any areas that you have missed covering. While painting the inside of the mouth with the dark pinkish purple color, work
from the gums first and be very careful to not paint over the teeth. Then
cover the rest of the inside of the mouth and tongue. So that you can get
as close to the base of each tooth as you can, paint from the inside of the
head.

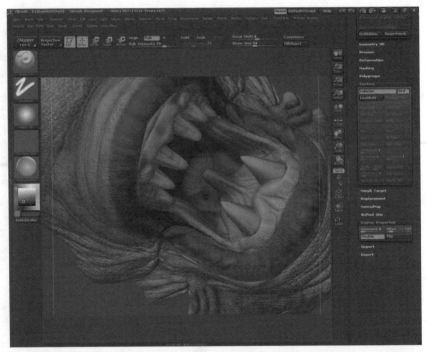

FIGURE 20-47

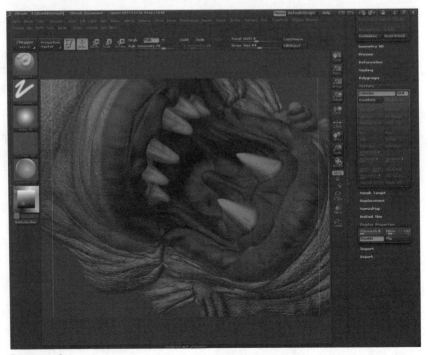

FIGURE 20-48

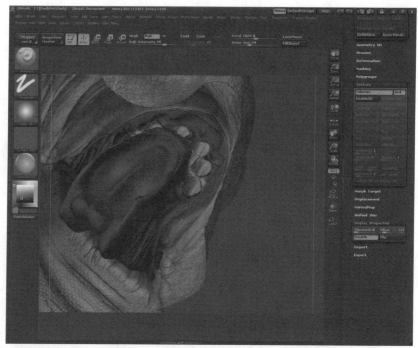

FIGURE 20-49

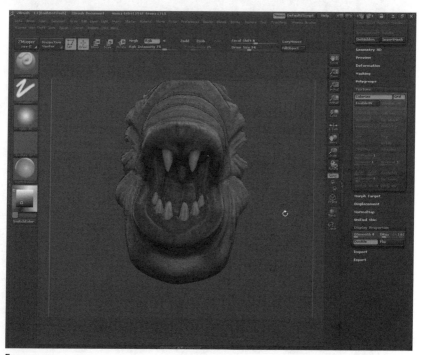

FIGURE 20-50

We can now start painting the highlights onto our texture using the light pinkish color (using RGB 138, 82, 91). You will need to turn the RGB Intensity down to **25** and use a very light touch as we don't want the highlights to be too obvious.

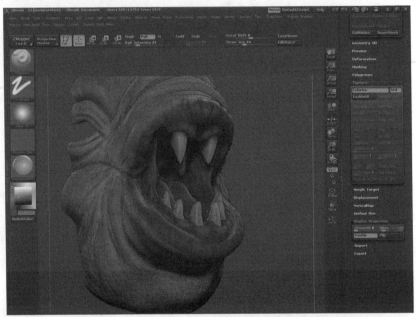

FIGURE 20-51

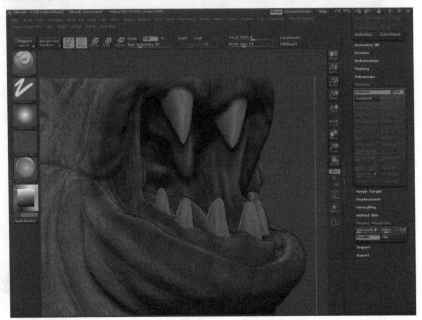

FIGURE 20-52

We are simply giving Mother Nature a helping hand and also making setting up the shader for our final render a little easier. Add the highlights as well as areas that are often a lighter color in real life anyway. Paint this color on every raised area in the mouth, on the gums, and particularly over each tooth.

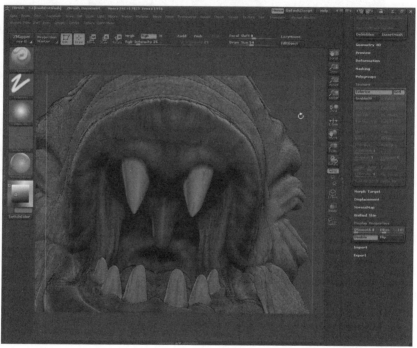

FIGURE 20-53

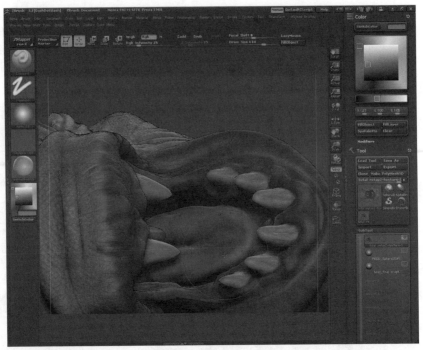

FIGURE 20-54

We are aiming for realism in this area or as near as we can get in the time available. For some areas that need variation but don't actually have any raised areas (such as the tonsils and certain places in the back of the mouth), we can fake the sculpting detail there using our color. So paint in the highlights on areas that you wish to "look" raised and you'll find at render time it will indeed look as if these areas were sculpted and not just painted onto our texture.

It is common to put as much information as possible into a texture, and if you can get away with not sculpting a detail but rather simply paint it on to the texture, then do it. While it is certainly fun and great practice to sculpt every single detail, sometimes in a work environment you have to use whatever shortcut you can find to meet deadlines. Paint over the entire tongue area to make it a more pleasing and realistic color as the purplish color is not doing it any favors on the realism front. Now darken the light pinkish color until it is darker than our other color and select **Alpha 17** (a small round alpha) and the **Color Spray** stroke type.

We are going to use this brush to create the look of taste buds and add texture to the tongue to help with its realism. But before doing so turn on **Zadd** with a ZIntensity of **13**, so we can both sculpt and add the color at the same time. I often like to add fine details like this by sculpting at the same time. Now switch to the light pinkish color and turn on Zsub with a ZIntensity of **25** to add some variation in color and depth to the inset areas.

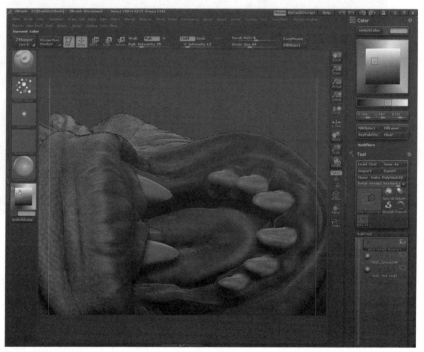

FIGURE 20-55

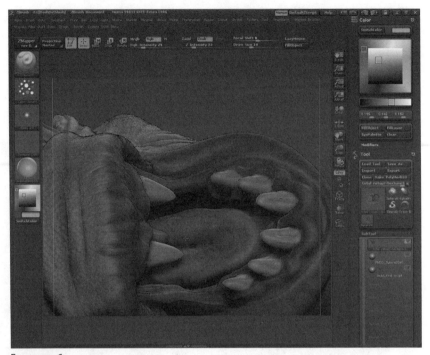

FIGURE 20-56

For the teeth I have a few colors I had sampled from photos of teeth and some darker colors I sampled from the horns of a strange-looking goat type animal. (I have no idea what type of animal it was, but the horns were certainly great.) The RGB values of the two colors are 178, 171, 163 (a very pale orangey color) and 58, 42, 29 (a dark brown color).

First use the pale color to cover the whole of each tooth. To get as near total coverage as possible you may need to paint from inside the head. Once you have this base pale color for the teeth we can add our second color to add some stains and help it look more realistic. Teeth are rarely if ever totally brilliant white; if they are too white it will make them look very false and ruin the believability of your digital sculpture. I'd like you to use this dark brown with a slightly larger brush than you may think you need when zoomed into the areas (the Draw Size I used was 74) and with a very light stroke add this color to the base of each tooth. Then start to paint some stains up along each tooth so the teeth actually appear to have some ridges. There is no valid reason to actually sculpt these shapes because no one is ever going to get close enough to check. Once this is done on all the teeth we can start to add a few finer details with this color.

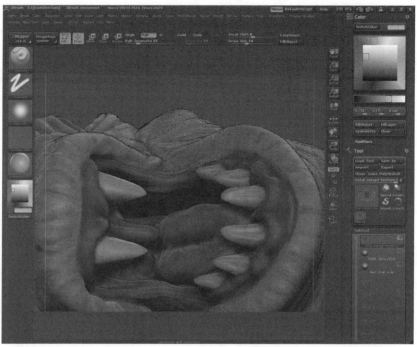

FIGURE 20-57

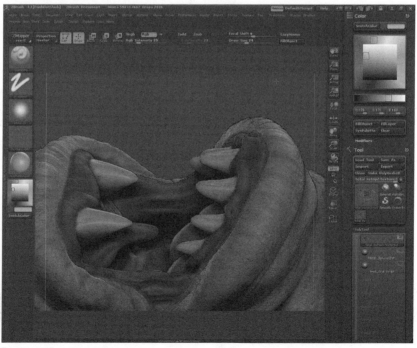

FIGURE 20-58

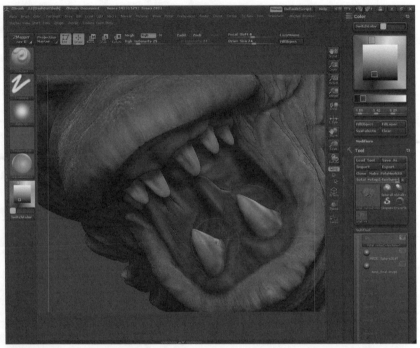

FIGURE 20-59

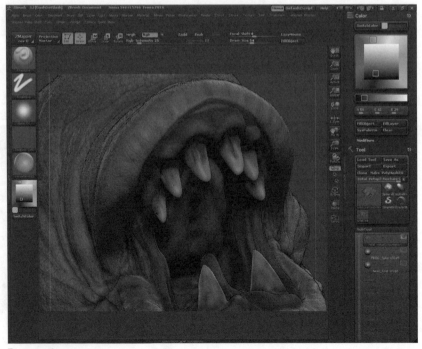

FIGURE 20-60

I'd now like you to change over to **Alpha 58**, change your RGB Intensity to **20**, and switch on **Zsub** with a ZIntensity of **14**. Making sure that your stroke type is set to the **FreeHand** stroke, start making some very light upward movements on each tooth to add some lines that will from a distance look like fine stains. We don't really need to add the sculpting with the Zsub setting, but as the light may reflect on the teeth and they are pretty visible, it is better to be safe than sorry.

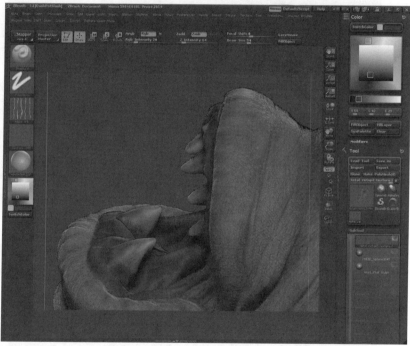

FIGURE 20-61

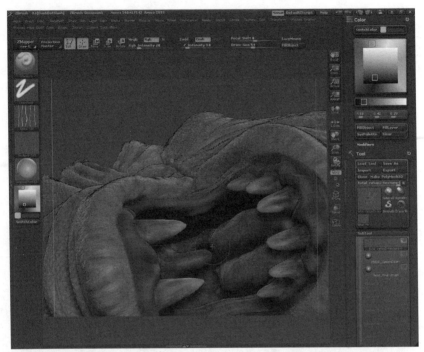

FIGURE 20-62

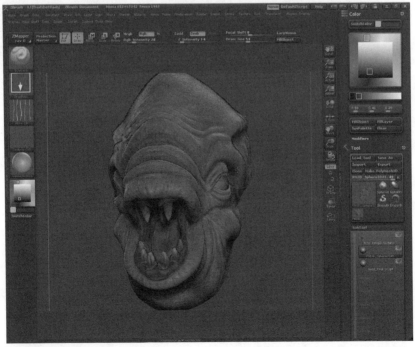

FIGURE 20-63

Now that the texture for the mouth and head is just about complete, it's a great time to set up a render with your lights. So turn up your light samples to about 200 or more, move your light to approximately 11 o'clock on the light ball, and make a test render. We do this to look for any issues that need to be addressed now instead of later on in the process. One thing I noticed straight away was that some areas of the gums that were light pink were not light enough. So I lightened that pink color and painted over all the previous light pink areas with this new lighter version (with a ZIntensity of **20** and both Zadd and Zsub turned off).

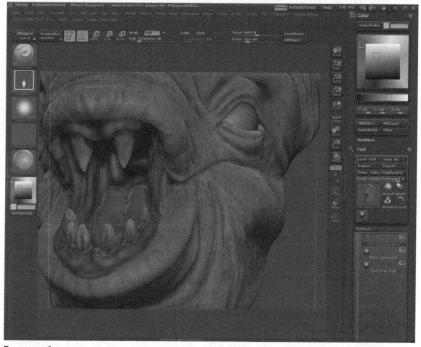

FIGURE 20-64

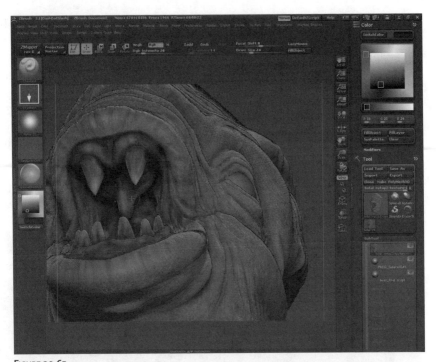

FIGURE 20-65

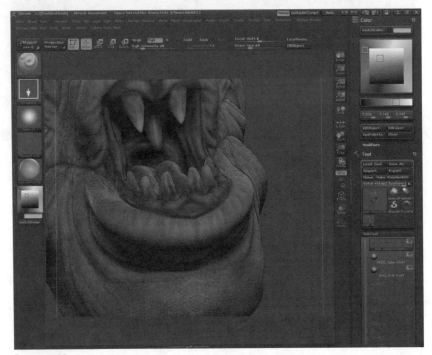

FIGURE 20-66

Finishing Touches to the Head Texture

As some final finishing touches to the head texture I selected **Alpha 46** (a small round alpha), a light pinkish color, and the **Color Spray** stroke type and added some very faint fine speckles over areas of the head such as the cheeks and chin for visual interest. I then changed my stroke type back to the **FreeHand** stroke, picked a nice dark brown color and **Alpha 01** again, and went over any wrinkles on the head I felt still needed to be darkened a bit.

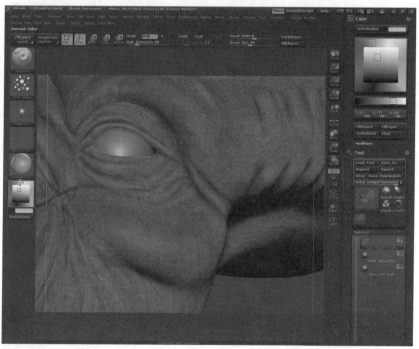

FIGURE 20-67

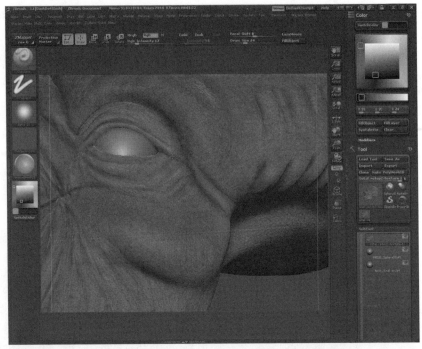

FIGURE 20-68

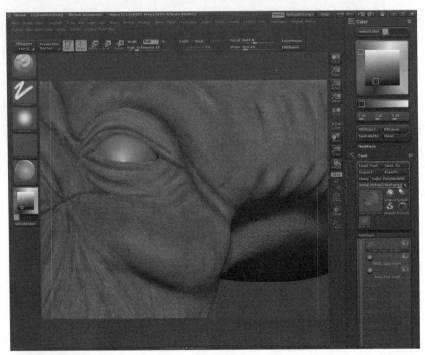

FIGURE 20-69

One of my final texturing jobs is to pick a very pale yellow color, almost an off-white, and paint the raised folds above and below the eye to make them a bit lighter and help the eye stand out a bit more. Then carefully and lightly go over some of the smaller folds with the same color to bring those out a bit as well. Finally, set up another render of the finished head texture and do one last check before calling it finished. We've now totally finished with the head texturing and only have a few small veins and minor details to color and sculpt on the body before moving on to the final scene.

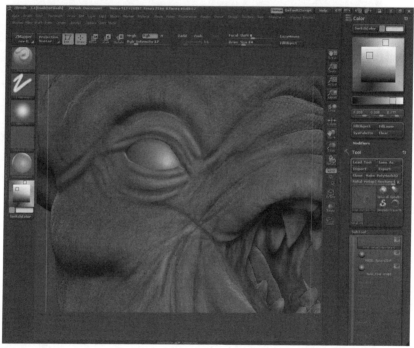

FIGURE 20-70

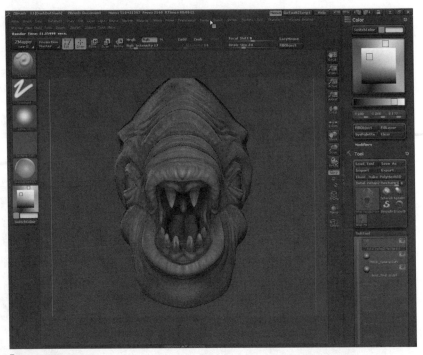

Figure 20-71

Coloring and Sculpting the Veins and Body Details

This is a very short section as there isn't a whole lot to cover really. I simply picked my **Displace** brush and picked **Alpha 41** along with a deep desaturated blue color, turned on **Zadd**, and set ZIntensity to **15**. I then proceeded to paint and sculpt at the same time the veins over the entire body of the Guardian. For reference I would advise doing an image search of bodybuilders because their veins are often visible. It is a good idea to put veins where they actually appear as opposed to where you might think they do. I would also suggest that you add them sparingly unless you are going for a more comic book look to your characters. Once this is done we can comfortably call the head and body of our digital sculpture done, on both the sculpting and texturing levels. Remember to save out multiple copies of it for safekeeping in several locations.

21 Sculpting the Accessories

The Guardian's Belt and Loincloth

The sculpting of the belt and loincloth should be fairly easy as they are not complex sculpting jobs. We add these items to complement the character and add some visual interest. First, we'll sculpt the belt, showing how to use masks to our advantage. We start with a base mesh made by retopologizing the body model and then exporting it to Silo to add some thickness to it. We could use the mesh extract feature in ZBrush, but this could leave us with a more polygon-heavy model than we need for use with a normal map.

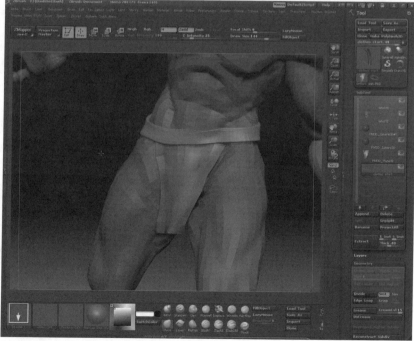

FIGURE 21-1

The loincloth is simply a polygon plane created inside of ZBrush that we will shape and add some folds to. Once we are done we use the same normal and cavity map extraction techniques that we used earlier to generate the maps. As usual, the base mesh for the belt (with full UV map) is available on the DVD.

Sculpting the Belt

The base mesh I used for this has been subdivided once before exporting from Silo to give us a set of evenly distributed polygons to sculpt on. Before subdividing your belt base, use the **Move** tool to tweak its position so that you get no interpenetration between it and the body, or the loincloth and the body. Then move to your main body base mesh and with it set to level 2, hide all but the sections that are close to the two parts we are about to sculpt.

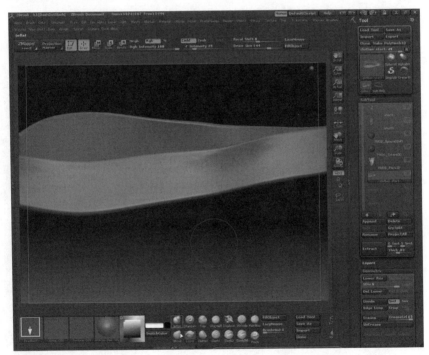

FIGURE 21-2

Move back to the belt and subdivide it to level 6, then take your **Layer** brush and **Alpha 12** and draw a diamond-shaped mask for what will eventually be the end of the belt, as shown in Figure 21-3. Once you've done this, use the Layer brush to add some mass to it, before stepping down to subdivision level 5 and smoothing the intersection out with the main part of the belt. (Leave the end of the belt looking like it has been wound around the body.) Then step up each subdivision level and smooth the same area out until it looks perfect at all levels.

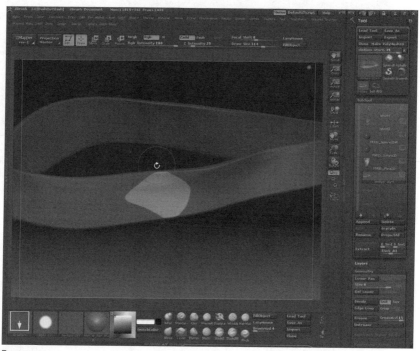

FIGURE 21-3

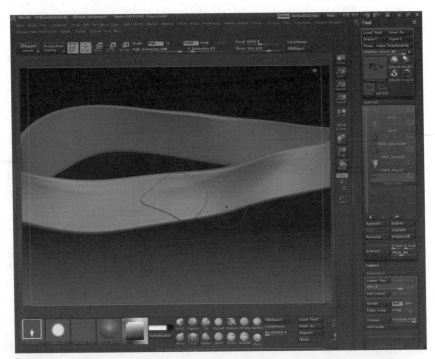

FIGURE 21-4

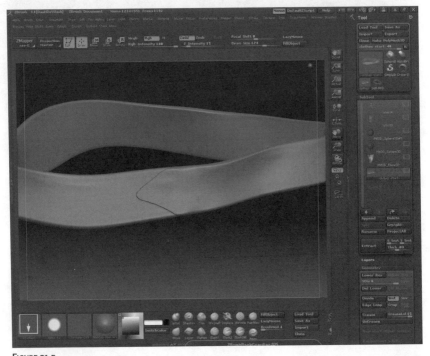

FIGURE 21-5

Now we will use a painted mask once again, but this time to add the belt buckle detail. So paint a mask on the belt's highest subdivision level in the shape shown in Figure 21-6. Then use the Layer brush to add some mass to this area, taking care that the mask is not painted over the edges and instead only meets the edges. Smooth out the edge into the belt as shown, then paint another for the pin part of the belt buckle and treat it the same way.

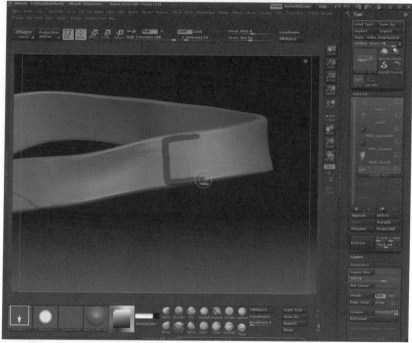

FIGURE 21-6

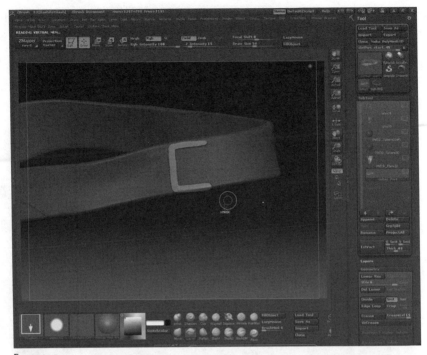

FIGURE 21-7

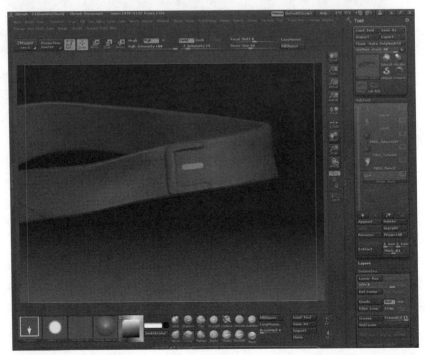

FIGURE 21-8

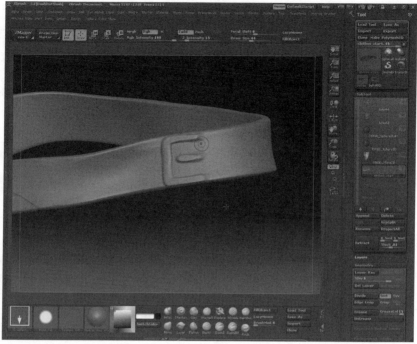

FIGURE 21-9

The holes are easy to create with **Alpha 12** and the **DragDot** stroke type. Set your brush to just slightly larger than the size of the belt buckle's pin to ensure that everything is to the correct scale before adding the belt holes. If you find that the belt buckle looks a bit soft around the edges, use either the **Slash1** or **Displace** brush with a very small alpha to carve some sharpness back in.

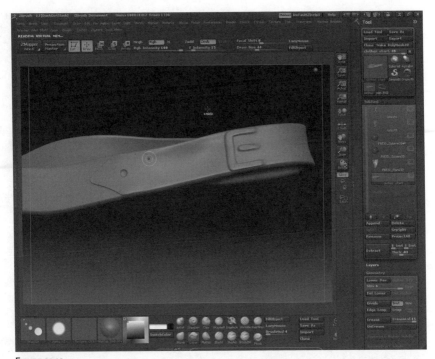

FIGURE 21-10

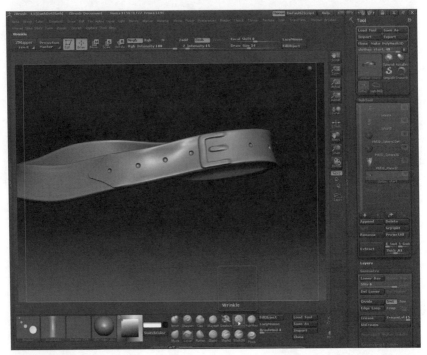

FIGURE 21-11

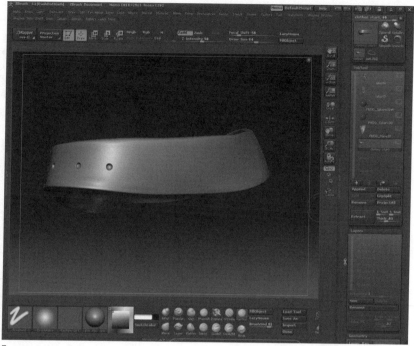

FIGURE 21-12

Now set your **Clay** brush to a ZIntensity of **50** and select **Alpha 01** and the **FreeHand** stroke type. To help this brush add a bit more mass when we sculpt the subtle folds in the belt, set its BrushMod to **81**. This will increase the amount that the brush will add and remove on each stroke. Sculpt in a few outward folds very lightly onto the sides of the belt, but do not go too crazy as belt leather doesn't fold much unless it is heavily worn. Once you've done the outward folds, subtract some of the mass between them until you have the look as shown. The belt is now ready for map extraction and later use.

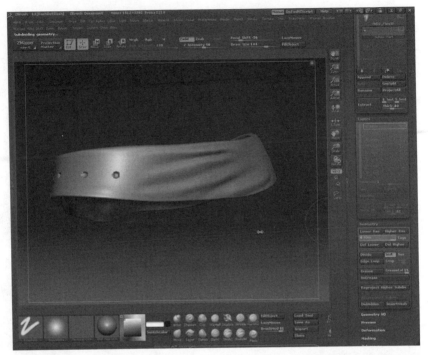

FIGURE 21-13

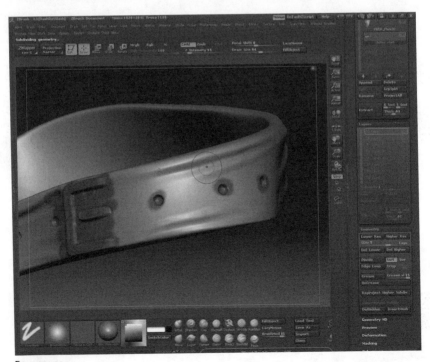

FIGURE 21-14

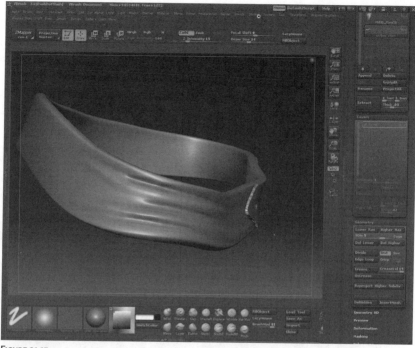

FIGURE 21-15

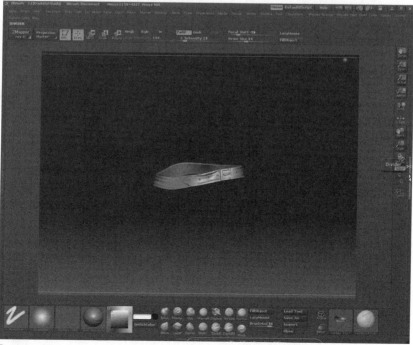

FIGURE 21-16

Sculpting the Loincloth

Subdivide the loincloth base mesh (created from a shaped **plane primi-tive** and made into a polymesh using the **Make PolyMesh3D** button) to level 6. Using the same brush as last time, start to work out where the folds are going to be in the loincloth. Add the outward folds first, going from the largest forms to the smallest, then remove the mass between them and refine the whole area.

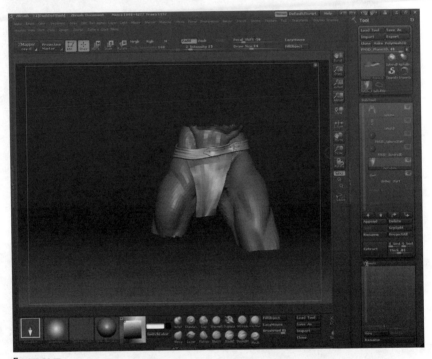

FIGURE 21-17

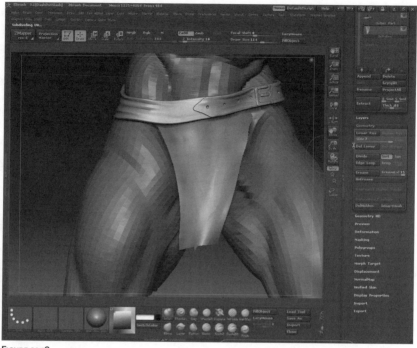

FIGURE 21-18

I like to sculpt in "passes" and refine each time I go over the form. As this is a small piece of cloth, there's not a whole lot of work in it. Just keep in mind where the cloth is pulling around the mass of the top of the legs and the stress points in the cloth that cause the folds themselves.

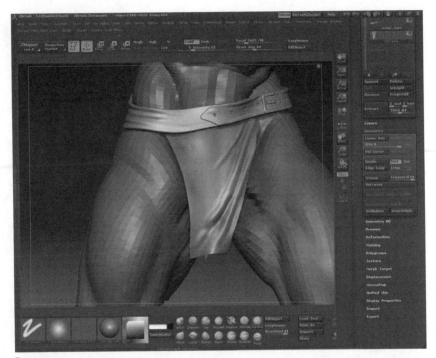

FIGURE 21-19

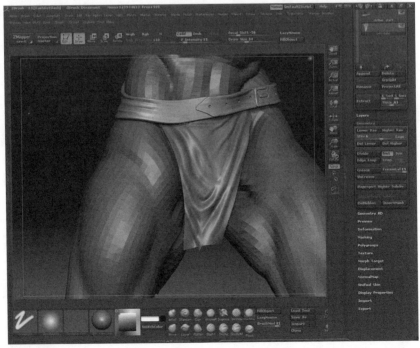

FIGURE 21-20

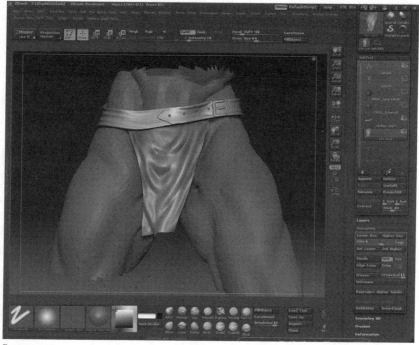

FIGURE 21-21

If in doubt about how to sculpt cloth folds, take a look at a piece of cloth that is of similar thickness and sculpt from life. This is a great way to learn because it's easier to sculpt from life rather than from theory.

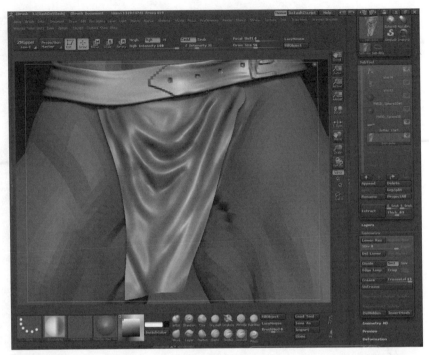

FIGURE 21-22

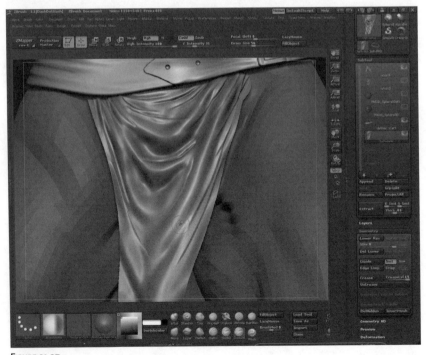

FIGURE 21-23

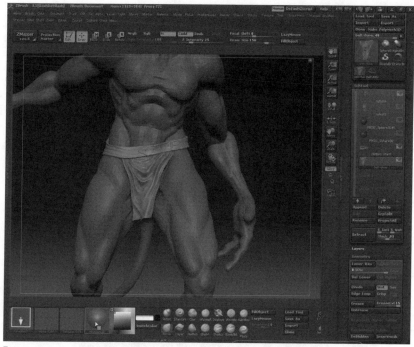

FIGURE 21-24

Once you are happy with the folds, generate normal and displacement maps and you are ready to move on to texturing each in Photoshop before using them in our final scene.

Photoshop: Texturing Both Items

What we will need is images of texture for cloth and leather, as well as cavity maps and normal maps for the belt and the loincloth.

The texturing in Photoshop is actually pretty easy to do and I'll outline how to go about it. Although I used textures from www.image-after.com and some of my own, you should have no problem rounding up the textures needed.

The Cloth

The loincloth is the easiest one to texture. Simply open your cloth texture and lay your cavity map on the layer above. Change its layer blending mode to **Multiply** and blur it a bit using **Filter > Gaussian Blur** until it loses some of its hard edges. You can add copies of the cavity layer if needed and of course color correct it using the **Filter > Hue /Saturation** controls. I left mine as is since there is no need for a specular map as the cloth is not reflective and specularity will be set to zero at render time.

FIGURE 21-25

FIGURE 21-26

FIGURE 21-27

The Belt

To texture the belt, open up your normal and cavity maps and put both into the same document with the normal map at the bottom. Ensure that all maps are facing the right way up and that none require vertical flipping. We will use the normal map to show us where each part of the model is and the cavity map to add the ambient occlusion effect to help with our texture.

FIGURE 21-28

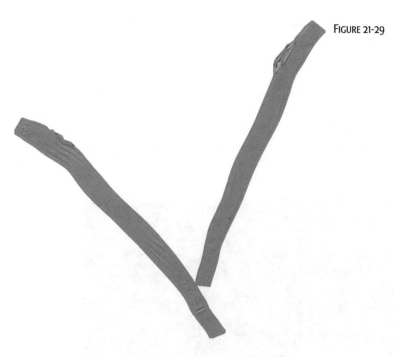

FIGURE 21-29

So open up a leather belt texture image (you can make your own by taking a photo of a belt and cutting a sample of it out). Use a section of this and simply cut and paste the sections, blending them together using the Erase, Burn, and Dodge tools.

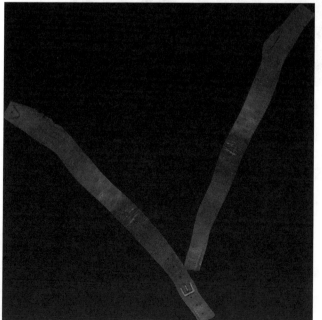

FIGURE 21-30

To make the belt buckle, just make a brand-new layer under the cavity map and paint the buckle area yellow, then darken the edges of it with your Burn tool and add highlights with the Dodge tool. You can also overlay a grungy texture in Multiply mode over the top of just the buckle by **Ctrl+clicking** on the buckle layer to select it and then using **Ctrl+I** to invert the selection and remove all of the grunge texture that is not part of the buckle.

You can also make a specular level map using your finished color texture map by desaturating it and darkening its levels quite a bit until it matches the one shown here.

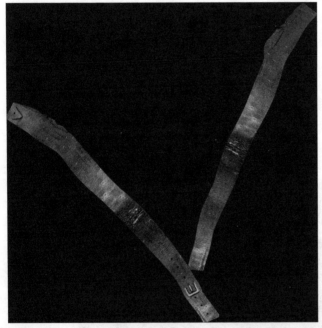

Figure 21-31

From there on in it is just matter of tidying up as you see fit and saving it out. Once you are done, you have all the resources needed for our final scene.

22 Rendering the Guardian Scene

To render out the final scene I decided to use Mental Ray inside of 3ds Max for several reasons. Although I am a big advocate of the power of ZBrush's own render engine, it simply would not (on my current machine) be able to handle the polygon counts of every item in the scene without dropping everything to 2.5D. So as such I knew when designing the scene that I would be using an external render engine. I went with Mental Ray because it's available in just about every major application, so you should be able to follow along fairly easily, regardless of the application you use.

Mental Ray has advantages for a ZBrush user in that the map interfaces for displacement and normal maps are well documented and it is a robust, production proven render engine. I also wanted to render out this scene with a lot of maps at a very high resolution for the cover picture. Some render engines may cope well with most render sizes, but once you get into very large 2, 4, or 8K renders, you'll find they are a bit less stable. Mental Ray has the benefit of a wonderful script that splits a truly massive render into sections for later slotting back together in Photoshop. The one I'm using is called **Splitrender** and you can find it with a quick Google search.

For this chapter I wanted to show you a workflow that is a bit different from the usual, as well as one that is robust and easy to learn. So instead of rendering out using displacement maps, we are going to be using a medium-res version of the body and head and a number of normal maps. This has the benefit of being faster to render, and there is also less chance that your machine will "max out" and be unable to render the scene at the size or quality that you wish.

You should have all the models and maps needed for this scene now, so I'll outline how I approached the render along with providing some tips on such things as handling subsurface shaders in Mental Ray correctly. You shouldn't have too much trouble converting this information to the application of your choice.

FIGURE 22-1

Importing the Models and Setting the Scene

It is important when you import your OBJ files that each is imported with the normals intact and not as multiple files. If we used 32-bit displacement maps for this scene, we would be unable to resize any of the meshes and the render settings we use would be incorrect. So by using normal maps we are getting around the problem, along with any scale related problems that you may experience.

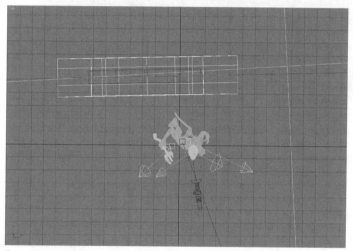

FIGURE 22-2

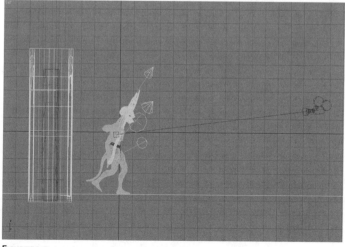

FIGURE 22-3

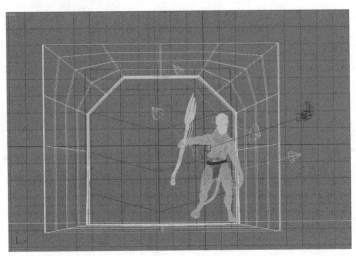

FIGURE 22-4

Models used:

Model	Subdivision Level	Maps Used
Guardian head	Level 2 of retopologized version	Color, normal, specular level, specular color
Guardian body	Level 2	Color, normal, specular level, specular color
Weapon	Level 1	Color, normal, specular level, specular color
Leather belt	Level 1	Color, normal
Loincloth	Level 1	Color, normal
Door of Secrets	Level 1	Color, normal, specular level, specular color
Frame for Door of Secrets	Level 1	Color, normal, specular level

Along with the above models, we will also make use of a couple of polygon planes with a few simple textures on them to help liven things up and fill out the scene a little. As they are barely visible in the final renders they are not of any real importance. The one we will use as a floor will have a simple repeating tiled texture and matching bump map, and the one we use as a wall to surround the door uses another simple tiled color map and matching bump map for the stonework.

As that is pretty basic stuff for any 3ds Max user I won't go into tremendous detail about those. One extra piece that you will notice in the render is the x-shaped leather chest piece. This was a last-minute addition; for those who want to recreate it, the workflow is identical to the leather belt you sculpted earlier.

Basic Material Creation

To create a material for an object in 3ds Max, all you have to do is open the Material Editor, click on the sphere with an arrow pointing to it, and choose a material. I'll be using a couple of types in this scene but let's start with a **standard** material. Along with changing the colors and levels in a material, you can also click on the small box next to it and add a texture map to it. Once you have the material set up, you simply select in the viewport the item or items that you wish to apply the material to and then click on the Sphere and Cube icon in the Material Editor.

While I realize this description is oversimplified, there are a wealth of tutorials available online and in print, so I'll save the space here.

The Mental Ray Subsurface Skin Shader (SSS)

The SSS material is probably the least understood material on the planet and one that many users have difficulty learning.

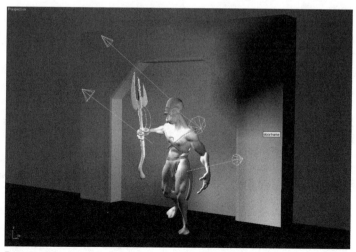

FIGURE 22-5

The secret to getting the subsurface skin shader to look good is scale. The size of your model and scene and its relation to real-world size is of primary importance for this shader family more than any other. If your model is too small in real-world units, the SSS effect will be a nightmare to control and you may have to wind the internal scale of the material down considerably. So the smaller the model is in relation to real-world size, the more sensitive (and hard to set up and control) it is. Therefore, you must scale the model correctly. Make the body for a human approximately 6 feet tall, with all other items in the scene of a relative size. I find it best to work in a unit scale of millimeters, so I make the height of the Guardian 1.5 meters.

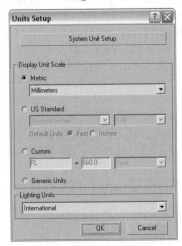

FIGURE 22-6

Once your model is the correct scale, you will find that with some maps the defaults look pretty good as a starting point for human skin. I would strongly suggest using the built-in specular controls, as the dual specular effect gives the skin shader a sort of reshaped specular highlight that is unique to skin. This can also be faked using a composited specular pass, but it's easier to get the best look using the SSS material for skin as a "unit."

Lights, Camera, Action!

Lighting for our scene is of primary importance, and it's easy to spend days tweaking a light setup to get something that not only looks good but also fits the scene. For ease of setup I've used a series of **Mental Ray area spotlights** for the whole scene, which gives us plenty of scope to tweak things.

I avoided using photometric lights such as the **mental ray sky portal,** as it simply sent render times sky high, although without doubt they give a much better final image. If you want to try them on your own projects, you will find that the exposure value you use is of great importance.

Figure 22-7

Of the four lights I used in the scene, all had Ray Traced Shadows enabled and a variety of falloffs and settings. So that you can quickly see my light setups, the following figures show each light along with its settings and a position reference. For exposure control I used the **mr Photographic Exposure Control** set to some custom values as you can see in Figure 22-11.

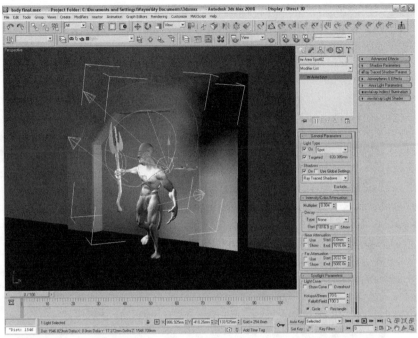

Figure 22-8

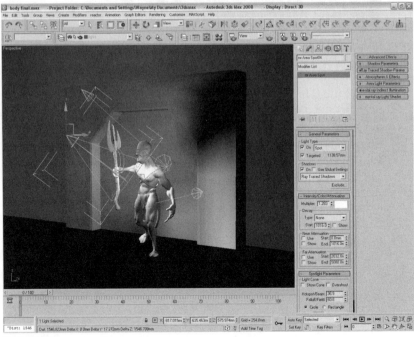

Figure 22-9

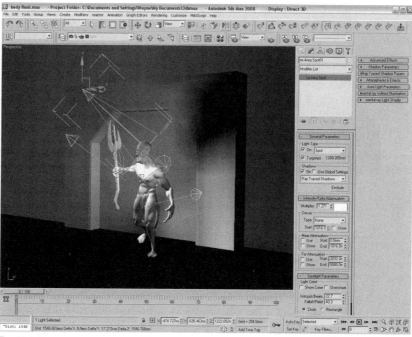

FIGURE 22-10

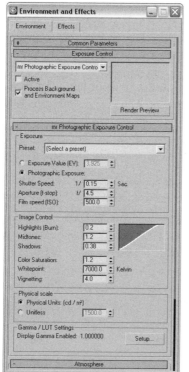

FIGURE 22-11

The camera I used was a target camera (two of them actually, one for a close-up shot that isn't visible in the screenshots) set to a lens size of **60mm**. No depth of field or other options were enabled, just a plain standard camera.

The Final Gather settings for the image were as follows:

Enable Final Gather: checked
Multiplier: 1.0
Initial FG Point Density: 0.5
Rays per FG Point: 100
Interpolate Over Num. FG Points: 27
Diffuse Bounces: 4 (You could increase this to 10 if you wish. I kept this low to speed up render times for the final large image.)
Weight: 1.0
Everything else was set to the default.

Now that you have all items in the scene and the lights set up, it's time for me to go through the materials I used. For most of them I'll provide screenshots so that you can quickly get the information that you need.

For the material for both the door and the surround, I also added the main color texture into the Additional Bump slot along with the normal map. For the floor tiles I used a setting of **30** in U and V mainly because the polygon plane I used was large so it wouldn't interfere with the rest of the scene when setting it up.

The Materials Used

The following screenshots show the Material Editor panel for each material used.

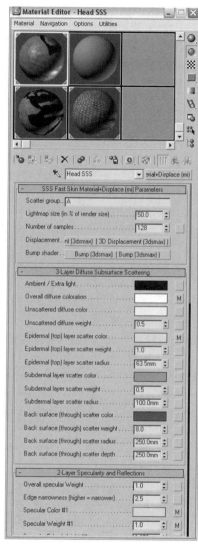

FIGURE 22-12

FIGURE 22-13

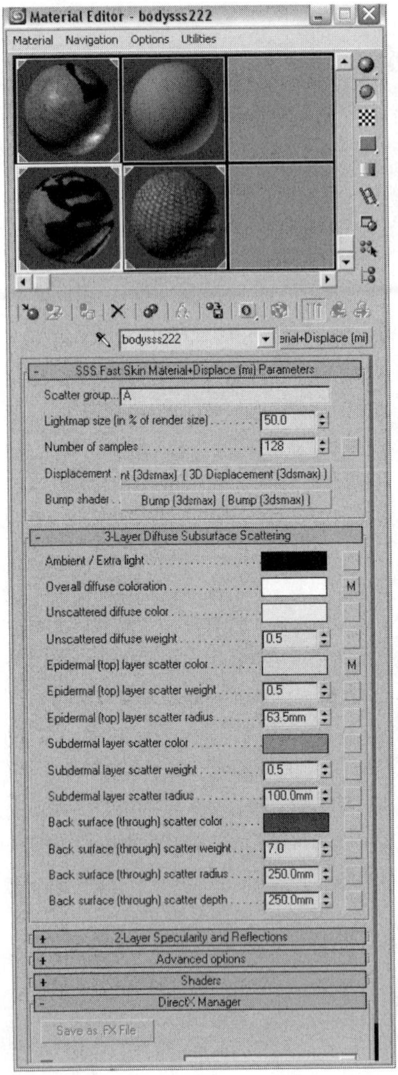

FIGURE 22-14

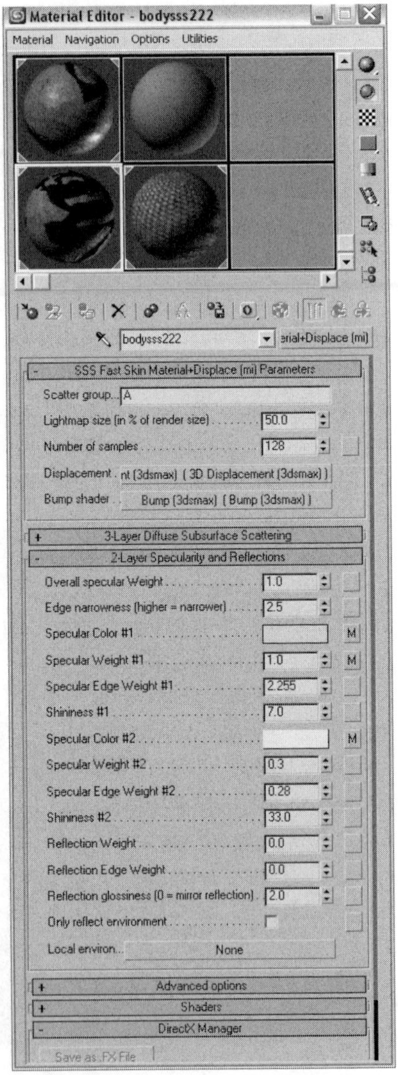

FIGURE 22-15

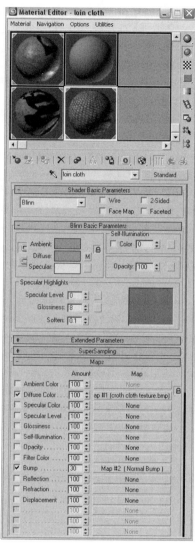

FIGURE 22-16   FIGURE 22-17

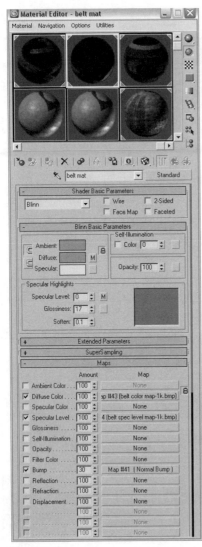

FIGURE 22-18

FIGURE 22-19

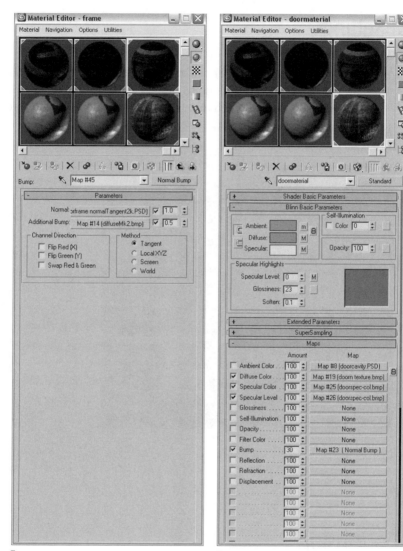

FIGURE 22-20   **FIGURE 22-21**

OBJ Settings

While for most of the parts on the Guardian I added a TurboSmooth modifier, I didn't for the body. For that I just selected all the body polygons and added a smoothing group to them. I left the surround, floor, and door as they were imported into the scene and didn't modify them in any way.

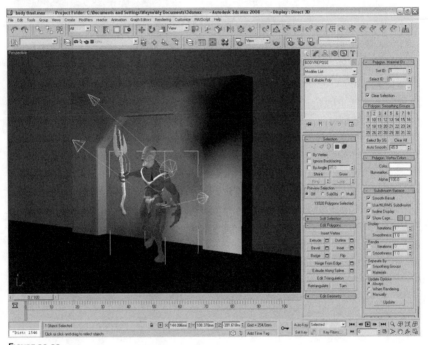

FIGURE 22-22

In Conclusion

I hope you have found this book informative and that you've learned some things you didn't know beforehand. In closing, I'd like to wish you all the very best of luck in your careers and your use of ZBrush. Be all that you can be, and never stop learning.

Index

Looking for More?

Check out Wordware's market-leading Graphics Applications and Development Libraries featuring the following titles.

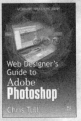

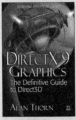

About the DVD

The companion DVD includes all the images in the book in full color, files and images needed to create the cover illustration, and video tutorials totaling more than 3 hours. The files are organized as follows:

- EXTRAS—Custom UI configurations, brushes, materials, and more
- Images—Full-color versions of the images used to create the cover illustration
- Images from book—Full-color versions of all the images in the book, compressed and organized by chapter
- Videos—Ten videos showing how to create and texture the Guardian
- WORK FILES—All the files needed to replicate the final cover render, along with the low-resolution work files for each piece

Warning: By opening the DVD package, you accept the terms and conditions of the DVD/Source Code Usage License Agreement.
Additionally, opening the DVD package makes this book nonreturnable.

DVD/Source Code Usage License Agreement

Please read the following DVD/Source Code usage license agreement before opening the DVD and using the contents therein:

1. By opening the accompanying software package, you are indicating that you have read and agree to be bound by all terms and conditions of this DVD/Source Code usage license agreement.

2. The compilation of code and utilities contained on the DVD and in the book are copyrighted and protected by both U.S. copyright law and international copyright treaties, and is owned by Wordware Publishing, Inc. Individual source code, example programs, help files, freeware, shareware, utilities, and evaluation packages, including their copyrights, are owned by the respective authors.

3. No part of the enclosed DVD or this book, including all source code, help files, shareware, freeware, utilities, example programs, or evaluation programs, may be made available on a public forum (such as a World Wide Web page, FTP site, bulletin board, or Internet news group) without the express written permission of Wordware Publishing, Inc. or the author of the respective source code, help files, shareware, freeware, utilities, example programs, or evaluation programs.

4. You may not decompile, reverse engineer, disassemble, create a derivative work, or otherwise use the enclosed programs, help files, freeware, shareware, utilities, or evaluation programs except as stated in this agreement.

5. The software, contained on the DVD and/or as source code in this book, is sold without warranty of any kind. Wordware Publishing, Inc. and the authors specifically disclaim all other warranties, express or implied, including but not limited to implied warranties of merchantability and fitness for a particular purpose with respect to defects in the disk, the program, source code, sample files, help files, freeware, shareware, utilities, and evaluation programs contained therein, and/or the techniques described in the book and implemented in the example programs. In no event shall Wordware Publishing, Inc., its dealers, its distributors, or the authors be liable or held responsible for any loss of profit or any other alleged or actual private or commercial damage, including but not limited to special, incidental, consequential, or other damages.

6. One (1) copy of the DVD or any source code therein may be created for backup purposes. The DVD and all accompanying source code, sample files, help files, freeware, shareware, utilities, and evaluation programs may be copied to your hard drive. With the exception of freeware and shareware programs, at no time can any part of the contents of this DVD reside on more than one computer at one time. The contents of the DVD can be copied to another computer, as long as the contents of the DVD contained on the original computer are deleted.

7. You may not include any part of the DVD contents, including all source code, example programs, shareware, freeware, help files, utilities, or evaluation programs in any compilation of source code, utilities, help files, example programs, freeware, shareware, or evaluation programs on any media, including but not limited to DVD, disk, or Internet distribution, without the express written permission of Wordware Publishing, Inc. or the owner of the individual source code, utilities, help files, example programs, freeware, shareware, or evaluation programs.

8. You may use the source code, techniques, and example programs in your own commercial or private applications unless otherwise noted by additional usage agreements as found on the DVD.

 Warning: By opening the DVD package, you accept the terms and conditions of the DVD/Source Code Usage License Agreement.
Additionally, opening the DVD package makes this book nonreturnable.